The Bible's Top Fifty Ideas
The Essential Concepts Everyone Should Know

Comments

What Rabbi Elkins does in this one volume window in the heart of the world's greatest Book is truly amazing. His discussions are engaging, inspiring, comprehensive and scholarly. I have found his book to be exceptionally accurate, thorough and comprehensive. This is a veritable treasure. I cannot praise this wonderful book enough.

> — **Prof. Shalom Paul**, *Chair, Department of Bible,*
> *Hebrew University of Jerusalem*

The Talmud teaches (Eruvin 54b) that "the Torah can only be acquired through simanim — abbreviations." This passage refers to lists of words which helped the rabbis memorize lists of laws and legends. If this was true then, it is even more true now in the age of soundbites.

Rabbi Dov Peretz Elkins has performed an important service. He has selected fifty essential verses from the Torah, which have had a profound influence on Judaism and on Western Civilization. He has examined those verses in an in-depth fashion, using a wide array of ancient and modern commentaries, while emphasizing their relevance to modern society. His book will benefit rabbis and teachers as well as laypeople who want to connect to the Torah and discover it's relevance to modern life.

> — **Rabbi Prof. David Golinkin**, *President*
> *Schechter Institute of Jewish Studies, Jerusalem*

Dov Peretz Elkins is a gifted rabbi and teacher who has authored a number of books which are very popular among his colleagues. They will find this volume particularly appealing as they seek to share their love of Judaism with their students. It is a wonderful text, highly appropriate both for post-confirmation and adult education courses, as well as for individuals who are interested in the traditional Jewish value system. The citations from Rabbinic texts and traditional commentaries, coupled with his own insights and those of modern thinkers provide the reader with a fine introduction to fundamental Jewish teachings and how they may be applied in our time."

> — **Dr. David L. Lieber**, *President Emeritus,*
> *University of Judaism*

Dov Peretz Elkins continues to educate and inspire us all. His unique talents and knowledge allow him to present the most important values and concepts found in the Bible to a wide audience of persons in a characteristically intelligent and accessible manner. This book is a jewel.

— **Rabbi David Ellenson**, *President,*
Hebrew Union College-Jewish Institute of Religion

Rabbi Dov Peretz Elkins brings his wealth of learning to bear on fifty key verses from the Torah. The method is an ancient one: posing crucial questions and scanning the tradition—from the Bible to the rabbis, to the medieval exegetes, to modern commentators—for insights, illuminations, even answers. Though his method is ancient, Rabbi Elkins' point of view is contemporary; he is well-informed by biblical scholarship and has a keen ear for dialogue between classical readers and modern ones. It's hard to imagine a book of Torah commentary both this substantive and this user-friendly. When word gets out, this book will be indispensable for all individuals and groups eager to get to the heart of the matter: what the Torah says, what it has meant, and what it continues to mean to us.

— **Esther Schor**, *Professor of English,*
Princeton University

For Jews, the transmission of Torah is our first duty and greatest joy. Among no other people has religious literacy been so prized. By expounding and interpreting critical Biblical passages so brilliantly, Dov Peretz Elkins has performed a great service for rabbis and teachers of Torah, who will seize upon this book, use it in their classrooms, and admire it for its scholarship, insight, and clarity. And he has helped the serious layperson as well, who will delight in the accessibility it provides to Judaism's most profound teachings.

— **Rabbi Eric H. Yoffie**, *President,*
Union for Reform Judaism

The Torah is a Tree of Life. Rabbi Elkins has harvested its fruit in a way that enables the reader to be enriched by its sweetness. His insights into this classic text make it come alive for the 21st century. This is a book that you will read many times and each reading will inspire you on a journey of life.

— **Rabbi Jerome M. Epstein**, *Executive Vice-President,*
The United Synagogue of Conservative Judaism

An excellent idea, and a fine execution. Dr. Elkins examines the biblical verses that have most reverberated throughout Jewish history and life, and shows how these verses still speak to us today.

— **Rabbi Joseph Telushkin,** *author,*
Jewish Literacy and The Book of Jewish Values

Appropriately viewing the Hebrew Bible as an anthology, Rabbi Dov Peretz Elkins, an extraordinarily gifted rabbi, scholar and teacher, has brought together a rich and suggestive tapestry of comment and reflection which accurately and artfully orchestrates the central themes of the Bible as they evolved since its composition and canonization. A great teacher does not simply inform, but brings students and readers into a dialogical relationship with the text being taught. Against the background of solid scholarship, Rabbi Elkins creates for the reader just such a dialogical relationship. This book represents a major achievement and will be invaluable both for individual readers and for younger adult and adult study groups.

— **David M. Gordis,** *Ph.D., President,*
Hebrew College, Newton, MA

By highlighting 50 key Torah verses, and expounding on their interpretations through the ages and their relevance today, Rabbi Dov Peretz Elkins re-emphasizes the Bible's centrality and its abiding wisdom. He also achieves what may perhaps have been one of his wider purposes: He reminds his readers of how much they have forgotten, or perhaps never learned, and sends us — questing and energized — back to the original.

— **David Horovitz,** *Editor, The Jerusalem Report;*
author, Still Life with Bombers: Israel in the Age
of Terrorism.

In this wonderful volume, Rabbi Dov Peretz Elkins asks — and answers — many of the questions about the central Biblical texts that have intrigued readers and commentators for centuries. His writing is accessible, inviting and insightful. A great text for sophisticated adult learners looking for a way into understanding the Bible!

— **Dr. Ron Wolfson,** *Vice President, University of Judaism;*
author, Shabbat, Hanukkah, Passover and A Time
to Mourn, A Time to Comfort

The Bible is a book for every generation but it takes special scholars and teachers to give it a contemporary voice. Dov Peretz Elkins is among the best such teachers and we are lucky to have his new book. It will educate and inspire.

> — **Ari L. Goldman**, *author,* **The Search for God at Harvard** *and* **Living a Year of Kaddish**

The Bible's Top Fifty Ideas is a delicious sampler of commentary and meditation on the Torah's most notable passages by the scholars and sages of past and present, presented and taught by a rabbi who is himself a wise commentator on, and teacher of, the sacred text.

> — **Raymond P. Scheindlin**, *Professor of Medieval Hebrew Literature, Jewish Theological Seminary of America; author of* **The Book of Job** *and* **A Short History of the Jewish People.**

For many, the Bible is a book more revered than read. Rabbi Dov Peretz Elkins' new book, *The Bible's Top Fifty Ideas,* should help change that. In a lively and lucid style, Elkins expounds some of the Bible's most memorable and important passages, the sources for so much of the wisdom and inspiration that continue to shape our lives and values. Masterfully bringing to bear traditional commentaries and contemporary insights, Elkins shows us why these verses matter and what they have to teach us about the essential truths and challenging questions that make the Bible the spiritual fount for Western civilization.

> — **Dr. Jonathan S. Woocher**, *President,*
> *JESNA (Jewish Educational Service of North America)*

It's fun to learn the real meaning of Biblical texts. Rabbi Dov Peretz Elkins is a great teacher.

> — **Edward I. Koch**, *former Mayor, New York City*

Rabbi Elkins' unique and accessible book, based on traditional commentaries as well as modern scholarship, will be a valuable resource to modern readers who are searching for meaning, inspiration and guidance for living an ethical Jewish life. Teens and adults will be able to use this text as a source for engaging and thought-provoking individual or group study.

> — **Helene Z. Tigay**, *Executive Director, Auerbach Central Agency for Jewish Education, Greater Philadelphia*

The Bible's Top Fifty Ideas is smart, well-written, and particularly useful to those for whom Jewishness is more familiar than Judaism.
— **Bret Stephens**, *Editor in Chief,* **The Jerusalem Post**

There are many experiences that make you fall in love anew with the Torah, among them: reading the parsha in shul each Shabbat: the biblical verses lifted out and inserted into the daily morning prayers: watching the second grade chumash play of your grandchildren: the Rashi commentary: and the ethical declarations and constitutions of all western societies.

This book, too. Dov Elkins takes an idea, a string of words. He focuses on the inner core, discovers the wider meaning, connects the words and ideas to our personal and communal lives. He shuttles gracefully between the worlds of Torah commentators, from Midrash to Chassidic rebbes to Nahum Sarna to the latest critical literature and back to the Talmud. In explicating his top 50, he fulfills the Talmudic dictum, *hafach bah ve hafach bah, dekulah bah*: he turns the subject around and around, examining it inside out, and then one more time, finding every association with that chosen string of words. In his depth analysis of these choice verses or those, he reminds us that the Torah is made up of 5,000 such ideas and that every word is precious. And like the great teachers that went before him, Elkins fills our hearts with great pride and with fresh awareness that this is our treasured inheritance, sign of our convenantal relationship with God, precious guidebook on our journey through life and history.

All this he does for us, and more. *The Bible's Top Fifty Ideas* is not a book to be read in one setting but rather to savor, paragraph by paragraph, as the beauty and richness of Torah keeps unfolding before our very eyes.
— **Blu Greenberg**, *author*

Books by Dov Peretz Elkins

The Bible's Top Fifty Ideas
Moments of the Spirit: Quotations That Inspire, Inform and Involve
Chicken Soup for the Jewish Soul (coauthor)
A Shabbat Reader
Moments of Transcendence
Jewish Guided Imagery
Forty Days of Transformation
Meditations for the Days of Awe
Shepherd of Jerusalem
God's Warriors: Rabbis in Uniform
So Young To Be a Rabbi
A Tradition Reborn
Prescription for a Long and Happy Life
My Seventy-Two Friends: Encounters with Refuseniks in the USSR
God's Warriors: Dramatic Adventures of Rabbis in Uniform
Four Questions on the Sidrah
Sidrah Sparks
More Sidrah Sparks
Clarifying Jewish Values
Jewish Consciousness Raising
Loving My Jewishness
Experiential Programs for Jewish Groups
Teaching People to Love Themselves
Glad To Be Me: Building Self-Esteem in Yourself and Others
Twelve Pathways to Feeling Better About Yourself
Self Concept Sourcebook

Translations

Melodies From My Father's House – by Simcha Raz
Hasidic Wisdom (translated with Jonathan Elkins) – by Simcha Raz

Children's Book

Seven Delightful Stories for Every Day

The Bible's Top Fifty Ideas

The Essential Concepts Everyone Should Know

Rabbi
Dov Peretz Elkins

with Abigail Treu

For further information, contact:

99 Spring Street, 3rd Floor
New York, NY 10012
Tel: (212) 431-5011
Fax: (212) 431-8646
E-mail: *publicity@spibooks.com*
Visit us at *www.spibooks.com*

10 9 8 7 6 5 4 3 2 1
First Edition

Library of Congress Cataloging-in-Publication Data available.

ISBN: 1-56171-878-5

To Maxine

Who is always tops in my book

Acknowledgments

My wife, Maxine, has been a partner in all my work, and has encouraged me to strive for perfection in all things. Words cannot express my gratitude for her companionship through all my work, as in all aspects of my life. My children helped in many ways, mostly by being there — but also for helping to find an appropriate title for this book — Hillel and Rachel, Jon and Rachel, Shira and Dany, Jamie and Abby, Jeremy and Yoni.

It is my deepest hope that my grandchildren will some day read this and my other books, since it is for them and their generation that all my labors are expended — Ari Jack, Mollie Jo, Leila Sol and Mia Eden.

I owe a deep debt of gratitude to the students in my adult classes at The Jewish Center of Princeton, New Jersey, who were first exposed to these pages in Xeroxed form.

Many scholars, colleagues and friends freely offered their advice and counsel in the preparation of this book. In its early stages, help was granted by Rabbis Reuven Hammer, Benjy Segal, and Shalom Paul. Later, I had the privilege of having some of the world's greatest teachers and scholars — whom I am also privileged to call friends — review the manuscript as it evolved. Rabbis David Lieber, Ray Scheindlin and Burton Visotzky read part or all of the manuscript and offered very useful suggestions.

It is impossible to mention every teacher to whom I was exposed, and with whom I studied Bible and Bible-related material from my youth to the present. I apologize if I omit any of the important people who influenced my learning in matters biblical and Jewish. First I offer thanks to my own rabbi at whose feet I sat as a child, and whose words I drank as from a deep well of wisdom — Dr. Mortimer J. Cohen, at Beth Sholom Congregation. Rabbi Sidney Greenberg influenced me in more ways than I can count.

At Gratz College in Philadelphia I was privileged to study with some wonderful teachers and seminal minds — including my classmate Shalom Paul, Ezra Shereshevsky, Leon Liebreich, and Shlomo Dov Goitein.

At The Jewish Theological Seminary, while I pursued my rabbinical studies, my classes and informal contacts with many giants of our generation brought me closer and closer to the meaning, inspiration and spirituality of the words of the Tanakh. Some of these are Louis Finkelstein, Gerson D. Cohen, Nahum Sarna, Mordecai M. Kaplan, Abraham Joshua Heschel, Shalom Spiegel, Robert Gordis, Mordecai Margaliot, Max Kadushin, Yochanan Muffs, and H.L. Ginsberg.

During the year 1962-63, when I studied at Hebrew University of Jerusalem, many teachers helped me develop a deeper appreciation of the biblical world, including Yigael Yadin, Menahem Haran, Moshe Goshen-Gottstein and Avraham Malamat.

The literary skill of Alys Yablon made this volume much more readable, and the knowledge of Bible and Midrash of Rabbi Melinda Levinson Zalma assured me that scholars of the highest level would find little to complain about.

I am grateful to the Jewish Publication Society, and especially its distinguished Editor in Chief, Ellen Frankel, for permission to reprint excerpts from *Tanakh* © 1985, The Jewish Publication Society with the permission of the publisher, The Jewish Publication Society; and *The JPS Bible Commentary: Genesis* © 1989, *Exodus* © 1991, *Leviticus* © 1989, *Numbers* © 1989, *Deuteronomy* © 1996 The Jewish Publication Society, with the permission of the publisher, The Jewish Publication Society.

We are deeply grateful to Yaacov Peterseil and Benjie Herskowitz of Devorah Press in Jerusalem for supplying the Hebrew text for each chapter. Without their kind, efficient and professional contribution, the book would not be as useful or attractive.

This work would never have been completed without the research, friendship, and able writing of Abigal Treu, whose contribution of a first draft of several chapters, allowed me to bring it to its proper conclusion, when my busy schedule prohibited me reaching all the way to the fiftieth verse.

I am grateful to Almighty God who granted me the gifts of mind and determination to bring this work to reality in the midst of a busy rabbinate, and in a world filled with boundless distractions.

Dov Peretz Elkins

The Bible's Top Fifty Ideas

The Essential Concepts Everyone Should Know

Contents

Preface xiv

Chapters 1-8
Ideas from **Genesis** 1

Chapters 9-16
Ideas from **Exodus** 56

Chapters 17-24
Ideas from **Leviticus** 108

Chapters 25-31
Ideas from **Numbers** 161

Chapters 32-50
Ideas from **Deuteronomy** 207

References
Traditional Commentaries 336
Bibliography 337

About the Author 343

Preface

Why do we find new meaning in the Bible each time we come back to its chapters, while we seldom find new meaning by rereading a novel? Perhaps it is because, like the old paintings of the great masters, the Scriptures "soak up" something from all the people who have interacted with them over the ages.

— Elie Wiesel

The Bible is mankind's greatest privilege. It is so far off and so direct, categorical in its demands and full of compassion in its understanding of the human situation. No other book so loves and respects the life of man. No loftier songs about his true plight and glory, about his agony and joys, misery and hope, have ever been expressed, and nowhere has man's need for guidance and the certainty of his ultimate redemption been so keenly conceived. It has the words that startle the guilty and the promise that upholds the forlorn. And he who seeks a language in which to utter his deepest concern, to pray, will find it in the Bible.

— Abraham Joshua Heschel

Seek out the book of the Lord, and read.

— Isaiah 34:16

But words are things, a small drop of ink,
Falling like dew upon a thought, produces
That which makes thousands, perhaps millions, think.

— Lord George Gordon Byron

Why is the Bible more famous than known, as Voltaire once asked?

Partly because it is an anthology of so many books, written over so many centuries, by so many different authors. It is like reading through the Encyclopedia Britannica, cover to cover. No one goes through an encyclopedic work like this page by page, book by book. Reading the Bible requires diligent study, infinite patience, a good teacher, and long years of commitment.

How sad, then, that the Book of Books, the literary legacy that Rabbi Heschel calls our "greatest privilege," is so little read, and even worse, so little known.

This vast collection of morals, poetry, laws, stories and divine revelation remains a hidden treasure for most people. Yet it forms the basis of all ethical standards ("Love your neighbor as yourself"), all great moral philosophy ("In the image of God was the human formed"), and legal majesty ("There shall be one law for you and for the stranger among you").

The question becomes, then, How do we transmit, teach and commend to the next generations this exquisite body which comprises the bedrock of modern civilized society?

When I was a child growing up in Philadelphia, our Confirmation Class text was the same book which most tenth graders all over North America used to study the Holy Scriptures, a book written by the rabbi of my own synagogue, Mortimer J. Cohen, titled *Pathways Through the Bible*. Written in the 1940s, *Pathways* is still in print, and is still one of the basic high school texts used in Religious Schools today. I am certain that there are other similar texts — perhaps not as good (Mortimer Cohen was a master of the English language and a teacher par excellence), but serviceable.

Nevertheless, what is needed today is a text that is accessible to the adult reader, and one that utilizes the historical, archeological, literary and exegetical insights of scholars and teachers right up until the early twenty-first century, as well as the vast compendium of commentaries and interpretations written over the last several millennia.

For many readers the pursuit of biblical knowledge is simply too daunting. The image of the Bible to many in today's world is that it is very old, very outdated, very thick and very boring. They may know that buried inside somewhere are deep and abiding truths, but they certainly are not about to spend the days, weeks, months or even years that it would take to discover them. For these reasons a book like Rabbi Cohen's *Pathways* is a marvelous tool.

For the same reason, I have approached teaching the Bible in my adult classes with an eye toward producing not a survey (like

Pathways), but an in-depth concentration on the most significant ideas to be found in it.

I have focused on the Torah, because it contains the laws and stories that are the foundation of the entire Hebrew Bible. Yet even within the Torah one can find some five thousand verses — not impossible to tackle, but also not a small bite, even for an interested reader.

Suppose, I thought to myself, I selected about one hundredth of this amount, and see if I can capture the very central ideas that a knowledgeable, educated and literate modern may want to be familiar with. Fifty verses, or verse clusters, out of five thousand. That surely would not be beyond the average English reader to nibble at, if it were provided with the proper historical, literary and legal background to make it readable, understandable and engaging. A reader can come to such a book and bypass the many verses which turn off the novice, such as "x begat y, and y begat z....; as well as passages which describe in gory detail how the priests lay goats on the altar, and chop them up to sacrifice; and other chapters which depict the splattering of blood around the sacrificial precincts for this or that ritual purpose.

For each of the fifty verse clusters the reader will find two translations. I have used the translations of the Jewish Publication Society (JPS), since Jewish scholars of the Bible have been its most loyal and determined readers, and are among the best, if not THE best in their respective fields of language, history and literary style. In 1917 JPS produced its first translation, based on the King James Version of 1611, but updated to reflect Jewish and scholarly points of view. It maintained the classical English style of "Thee, Thou, Thy," etc. A book review of the newer JPS translation of 1961, written by the late master of classical English literary skill, Abba Eban, complained that the newer translation lost much of its established literary majesty by trading in these antiquarian phrases. This may be so, but the newer translation of 1961, though lacking a bit in elegance, presented the modern reader with a Bible (or, better, a Tanakh) that is more in keeping with the reading habits of the twentieth century reader, as well as updating the Torah with the vast amount of historical, archeological, literary and linguistic information available a half century after the first translation. We shall refer to the two translations as JPS does, and as has become the conventional method of reference, as follows: the 1916 translation is called "JPS" and the 1961 edition as NJV — or New Jewish Version.

My goal in selecting the commentaries and interpretations consulted and presented, woven in the commentary that follows each verse is first to make the text clear, readable and under-

standable for our age and for the modern reader. So much of the
Torah, an ancient book whose language, thought and concepts
are difficult to parse even for the most trained Hebrew authority,
is inaccessible simply because of the distance of three or four millennia between the writer (or Writer?) and us.

Secondly, my hope is that this book will help the reader see
that one cannot comprehend an ancient book like the Torah
without the context of the broader ancient world of Mesopotamia, Assyria, Sumer, Ugarit, and the entire ancient Near East.
This is one of the main differences between the 1916 translation
and the more up-to-date version of 1961.

A third goal is to bring not only the newest linguistic and archeological light to these hoary chapters, but to enable the modern reader to absorb the full impact of the Torah's message on the
moral and ethical values of people who have read and lived by
these texts for centuries since their writing.

Finally, I wanted to show that both Jewish and non-Jewish
commentaries — ancient, medieval and modern — contain what
Jewish tradition calls *peshat* (the simple, straightforward meaning of the text) and *drash* (the homiletical, imaginative extension
of texts that served readers for so many years in so many places,
as their guide book to how to live their daily lives). To show, in
other words, how the Tanakh, both in ancient times and today,
can serve as a Book to light for us a path through the black thick-
ness of our personal and communal lives; to see the Torah as a
book not only to read, study and titillate our intellect, but also to
prod us, challenge us, to see the world from its perspective, and
to push us into new and daring paths of a good life, a serious life,
a life with meaning, purpose, direction, value and hope.

Were the Torah for me just a book of history and law, I may
not have undertaken to teach it in my adult classes, nor would I
have bothered to spend the days and weeks I have to mold my
scribbled teaching notes into what I hope will be a useful book
for people of all faiths and ages. A book to help us re-ignite our
view of The Book as a modern Guide for the Perplexed, a collection of ideas and moral principles that may help us add value to
our lives, and meaning to our existence.

So here it is, *The Bible's Top Fifty Ideas*. The fundamental
ideas and concepts that have moved four thousand years of civilization to produce a moral, legal and literary framework that
has stood the test of time, and remain the basis of all democratic
and principled society to this day.

Dov Peretz Elkins
Princeton, New Jersey
Yom Ha-Atzmaut, 5764

1

Genesis 1:1

בראשית א,א:

בְּרֵאשִׁית בָּרָא אֱלֹהִים אֵת הַשָּׁמַיִם וְאֵת הָאָרֶץ.

JPS (1917) — "In the beginning God created the heaven and the earth."

NJV (1962) — "When God began to create heaven and earth ...."

Many commentaries point to the fact that the Torah begins with the second letter of the alphabet, *bet*, rather than *alef*, the first letter. Some say this is to teach us that we can never know everything. (A similar explanation is given for the Talmud's first page always having the number two, or *bet*, rather than *alef*, or one). Others point out that the last and first letters of the Torah (*lamed* and *bet*) spell the Hebrew word *lev*, heart. One cannot really understand the Torah without coming to it with an open heart.

The Gaon of Vilna (Poland, 1720-1797) suggests fancifully that the first word of the Torah, B'R'SH'I'T, can be read as an acronym, each letter suggesting a complete word: *bitahon*, faith in God, *ratzon*—a willingness to follow the *mitzvot*; *ahavah*, love of God; *shtikah*—quiet acceptance of our lot in life; *yirah*, fear of God; and *Torah*, study and knowledge of the sacred Scriptures.

Some interpreters take note of the fact that the subject-verb order is reversed; i.e., in the Hebrew, the word "created," the verb, precedes the noun, "God." While to us this may seem to be normal poetic usage, the rabbis always looked to grammatical oddities in the text for a peg on which to hang their creative thoughts. One suggestion for word order reversal is that "creation" itself is God's primary attribute, and is the only way for us to recognize God's power and awe. What God *does* is more important than who God *is*. Thus the action word precedes the Being who performed the action, to show us what is most important about God.

It is widely accepted that the biblical creation story is copied in content, (pseudo-) scientific approach to creation, and somewhat in vocabulary, from an earlier Babylonian account, *Enuma Elish*, written some 6 or more centuries before. The biblical Hebrews accepted the Babylonian "science." Babylonian culture was highly advanced long before Hebrews came upon the scene of history, as the discovery of their cuneiform literature demonstrates. Remember also that Abraham came from that part of the world, Mesopotamia, and the Creation story is an introduction (Genesis chapters 1-11) to the appearance of Abraham in the Bible, tracing the history of the Hebrews back from the beginning of the entire world.

Let's compare and contrast the Babylonian story of Creation with ours. In both stories there was at first chaos in the *deep* (Hebrew: *tehom*). In the Babylonian story the goddess Ti'amat was enveloped in darkness. In our story light was the first substance to appear. In the Babylonian account light emanates from the gods. And so on, both accounts following the same order: creation of the firmament, dry land, the sun, moon and stars, the human being, followed by rest and celebration.

The one difference, and not a small one to be sure, is that in the Babylonian story it is the rival deities locked in cosmic combat, who succeed in bringing about the parts of creation. In the Bible there is a single God doing the creation. In biblical scholar Ephraim Speiser's words, "Thus the two are both genetically related and yet poles apart."[1] In short, the Hebrew writer borrowed a primitive scientific and polytheistic account, and turned it into a major premise for the beginning of uncompromising monotheism. By doing so it provided for the creation of a religion, and a revolutionary philosophy of life, with depth, meaning and sanctity. According to Nahum Sarna, this Creation account's "quintessential teaching is that the universe is wholly the purposeful product of divine intelligence, that is, of the one self-sufficient, self-existing God, who is a transcendent Being outside of nature and who is sovereign over space and time."[2] What the Bible did to the Creation story is something akin to what Shakespeare did when he borrowed most (or all?) of his plots from earlier authors and turned them into "Shakespeare."

The Documentary Theory

Scientific scholars claim that the Torah is composed of four major sources which they call J, E, P, and D and edited by R. J is the source which uses God's ineffable name, YHWH; E, which uses *Elohim* until God reveals God's self to Moses, and then uses both names; P, the Priestly documents, mainly the Book of Leviticus and parts throughout Genesis, Exodus and Numbers, which deal with the sacrificial system and the establishment of the sanctity of Israel; D, the source of the book of Deuteronomy;[3] and R, the Redactor (editor), or, as early 20th century philosopher Franz Rosenzweig (Frankfurt, Germany) called more respectfully, "*Rabbenu* (Our Teacher)."

Ephraim Speiser says:

> This opening statement about the creation of the world is assigned by nearly all critics to the P(riestly) source.... The version...displays, aside from P's characteristic vocabulary, a style that is impersonal, formulaic, and measured to the point of austerity. What we have here is not primarily a description of events or a reflection of a unique experience. Rather, we are given the barest statement of a sequence of facts resulting from the fiat of the supreme and absolute master of the universe. Yet the account has a grandeur and a dramatic impact all its own.... The ultimate objective was to set forth, in a manner that must not presume in any way to edit the achievement of the Creator — by the slightest injection of sentiment or personality — not a theory but a credo, a credo untinged by the least hint of speculation.[4]

How Do We Explain the Different Translations of This Verse?

The first word of the Hebrew Bible is "Bereshit." The form of the noun is a "construct" form, which translates literally as "in the beginning of." In Hebrew the construct form of a noun is generally followed by another noun. For example: Bet Sefer, literally, "House of the Book," or "school." *Bayit* is regular form, meaning "house." *Beit* is the construct form, meaning "the house of." *Beit*, "the house of" must be followed by another noun—i.e., the house of the book.

This irregular noun form has provided an open field for commentators throughout the centuries, and has led to a variety of attempts at translation. After all, how can one translate an incorrect grammatical form? We must guess at what the author (Author?) meant.

The two translations above are examples of the two most prominent attempts. The NJV translation "corrects" the vocalization of the following Hebrew word, *"bara"* to force the verse to make sense. Their translation is based on a literal meaning, i.e., "In the beginning of the creation by God of the Heaven and the Earth," — or in better English, "When God began to create the Heaven and the Earth." Taking the liberty to amend the vocalization of the text is somewhat risky — first because it is a guess, albeit an educated guess; and second because it "tampers" with the traditional text, which only scholars who accept a "scientific approach" to textual study can permit themselves. However, since the vowels were placed in the text many centuries after the consonants, and the original, ancient text of the Torah only has consonants, modifying the vowels is nowhere near as serious as changing the consonants would be.

While it is possible to accept the vocalized text as is, since grammar rules have many exceptions, the traditional translation, "In the beginning God created the heaven and the earth," would imply that God's initial performance was inadequate; namely, that even after the first stages of Creation, there was only chaos and formlessness. In the NJV translation, now widely accepted, it is easier to see God in the process of taking formless matter and turning it into something useful.

Who is God in the Creation Account?

In the Mesopotamian stories much space is given to naming, defining and describing the origins of the various gods who are competing with each other. In our account God's existence is not questioned, defined or explained. God is known not for any philosophical, speculative thought, but merely because of the actions that are performed (and later by the demands God makes on human beings in their actions).

God's nature by assumption is in this verse that of Creator. The Hebrew word which follows God's name, *"bara,"* is used in the Bible only in reference to God's creativity. God's creativity is a model for human creativity, but differs from it. Humans create from raw material, while God's creation is *creatio ex nihilo*, creation out of nothing, an act that is *sui generis*, unlike anything a human can perform. According to Sarna, the pagan cosmologies (of which there were many) place great importance on preexisting matter, while in our account, there is no such raw material. God's act of creation is totally unique, and is "utterly beyond all human comprehension."[5]

Homiletical Hasidic commentaries on the word *Bereshit* suggest that God created the world "*Bereshit*" in a state of beginning, and that consequently the task of humankind is to be God's partner (*shutaf*) in the ongoing, never-ending process of continuing creation. The human role as a creative being, formed in the image of God, is an exalted one, and is based on an ancient Talmudic idea. The idea of our being God's partner in a still-being-created world is also reflected in several passages of the Siddur ("God who daily renews creation" — before the *Shema*, and similar ideas elsewhere). David Leiber didn't see how this prayer references our partnership with God, only that Creation is renewed. I guess you can say that means it is ongoing and therefore if it is ongoing than we must be a part of it. Except the prayer seems only to speak about God's role and not ours. Perhaps you can find a more straightforward prayer to illustrate your point.

In Jewish tradition, God has three major roles: Creator, Revealer and Redeemer. One can interpret the phases of Shabbat according to these three concepts. Friday night, in the words of the *kiddush*, God's role of Creator is prominent. On Shabbat morning, when the Torah is read, God's role of Revealer is uppermost. Finally, as Shabbat draws to its end, and dark sets in, when we sing of Elijah and the future Messianic age, the Talmud tells us Shabbat late afternoon is most like the days of Redemption.

In this first verse of the Torah God's name, *Elohim*, is given in the Hebrew plural form, yet the verbs following God's name are always singular. This is the plural of majesty, or the "editorial" we — giving added significance to the word. Sarna believes that *Elohim* is used instead of the sacred divine name *Adonai*, because *Elohim* connotes universalism and abstraction, most appropriate for the transcendent God of Creation.

Rashi explains that the use of *Elohim* here, and *Adonai Elohim* in the second Creation account (Genesis chapter 2) in the following way. According to rabbinic tradition when the Torah uses the word *Elohim* it reflects one side of God's nature: the quality of judgment. When the Torah uses the word *Adonai* it reflects God's mercy, the opposite characteristic. In the verse in the Torah, God created the world, hoping that it could be ruled by strict justice, thus the use of the name *Elohim*. But when God realized that the world could not survive with strict justice alone, the Torah begins the second account of creation after God had employed the other side of Divinity, the quality of mercy (cf. Genesis 2:4). What seems most interesting about this comment is that the rabbinic commentators (and Rashi is the most famous and important of the traditional commentaries) did not hesitate to assume that even God can change God's mind, and often did so!

Is the Creation Story Scientific?

Science tells us that the stars were created well over 10 billion years ago. Many people have tried to reconcile the biblical account of creation with science. This is unnecessary and unfair. Our biblical ancestors could not have known what we know today after centuries of scientific exploration. The creation story is a theological poem, not a scientific or historic account. Rabbi Harvey Fields points out that one can find even in the writings of the ancient rabbis of the Midrash varying scientific explanations of the Creation story that are not literally scientific. He writes: "...some of the rabbis argued that God had created everything on the first day. Then, on each of the five following days, God introduced what had already been formed. Other rabbis disagreed. They believed that the creation of light came before everything else. Still others taught that God, like an unsatisfied artist looking for perfection, had created and destroyed many worlds before deciding that this one was acceptable. (*Genesis Rabbah* 1:15; 3:1,7; 9:2; and 12:14)." [6]

Rashi argues that the Hebrew word for day, "*yom*," might contain thousands of years. However, the many attempts of traditionalists and literalists to reconcile the Bible with science are exercises in futility, and more importantly, misperceptions of the purpose of the Book of Books. Which is ...

Anyone has the right to interpret any verse of the Bible in any way one sees fit. I believe that the only obligation of an interpreter is the clear (even if unspoken) implication that their interpretation is figurative, metaphoric, symbolic and homiletical, rather than literal. This is the traditional function of *Midrash*, i.e., to expand on a biblical verse to bring new interpretations that the author may never have had in mind, but which tells us an important idea. This new idea tells us more about the author of the commentary than that of the original text, but it is attached to the text in that it establishes the chain of historical tradition connected to our sacred past. This is how any sacred work of law or theology maintains its viability in passing generations.

In this vein, a Hasidic sage, Rabbi Moshe Leib of Sassov, interprets the word *Bereshit* to mean that the first and foremost thing with which a Jew should begin one's thinking is that God created the world. This idea of God as Creator is primary, it is the "beginning" idea of all Jewish wisdom and theology.

Notes

[1] E. A. Speiser, *The Anchor Bible: Genesis* (Garden City: Doubleday, 1995) 11.

[2] Nahum Sarna, *Genesis: The Traditional Hebrew Text with New JPS Translation, The JPS Torah Commentary* (Philadelphia: Jewish Publication Society 1989) 3-4.

[3] Moshe Weinfeld, "Pentateuch," *Encyclopaedia Judaica* 1972.

[4] Speiser 8.

[5] Sarna 5.

[6] Harvey J. Fields, *A Torah Commentary for Our Time* (New York: UAHC Press, 1990) I, 23.

2

Genesis 1:27

בראשית א,כז:

וַיִּבְרָא אֱלֹהִים אֶת הָאָדָם בְּצַלְמוֹ בְּצֶלֶם אֱלֹהִים בָּרָא אֹתוֹ
זָכָר וּנְקֵבָה בָּרָא אֹתָם.

*JPS (1917) – "And God created man in His own image, in
the image of God created He him; male and female created
He them."*

*NJV (1962) – "And God created man in His image, in the
image of God He created him; male and female He created
them."*

Only with regard to the creation of humans does God announce his plan, or intention, to create something (cf. v. 26).
Nahmanides points out that this sets apart the special quality of
this creature as compared to the rest of creation. This particular
verse evokes the sense of a more intimate and intensive involvement of God in this specific act of Creation.[1]

In the Mishnah, *Pirke Avot* 3:18, Rabbi Akiva (2nd century)
takes special note of the fact that not only is the human being
made in the image of God, but he is *conscious* of the fact that he is,
and is told so by the Torah. Says Akiva: "Beloved are humans,
who are created in the image of God. They are exceedingly beloved, for it was made known to them that they were created in
the image of God; as it is written (Genesis 9:6) 'For in God's image did God make humans.'"

Another explanation, by Rabbi David Kimhe, suggests that
the uniqueness of the creation of humans was that he/they were
created last, at the peak of creation.[2] In Psalm 8 we find that the
human was created "but little lower than the angels," suggesting
that although humans are not immortal like angels, they do pos-

sess an immortal soul and are capable of recognizing their Creator.

Still another explanation is that only in the case of the creation of human beings is the verb of creation (*bara*) repeated three separate times, and furthermore, in poetic fashion (3 lines of four beats each). Our verse states:

> And God created the human in God's own image;
> In the image of God was the human created;
> male and female God created them.

As Sarna notes, "Human beings are to enjoy a unique relationship to God, who communicates with them alone and who shares with them the custody and administration of the world."[3]

What is the Implication of Being Created in the Image and Likeness of God?

Maimonides deduces that it is only the human being who is endowed with a sense of "morality, reason and free will."[4] Humans alone can love God and can maintain a spiritual dialog with God. Humans alone of all creatures can guide their actions through reason.

Naomi Pasachoff explains Maimonides views on our verse in these words:

> ...if God is purely spiritual and invisible, how can there be a divine image? Maimonides searches the text of the Torah itself for a solution to this problem. He discovers one in a second Hebrew word, *to'ar*. When the Torah is referring to an object's actual shape, image, or form, it uses the word *to'ar*. For example, when Joseph's good looks are being described (Genesis 39:6), we find the word *to'ar*. . . Maimonides concludes that *to'ar* cannot be used for God, because God has no shape. Instead, the Bible uses *tzelem*, because that word points to an object's *essence*. When God made human beings in his *tzelem*, they were made to reflect the essence of godliness—namely, perception and intellect.[5]

According to Sarna, there are several implications of humans being created in the image of God: a) that the human being is above the animal kingdom, b) that only humans can be *murdered* (cf. Genesis 9:6 – "Whoever sheds the blood of a human, By a human shall his blood be shed; For in God's image did God make the human." c) it asserts human dominance over nature (cf. 1:26), d) that the human being is the symbol of God's presence on earth. "While he is not divine, his very existence bears witness to the activity of God in the life of the world. This aware-ness inevitably entails an awesome responsibility and imposes a code of living that conforms with the consciousness of that fact."[6]

Betzelem Elohim, "in the image of God," surely includes many different kinds of spiritual similarities to the Transcendent Being: the ability to think, reason, communicate, and ultimately to transcend oneself.

Why Does Verse 26 Refer to God in the Plural ("Let *us* make man...")?

In the preceding verse (1:26), we read: "And God said, 'Let us make man in our image, after our likeness.'" Much has been written about this peculiar use of the plural. As Harry Orlinsky writes, "It may well be that the plurals here reflect ultimately an older Mesopotamian version of creation according to which a chief god and his assembly of gods took part in arriving at deci-sions.... In Jewish tradition, the phrase denoted God and His an-gels."[7]

The Hebrew Bible has many references to a Heavenly Court whom God consults for advice in various actions. See, for exam-ple, I Kings 22:19 ff., Job 1, and Isaiah 6). Targum Yonatan ben Uzziel (2nd century B.C.E.) paraphrases the verses as follows: "And God said to the ministering angels who had been created on the second day of Creation of the world, 'Let us make a hu-man.'"[8]

In the early traditions of Israel, God was viewed as organiz-ing the cosmos with an army of divine helpers. The members of this divine platoon were called "divine beings" and "morning stars" (Job 1:6, 38:7), "gods" (Psalm 82) or the "host of heaven" (Nehemiah 9:6ff.), and their task was to be God's lieutenants and administrators in a hierarchical bureaucracy (Deuteronomy 32: 8ff.). When the pagan neighbors of Israel saw these creatures as simply members of the pantheon, the Tanakh depicts them as subordinate, and not at all comparable to the Israelite God."

Homiletically, one can use the verse as a jumping off point for teaching that any time an important decision must be made, one should consult with other wise people and not rely on one's own judgment. Such cooperative decision-making will also help those who must accept the consequences of the decision to feel part of the process. Thus God is a model decision-maker, a dem-ocratic Leader par excellence, who "empowers" followers to be part of a decision.

What is the Meaning of Mentioning the Creation of Both Sexes?

This version of the creation of man and woman contrasts with the version in Genesis 2:21-22, in which woman is created from Adam's rib. In this verse, both sexes are created equally, both are mentioned in the same phrase; both are the pinnacle of creation on the sixth day; both are created by the same single God "in God's image."

Rabbi Samson Raphael Hirsch points out that although all living creatures were created both male and female, it is specifically mentioned only in connection with humans to emphasize that God created both sexes in the Divine Likeness.[9]

Rashi used an ancient Midrash (*Genesis Rabbah* 8:1) to explain that God created one being with two faces, which was afterward separated into two parts, male and female. Another interpretation given in the Midrash in *Genesis Rabbah* is that God created one combined bisexual creature, a hermaphrodite, which was then split into two beings. The idea present in both interpretations is similar to the Greek legend of Janus, in which the original creature was first created single, and split into two halves. Are there implications here that every creature has both male and female parts (hormones?), and that the male has mostly male parts (but some female qualities), and vice versa? Jungian psychoanalytic theory is based on the notion that all humans are to some degree androgynous. A truly fulfilled human person makes full use of both aspects of his/her nature, the male (aggressive, penetrating) and female (receptive, compassionate) qualities. Others disagree and claim that the fact that God created "male and female" intends to convey the idea that *two* creatures were originally created, not one androgynous being.

How Did Other Biblical Writers and the Rabbis of the Talmud View the Creation of Humans?

Other accounts of Creation are contained in Genesis 2, Psalms 8 and 104 and Job 38. In general the Bible sings of the glory of Creation as an awe-filled achievement, crowned by the creation of the Human Being, God's partner in Creation.

In the Talmud, we find two main sources referring to the creation of humanity. The first is M. Sanhedrin 4:5; Talmud, Sanhedrin 37a, which reads:

Only one single person was created in the world, to teach that if anyone has destroyed a single life, Scripture imputes it to him as though he had caused a whole world to perish, and if anyone saves a single life, Scripture imputes it to him as though he had saved a whole world. . . . Again, the human being was created singly for the sake of peace among humanity, so that no one can say to another: "My parent was greater than your parent." . . . Also so that the heretics should not say: "There are many ruling powers (gods) in Heaven." . . . Again, but a single person was created to proclaim the greatness of God, for a human stamps many coins with one die, and they are all exactly alike. But God stamped every person with the die of the first person, yet not one of them is like anyone else. [cf. examples: finger prints, DNA, etc.] . . . Therefore every human being must say: "For my sake was the world created."

The second source is *Genesis Rabbah* 8:11:

The angels are created in the image and likeness of God, but they do not increase and multiply. The animals increase and multiply, but they are not created in the image and likeness of God. So God said: 'I will create a human being in the image and likeness of the angels, but he shall increase and multiply like the animals.' And God said: "If I were to create him entirely according to the nature of the angels, he would live forever, and never die. If I were to create him entirely according to the nature of the animals, he would die, and not live again. So what I will do is to create man with something of the natures of both. If he sins, he shall die; if he does not sin, he shall live."

The mystery of creation, as we have seen above, has been the preoccupation of writers, thinkers, artists, poets and philosophers all throughout living history. The attention given to the conception of the universe has called forth from the soul of humans the deepest desire to know more about our origins. Doubtless the Muse of human imagination will continue to speculate on how our planet and our galaxies came to be for centuries and millennia to come.

What Impact Has This Verse Had in History?

The idea that humans were created in the likeness of God has had a far-reaching influence on thinkers, heads of state, leaders in every field of science, medicine, academia, human rights organizations, clergy, teachers, journalists, artists, laborers, including "drawers of water and hewers of wood."

During World War II President Roosevelt was asked why America was involved in the war. He answered: "To defend one verse in the Bible, namely that 'the human being was created in the image of God.'" In other words, the War was fought to pre-serve human dignity and the divine image which every human being carries within as part of our God-given right to freedom and justice.

A human rights organization in Israel, called *Betzelem*, has adopted its name from this verse. It is easy to see why. In the view of some *Betzelem* does not have an unblemished record in its human rights work. Israelis and others have complained that it exaggerates Israeli violations of Arab rights, and ignores Pales-tinian violations of Israeli and Palestinian rights. Nevertheless, its desire to create equality between Israelis and Palestinians is admirable, and it is not at all surprising that their name is drawn from this biblical notion that the rights of human beings are based on the philosophy of the Tanakh.

Philip Gourevitch was hardly the only reporter who held the view that "...the Bible has it that God made us in his own im-age. That means we are made in the image of the creator, and our work is his work—to perpetuate creation by casting our images over and over again in new histories against the screen of the world" (*Forward*, November 1993).

In the introduction to his final annual report as Secretary General of the UN, U Thant wrote: "I feel more strongly than ever that the worth of the individual human being is the most unique and precious of all our assets and must be the beginning and the end of all our efforts. Governments, systems, ideologies and institutions come and go, but humanity remains. The nature and value of this most precious asset is increasingly appreciated as we see how empty organized life becomes when we remove or suppress the infinite variety and vitality of the individual" (*New York Times*, September 21, 1971).

In recalling his painful days as a "refusenik" in the former Soviet Union, Natan Sharansky, now a prominent Israeli states-man, wrote that the "Jewish faith came to mean more to me than simply a part of my cultural background in the days after I was sentenced. It was at that time that I made my decision not to compromise. It wasn't a decision that I reached in any rational way. Rationalization wasn't enough, it was based on an irratio-nal—even mystical—feeling of myself as a Jew created in the im-age of God. And as that was the case, then there could be no possibility of compromise" (*Zionist Forum*, Jerusalem).

Notes

[1] As cited by Nehama Leibowitz, *Studies in Bereshit (Genesis): In the Context of Ancient and Modern Jewish Bible Commentary* (Jerusalem: World Zionist Organization, Department for Torah Education and Culture, 1974) 1.

[2] Ibid. 1-2.

[3] Sarna 1.

[4] Rabbi Nosson Scherman, ed., *The Chumash: The Torah, Haftaros and Five Megillos with a Commentary Anthologized from the Rabbinic Writings* (Brooklyn: Mesorah Publications, Ltd., 1994) 9.

[5] Naomi Pasachoff, *Great Jewish Thinkers: Their Lives and Work* (West Orange: Behrman House, 1992) 34.

[6] Sarna, 12.

[7] Harry M. Orlinsky, *Notes on the New Translation of The Torah* (Philadelphia.: Jewish Publication Society of America, 1969) 58.

[8] Scherman 8.

[9] Samson Raphael Hirsch, *The Pentateuch* (London: Isaac Levy, 1959) I, 33.

3

Genesis 2:24

בראשית ב,כד:

עַל כֵּן יַעֲזָב אִישׁ אֶת אָבִיו וְאֶת אִמּוֹ וְדָבַק בְּאִשְׁתּוֹ
וְהָיוּ לְבָשָׂר אֶחָד.

JPS (1917) — "Therefore shall a man leave his father and mother, and shall cleave unto his wife, and they shall be one flesh."

NJV (1962) — "Hence a man leaves his father and mother and clings to his wife, so that they become one flesh."

The context of this verse, in verses 22 through 25 of Genesis 2, describes the initial relationship between Adam and Eve. One's wife is bone of his bone and flesh of his flesh, and as we read in verse 25, which describes the nakedness of Adam and Eve, they were "not ashamed" of their sexuality. "Sex is not regarded as evil but as a God-given impulse that draws a man and a woman together so that *they become one flesh*. The two were unashamedly naked, a symbol of their guiltless relation to God and to one another."[1]

One of the main points the narrator is trying to make here is that since woman was originally a physical part of man (she was created from his rib, according to the account in this chapter, or split from one being, according to a Midrash on the account in Chapter One), they are literally *one flesh*, and by destiny they belong together. Their normal, innate sexual drive stems from this original union. This is a theological observation, justifying the well-recognized libido in all creatures ("love is strong as death," Song of Songs 8:6).

What Does this Verse Teach us about the Relationship between a Husband and Wife?

Note the assonance of Hebrew *ish* (man) and *ishah* (woman). The same play on words can be found in English: *man* and *woman* (derived from "wife of man"). Sarna explains Adam's naming the woman *ishah*, related to his own designation *ish*, as an acknowledgment that she is his equal. Prior to this verse he is called *Adam*, and now changes his own designation to match hers. "Thus he discovers his own manhood and fulfillment only when he faces the woman, the human being who is to be his partner in life."[2]

There is an old midrash, often quoted at weddings, pointing out the connection in the similarity between the Hebrew words for man and woman (*ish* and *ishah*). The two words, *ish* and *ishah*, share two Hebrew letters and each have one Hebrew letter the other does not have. They both have the *alef* and the *shin*. The word for man, *ish*, contains a *yod*, which *ishah* does not; and the word for woman, *ishah*, contains a *heh*, which *ish* does not. The midrash explains that the letters which are *not* in common, i.e., the *yud* and the *heh*, spell God's name, *Yah* (as in Hallelu*yah*, "praise the Lord"). The obvious lesson is that if you remove God (*Yah*) from the two words, i.e., if you remove God from the relationship between husband and wife, what is left? *Alef* and *shin*, or the Hebrew word for fire, *esh*.

The midrash implies then that without the Godly presence, a marriage will be consumed like fire. But with the right approach to the relationship, a man and woman will be as "one flesh." What does this phrase actually mean? First, there is the obvious sexual connotation as alluded to above. In other words, through sexual intercourse, and through the creation of progeny through intercourse, they combine their "bones and flesh" to make a shared creature, and to share their very essence.

But there is also the metaphoric connotation. Sometimes we refer to a married couple as being "like one person." This means that they share so much of their life, their values, their attitudes, their hopes and dreams, their energy and commitments, that it almost seems as if they were "one person," or "one flesh."

There is an implicit admonition to young people to select someone for a life mate who shares common background, heritage, outlook and values. The more things a marrying couple have in common, the more likely is their union to last.

The medieval Italian commentator Ovadiah ben Yaakov Sforno (1475-1550), makes this comment: "A man should seek to marry a woman harmoniously suited to him, so that together they form *one flesh*, a perfect whole."[3]

It is related that in the high society column of a prominent British newspaper, on the page in which weddings were listed, the following description was given: "The bride and groom were joined in holy matrimony and the two became one. Which one has not yet been determined."

That said, the question remains: In order to cling together, two beings must be separate, individual creatures. How then can they be "one flesh?"

Sarna explains: "There is a seeming contradiction here since Hebrew *d-v-k*, 'to cling,' essentially expresses the idea of two distinct entities becoming attached to one another while preserving their separate identities. To become 'one flesh' refers to the physical aspects of marriage, as though the separated elements seek one another for reunification. The underlying meaning of the paradox is clear, if it is noted that the verb *d-v-k* is often used to describe human yearning for and devotion to God. Sexual relations between husband and wife do not rise above the level of animality unless they be informed by and imbued with spiritual, emotional, and mental affinity."[4]

Does Our Verse Imply a Requirement for Monogamy?

The verse clearly uses the word for woman, or wife, in the singular. That is, a man should cling to his wife (not *wives*). Is the Narrator requiring man to have only one wife? This could not be possible, since even the patriarchs, paradigms of virtue (though not without faults, as we well know from reading their biographies in chapters 12 ff.) have many wives, and never is a shred of criticism suggested by the Torah about their polygamy.

Hertz sees this verse as expressing an *ideal*, even though it was not lived out in the biblical period. "The sacredness of marriage relations, according to Scripture, thus goes back to the very birth of human society; nay, it is part of the scheme of Creation. The Rabbinic term for marriage is *kiddushin*, sanctification; the purpose of marriage being to preserve and sanctify that which had been made in the image of God...."[5]

Thus, the biblical writer is teaching an important lesson that even he may not have completely understood when he wrote it.

Why Does the Torah Require that Man
Leave His Parents?

Verse 23 begins by saying "Then the man [Adam] said...." One might assume that verse 24 is therefore a continuation of Adam's words. Rashi argues that only verse 23 contains Adam's words. Verse 24 begins a new thought, not part of Adam's statement, and is an addendum by God himself (*Ru'ah Hakodesh* — the Holy Spirit, in Rashi's words), Who is teaching this important lesson about man leaving his parents and clinging to his wife. This verse, and the message it contains, is too important to be ascribed to Adam alone.

Rabbi Samson Raphael Hirsch, taking a leaf from an earlier idea in the Talmud, suggests that we have here the basis for the prohibitions in Leviticus 18:6-18 of incestuous relations, and hence non-binding marriages, whose children are in the category of *mamzer* (illegitimate in Jewish Law). The Torah in Leviticus and in later embellishments of this passage, seems to sense, far ahead of its time, both the biological (genetic) and psychological dangers of marital bonds between close relatives. Hirsch is suggesting that this verse is warning us to go far from our parental homestead in seeking a mate.[6]

But as every married person knows, the process of shifting primary loyalties from parents to spouse is a gradual and difficult one and is far more involved than simply physically leaving the parental home. For many people it never happens completely, and thus has the potential to cause repetitive and severe conflicts between oneself, parents and spouse. To whom is our greater loyalty: the man and woman whose physical union gave us our very life and breath (flesh and bones), who raised, natured and loved us, and launched us into the world, or to the person we choose as our mate, and with whom we will in turn raise our own family and with whom we will spend most of our mature lives? In some cases it feels as though we are between a rock and a hard place, trying to make such a difficult decision between two loyalties.

The Torah is clearly telling us that shifting our primary loyalty at a designated point in our lives from our parents to our spouse is built into the design of the universe. In a sense this should make it easier for us, knowing that this is what God and our Tradition demand of us. The Torah expresses this demand very clearly, by telling us in no uncertain terms that we must *leave* our parents (our parents' home) and *cling* to our spouse.

Modern psychologists have expended a great deal of energy on this problem. Moving from one's parental home to one's own intimate relationship and home is part of the long, slow process of maturation. In our young, helpless years, we are clearly dependent on our parents and other caregivers. During adolescence it is the task of the healthy, mature parent to prepare us to go off on our own, for them to "let go" of our dependence on them, and let us go off into the world. The parents' task has been described eloquently in these words: to give their children roots and wings—a solid grounding during our growing-up years, and the capacity to fly on our own at the end of adolescence.

The process of raising children to the point of their independence is a natural and wholesome part of the child-rearing process. It is healthy and necessary for both parent and child to reach the point at which the detailed daily process of nurturing comes to a reasonable end. As adults we continue to grow, but our guides and mentors expand considerably from the narrow circle of parents, significant relatives, teachers and friends who brought us to the point of emotional, spiritual and financial emancipation.

The clear and unequivocal emphasis that the Torah places on this point of personal maturity and autonomy is necessary for both parents and children. It is a two-sided action that is required for the ultimate welfare of both parents and children. Parents must accept their "empty-nest" status, and children must begin a life that is totally their own. Any obstacles in this process of psychological separation, what Jung calls "individuation," will impede the further growth of both sides of the equation—parent and child.

For the Torah to have recognized this crucial, difficult and definitive turning point in the normal life cycle of the generations, is further evidence of its far-sighted psychological and spiritual wisdom, centuries ahead of its time. It is one small detail which gives the Creation Myth in Genesis 1 and 2 the spiritual credibility wherein lies its greatest wisdom and value, and more than makes up for what it may lack in scientific accuracy. It is, after all, the ultimate purpose of God's creation to have each creature set out on the life-long journey of self-reliance, self-realization and self-fulfillment. The Torah has now clearly legitimated this process, and laid the groundwork for the unending journey to commence in its fullest sense.

Notes

[1] Bruce M. Metzger and Roland E. Murphy, eds., *The New Oxford Annotated Bible with the Apocryphal/Deuterocanonical Books* (Oxford, New York: Oxford University Press, 1991) 4-5.

[2] Sarna 23.

[3] A. Cohen, ed., *Soncino Books of the Bible* (London, New York: Soncino Press, 1947) I, 12.

[4] Ibid.

[5] Joseph H. Hertz, *Pentateuch and Haftorahs: Hebrew Text, English Translation and Commentary* (London: Soncino Press, 1960) 10.

[6] Hirsch 70.

4

Genesis 6:9

בראשית ו,ט:

אֵלֶּה תּוֹלְדֹת נֹחַ, נֹחַ אִישׁ צַדִּיק תָּמִים הָיָה בְּדֹרֹתָיו
אֶת הָאֱלֹהִים הִתְהַלֶּךְ נֹחַ.

JPS (1916) — "These are the generations of Noah. Noah was in his generations a man righteous and whole-hearted; Noah walked with God."

NJV (1961) — "This is the line of Noah. — Noah was a righteous man; he was blameless in his age; Noah walked with God."

"**T**hese are the generations of Noah" — our verse begins with the standard formula introducing a Biblical lineage. However, the lineage is interrupted before it even begins, with a comment about Noah's righteousness. The lineage is in fact given later. In the very next verse, the Torah tells us about Noah's three sons, and in chapters 10 and 11 a full lineage stretching 10 generations from Abraham to Noah is given. However, the entire story of Noah and the flood takes place between the introductory statement, "These are the generations of Noah," and the actual list of descendants, and the introduction "these are the generations of Noah" and the listing of Noah's sons is interrupted with a description of Noah's moral character.

Many scholars, stretching from medieval Bible commentators like Rashbam to modern scholars like Nahum Sarna, feel that "these are the generations of Noah" should be understood as the text's way of introducing the story of Noah and the flood. Although the phrase is the one used elsewhere in the Bible to introduce genealogies, here, they argue, it is being used to introduce a story, one that features a genealogy as a sort of epilogue. As Sarna notes in the *JPS Commentary* to Genesis, the verse would be better read as " 'This is the story of Noah.'[1] — Noah was a righteous man...." As a way of setting the background for the story of Noah and the flood, the Torah tells us that Noah was righteous and walked with God. It then explains that Noah had three sons, and then delves into the story of the wickedness that reigned on earth at that time by Noah's contemporaries. Maimonides aptly comments that the note regarding Noah's moral strength explains to the reader why God spared Noah and commanded him to build the ark; without it, the story would lack crucial information about its hero and the reason he was chosen to be saved by God.

Other commentators have seen a broader teaching in the verse's structure. Rashi writes that "because the text mentions Noah, it praises him" — which follows the teaching of Proverbs 10:7 that one should always praise good people when speaking of them, and not skip over their merits. After all, had the Torah not explicitly stated that Noah was righteous and blameless, God's choosing him as the survivor of the great deluge would be inexplicable. So too when we speak of others, we should be careful to recognize that if we don't sing their praises, we may lead others to think more poorly of them than they deserve.

Rashi also suggests that the juxtaposition of "these are the generations of Noah" and the description of Noah's righteousness teaches that "the main progeny of the righteous are good deeds." Indeed, Rabbi Moshe Feinstein, a modern orthodox rabbi, compared the love one has for one's children to the one s/he should have for good deeds. First, a person should perform good deeds out of love, not just out of duty, just as one acts as a parent out of love and not just duty. Moreover, just as a parent loves a child who lacks some ability just as much as he or she loves an exceptionally gifted child, so too no good deed should be disparaged. Finally, a person should strive to perfect his or her own good deeds with as much love and care as he or she puts into raising and perfecting his or her children.[2]

Righteousness in the Bible

The verse uses the words *tzaddik*, translated as "righteous," and *tamim*, translated as "whole-hearted" or "blameless" to describe Noah. What qualities do these terms signify?

In contemporary usage, a *tzaddik* is a person of great piety, integrity, and honesty. The *Alcalay Hebrew-English Dictionary* translates it as "right, righteous, just, innocent, honest, upright, pious, God-fearing, correct, acquitted, *Zaddik (Hassidic Rabbi)*."[3] Indeed, the last entry reveals how the term has become a title of respect bestowed on great rabbis in some circles. The word is used often in the Bible, and as Nahmanides points out, it often has a legal connotation (see, for example, Exodus 23:7, Deuteronomy 25:1, or Proverbs 17:15).

Tamim is harder to define, which explains the varying translations of the JPS and the NJV. The word is usually used regarding ritual animal sacrifice, to denote an animal without blemish and therefore worthy of God (see, for example, Exodus 12:5 or Leviticus 1:3). Used as it is here regarding a person, then, it may mean "morally unblemished" — or as the *JPS Commentary* puts it, "a person of unimpeachable integrity."[4] The adjective can also mean whole or complete, hence the translation as "whole-hearted". One midrash, cited by Sforno in his commentary on the verse, held that Noah's being called "*tamim*" meant that he was born already circumcised.

Taken together, the terms complement one another and paint an inspiring moral portrait of Noah. Sforno writes that Noah was *tzaddik* in his actions, and *tamim* in his thoughts. Nahmanides notes that because Noah was *tamim* — here he takes the term to mean whole, complete, pure – in his righteousness, he did not deserve punishment for any misdeeds. God therefore spared Noah's wife and sons along with Noah himself, because it would have been an unwarranted and cruel punishment to have Noah survive the flood without them. (Another explanation as to why Noah's whole family was saved, Nahmanides writes, is that Noah taught them all to be as righteous and "whole-hearted" as he was, so that they too did not deserve punishment.)

Ibn Ezra's comment on the verse includes a beautiful formula: "righteous in deeds, complete in his heart." This reading of the text can be read in two directions. One who does good deeds and acts justly lives in peace with him or herself. In the other direction, one who is "complete" in his or her heart, is inspired to behave justly and kindly. The example set by this description of Noah in his generations can serve to inspire us to be *tzaddik* and *tamim* in our own.

Who was more righteous, Noah or Abraham?

A battle of reputations has been waged from the comparison of the verse at hand, in which Noah is described as "righteous and whole-hearted" and "walking with God," to Genesis 17:1, which uses similar language to describe Abraham:

> And when Abram was ninety-nine years old, the LORD appeared to Abram, and said to him: "I am God Almighty; walk in My ways, and be blameless."

In Genesis 18:19, God calls Abraham "righteous," so both he and Noah seem to possess similar ethical qualities of righteousness and whole-heartedness. The debate stems from the fact that Noah walked *with* God, while Abraham walked *before* God. Does one image imply a higher standard of righteousness or whole-heartedness than the other?

Several midrashim seek to explore the shades of meaning suggested in the different images of walking with or before God. One midrash (recounted by Rabbi Hertz) envisions a father walking with a child. If the child is young, the father takes that child by the hand, so that the child walks with him. With an older, more mature child, however, the father allows her to walk in front of him.[5] Rashi, evoking this midrash in his comment to Genesis 6:9, writes that Noah needed God to help him in his righteousness. Abraham was strong enough to walk "by himself," but Noah needed God's strong support in order to stay on God's path.

Another midrash compares Noah to a friend of the king, whom the king finds sinking in the mire. The king says to his friend, "Before you sink into the mire, walk with me," saving his friend from disaster through companionship and a supportive presence. Of this midrash, Nehama Leibowitz writes:

> How apt is the parable used by our Sages. One who is sinking in the mire wishes to extricate himself, but cannot on his own. Noah possessed the will to extricate himself from the corruption of his generation. Because he possessed the initial desire to do so, the Almighty came to his aid, saying "come and walk with Me." But Abraham was in no need of help.[6]

In other words, the only reason Noah needed God's help — and needed to walk *with*, and not *before*, God — was because he was surrounded by corruption and violence.

These midrashim seem to place Abraham at a higher level of righteousness or "whole-heartedness" than Noah. This attitude is bolstered by the reactions the two had to God's news of impending destruction. When Abraham was told of God's plan to destroy the wicked cities of Sodom and Gemorrah in Genesis 18, he argued with God on behalf of the innocent. Noah, however, says nothing upon learning of God's plan to bring a flood which will destroy nearly all of humanity. As Nehama Leibowitz put it, "Noah was limited in his horizons and belonged to those who were satisfied to save their own souls."[7] Abraham and Noah's differing reactions indeed show differing levels of righteousness and courage before God. Abraham, billed as "strong" and "independent" in the above midrashim, has the courage to plead for God's mercy on behalf of others he does not know. Noah, who needed God's help and support to maintain his righteousness, lacked the spiritual strength or courage to plead for mercy for his fellows.

The midrash, aware and uncomfortable with this unkind picture of Noah—after all, Noah is called "righteous" and "blameless," and his being singled out by God to survive the flood is predicated on those positive qualities—fills in this "gap" with stories of Noah warning his fellow contemporaries of the impending disaster and encouraging them to change their ways.[8] Sforno picks up on these stories when he writes in his commentary to Genesis 6:9 that Noah "walked in God's path to do good to others and to persuade the people in his generation" of God's goodness.

Nehama Leibowitz sees in Noah's silence not a failure, but a signal that Noah and Abraham were given different missions from God according to their different capacities. "Noah is singled out for survival, Abraham for a mission," she writes.[9] Abraham walked in front of God in order to spread the message of God's coming before God's arrival. Noah, who didn't have the capacity to save others, had a different Divine mission: to save himself and his family in order to bring a new start to humanity. God, who has created each of us according to God's image and will, knows our individual strengths and capacities, and asks of each of us only what we can handle. The stronger among us are asked to walk before God, alone; many of us, however, require God's comforting presence and seek only to walk with God as we, like Noah, seek to maintain a righteous and blameless path through life.

Noah: Righteous "in his Generations"

If the Torah is trying to paint Noah as "righteous" and "blameless," then why include the qualifying phrase "in his generations"? Does "in his generations" somehow lessen the compliment paid to Noah's character? Or is it teaching something else?

Since the earliest discussions of this text, there has been disagreement as to what "in his generations" implies. The Talmud (BT *Sanhedrin* 108a) records a dispute among the Sages on this very point. Some rabbis argued that "in his generations" was a compliment to Noah. Noah, they argued, was a perfectly righteous man. In fact, he would have been even more righteous if he had lived in a more righteous generation. "In his generations" teaches that Noah's righteousness would only have grown had he lived among more righteous people than he did.

Against this position, other rabbis argued that "in his generations" is a phrase discrediting Noah. According to this opinion, Noah was called righteous only in comparison with the wicked people among whom he lived. Had he lived in Abraham's generation, this argument goes, Noah would not have been counted as righteous at all. Building on this idea, a midrash (recounted by Nehama Leibowitz)[10] compares Noah to a silver coin found in a pile of copper coins. Even though there are coins more valuable than silver, the silver coin stands out for its beauty and rarity and comparative value when surrounded by the dull, inexpensive copper ones. So too, Noah stood out as righteous and even "blameless" in the context of his corrupt and violent contemporaries; however that description says little about his character relative to other, much more righteous people.

At the very least, "in his generations" implies that Noah must be judged in terms of his situation. Given that Noah's generation was corrupt and violent, so much so that God decided to destroy all of humanity rather than let them continue their wickedness, Noah maintained "civilized standards of behavior."[11] Nahmanides wrote that Noah's righteousness was in his following only the one true God, even in his evil generation. Noah was not swayed by astrologers, soothsayers, sorcerers or idol-worshippers, all of whom (in the rabbinic imagination) prevailed at that time. Noah had the strength of character, the moral integrity, and the firm faith to "walk with God" at a time when no one else was. For that, Noah stood out alone in his generation in God's eyes, and was chosen by God to be the one from whom all future humanity would be born following the flood. As the *Sefer HaParshiyot* states the righteous—and the not-so-righteous— should be judged in terms of his or her circumstances, including the time and place and situation in which a person lives.[12] All of these influence one's behavior and have an important hand in our relationship to each other, to Judaism and to God.

Furthermore, if the phrase "in his generations" is confusing conceptually, it is also confusing grammatically. Why is the word plural?

While there is no good *pshat* or literal explanation, there are several more midrashic ones seeking to explain the grammatical oddity. Maimonides teaches that "generations" is in the plural because Noah was the most righteous man to live for many generations, not just his own. This puts Maimonides on the side of those who argue that "in his generations" is a compliment to Noah's character. "Noah was in his generations a man righteous and whole-hearted" is the Torah's way of telling us that there was no other person for many generations worthy of being saved from the Flood.

Another medieval commentator, Ibn Ezra, used the plural "generations" as a springboard from which to further connect Noah with Abraham. Abraham, he notes, was 58 years old when Noah died (the letters spelling Noah's name in Hebrew add up in numerology, or "Gematria," to 58). The text therefore writes "generations" in the plural, to show that Noah was the most righteous for all of the 10 generations stretching between them.

What does it mean that "Noah walked with God"?

The phrase *"hithalekh et Elohim,"* meaning "walked with God," is used three times in the Bible. It is first encountered in Genesis 5:22 and 5:23, regarding the figure of Enoch. In the midst of a genealogy stretching 10 generations from Adam and Eve to Noah, the Torah offers a mysterious and tantalizing tidbit regarding Enoch:

> When Enoch had lived 65 years, he begot Methuselah. After the birth of Methuselah, Enoch walked with God 300 years; and he begot sons and daughters. All the days of Enoch came to 365 years. Enoch walked with God; then he was no more, for God took him.

No more is said of Enoch, though midrashim based on this unusual description of his "walking with God" paint various pictures of him.

The second time the Torah uses the phrase is here, in Genesis 6:9, regarding Noah. Here it seems part of a compliment, including in the praises "righteous" and "whole-hearted," and used to account for God's sparing Noah and his family from the flood. Finally, the phrase is used in Malachi 2:6, as part of a description of an ideal priest:

> Proper rulings were in his mouth;
> And nothing perverse was on his lips;

He walked with Me with complete loyalty
And held the many back from iniquity.

Here too, the phrase is a positive one. The JPS *Torah Commentary* describes it as "expressive of a life spent in full accord with God's will and in closest intimacy with Him."[13] Saadya Gaon wrote in a similar vein that "walking with God" means "with awe of God."

The phrase in 6:9, however, features an unusual word order. The order of the phrase is inverted, so that it would be translated literally as "with God walked Noah." Perhaps, suggests Nahum Sarna, the placing of God at the beginning of the phrase emphasizes the centrality of God's presence in Noah's life. The unusual turn of phrase, he writes, "accentuates the fact that the standards by which Noah's righteousness is judged are divine, not human."[14] The medieval commentator known as Radak (Rabbi David Kimhi) argued that the phrase, as applied to Noah, calls attention to the fact that Noah had to be strong in order to overpower his own human nature and the bad influence and example of his friends and neighbors. Since he was living among corrupt people, he had to maintain the strength to resist learning their ways, and to isolate himself from worshipping their gods and lowering himself to violence and depravity. "With God Noah walked" emphasizes that Noah dedicated his life only to God and the amount of strength such resistance to the ways of those around him required.

Notes

[1] Sarna 50.
[2] As paraphrased in the Scherman 30.
[3] Reuben Alcalay, *The Complete Hebrew-English Dictionary*, (Brooklyn: Hamed Books New York Branch, 2000) II, 2153.
[4] Sarna 50.
[5] Hertz 26.
[6] Leibowitz 63.
[7] Ibid. 61.
[8] Sarna 50.
[9] Leibowitz 64.
[10] Ibid 59-60.
[11] Sarna 50.
[12] as noted in Scherman 31.
[13] Sarna 43.
[14] Ibid. 50.

5

Genesis 12:1

בראשית יב,א:

וַיֹּאמֶר ה' אֶל אַבְרָם, לֶךְ-לְךָ מֵאַרְצְךָ וּמִמּוֹלַדְתְּךָ
וּמִבֵּית אָבִיךָ אֶל הָאָרֶץ אֲשֶׁר אַרְאֶךָּ.

*JPS (1917) – Now the Lord said unto Abram: 'Get thee out
of thy country, and from thy kindred, and from thy father's
house, unto the land that I will show thee.*

*NJV (1962) – The Lord said to Abram, "Go forth from your
native land and from your father's house to the land that I
will show you.*

The next two verses, clearly part of this one indivisible unit,
read:

> JPS—*And I will make of thee a great nation, and I will bless thee,
> and make thy name great; and be thou a blessing. And I will bless
> them that bless thee, and him that curseth thee will I curse; and in
> thee shall all the families of the earth be blessed.*

> NJV—*I will make of you a great nation,
> And I will bless you;
> I will make your name great,
> And you shall be a blessing.
> I will bless those who bless you
> And curse him that curses you;
> And all the families of the earth
> Shall bless themselves by you.*

This verse and the chapter of which it is part turns the biblical narrative to a new phase of human history, and makes way
for the entrance of a new people/nation in the family of peoples
and nations.

The importance of God's selection of Abraham to be the Progenitor (with Sarah) of the Jewish People foreshadows the three major components of Judaism as it developed in biblical history: The creation of a new religion (ethical monotheism), a new people (the Hebrews, later called Israel, and, finally, the Jews), and a Land (Eretz Yisrael) which was to be central to the nationality and religion of Israel. This tripartite value system of God, People and Land was to be the hallmark of this universal people that changed human history in such radical ways in the millennia following its Founding Parents, Abraham and Sarah.

Forgiving the anachronism, Abraham has often been called the first Zionist in history. His radical relocation of place, belief and ethnic identity was a total transformation in his life. The typology of such a total transformation of one's life and lifestyle, belief system, values, loyalties and goals in life, falls into the category of what has been called a religious conversion, in the fullest technical sense of that term. William James in his classic study, *The Varieties of Religious Experience*, explains in depth the significance of the transformation that happens to people when they discover, usually in some kind of mystic vision, an entirely new direction in their life.[1]

Such religious conversions are not uncommon today, and have been described in Hasidic literature as the moment in which certain individuals "see the light" of a new philosophy or *Weltanschauung*. Their entire life finds a new direction and purpose, and everything about them is focused on this new and powerful belief that seizes them with a totality and passion that is unsurpassed in anything previously experienced. Such a phenomenon is present in the modern day Baal Teshuvah Movement among Jews, and among Christians (born-agains) and Moslems in their respective traditions.

Rashi explains the Hebrew words "*Lekh Lekha,*" — i.e., "Get thee," or literally "Go to yourself" — to mean that it will be for Abraham's own benefit to do as God commands. The normal Hebrew grammatical construction, meaning "take leave," is here over-literalized to mean midrashically that by acceding to God's call, Abraham ultimately benefits himself (Lekh *lekha*). A Hasidic interpretation plays on the same Hebrew grammatical construction, and translates the verse "Go to yourself," i.e., Go inwards, go to your innermost being, to find your destiny, vision and calling in life.

God's promise to Abraham, which we shall examine in greater detail a bit further on, contains an important and well-known Hebrew word, *goy*. God promises to make Abraham the head of a great "*goy,*" or *nation*. The Torah does not use the other possible word here, *am* — or people. The word *goy* suggests a political entity, and requires land to complete its full nature. Some scholars suggest that this verse was written when a more highly developed national consciousness had come into existence during the period of the early monarchy, when this story was retold and set into its present form. (Namely, the days of the first Kings of Israel, Saul, David, Solomon).

The use of the word *goy* clearly reflects the important tie that the Land of Israel has had in Jewish consciousness from the earliest days of Jewish history. Even more important, of course, is the integral connection between Abraham's call and mission of serving God by going to the special land that was to be the home of the nation Abraham is commanded to establish.[2]

Who is Abraham and Why Did God Choose Him?

Nothing is stated about the first seven and a half decades of Abraham's life. Suddenly, with a terse statement, Abram is called by God to be the Founder of the Jewish People, at the age of 75.

Why was Abraham chosen for this exalted role? Christian interpretation suggests that it was purely out of God's grace, and that Abraham did nothing special to deserve this merit. One source in the Midrash seems to agree (*Midrash Tanhuma*, Lekh Lekha, 9). But most Jewish commentators find Abraham to be a special individual who, through his life's actions, his sincere search for a monotheistic faith, and for his special moral qualities (as seen from future chapters in his biographical narrative), he was elected by God to begin a new direction in human history and religious belief.

Abraham's call by God is one of many examples in the Tanakh of special people being called to fulfill a unique mission by their Creator. Moshe's call was at the burning bush (Exodus 1); Isaiah's in the Temple in Jerusalem (Isaiah 6). The "call" experience is a religious genre, a model for every human being (or group) who is called by God to fulfill their own special task that only they can fulfill in this universe.[3]

Abraham's Exit from Babylonia: Where, When, and How?

There is a difference of opinion as to whether Abraham is being commanded to leave Ur of the Chaldees, his birthplace, or Haran, the city where he and his father, Terah, paused on their journey from Ur (see the previous chapter, 11:28). In any case, Abraham is being told to leave Babylonia, and the exit is described in three Hebrew phrases.

JPS translates these literally as three stages: thy country, thy kindred, and thy father's house. Modern Hebrew grammarians lump the first two Hebrew words as if it were one noun with a modifying adjective (called by the technical term *hendiadys*) — in which two nouns connected by an "and" are really one modified noun. In our case, NJV translates the phrase *me'artzekha umimoladetekha*, as "your native land." (In other words, "the land of your birth," rather than "your homeland *and* your birthplace").

Traditional commentators see three separate stages of leaving mentioned here, often read as the reverse of the logical order of leaving. After all, to go on a journey, one must first, logically, leave one's specific home, then one's city, and lastly one's country. Why then is the order given in the reverse here? Some see an ascending order of difficulty — to leave your Homeland, then your own city, and finally, hardest of all, to leave your household. Another way to put it would be to say that this ascending order of difficulty is leaving your country, your extended family, and your nuclear family.[4] The main point here is the difficult chore which God is placing on the shoulders of Abraham — to make a radical change in his life and lifestyle.

Rabbi Hertz suggests that the fact that Abraham does not know his specific destination, that it is merely called "the land," raises his spiritual status, because it increases "the test of [his] faith in the Divine call."[5] In other words, Abraham's willingness to go wherever God wants him, regardless of the locale or circumstances, makes his trust in God all the more convincing and authentic. In verse 4 the text simply reads, "And Abram went forth, as the Lord had commanded him...." No questions asked.

Rashi gives another reason. "God did not reveal to him at once which land it was in order that he should hold it in high esteem and in order to reward him for complying with each and every command [such as the sacrifice of his only son in Genesis 22]." Rashi attributes to God a psychological sophistication, knowing that something that is unknown and mysterious will make the place even more special and precious, enabling Abraham to elaborately fantasize about some special land of dreams.

Blessings and Curses

JPS translates the culminating blessing to Abraham and the Jewish People in this way: "And in thee shall all the families of the

earth be blessed." NJV (1962) translate it this way: "And all the families of the earth/Shall bless themselves by you."

Because the Hebrew verb for bless is in the passive, *ve-nivrekhu*, it is not clear whether it has the connotation that others will *be blessed* through Abraham and his descendants; or that the families of the earth (understanding the Hebrew verb as having a reflexive usage, which the passive construction *nifal* often has) will *bless themselves* by using Abraham's name.

Let's try to understand the difference between the two translations. If we follow JPS, the meaning is that the greatness of Abraham and his descendants, the Jewish People, will be such that other nations will be able to copy it and derive benefit from it. In other words, all the nations of the earth will be blessed to have Abraham and his people among them on this earth—by learning from them and using them as role models. This is a high compliment. The Jewish People will do such wonderful things, and be such a wonderful people of extremely high standards, that all other groups and communities will learn from them, and their greatness will spread to others.

If we follow the NJV (1962), considering the verb "bless" to be reflexive, then what the verse means is that groups will point to Abraham and his descendants and say: "May we be like Abraham and the Jewish People." Or, alternatively, say to other nations, "May you some day be as great as the Jews!" In other words, they will use Abraham's name and the name of the Jewish People as a source of blessing and as an ideal role model.

Both translations clearly place a wonderful blessing on Abraham and his future progeny. However, the older translation, that of JPS (1917) gives a greater sense that it is God who will be the one to spread Abraham's blessings gradually to the rest of the world.

Sarna sees verse three as a three-staged blessing to Abraham, from the particular to the universal. First Abraham is blessed (verse two); then anyone coming into contact with him (verse three); and finally all the families of the earth (end of verse three).[6] He divides God's blessing in verse 2 into 7 segments:

1) "I will make of you a great nation"—great in both number and importance.

2) "I will bless you"—with material prosperity (the word *b'rakhah* often has this specific connotation.)

3) "I will make your name great"—the importance of one's name in the Ancient Near East has a significance far beyond what it meant at other times and places. Here it designates

that Abraham "will acquire fame but also that he will be highly esteemed as a man of superior character."

4) "You shall be a blessing." Abraham will be the standard by which blessings are invoked.

5) "I will bless those who bless you" — Anyone who joins you will share God's blessings.

6) "And curse him that curses you." — Note that those who bless Abraham will be many, and his curser is in the singular ("him that curses you"). Those who curse Abraham will be punished appropriately.

7) "And all the families of the earth/Shall bless themselves by you." All God's children will ultimately share Abraham's blessings by God.[7]

Rabbi S. Singer declares:

> The germ of the idea underlying the fuller conception of a Messianic Age was in existence from the time of the founders of the race [sic] of Israel. *In thy seed shall all the families of the earth be blessed*, was the promise given both to Abraham and Isaac. It as a promise that reached far beyond the lifetime of each, farther than the limits of the temporal kingdom their descendants founded; that has obtained but partial fulfillment up to our time, and looks for fullest realization to that future towards which each of us in his measure may contribute his share.[8]

By declaring that the influence of Abraham and his children and children's children will have such a powerful influence for good on the world, the Torah foreshadows the notion that some day all God's children will be blessed like Abraham, and that the qualities of Abraham's descendants will some day spread to the entire world. This is identical to the idea of the coming, at some future age, of the Messiah.

Notes

[1] William James, *The Varieties of Religious Experience* (New York: Random House, 1929) 213-26.

[2] One further interesting note. In modern Yiddish parlance, the word *goy* refers to a *non*-Jew, though in the Bible the word simply means "a nation." Over time, the Hebrew term came to mean "other" nations, or non-Jews, while in our verse, it is the Jews who are referred to as "goy," before the term took on its expanded and separate meaning of non-Jew.

[3] For fuller descriptions of the nature of Abraham's call see Yehezkel Kaufmann, *The Religion of Israel* (Chicago: University of Chicago Press, 1960) 221-231; Adin Steinsaltz, *Biblical Images: Men and Women of the*

Book (New York: Basic Books, 1984) 13-19. All heroic beginnings in ancient mythology can also be compared in Joseph Campbell's classic study, *The Hero With A Thousand Faces* (Princeton: Princeton University Press, 1972), in which he says that the call of the Hero is the essence of all ancient mythology, in which the Hero in every myth is the creator of a new vision, the founder of an institution, and the giver of life and vitality to his community.

[4] Sarna 88.

[5] Hertz 45.

[6] Sarna 89. Additionally, Rabbi W. Gunther Plaut, in his highly acclaimed *The Torah: A Modern Commentary* (New York: Union of American Hebrew Congregations, 1981), explains the verse in these beautiful words:

> Few biblical dicta have been more clearly reflected in history than the statement that those who bless Israel will be blessed and those who curse it will be cursed, or that those who are blessed bless Israel and those who are cursed curse Israel. The decline of a nation can often be clearly related to the way it has treated the Jew, and its prosperity stands in direct proportion to its sense of equity and human dignity. For if the Jew rests indeed at the fulcrum of spiritual history, his condition must be essential to the welfare of his environment. Enough historical evidence can be advanced — from the appearance of the Prophets to the events of the holocaust — to make a persuasive case for the archetypal significance of Jewish existence in the world, a significance that Jews themselves have considered central ever since patriarchal days. 119

[7] Sarna 89.

[8] As quoted by Hertz 45.

6

Genesis 18:25

בראשית יח,כה:

חָלִלָה לְּךָ מֵעֲשׂת כַּדָּבָר הַזֶּה לְהָמִית צַדִּיק עִם רָשָׁע
וְהָיָה כַצַּדִּיק כָּרָשָׁע חָלִלָה לָּךְ הֲשׁפֵט כָּל הָאָרֶץ
לֹא יַעֲשֶׂה מִשְׁפָּט.

*JPS (1917) – "That be far from Thee to do after this man-
ner, to slay the righteous with the wicked, that so the righteous should be as the wicked; that be far from Thee; shall
not the Judge of all the earth do justly?"*

*NJV (1962) – "Far be it from You to do such a thing, to
bring death upon the innocent as well as the guilty, so that
innocent and guilty fare alike. Far be it from You! Shall not
the Judge of all the earth deal justly?"*

Abraham's plea, nay, argument with God over the fate of the
wicked city of Sodom is one of the classic passages in biblical literature. Israel Zangwill called the verse an "epochal sentence in
the Bible."

Because this is the first "argument" with God, it sets the
standard by which we learn that such challenges to God are not
only permitted, but perhaps expected, the assumption being that
not even the Infinite is incapable of making a mistake in judgment. At the very least, we may learn from this story that in order to understand God's judgment, we must argue with God to
ascertain for ourselves the justice of the decision. In any case,
Abraham's actions distinguish his faith from other traditions of
his time in that he is unwilling to blindly accept Divine Will. In
the 18th century, when the Hasidic Movement was founded in
Eastern Europe, it became standard to argue with God and the
world's justice.

That the Bible enables people to argue with the Almighty, with no hint of this being an improper, blasphemous or heretical act, is an enormous vote of confidence in the powers of the divinely-bestowed cognitive ability of humans. To the contrary, it is almost expected of one of God's elite. For other examples of prophets challenging God, see the arguments of Jeremiah, Habakkuk, and Job.

What Were the Sins of the People of Sodom and Gomorroh?

Rabbi Harvey Fields summarizes six sins that are mentioned in many Jewish traditional commentators as the reasons for which the people of Sodom and Gomorroh were to be punished:

1) They refused to share their wealth and abundant riches with others.

2) They made fun of those in need and deliberately made their lives more miserable.

3) They refused to care for the sick, aid the poor, help the needy, or offer hospitality to the immigrant or stranger in their midst.

4) Their leaders were so greedy and selfish that they made cruelty a public policy.

5) They went so far as to punish their own citizens who reached out to feed the hungry or provide shelter to the homeless.

6) Their judges practiced dishonesty and robbery, and their courts offered no fair treatment for victims of oppression or injustice.[1]

Clearly, such a society would have to be punished. But the question remains: Why doesn't God or Abraham demand that the people of Sodom and Gomorroh repent, before pronouncing the final decision of doom?

Jonah gave the people of Nineveh 40 days to change their ways, and by doing so they were able to avert their terrible disaster. Why not the same here in our case? Furthermore, throughout the writings of the biblical prophets, the world's supreme models of teachers of morality, the theme of the possibility of change and *teshuvah* is ubiquitous. Why not here?

Very simply, the grand humane conception of repentance is an idea that did not develop until after the early period of patriarchal times with which we are now dealing. It may be startling for some to accept, but it is a fact that in this early stage of biblical theology, the notion of the possibility of change and repentance simply was not sufficiently crystallized in the mind of the biblical writer. Part of the secret of understanding the Book of Jonah lies in the fact that while God is perfectly content to have the Ninevites repent, Jonah is not yet ready to accept such a revolutionary concept in his theology. He thus refuses to do God's mission.

Why Is Abraham Concerned about God's "Reputation?"

In biblical theology, one's religion was closely tied with the personal qualities of the God (or gods) one accepted. Is there a suggestion here that a questionable act by Abraham's God would not only reflect ill on Abraham, but on God as well? Rashi expresses the concern that if people would see the unfair punishment by lumping together the good and evil people in the destruction of Sodom and Gomorroh, they would associate that with God's destruction of the generation of the Flood (perhaps also a conglomeration of good and bad people?), as well as God's actions regarding the dispersal of the builders of the Tower of Babel, and conclude that this God is some capricious potentate.

It is clear that the Bible as a whole is a book permeated by the foundations of universal ethical monotheism, which allows for the highest standards of justice and equality to be applied to all creatures made in the image of God. This broad pattern of universal justice is one of the extraordinary hallmarks of biblical literature, centuries before the notion of human oneness entered into the consciousness of society at large. Consider Malachi's uplifting doctrine: "Have we not all one Father? Did not one God create all of us?" (2:10). Any charge of parochialism against the Israelite or Jewish tradition can be forcefully undermined by many such passages in Jewish literature, beginning with the Founder of Judaism, Abraham.

What is the Biblical View of the Relation Between the Individual and Society as Reflected in this Verse?

In Speiser's view the author of this passage ("J") takes the position that the saving grace of the just individual (Abraham) is sufficient to bring salvation to the entire community.[2] He also points out that even though any very small deserving minority is not large enough to save the entire community, nevertheless there are some who are saved—namely, Abraham, his nephew Lot and Lot's daughters. He also notes that this theme of the "Suffering Just" is also discussed in other pre-Israelite Babylonian literature. The most well-known treatment of this subject in the Bible is, of course, in the Book of Job.

Sarna points out that it is both Abraham and God whose ethical standards are being tested. As in other biblical passages, God takes a trusted servant into confidence. In Amos (3:7) we find: "Indeed, My Lord God does nothing without having revealed His purpose to His servants the prophets." Jeremiah points out that God never makes important decisions without consulting the one "who has stood in the council of the Lord, and seen and heard His word" (23:18). As Sarna puts it, "...the divine foretelling is an expression of God's love for humanity, meant to warn of impending calamity in the hope of bringing about repentance and the enhancement of the human condition. Such was the case, for instance, in the Book of Jonah. In this prior revelation to Abraham of God's intentions toward Sodom, both the patriarch's humanity and God's morality are put to the test."[3]

In other words, if Abraham (and his descendants) are to be the source of blessing to the entire world, he cannot be impervious to the fate of humanity at large. In this story Abraham proves himself to be worthy to carry on the tradition of "the way of the Lord" (Genesis 18:19). Verse 19 in our chapter clearly adumbrates Abraham's role in being chosen by God to spread the highest standards of justice and ethics in the world. Note the comment in the Talmud (Tractate *Beitzah* 32b): "Whoever is merciful to his fellow beings is without doubt of the descendants of our father Abraham, and whoever is not merciful to his fellow beings certainly cannot be of the descendants of our father Abraham."[4]

Sarna distinguishes two separate issues here—the justification of exonerating the evil by not destroying the city, and the morality of punishing the good by destroying the city. God is being called to the standard of justice in the former case, and mercy in the latter. In both, Abraham and God emerge triumphant.

What Significance Does the Number "Ten" Have in Our Story?

There is an implication in the story that if there is not a minimal sense of community among a number of righteous people, that justice cannot sustain itself. That indeed, there is some limit beneath which the principles of justice would be swallowed up by the larger majority. That magical number (is it arbitrary?) is ten, a number not without significance in Jewish tradition. According to the tradition, certain prayer services may only be conducted in the presence of ten men (or in modern liberal communities, ten men and women). The Midrash (*Bereshit Rabbah* 49:13) is worth quoting on the subject of the *minyan*:

> And why ten? So that there might be sufficient for an assembly [of righteous men to pray] on behalf of all of them. Another reason, why ten? Because at the generation of the Flood eight righteous people yet remained [Noah, his wife, three sons and their wives], and the world was not given a respite for their sake.

The tradition does not feel it possible to permit a group smaller than ten to act strongly enough against a larger majority to ward off the evil consequences of a mob psychology. With a minimal number of ten, it seems, the sense of community among the righteous is strong enough to sustain itself.

Notes

[1] Fields 50.
[2] Speiser 135.
[3] Sarna 131.
[4] as quoted by Sarna 132.

7

Genesis 28:16-17

בראשית כח,טז-יז:

וַיִּיקַץ יַעֲקֹב מִשְּׁנָתוֹ וַיֹּאמֶר אָכֵן יֵשׁ ה' בַּמָּקוֹם הַזֶּה
וְאָנֹכִי לֹא יָדָעְתִּי: וַיִּירָא וַיֹּאמַר מַה נּוֹרָא הַמָּקוֹם הַזֶּה
אֵין זֶה כִּי אִם בֵּית אֱלֹהִים וְזֶה שַׁעַר הַשָּׁמָיִם.

*JPS (1917) – "And Jacob awaked out of his sleep, and he
said: 'Surely the Lord is in this place; and I knew it not.'
And he was afraid, and said: 'How full of awe is this place!
This is none other than the house of God, and this is the
gate of heaven.'"*

*NVJ (1962) – "Jacob awoke from his sleep and said, 'Surely
the Lord is present in this place, and I did not know it!'
Shaken, he said, 'How awesome is this place! This is none
other than the abode of God, and that is the gateway to
heaven.'"*

Jacob's famous dream, which occurs between Beersheva and
Haran as he flees from Esau (having just stolen their father's
blessing), is a classic image in world literature, and has been the
subject of much mystical, philosophical, literary, and artistic
speculation.[1]

The connection between the words "Shaken" and "Awesome" in verse 17 set the tone for much of the commentaries on
this excerpt. Both words derive from the same Hebrew root, *yod,
reish, alef*. As in all translations, there is no exact equivalent to any
one word in another language. The Hebrew words *vayira* and
nora have a multitude of connotations, but both clearly connote
the sense of religious awe and reverence which Jacob is experi-
encing. There is no doubt that this is a "conversion experience"

in the sense that William James wrote about in his classic text, *The Variety of Religious Experience.*[2]

The word and concept have been translated in different ways by different theologians over the centuries, in a variety of traditions, in a multitude of ways. The 19th century scholar Rudolph Otto called it the sense of the *numinous*, and it is probably what Kierkegaard meant in his book about *Fear and Trembling.*[3] Rabbi Abraham Joshua Heschel refers to it as "radical amazement," and "the sense of the ineffable." It is a religious feeling that is so deep and powerful that it is impossible to describe in words. It is what mystics throughout the ages have attempted to describe in a voluminous literature that was revived in the latter part of the 20th century, in our post-modern quest for the spiritual, partly in what is sometimes referred to as "New Age."

What Can We Understand From the Expressions: "The House of God" (Beth El) and "The Gateway to Heaven"?

The name of the city of Bethel (the House of God) is explained by this verse. The narrator is explaining that the famous city of Bethel was first called by that name because of this famous encounter between Jacob and God in Jacob's famous dream: "He [Jacob] called that place Bethel; but previously the name of the city had been Luz" (verse 19).

The midrash (Talmud *Pesahim* 88a and *Pirke deRabbi Eliezer* 35, etc.) likes to connect significant biblical events with others that occurred at the same place. It therefore associates Bet El, the House of God, not with the well-known city of that name in biblical times, but with the true "House of God," namely, the Temple in Jerusalem. The midrash explains that Jacob's head was actually lying, while he slept, on the Holy of Holies where the Tablets of the Ten Commandments later rested in the Holy Temple. It is not likely that this is so, since Jerusalem is a good forty miles from Be'ersheva, and the text seems to indicate that this was Jacob's first stop on the journey to Haran. Also, modern scholars have located Bet El north of Jerusalem. But the Midrash is more concerned with fanciful ideas embodying homiletical truths than with dry scientific facts.

Archeologists tell us that Bethel, located about ten miles north of Jerusalem, was a holy site to the pre-Abrahamic Canaanites, sacred to the Canaanite God *El*. It remained a sacred site in Israelite history during the period of the Judges (Judges 20:18-28, 21:2-4), later in the time of the prophet Samuel (I Samuel 10:13), until King Josiah, of Judea, destroyed the city during his religious reforms because it had become a site of pagan worship (cf. II Kings 23:15). The interesting thing is that to the biblical narrator, the only importance it has here is its connection with the important theophany to Jacob in his famous dream.

Many synagogues today call themselves Beth El, both because of the meaning of the words, "House of God," as well as because of the historical association with Jacob's encounter with God at this holy place.

As for the *sha'ar hashamayim*, the Gateway to Heaven, this is taken to mean a place where humans can have entree to God. The term "gateway" is used even today in the Yom Kippur Ne'ilah Service. *Ne'ilah* is short for the full expression *Ne'ilat She'arim*, locking of the gates. Literally it meant locking the gates of the ancient Temple at the end of Yom Kippur, but it contains more metaphoric overtones of the closing of the Gates of Heaven after which the period of Repentance is finished.

A Gateway is an important bridge between two normally unconnected areas — in this case that of the human and the Divine. The Gateway in our passage refers to the "Stairway" (Hebrew *sulam*) mentioned in verse 12. Ladders from earth to heaven are commonly mentioned in pre-biblical Egyptian and Hittite sources.

In the Bible a famous stairway is alluded to in the story of the "Tower of Babel" (Genesis 11). Scholars recognize in this "tower" the famous Mesopotamian temple tower known as a *ziggurat*, with its base on the earth and its roof in the sky, with stairways linking each stage of the tower with the one higher, until its very top reached into heaven itself (Genesis 11:4 — "a tower with its top in the sky"). According to Speiser, the function of the *ziggurat* is to be a place connecting human beings on earth and the gods in heaven; namely a place where people could talk with the gods, or a "spiritual symbol, in short, of man's efforts to reach out to heaven."[4] Speiser pays special attention to the fact that Jacob was traveling at the time toward Mesopotamia.

Numerologists point out that the Hebrew words for stairway, *sulam*, and "Sinai" both add up to 130 in *gematria*. Thus, the stairway is connected again with the place where humans meet God.

Why Does Jacob Seem Caught by Surprise and Express Such Deep Emotion at the Presence of God in This Place?

Sarna notes that in the case of no other patriarch is there a reaction of amazement, or of exceptional emotion when confronted by God. Why, then, does it appear here in Jacob's case? Sarna's suggestion is that because of Jacob's immoral and deceptive behavior in stealing the patriarchal blessings, he would naturally think that God would have deserted him. "Having fallen prey to guilt and solitary despair, he is surprised that God is still concerned for him."[5]

From a theological point of view, we can generalize that in any time and place, human beings can find God when they open their eyes and souls, and become aware of the Presence. In John Ruskin's *Crown of Wild Olive*, we read of the Place where Jacob met God: "...*any* place where God lets down the ladder. And how are you to know where that will be? Or how are you to determine where it may be, but by being ready for it always?"[6]

It is interesting to note that the Hebrew word *HaMakom*, the Place, is one of the dozens of names used in biblical and rabbinic literature for God. Verse 10 could then possibly mean "Jacob came upon *HaMakom* (God)."[7] Similarly, the commentary *Panim Yafot* (Rabbi Pinchas Halevi Horowitz, 16th century) explains the phrase "I [Jacob] did not know" (verse 16) to mean: "When can people experience God's nearness? Only when one is suffused by 'I don't know,' i.e., when one realizes that one knows she does not know, and does not pretend to have wisdom and insight. In other words, humility is a prerequisite for meeting God."

What Significance Is There to the Fact That Jacob's Vision Occurred During a Dream?

Freud, of course, informed us that the dream is the royal road to the unconscious. Others have helped us understand that the importance of dreams in our lives–especially in our spiritual lives–goes well beyond the unconscious. John A. Sanford, an Episcopal priest who became a Jungian analyst has written many books on the Bible and religion from the point of view of Jungian psychology. He points out that "dreams and their companion experience, visions, are regarded in the Bible as the way par excellence in which God speaks to man."[8] In his view, dreams lead us toward the transcendent and spiritual meaning that lies beyond our own narrow selves. Jacob's dream is, in his opinion, one such experience. It is a powerful experience that helps Jacob develop from the self-absorbed child who stole his brother's birthright to a responsible, sensitive adult.

The fact that Jacob's dream occurred at a moment of severe psychological crisis is the first hint of its significance. Further, the inclusion in the dream of the staircase, or ladder, is an important factor because it draws from "the great storehouse of mythological and religious symbols deep within the unconscious," making it not just an idiosyncratic experience, but an archetypal dream which fits into the mythology of what all heroes must undergo on the path to leadership. Through the exposure of Jacob's unconscious mind to the higher realm, he is now exposed to a new dimension in his life. It is a prerequisite to living the highest form of spiritual life. Later experiences in Jacob's life will complete the important transition he has to make before he reaches his full potential of spiritual leadership.

In a commentary quoted in *Ma'ayanei HaTorah*, the author suggests that when Jacob awoke, and said "Surely the Lord is in this place," what he meant was that he realized that God's presence would follow him from Eretz Yisrael to the Diaspora. In other words, that even in Mesopotamia, or anywhere in the *Galut* (exile), God's presence would not desert the Jewish people. This is meant to be a foreshadowing of future Jewish history — that God's holiness would also be available to the Jewish People wherever they settled, through their synagogues and houses of study, even in the Diaspora. Until this moment, Jacob was not aware of this fact.

What Influence Has This Passage Had on Jewish Mysticism and Art?

Many writers and theologians have taken this seminal story as a symbol for the ever-reaching climb of humans toward the divine. Lawrence Kushner's book is a prominent example (see note 1). Dr. Edward Hoffman's book on Jewish mysticism, *The Heavenly Ladder*, describes the importance that the image of the ladder has had on mystics throughout the ages:

> Over millennia, many Jewish commentators have offered their interpretations on the symbolic importance of this narrative. They have consistently viewed the ladder in particular as both a vivid depiction of the human condition and a prescription for reaching the transcendent world. Kabbalists have specifically seen the ladder as radiant with subtle and sublime meanings for imparting a deeper understanding of the cosmos. Not surprisingly, Hasidic and *musar* leaders have often alluded in their public talks and writings to the celestial ladder; they have also valued it as an image for guided meditation. Indeed, the heavenly ladder has probably stood for the nature of individual advancement more centrally than any other symbol in Judaism.

But what does Jacob's starry vision say to us in the late twentieth century? Does it really have much relevance for our own needs and aspirations? It is a basic dictum of Jewish mystics that the sacred tradition speaks simultaneously on many levels—and to every person in every generation. Therefore, if this intriguing account in Genesis has inspired countless men and women around the globe for centuries, then it undoubtedly possesses the same archetypal power today. Later in this book you will be invited to meditate in a personal way upon the celestial ladder....[9]

Hoffman then goes on to describe the many and varied aspects of the implications of living a life imbued with transcendence.

The symbolism of these verses has given much raw material to the creative muses of many generations in many fields of literature, music and art. As the famous African-American spiritual song goes, "We are climbing Jacob's ladder." In a sense, all religions are "climbing Jacob's ladder."

As *The Interpreter's Bible* points out, the story resonates with most readers because in it Jacob begins as a wanderer, and we are all wanderers through life, people who often feel that they are in spiritual exile. All of us at times long for an experience similar to Jacob's which will demonstrate to us that in the most desolate place, "there can be a shining something which bridges the gap between earth and heaven so that henceforth all the horizons of hope and trust are lifted and enlarged."[10]

The quest for the sense of mystery inherent in life, portrayed in Jacob's dream, has been the essence of what distinguishes a society searching for a sense of transcendence, from one whose sole purpose is having fun and amassing wealth. T. S. Eliot described the latter kind of society in his poem, *The Rock:*

> There is no beginning, no movement, no peace
> and no end
> But noise without speech, food without taste.
> And the wind shall say: "Here were decent godless people:
> Their only monument the asphalt road
> And a thousand lost golf balls."

Notes

[1] Hazlitt called the description of Jacob's dream the most beautiful in literature. Rabbi Lawrence S. Kushner, of Sudbury, MA, has written an entire book on this passage, *God Was in This Place and I, i Did Not Know* (Woodstock, Vermont: Jewish Lights Publishing, 1991), taken from the conclusion of the episode.

2 James 186-253.

3 Soren Kierkegaard, *Fear and Trembling* (New York: Penguin Books, 1985).

4 Speiser 220.

5 Sarna 199.

6 As quoted by Solomon Goldman, *The Book of Human Destiny* (Philadelphia: Jewish Publication Society, 1949) II, 611.

7 Plaut 283.

8 John A. Sanford *Dreams: God's Forgotten Language* (Philadelphia and New York: J.B. Lippincott Co., 1968) 23-9. See also chapter VI in his *The Man Who Wrestled With God: Light from the Old Testament on the Psychology of Individuation* (New York: The Paulist Press, 1981).

9 Edward Hoffman, *The Heavenly Ladder: A Jewish Guide to Inner Growth* (San Francisco: Harper & Row, 1985) 58.

10 George Arthur Buttrick et al., eds., *The Interpreter's Bible: The Holy Scripture in the King James and Revised Standard Articles and Introduction, Exegesis, Exposition for Each Book of the Bible* (New York, Nashville: Abington Press, 1952) I, 688.

8

Genesis 32:29

בראשית לב,כט:

וַיֹּאמֶר, לֹא יַעֲקֹב יֵאָמֵר עוֹד שִׁמְךָ כִּי אִם יִשְׂרָאֵל
כִּי שָׂרִיתָ עִם אֱלֹהִים וְעִם אֲנָשִׁים וַתּוּכָל.

JPS (1917) – "And he said, 'Thy name shall be called no more Jacob, but Israel; for thou hast striven with God and with men, and hast prevailed.'"

NJV (1962) – "Said he, 'Your name shall no longer be Jacob, but Israel, for you have striven with beings divine and human, and have prevailed.'"

Jacob returns from twenty years of exile, and is about to cross the border into Eretz Yisrael. At the ford of Jabbok, left alone, he wrestles with a man until the break of dawn. This encounter changes Jacob's name and his life. In verse 25 we are told that Jacob wrestled with "a man." Yet in verses 29 and 31 the same individual is termed "a divine being" (*Elohim*). Hosea (12:4-5), centuries later, refers to this incident and mentions a struggle with an angel (*mal'akh*).

The terms for God and angels are frequently interchangeable in the Bible. For example, Hagar, Sarah's Egyptian handmaid, is addressed by an angel, and yet she responds directly to God (Genesis 16:8-13). In the case of the three angels who visit Abraham, the Narrator tells us that they take the form of men (which angels often do) so that Abraham is unaware of their angelic nature (Genesis 18 and 19).

As Sarna points out, angels are basically messengers of God. Sometimes ordinary people, such as a priest or prophet, are called "angels of God." Angels are usually nameless, and without any mythological qualities. They have "neither individuality nor free will, and...their sole function is as the emissary of God to carry out His specific charge."[1] Sarna also notes that the appearance of angels frames the Laban-Jacob cycle. In Jacob's dream at Bethel (Genesis 28) and here (Genesis 32), angels figure prominently.[2]

In short, when the Bible refers to an angel, it can be a person, or a spiritual (divine) being. Angels may look like normal humans, or have a supernatural appearance. Sometimes they are called "divine," with the implication that they are heavenly emissaries of God taking a human form, and sometimes they are simply human beings acting as God's messengers. In all cases the Bible has de-mythologized the pre-biblical angels who are semi-divine/semi-human ministers to the gods. The role of angels rises and falls in different biblical periods. They disappear in the epoch of the classical prophets (8th century B.C.E.), and return in more complex forms in the fifth century.

It is clear that in our story Jacob is wrestling either with a heavenly emissary of God who takes a human form, or an angelic human messenger who is acting on God's behalf. The statement, "You have striven with *beings divine and human*, and have prevailed" most obviously suggests that Jacob has striven with beings divine—namely, this angel at the River Jabbok, and human—with Laban and Esau.

Sarna offers an alternative suggestion, namely that the phrase "beings divine and human" may be another example of a *merism*, meaning everything from beginning to end—all inclusive. Thus "beings divine and human" would mean "You have struggled with all and sundry"[3] beings—with every kind of possible being—and you have nevertheless prevailed.

What is the Meaning of the Frequently Occurring Change of Names in the Bible?

In our story Jacob becomes Israel. Previously, Abram and Sarai became Abraham and Sarah (Genesis 17:5, 15), indicating the new covenantal relationship with which they entered to be God's appointed progenitors of a new and great nation. Israelite and foreign Kings in the Bible often taken new names upon ascending the throne, indicating their new status. This custom prevails today in the Catholic Church, when the Pope takes a new name upon being elected to the throne of St. Peter.

In the Bible, names carried enormous theological significance, and were not merely convenient methods of differentiating people. A name was actually part and parcel of one's essence.

In ancient times, people believed that knowing one's name therefore bestowed power over the individual. (Thus, the angel refuses to give Jacob his name). A change in name implied a significant change in religious and historical status. So it is that Jacob's new name, Israel, gives him an entirely new status in God's eyes. His mission to be the leader of the tribal confederacy, and thus the father of the nation of Israel, is now divinely confirmed.

Furthermore, Jacob's change of name indicates the necessary prerequisite shift in character in order for him to be worthy of his divine mission. His given name, Yaakov (Jacob), connotes "the supplanter," and is redolent of his crafty dealings with his brother and father in stealing the birthright and the blessing of the first born (which rightfully belonged to his older twin brother, Esau). His shrewd negotiations with treacherous Laban, though warranted, also demonstrate this side of his character.

As Speiser and others point out, Jacob's struggle with the "angel" proved him worthy of the significant divine mission he was to carry out—being the father of the twelve tribes of Israel and hence of the entire Jewish People.[4] The shift is clearly seen two chapters later (Genesis 34) when Jacob condemns the vengeful deed of Simeon and Levi, and invokes a higher concept of morality (Genesis 49:5-7). Being left with a permanent scar from the struggle in his hesitant limp, Jacob will now be more humble, having lost his youthful hubris.

It is interesting to note that in modern Zionist history, a similar change in names, from exilic naming customs to biblical and other Hebrew names, connotes an ideological shift from the dependent mentality of the *galut* (exile) to the frame of mind of a free, independent nation with its own literary and religious history. For example, David Green became David Ben Gurion, Golda Myerson became Golda Meir, Levi Skolnick became Eshkol, Yigael Sukenik became Yadin, and so on. These new names were taken on when "Israel" once again became a viable political force on the world scene.

Before examining the meaning of the name Israel (*Yisrael*), the point must be emphasized that by taking on this new name, Jacob was reassured that Esau would not attack him and destroy his family, as he deeply feared, and that he would indeed become the father of a great nation. Verse 33 is the first mention of *Benei Yisrael*—no longer just the twelve sons of Jacob, but the People of Israel—the usage that the phrase has taken ever since.

Speiser follows the Christian Bible scholar S. R. Driver in giving an etymology of Israel that means "May El persevere." He notes, though, that both the names Jacob and Israel are used symbolically. Jacob, the "Supplanter," now becomes Israel, a forthright and resolute fighter for the values of God.[5]

Sarna deals with the name Israel at length, clarifying that the Torah wants us to understand the name to mean that Jacob is now one who has striven, or struggled, with God. Sarna quotes Rambam and the Midrash who contrast Jacob the deceiver with Yisrael, one who is upright (*yashar*) with God. He also brings the interpretation of Philo and Seder Eliyahu Rabba who regard "*yisra'el* as a contraction of *ish-ra'ah-'el*, 'The man who saw a divine being,'"" derived from Genesis 32:31.[6]

Ralbag explains the latter part of the verse, not in the conventional way, "you have *struggled* with God and humans," but you have become a prince (*sar*) among the angels and among humans. Just what Hebrew root is involved in the name Yisrael is very problematic. Still others derive it from *sarar*, to rule.[7]

What Is the Significance of Jacob's Battle Taking Place at Night and at a River?

Sarna takes note of the popular mythology of a demonic being whose power is restricted to the night, and who cannot face the coming of the rays of sun at dawn.[8] Remember Dracula, who had the same problem, and Hamlet's ghost, who had to flee at dawn? If Jacob could persist in the fight until dawn, he could extract some gift, or blessing, from the angel, which he does. Sarna uses the comparison of the river demon to point out again how the Bible has demythologized our account, though some of its narrative elements remain. Jacob does not propitiate any river demon, nor does the angel interfere with Jacob's retinue, who have already crossed the ford before him. Furthermore, the angel does not take a symbolic form such as an animal, serpent or monster. All non-monotheistic elements have been purged from our story. The only importance of the river here is that it is the border of the Land of Israel.

At dawn, the angel demands that Jacob release his assailant (v. 27). In the light of day Jacob can recognize that he has been fighting with a divine being, not a mere human. If we remember that the Bethel story and this story at Peniel frame the Laban-Jacob cycle, it makes sense to understand that Jacob ran away as the sun set, just as he arrived at Bethel. His act of shameful flight took place at night, and his return, entering a new chapter in his life, now cleansed of his childish narcissism, occurs at daylight, at the end of a long, hard night.

Both the dream at Bethel and the return at Peniel take place at night, when dramatic changes of consciousness are most likely to occur. What happened in between these two nocturnal episodes, according to Jungian analyst John Sanford, is that Jacob fell in love (with Rachel), and learned how to give to others instead of merely being the recipient and taker. He is now ready for a complete reconciliation—with his brother, with himself, and with God.[9]

Elie Wiesel adds that it was only at night that Jacob could confront God. Jacob, who avoided confrontations during the day, who let his mother pamper him and help him be the "supplanter," and the "heel," was able to achieve grander visions at night. His tormented dreams did not permit him to remain a child. At Peniel he decides to fight the fight, alone, and come into his own power and ability, to regain his self-confidence and his sense of moral vision. He is transformed from Jacob to Israel.[10]

How Did Later Commentaries Define the Creature Who Wrestled with Jacob?

Wherever the Bible is silent on important matters, there is created a vast field of potential imaginative reconstruction available to later commentators. The outline of the story in chapter 32 is so bare that the interpreters have a field day with all the spaces between the lines. One such issue is the identity of the "Angel" who wrestled with Jacob.

Rashi cites a Midrash in *Bereshit Rabbah* 77:3), and the Zohar, which suggest that the angel was in fact Samael, the Guardian Angel of Esau, and the incarnation of Evil. The blessing of Jacob by Esau's Guardian Angel acknowledges that it was God's intention to have Jacob receive the blessing of Isaac. This is the Midrash's way of justifying the unseemly deeds of the heroes of Israel. The Torah itself implies an overall Divine Plan that carries the narrative on a different plane than the human drama that is often unrelated in its details. The Midrash sometimes states explicitly what the Torah merely implies. But in doing so the Midrashic rabbis expose their own biases and preferences in stories that may take different explanations depending on the reader. Here the rabbis are trying to show that Jacob deserves the position of prominence between the brothers, having earned it through his Herculean strength (see Genesis 29:10, where Jacob rolls the stone from covering the well of Laban) and bravery.

Sarna points out that the angel being the celestial patron of Esau-Edom, the archenemy of Israel, makes perfect sense in the biblical context. Jacob is crossing into the territory of Esau, and meets Esau's angel in a struggle that foreshadows the relationship between the peoples of Israel and Edom (the archetypal enemy of Israel).[11]

Several medieval commentators, including Nahmanides and Sforno [Cf. comments on Genesis 32:21], see Jacob as struggling with the impurities of his own soul; i.e., fighting with his own dark side, his *Yetzer Hara*, or his conscience.

Elie Wiesel prefers this explanation, and argues that Jacob was diffident; he had lost his self-confidence. Not thinking he was worthy of celestial blessing, and unworthy of his distinguished ancestors, unworthy to be the patriarch to pass on the message of ethical monotheism[12], he overcame his self-doubts and fought off the part of himself who was the "inveterate fugitive." Wiesel claims that this is the primary meaning of this story, namely that 'Israel's history teaches us that one's true victory is the victory that a person achieves over oneself.[13]

In similar vein, Targum Yonatan and Midrash Tanhuma suggest that the combatant was a holy angel, foreshadowing Jacob's (and the Jewish People's) future struggles between their tendency to sin and their spiritual side. Rabbi Samson Raphael Hirsch points out that the Torah states that it was "the man" who "struggled with Jacob," and not the reverse. He sees this as symbolic of the struggle of the People of Israel through the ages. Israel (Jacob) is the victim, not the aggressor. Jacob fights only in self-defense.[14] He further explains Jacob's name, *Yaakov*, or heel, to mean that the people of Jacob were under the heel of its oppressor.[15]

What Other Midrashic Interpretations Illuminate This Passage?

The Talmud (*Hulin* 91) interprets the nature of the "man" who struggled with Jacob in at least two different ways. Some, says the Talmud, suggest that the man appeared to Jacob as a heathen, and some say he appeared as a Torah scholar. Aharon Greenberg in *Iturei Torah*, his commentary on the Torah, quotes Rabbi Y.I. Herzog on this Talmudic passage with the following comment: "Our enemies attack us in two completely different ways, both with the same end in mind. Sometimes they appear as a heathen, using physical violence to destroy us. At other times, they try to annihilate us spiritually, as when they forced us in the Middle Ages into public debates to prove our religion false. Sometimes they appear as a 'Torah scholar' and argue with us from within our own system."

The five letters of the Hebrew name *Yisrael* have been interpreted to be an acronym for all seven patriarchs and matriarchs. The *Yod* stands for Yaakov (Jacob) and Yitzchak (Isaac). The *Sin* stands for Sarah. The *Resh* is for Rivkah (Rebecca) and Rachel. The *Alef* is for Avraham. And the *Lamed* is for Leah. All seven are accounted for!

Rabbi Abraham Isaac Kook, beloved first Chief Rabbi of Eretz Yisrael under the British Mandate (1865-1935), was a mystic, poetic soul, whose abundant writings left an undying legacy to future generations. Rabbi Kook has written a passage on the name *Yisrael*. He describes four different kinds of people — or levels of spirituality. First is the person who sings the song of his own life and finds full spiritual satisfaction therein. Next, on a higher level, is the one who sings the song of his people, who leaves the narrow circle of self and reaches toward the community of Israel in love. Third is the one who goes to more distant realms and binds oneself to all humanity by singing the song of all God's children. Fourth, and highest, is the one who links oneself with all humanity, all God's creatures and all worlds, and sings the song of all of life. "It is of one such as this that tradition has said that whoever sings a portion of song each day is assured of having a share in the world to come."16

When all four voices join together, and each lends its beauty and vitality to the other, there comes a sound of jubilation, ecstasy and holiness. This united song is the song of God, and the song of Israel. Rabbi Kook, drawing from the Zohar and an ancient midrash, which interpret God's four-letter ineffable name (*yud hei vav hei*) as the basis of these four levels of spirituality, explains that the highest song of all of God's creatures is what is implied in the phrase "Song of Israel," or, in Hebrew "**Shir El**" — which include the letters of Yisrael, and point to the true meaning of *Yisrael*. I believe that Rabbi Kook's comment means that the highest destiny of the Jew is to reach for the holiness of all of life, and that is "The Song of God," (Yisrael), and the purpose of Jewish existence. It is a noble vision, worthy of Jacob's encounter with God.

Notes

1 Sarna 383-4.
2 Nahum Sarna, *Understanding Genesis* (New York: Schocken Books, 1966) 202-206.
3 Sarna, *JPS* 227, 5.
4 Speiser 227.
5 Ibid. 255.

6 Sarna, *JPS* 404-405.

7 cf. notes on Genesis 32:29 in Aryeh Kaplan, *The Living Torah: The Five Books of Moses* (New York: Maznaim, 1981) 88.

8 Sarna, *JPS* 403-404.

9 Sanford, *The Man Who Wrestled* 28-9, 36-43.

10 Elie Wiesel, *Messengers of God* (New York: Random House, 1976) 128-132.

11 Sarna, *JPS* 404.

12 Wiesel 124.

13 Ibid. 125.

14 Hirsch 504.

15 Ibid. 506.

16 Abraham Isaac Kook, Abraham Isaac Kook: The Lights of Penitence, The Moral Principles, Lights Of Holiness, Essays, Letters, And Poems (New York: Paulist Press, 1978) 228-9.

9

Exodus 3:2

שמות ג,ב:

וַיֵּרָא מַלְאַךְ ה' אֵלָיו בְּלַבַּת אֵשׁ מִתּוֹךְ הַסְּנֶה
וַיַּרְא וְהִנֵּה הַסְּנֶה בֹּעֵר בָּאֵשׁ וְהַסְּנֶה אֵינֶנּוּ אֻכָּל.

*JPS (1917) – "And the angel of the Lord appeared unto him
in a flame of fire out of the midst of a bush; and he looked,
and, behold, the bush burned with fire, and the bush was
not consumed."*

*NJV (1962) – "An angel of the Lord appeared to him in a
blazing fire out of a bush. He gazed, and there was a bush
all aflame, yet the bush was not consumed."*

Chapter three of Exodus might be titled "The Call of Moses."
Moses' experience of God's Call, and his resistance (found
among most biblical prophets) is found in chapters 3 and 4 of Exodus. The opening segment of the Call, the story of the Burning
Bush, is found in 3:1-10.

This verse is particularly rich in its symbolism and metaphor. But like so many other famous and colorful verses it cannot
be read out of context. In the end of the previous chapter, 2:23-25,
the scene is set for God's appearance at the thorn bush in that
God hears the moaning of the slaves, remembers the Covenant
with the patriarchs, looks down upon suffering Israel, "and God
took notice of them." The story of salvation now resumes, with
the drama of the Call of Moses at the burning bush in chapter
three.

Why Does God Speak to Moses at the Burning Bush and through an Angel?

It seems odd that God would choose a lowly bush through which to speak to Moses, but perhaps the Hebrew word for bush, *sneh*, is related to *Sinai*, a premonition of the future theophany that will take place there.[1]

The rabbis have written extensively on the metaphoric significance of the bush. Midrash suggests that God speaks from lowly places to reinforce the importance of human humility. Mt. Sinai was also not the highest mountain in the Sinai desert. As Nehama Leibowitz writes, "outward distinction and grandeur bear no relation to inner greatness."[2]

We also read: "Rabbi Eliezer said: Just as the thorn bush is the lowliest of all trees in the world, so Israel were lowly and humble in Egypt; therefore God revealed Himself to them and redeemed them, as it is said — "And I have come down to deliver them from Egypt (Exodus 3:8)" (Midrash, *Exodus Rabbah* 2:5). Rashi quotes a midrash in his commentary which reflects this simple message: God selected the thorn bush through which to speak to confirm the verse in Psalms (91:15): "I shall be with him [Israel] in trouble."

In another midrash, a heathen approached Rabbi Joshua ben Karhah and asked:

"'Why did God choose a thorn bush from which to speak to Moses?' The rabbi replied: 'Were it a carob tree or a sycamore tree, you would have asked the same question. But I will answer you anyway. He picked a thorn bush to teach you that no place is devoid of God's presence, not even a thorn bush.'"[3]

Perhaps the most well-known and profound interpretation explaining the burning bush as a metaphor is that of the Midrash in Yalkut Shimoni: "It is the nature of a thorn bush, that if one thrusts one's hand into it, the hand suffers no hurt because its thorns are bent downwards. But when one tries to pull out the hand, the thorns catch it and one cannot withdraw it. So it is with Egypt. At the beginning they welcomed Israel. But when they wanted to leave, they would not let them. A situation reminiscent of Jews in Europe in the mid-twentieth century."[4]

Similar in intent to the above is another Midrash that explains: Why did God show Moses this symbol [the burning bush]? Because Moses had thought to himself that the Egyptians might consume Israel; hence did God show him a fire which burnt but did not consume, saying to him: Just as the thorn bush is burning and is not consumed, so the Egyptians will not be able to destroy Israel (Midrash Rabbah 2:5).

As masters of Gematria (Hebrew numerology), the rabbis also taught that God's speaking from *hasneh*, the bush, was to hint to him that he would live for 120 years (*hei* is 5, *samekh* is 60, *nun* is 50, and *hei* five = 120 (*Exodus Rabbah* 2:5). Still another midrash suggests that the thorn bush was chosen because it needs much water to survive [Moses probably took his flock there because of the proximity of water], so too the people of Israel can flourish only by drawing deeply from the wells of salvation, Jewish knowledge, Torah. [5]

As to why an angel is used to convey God's message, the Narrator may have wanted to avoid anthropomorphism (making God appear in human terms, or, even worse, in a bush), although such cases do appear throughout the Bible (God's anger, God's voice, God's finger, for example). Since angels are used in the Biblical stories interchangeably with God, this example is not out of the ordinary. The meaning clearly is that God is about to speak to Moses. Perhaps the angel is easing the reader into the Presence of God's revelation to Moses.

Noticing that first the angel addresses Moses (verse 2), and only afterwards did God speak (verse 3), the rabbis suggest that this was done intentionally, to prepare Moses gradually for the conversation with God. The angel acts as an intermediary to ease Moses into the divine conversation (*Exodus Rabbah* 2:5). Rabbenu Bahya picks up on this theme and suggests that no one should try to achieve a full, clear revelation of God all at once, suddenly, but only gradually and slowly. He compares it to a person in a dark room, who must adjust his eyes to the light in slow stages. It takes a lifetime to know God, and even then our knowledge is quite limited and imperfect.[6]

Why Does God Speak Through Fire?

Fire is frequently present when the Bible describes an appearance of God. In Psalm 104:4 we read: "God makes the winds God's messengers/ fiery flames God's servants." Fire has a magical, formless, luminous quality to it, and is the source of enormous power. Even to this day people are drawn to fires — in the hearth or fireplace, a blazing furnace, a burning building, or an exploding volcano. It makes sense that if God is to be represented in any physical way, it would be with something as powerful, mysterious, and shapeless as fire. Moving away from the symbolism of fire as a manifestation of God's presence, the interpretation of the midrash and many other later commentators is that the fire also has a secondary, and more specific symbolism, that of the enemies of Israel who try to consume her. In Deuteronomy 4:20, the Egyptian exile is referred to as an iron furnace.

Rabbi Samson Raphael Hirsch sees the fire as symbolic of God's presence and as the Law (Torah) which is meant "to penetrate us, to refine and purify us, to warm us, and to quicken and enliven us."[7] As bearers of godliness, it is our task to spread the fire of Torah and divinity far and wide.[8]

The Torah states that the angel spoke through a *labat esh*, which is variously translated as a flame of fire, from the midst (heart — Hebrew *lev*) of the fire; or the *essence* of the fire. NJV translates "a blazing fire." Perhaps the flame took the **shape** of a heart.

Aware of the fact that fire was also present at the later theophany at Sinai, the rabbis suggest that the fire here is to give Moses courage, so that when he later meets God at the same mountain, he will be ready for the fires, and not be afraid (Exodus Rabbah II, 5). In the same passage the rabbis explain that the burning bush was an attention-grabber, to force Moses to pay strict attention to the divine message. In another midrash we are told that Moses was too deeply concentrating on the work of shepherding to pay attention to the voice of the angel, until God startled him with the wonderful phenomenon of the burning thorn bush.[9]

Nehama Leibowitz, Israel's late, premier Bible teacher, points out that unlike other divine revelations to the patriarchs before him, God's first appearance to Moses is not only auditory but visual as well.[10]

Why Goes God Speak to Moses While He is Shepherding His Flock?

As Rabbi Plaut notes, the shepherd theme is common in ancient Neareastern literature.[11] For example, in the opening of the Code of Babylonian King Hammurabi, the king is called a shepherd. King David is also shepherding the flock when called to become King of Israel. The metaphor is obvious and universal. Modern Christian clergy are often referred to as *pastors*.

The Psalms use the metaphor of God being Israel's shepherd ("The Lord is my shepherd, I shall not want," Psalm 23:1). The shepherd is a loving and nurturing figure for those who wander aimlessly without a leader or care-giver. The midrash tells that Moses was selected because of his qualities of compassion, in the following tale: When Moses was tending the flock of Jethro, a kid escaped and Moses chased it until he found a shady place near a pool, and the kid stopped to drink. Moses said to the kid, "I did not know you were so thirsty, you must be very tired." Moses then placed the kid on his shoulder and carried him back to the flock. Thereupon God said: "Because you have shown mercy in leading the flock of a mortal, you will surely tend my flock Israel" (Midrash, Exodus Rabbah 2:2).

What was the "Miracle" of the Burning Bush?

The simple explanation is that God drew Moses' attention to the burning bush because of its miraculous nature — if there is fire, the bush should be destroyed. But there was a second miracle. If the bush was not consumed by the fire, the fire was burning without any fuel. Such an independent fire is obviously the symbol of God's presence. The unconsumed bush, then, is the symbol of the people of Israel that is never destroyed no matter how evil its enemies' designs. In short, then, there are *two* miracles. The miracle of the fuel-free fire symbolizes God, while the miracle of the unburned bush represents the invincible people of Israel.[12]

There is little use in trying to explain in scientific terms the miracle of the burning bush which was not consumed.[13] Neither does it make any sense to justify scientifically any other miracle of the Bible, such as the parting of the Reed Sea, or the delaying of the setting sun for Joshua. The biblical writer meant these events to be miraculous experiences of God as perceived by the people present.

Writers who lived thousands of years ago could not have understood the world as we know it scientifically, and it is foolhardy to try to impose 20th century scientific standards on writers who lived millennia ago. To their way of thinking, these things occurred because of God's divine intervention, and for no other reason. It is unfair to them to do intellectual cartwheels and explain away these biblical perceptions with convoluted scientific explanations.

Plaut puts it well:

> Those who deny that God can address man will not be convinced by any assertion to the contrary; whereas those who believe in a God who can be heard by man will likely find the account a realistic description of the encounter. The circumstances are marvelous and mysterious, and Moses is afraid. . . The divine self-disclosure reveals a God who cares for man and is attracted to him; who takes account of his frailty, yet holds him in high regard. It is a relationship based on divine love, given freely and, at this juncture, outside a framework of reciprocal obligation.[14]

What is the Location of Mt. Horeb, Where the Burning Bush Appeared?

Horeb and Sinai are used interchangeably in the Bible. Hertz suggests that Horeb is the mountain range in the Sinai desert, and the term Sinai designates the particular summit where Moses ascended to receive the Ten Commandments. Alternatively, he says perhaps both Horeb and Sinai are two separate peaks in the same mountain range.[15]

From verse one we learn that Horeb is also known as the "mountain of God." Rashi suggests that it is so called because of the Great Revelation that will take place there when the Ten Commandments are given to Moses. This leaves us with the question as to whether it was *later* called the mountain of God, and the narrator is reading this name back into the story anachronistically; or, whether it was already a holy spot known to be a place where God communicates with humans.

If the latter is true, it may have been a Midianite holy place, since what brought Moses there in the first place was to tend the flock of his father-in-law, Jethro, who is a Midianite priest. S. R. Driver suggests that ancient Semitic tribes often regarded lofty mountains as sacred, and reminds us that the name "Sinai" suggests a derivation from *Sin*, the name of the moon-god in Babylonia.[16] The Torah makes no mention, however, that Moses had been aware of the place as already being a holy site, as one would expect in a narrative that gives no credence to other gods.

In either case, Sinai/Horeb is an appropriate place for God to speak to Moses, because at this point God announces the physical liberation of the People of Israel, and later, at the Great Revelation, the giving of the Decalogue, the spiritual liberation takes place.

Rabbi Abraham ibn Ezra suggests that Horeb comes from the root *harav* meaning dry — appropriate for a desert area. A modern traditional Israeli commentary, *Da'at Mikra*, suggests that Horeb comes from the root *horvah*, ruins, because the barren rocks there may have resembled the ruins of houses, or the ruins of a pre-existing habitation.[17] Fourth century sources identify the site with Jebel Musa, or Mt. Catherine (the site on which Justinian built the convent of St. Catherine in 527 C.E., still standing today) in Southern Sinai. This would define the route of the Exodus as traveling south to the apex of the desert, and then north again. Since we are told later that Sinai was only a three-day journey (perhaps a generic term for a moderate voyage?), it is not likely that Jebel Musa ("the mountain of Moses") is the correct location. A more logical location is in the northern part of the Sinai desert, close to Kadesh-Barnea. The Book of Judges offers strong evidence in 11:16: "When they came up from Egypt, Israel walked through the wilderness to the Sea of Reeds, and came to Kadesh...."[18]

It is difficult for the modern tourist to accept the fact that many of the so-called holy sites of biblical Israel were given their identities at much later periods in history by a wide variety of Byzantine, Ottoman and other spiritual searchers. It is doubtful if we will ever know the exact location of the site of the burning bush or of the Revelation at Mt. Sinai, as painful as that fact might be for some moderns to accept.

Notes

[1] The Midrash in *Exodus Rabba* 2:4 also relates the Hebrew word *sinah*, hatred, to Sinai, and says that hatred of Jews began at Sinai because of the Torah—in other words, because of the strict moral code given at Sinai, which Israel imposed on the world.
[2] cf. Nehama Leibowitz, *Studies in Shemot (Exodus): In the Context of Ancient and Modern Jewish Bible Commentary* (Jerusalem: World Zionist Organization, Department for Torah Education and Culture, 1976) 56-57.
[3] Midrash Exodus Rabbah, 2:5.
[4] as quoted by Leibowitz, *Shemot* 57.
[5] as quoted from a midrash by Ellen Frankel, *The Classic Tales: 4000 Years of Jewish Lore* (Northvale: Jason Aronson, 1989) 108.
[6] Leibowitz, *Shemot* 52-3.
[7] Hirsch II, 25.
[8] Ibid.
[9] as quoted by Louis Ginzberg, *Legends of the Bible* (Philadelphia: Jewish Publication Society of America, 1956) 311.
[10] Leibowitz, *Shemot* 53.
[11] Plaut 396.
[12] Nahum Sarna, Exodus: The Traditional Hebrew Text with New JPS Translation, The JPS Torah Commentary (Philadelphia: Jewish Publication Society 1991) 14.
[13] Plaut 403.
[14] Ibid.
[15] Hertz 213.
[16] S. R. Driver, ed., *The Cambridge Bible: The Book of Exodus in the Revised Version* (Cambridge:The University Press, 1911) Xa, 18-19.
[17] Yehudah Kil, ed., *Torah, Nevi'im, Ketuvim 'im perush Rashi ve'Da'at Mikra'* (Jerusalem: Mosad haRav Kook, 1969) II/1 38, note 5.
[18] For a full discussion of the location of Mt. Sinai, cf. Dov Peretz Elkins, *So Young To Be A Rabbi* (New York: Thomas Yoseloff, 1969) 122-128.

10

Exodus 3:14

שמות ג,יד:

וַיֹּאמֶר אֱלֹהִים אֶל מֹשֶׁה, אֶהְיֶה אֲשֶׁר אֶהְיֶה
וַיֹּאמֶר כֹּה תֹאמַר לִבְנֵי יִשְׂרָאֵל אֶהְיֶה שְׁלָחַנִי אֲלֵכֶם.

JPS (1917) – *"And God said unto Moses: 'I AM THAT I AM'; and He said, 'Thus shalt thou say unto the children of Israel: I AM hath sent me unto you.'"*

NJV (1962) – *"And God said to Moses, 'Ehyeh-Asher-Ehyeh.' He continued, 'Thus shall you say to the Israelites, "Ehyeh sent me to you." '"*

Following the theophany at the Burning Bush, Moses raises several objections as to why it will be difficult for him to fulfill God's mission. First, he complains that he is not adequate for the job. God reassures him that God will be with him. Next, Moses asks, Who shall I say has sent me? What will I say when the Israelites ask me the name of the God who is sending me? God answers with this mysterious name — "*Ehyeh-Asher-Ehyeh.*"

While the JPS translates the Hebrew phrase "I AM THAT I AM," the NJV doesn't even try to translate such an enigmatic phrase, but rather *transliterates* it. In a note, the NJV, with a sense of exasperation, explains: "Meaning of Heb. uncertain; variously translated: 'I Am That I Am'; 'I am Who I am'; 'I Will Be What I Will Be'; etc.

Although in verse 14 God is called *Ehyeh-Asher-Ehyeh,* in verse 15 the text reverts to YHVH, God's special four-letter Hebrew name (*yud hei vav hei*), also known as the Tetragrammaton, since we no longer know exactly how it was pronounced. It is also referred to in traditional Hebrew as *HaShem Hameforash,* literally,

"God's name, as it is written," and referred to in English as the Ineffable Name. Most modern Biblical scholars either use the equivalent English letters, YHVH, without vowels, or refer to this word as YAHWEH, a scholarly hypothesis, based on Greek transcriptions and other evidence. Since the Bible was written without vowels, and since God's "official" name was too holy to pronounce outside of certain special sacerdotal occasions, we no longer know exactly how this name was pronounced in Biblical times.

When we read the Hebrew Bible today, we use the phrase "Adonai" instead, and insert the vowels for "Adonai" wherever YHVH appears -indicating that the word should be pronounced ADONAI, even though it is written YHVH. When one combines the consonants of YHVH and the vowels of ADONAI, the result is JEHOVAH, a hybrid word which was never meant to be pronounced. Today, even the word for God in Hebrew, ADONAI, has become so sacred, that Jewish law dictates that one may not pronounce that name either — unless pronouncing a statutory blessing (*berakhah*) with its appropriate consequent action, or in reading a full verse of the Bible. People substitute the word *HaShem*, or "The Name" whenever they want to avoid the sacred name ADONAI. Modern Jews are less careful about this distinction, and the name ADONAI has found its way into modern English liturgy, especially as a device for avoiding gender-specific names for God, such as "The Lord."

In Second Temple times the name took on even more important metaphysical power. Only the Kohen Gadol was permitted to recite the correct pronunciation of the Tetragrammaton, and then only on Yom Kippur in the *Kodesh Kodashim* (Holy of Holies). It was considered too sacred to pronounce the name elsewhere or on other occasions. It was then, apparently, that ADONAI was substituted for YHVH in speech. After the destruction of the Temple, the correct pronunciation of the Name was lost.

What is the Significance of the Two Different Names in Verses 14 and 15?

A comment by the Maharal of Prague (1526-1609) explains that God wants to be known in two different ways — as a close friend, (EHYEH), a Redeemer who cares about God's Chosen People; and also as an ineffable, mysterious, unknowable abstract Being (YHVH).

Some see in the standard statutory blessings, the formula with which every *berakhah* begins, in the same light. Ironically, we begin to address God in the first person, as a friend and close

Intimate—i.e., *Barukh Attah*—blessed are *You*. Then, in the middle of the same sentence, we refer to God in the third person, "Who has commanded us...," placing God in a more distant, remote position. In theology we refer to these two relationships with God as "immanent," (close) and "transcendent," (above, beyond). In the recitation of a *berakhah* we are capturing *both* of these aspects of God's essence and God's relationship with God's creatures.

It is interesting to note that in addition to being called YHVH in verse 15, God is next referred to as "the God of your fathers, the God of Abraham, the God of Isaac, and the God of Jacob." The *Mekhilta* (a midrashic collection) points out in Parashat Bo, 16, that it is from this verse that we recite the names of the patriarchs in the first paragraph of the Amidah.

Students of Gematria point out that the word *Ehyeh* equals 21, and so do the first letters of the names of the three patriarchs [*alef* is 1, *yud* is 10, and *yud* again is 10, totaling twenty-one]. Rabbi Kasher also brings this Gematria (p. 107): *Ehyeh* stands for many important ideas: *alef* (of *Ehyeh*) is One, denoting God's Unity; *heh* (5) is the five books of the Torah, *yud* (10) is the Ten Commandments; and the final *heh* (5) represents five ancient leaders—Abraham, Isaac, Jacob, Moses and Aaron.[1]

Interestingly, in our verse we see that God answers Moses, "*Ehyeh Asher Ehyeh*." God then tells Moses to report to the people: "*Ehyeh* sent me to you." The modern Israeli commentary *Da'at Mikra*, suggests that it is easier just to say to the people, "I will be" sent me to you, meaning, "I will be with you!" Fear not, I am a God who is with you, and will redeem you.[2]

What is the Significance of God Telling Moses This Name/Phrase?

Nahum Sarna claims that the revealing by God of this special name, beyond comprehension as it may be, "registers a new stage in the history of Israelite monotheism."[3] If we recall the importance of names of humans, in earlier discussions on previous verses (for example, Jacob/Yaakov to Israel/Yisrael), we can understand better how the name of God had even more special significance. Names carried within them the very essence of the being (Being) they identified. Thus, the name YHVH, coming as it does from the Hebrew verb *to be*, carries the significance of Being itself. Rabbi Ovadiah Sforno takes the verb "to be" (*hayah* or *Ehyeh*) to mean that God will remove any obstacles to being, including any oppressive power that threatens the *being* of the Jewish People. In the context of Moses' question, the answer is designed to give the questioner reassurance, that God will be at his side, help him, and save him and his people.

It seems that in the biblical belief system, Moses felt that he could not convince the people to follow a God without a specific name. The name being the essence of the God, it carried enormous significance and credibility.

In Martin Buber's *Moses*, the philosopher explains: "The 'true' name of a person...is the essence of the person, distilled from his real being, so that he is present in it once again. What is more, he is present in it in such a form that anybody who knows the true name and knows how to pronounce it in the correct way can gain control of him. The person himself is unapproachable, he offers resistance; but through the name he becomes approachable, the speaker has power over him."[4] In our verse, it is not that the Israelite people would want to have power over God, but to risk escaping from Egypt, they had to have some strong connection and belief in the approachable God of whom they had no previous knowledge.

In Plaut's words, "It is an aspect of God's freedom to conceal His essence, and hence Ehyeh-Asher-Ehyeh must remain elusive."[5] Plaut also quotes a different interpretation of the prominent biblical scholar Samuel Sandmel, who sees in God's answer "not theology but a bit of wry humor, designed to help Moses over his fright."[6] The passage doesn't seem to lend itself to a humorous answer, and it is more likely a very modern literary reading that sees it that way.

How Can We Understand God's New Name, *Ehyeh*?

The collection known as *Midrash Rabbah* (*Exodus* 3:6) sees an action component as the key to the phrase *Ehyeh*. In this midrashic text, first God lists many of the different names by which Divinity is called in order to demonstrate the diversity of ways in which God is known, according to the name by which one calls God. God is called variously Almighty God, Lord of Hosts, God, Lord, according to the task referred to. For example, the name YHVH is usually associated with God's mercy; Elohim with God as Judge. When waging war, God is called "Lord of Hosts." When forgiving, God is called "*El Shaddai*," Almighty One. In this case, says the Midrash, "I am Who I am" refers to My *deeds*. Rabbi Isaac explains: God said to Moses: "Tell them that I am now what I always was and always will be;" for this reason is the word *Eheyeh* written three times (noting continuity, or eternality).

In another midrashic anthology, Rabbi Menachem M. Kasher elucidates the connection between our verse and the giving of the Ten Commandments: "At various times God gave various names to the People of Israel—in Egypt, I told you I was the God of your fathers, and when you asked My name, I told you *Ehyeh Asher Ehyeh*, but now, here we are at Mt. Sinai, and you are hearing God's own voice from God's very mouth: I am the Lord your God...."[7]

In the commentary of Rabbi Aryeh Kaplan, we read: "According to the Kabbalists, this Name denotes the Crown (*Kether*) of creation, that is, the very first thought and impulse of Will that initiated the creative process. Hence it is 'I will be,' since at the time of that impulse, everything was in the future.... This name was revealed now that God was about to create the nation Israel."[8]

In other words, the kabbalists emphasize the fact that the Hebrew word *Ehyeh* is in the future tense, meaning that it goes back as far as creation. It is then related to one particular instance of creation, that of the Jewish People. By indicating to Moses God's creative powers, God is intending to explain to him that just as God created the world, and the Jewish People, God will also in the near future redeem Israel, and continue its creative development in the future. It is a name filled with hope for tomorrow.

Kaplan also quotes medieval sources that suggest that since God was, is and will be, God's special name of YHVH points to that unknowable place where past, present and future are all the same.

Is the Phrase Meant to Convey A Vague Philosophical Indeterminacy?

Rabbi Joseph Hertz suggests that the phrase implies more than some abstract philosophical concept. "...The emphasis is on *the active manifestation* of the Divine existence;.... To the Israelites in bondage, the meaning would be, 'Although He has not yet displayed His power towards you, He will do so; He is eternal and will certainly redeem you.'" Explaining that the Hebrew root is *hayah*, to be, Hertz argues that the phrase "gives expression to the fact that He was, He is, and He ever will be."[9]

The expression is clearly related to the common name for God in Hebrew, *yud hei vav hei*, which is a form of the verb to be (*hayay*). In Nahum Sarna's explanation, "Either it expresses the quality of absolute Being, the eternal, unchanging, dynamic presence, or it means, 'He causes to be.'"[10] As Rabbi Abraham Ibn Ezra points out, Moses, in addressing God, always uses the name YHVH, and not ELOHIM.

Coming from the Hebrew verb "to be," God's name probably has something to do with the "One Who Causes Being," or "the Creator." It stresses God's active role in making the world *be*, and suggests to Moses that God will also be his and Israel's Redeemer.

Rabbi Isaac Abravanel explains God's answer to the question, "What is Your Name?" in the following words: Why should they ask My name, which is in the realm of mystery and the unknowable? Just tell them that the Being Who is called "I am", the hidden Being who cannot be understood, has sent me to you. The main thing they need to know is that I am the God of their ancestors. They don't need to know my name, or anything else.[11]

Notes

[1] *Otiot deRabbi Akiba.*
[2] *Da'at Mikrah* II/1, 50.
[3] Sarna, *Exodus* 18.
[4] Martin Bubuer, *Moses: The Revelation and the Covenant* (New York: Harper & Row, 1958) 51.
[5] Plaut 405, 1709, note 24.
[6] Ibid.
[7] Menachem M. Kasher, *Encyclopedia of Biblical Interpretation* (New York: American Biblical Encyclopedia Society, 1967) VII, 105.
[8] Kaplan 152.
[9] Hertz 215.
[10] Sarna, *Exodus* 17.
[11] Rabbi Yitzhak Abravanel: Commentary on Exodus 3:13.

11

Exodus 19:5b-6

כִּי לִי כָּל הָאָרֶץ: וְאַתֶּם תִּהְיוּ לִי מַמְלֶכֶת כֹּהֲנִים וְגוֹי קָדוֹשׁ
אֵלֶּה הַדְּבָרִים אֲשֶׁר תְּדַבֵּר אֶל בְּנֵי יִשְׂרָאֵל.

*JPS (1917) – "For all the earth is mine; and ye shall be unto
Me a kingdom of priests, and a holy nation. These are the
words which thou shalt speak unto the children of Israel."*

*NJV (1962) – "Indeed, all the earth is Mine, but you shall
be to Me a kingdom of priests and a holy nation. These are
the words that you shall speak to the children of Israel."*

Moses and the Israelites have reached Mt. Sinai, and Moses
is about to ascend the mountain to receive the Ten Commandments. In preparation for the receipt of the Tablets and the forg-
ing of this sacred spiritual Covenant (*brit*, v. 5), God instructs
Moses to tell the Israelites that they are to be a special, chosen,
people: "My treasured possession among all the peoples" (Exodus 19:5). This is to be their Mission as a People of God. The Israelites are referred to in Deuteronomy (7:6; 14:2; 26:18-19) as
God's Treasured People.

In order to carry out God's sacred mission, the Israelite people must attain national independence. Without the authority to
live the lifestyle and value system which are commanded by
God in the Covenant, and which are uniquely that of the Israelite
nation, they would be too much subject to the forces of surrounding nations to carry out their God-given task.

What is Meant by the Phrase "*Kohanim*"?

The Torah is making the following analogy: *Kohanim* are the spiritual leaders of the Israelite People. In like manner, the Israelite

people should be the spiritual leaders of the nations of the world. In logical terminology we can put it this way: As priests are to Israel, so Israel is to the world. The meaning is clear. But does the text take the word *Kohanim* literally?

The *Stone Chumash* translates *Kohanim* as "ministers," and makes the following comment: "...the word *kohanim* in the context of this verse means that the entire nation of Israel is to be dedicated to leading the world toward an understanding and acceptance of God's mission. In the ritual sense, priests, too, can be seen as having this function."[1] In other words, the role of the Israelites as *kohanim* in this verse is not meant in the *ritual* sense, but in a spiritual sense, as moral leaders.

Some prominent Christian translations, including the prestigious "New Revised Standard Version" use the phrase "a priestly kingdom."[2] This gives a better sense of the use of the word *kohen* than the Jewish versions. The Israelites are not to *be kohanim*, but to be *like kohanim*, or priest*ly*. The role of the *kohen* in their understanding is that the Israelites are to be "the covenant *mediator*"[3] (italics mine), representing God's word to the people, and likewise representing the people before God. This flows logically from the next two verses (Exodus 19:7-8).

Rashi refers to another use of the term *kohanim* in II Samuel 8:18, "and David's sons were priests." David, of the tribe of Judah, not Levi, could not have had sons who were true *kohanim*. The verse in II Samuel obviously uses the expression *kohanim* in another, metaphoric sense. Rashi uses the word *sarim*, or princes, to explain the usage of *kohen* in our verse. *Kohen*, to Rashi in this verse, means a leadership role.

Nahmanides gives more color to the metaphor, when he explains that the *kohen* symbol here means a people living a holy life devoted to the service of God. Rabbi Ovadiah Sforno suggests that Israel be an inspiration and model people to all humanity.

The traditional Israeli commentary, *Da'at Mikra*, details what the task of the *kohen* is, and thus how this should apply to Israel: The *kohen* is *closer* to God than the rest of the people; so is Israel closer to God than other nations; The *kohen* accepts *more obligations* than other members of the people. So too do the Jewish People accept upon themselves more religious responsibilities than other nations (*kashrut, Shabbat, brit milah*, etc.). The *kohen* atones for the people; so Israel atones for the nations through its exemplary behavior. The *kohen* teaches the people respect for God; so the Jewish People is to teach the nations of the world respect for God and God's ethical laws.[4]

Another creative interpretation of the phrase "kingdom of priests" is brought by Rabbi Levi Yitzchak of Berditchev, famous Hasidic sage (1740-1809) in his commentary *Kedushat Levi*. First Reb Levi quotes the old idea that there are three crowns of the people of Israel: of Torah, of priesthood, and of royalty. The only one that is hereditary is that of *kehunah* (priesthood). But Reb Levi claims that along with the hereditary nature of the priesthood comes the ability to pass on the *holiness* of the *kehunah*. His biblical prooftext: "The Lord's portion is God's people, Jacob God's own inheritance" (Deuteronomy 32:9). God chose Israel because they can pass their holiness from one generation to the next. That's the meaning of "a kingdom of priests."

What is the meaning of the phrase *"Goy Kadosh,"* a holy nation?

The Hebrew *goy* in the Bible means nation, not Gentile, as in post-biblical parlance.

The Midrash—*Mekhilta de Rabbi Shimon bar Yochai* (ed. 4th century)—says this implies that Israel will be a *united* nation, as "one body and one soul." The biblical prooftext is Chronicles 17:21 (quoted in the Shabbat *Minhah Amidah*): "Who is like Your People Israel, a single nation [*goy*] on earth?" Further implied in the word *goy*, with other prooftexts mentioned, is that whenever one Israelite sins, all are punished; and when one Israelite is hurt, all feel the pain. This is unlike other nations, whose members sometimes rejoice in the pain of their neighbors.

The word *holy* means many things in the Bible. Rudolph Otto, as we pointed out above (Verse #6) describes the *numinous*, or the *mysterium tremendum*, the ineffable mystery of God. But when applied to the people of Israel, the term holy clearly has another connotation.

The term is used in many passages throughout the Torah and the rest of the Tanakh. These passages uniformly point to the connection between Israel's carrying out the terms of the Covenant, that is, imitating God and obeying God's Law. Such is the path to holiness. "You shall be holy, for I the Lord your God am Holy" (Leviticus 19:1); "For I the Lord am your God; you shall sanctify yourselves and be holy, for I am holy.... For I the Lord am He who brought you up from the land of Egypt to be your god; you shall be holy, for I am holy" (Leviticus 11:44-45); "You shall sanctify yourselves and be holy, for I the Lord am your God. You shall faithfully observe My laws; I the Lord make you holy" (Leviticus 20:7-8).

The Covenant is two-sided. Israel's part is to emulate God and obey God's *mitzvot*. God's part is to watch over and protect God's treasured, chosen People.

Perhaps the clearest meaning of the word "holy" in the context of this passage is the Aramaic translation of the verse in Sidrah Kedoshim, Leviticus 19:1, "You shall be holy," which Onkelos, the authoritative Aramaic translator of the Bible (c. 90 C.E.) renders as *perushim*, or "separate." Onkelos uses the same Aramaic word that the Pharisaic rabbis took for themselves – *Perushim*, "separate." The Pharisees separated themselves from other Israelites through a series of rituals of purification. In this sense, the Israelites are to be separate from the nations of the world in their moral behavior, their emphasis on ethical monotheism, and their commitment to the sacred Covenant with God.

Rabbi Ovadiah Sforno has a still different meaning for *holy*, emphasizing that the Israelites would not perish but last forever. Holiness is synonymous with eternal in his interpretation.

Da'at Mikra brings another interesting aspect of being a "holy nation." Namely, that it provides divine protection. In support of this, it brings the verse from Jeremiah 2:3: "Israel was holy to the Lord/ The first fruits of God's harvest./ All who ate of it were held guilty; Disaster befell them...."[5]

The notion of a holy nation became part of the prophetic dream for the future, when it would be ultimately realized in all its fullness. Compare Isaiah 62:12: "And they shall be called 'The Holy People, the Redeemed of the Lord'...." The holy-nation concept became in prophetic times an ideal to be sought after at the end of days, while the seed idea was laid during the period of the wilderness.

The *Midrash Hagadol* (13th century) points out that the word "*kadosh*," "holy," applies to many entities in the Bible—to the people of Israel (in our verse—a holy nation); to the Shabbat, etc. But these references do not imply that the holiness of God is of the same caliber. God's holiness is in a separate, higher category altogether, as it says "There is no holy one like the Lord" (I Samuel 2:2).

What Was the People's Response to God's Call to Be a Kingdom of Priests and a Holy Nation?

In verse 8 we see that the response of the people was strong and immediate. "All the people answered as one, saying, 'All that the Lord has spoken we will do!'"

Rabbi Abraham Joshua Heschel puts great emphasis on the people's acceptance in this biblical account. "The wonder of Israel's acceptance was a decisive as the wonder of God's expression....Without that power to respond, without the fact that there was a people willing to accept, to hear, the divine command, Sinai would have been impossible."[6]

A well-known Talmudic legend relates that God first offered the Torah to several other nations. Each one asked the content of the Torah, and when told that it prohibits murder, adultery, theft, lying, etc. each of 70 nations replied negatively. When Israel asked what's in the Torah, God replied: 613 commandments! Immediately all Israel replied with one voice: "We shall obey and we shall hear" (Exodus 24:7). Thus, God was pleased and selected Israel who would be the "treasured nation," "a kingdom of priests and a holy nation."[7]

Why Has the Concept of the "Chosen People" Taken on an Elitist Notion Among Many Non-Jews?

That the idea of chosenness was never meant to be elitist is clear from our verse, and from many other biblical passages. It is a given that there is more a sense of *obligation* than *privilege* in the biblical message.

The most powerful reminder of that idea is found in the third chapter of Amos, when the prophet reminds the people that they were chosen for extra punishment (i.e., held to higher standards) rather than any special reward:

> You alone have I recognized
> Of all the families of the earth,
> That is why I will punish you
> For all your iniquities. (Amos 3:2)

The famous Hasidic teacher the Seer of Lublin (Poland, 1745-1815) points out that Israel's chosenness and holiness is to be spread to all peoples, as it states in Isaiah 2:3: "And many peoples shall go and say: 'Come, let us go up to the Mount of the Lord, to the House of the God of Jacob, that God may instruct us in God's ways, and that we may walk in God's paths.'" In other words, Israel's chosenness is the first step toward all people rising to the level of holiness of Israel.

Rabbi Samson Raphael Hirsch draws the explicit implications of being a "holy nation": "...a nation which does not exist for its own fame, its own greatness, its own glory, but the foundation and glorification of the Reign of God on Earth, a nation which is not to seek its greatness in power and might but in the absolute rule of the Divine Law...."[8]

When God calls Israel God's "treasured people," and "a kingdom of priests and a holy nation," in Exodus 19, these terms are immediately followed by Exodus 20, the Ten Commandments. They are all part of the same indivisible Covenant. God's love and protection follow upon Israel's obedience to their side of the Covenant, following the *mitzvot*.

Notes

[1] Scherman 403.

[2] *The Holy Bible: New Revised Standard Version* (New York: National Council of the Churches of Christ, 1989).

[3] Ibid.

[4] *Da'at Mikra* II/1, 361.

[5] Ibid.

[6] Abraham Joshua Heschel, *God in Search of Man: A Philosophy of Judaism* (New York: Farrar, Straus and Cudahy, 1955) 259-260.

[7] Cf. Louis Ginzberg, *Legends of the Jews* (Philadelphia: Jewish Publication Society of America, 1909-1938) II, 80-82.

[8] Hirsch 251. For extended treatment of the Chosen People concept see Plaut 526-7, and "Chosen People" by Henri Atlan, in *Contemporary Jewish Religious Thought*, ed. Arthur A. Cohen & Paul Mendes-Flohr (New York: Scribner's Sons, 1987) 55-59.

12

Exodus 20:8

שמות כ,ח:

זָכוֹר אֶת יוֹם הַשַּׁבָּת לְקַדְּשׁוֹ.

JPS (1917) – "Remember the Sabbath day, to keep it holy."

NJV (1962) – "Remember the Sabbath day and keep it holy."

After the first three commandments which dictate the belief in only one God, to whom we are to make no graven images, we proceed to honor God's resting after creation by remembering and observing Shabbat. The Talmud teaches (Tractate *Hulin* 5a) that Shabbat is equal to all the other commandments.

We are told in the creation story in Genesis that God rested on the Sabbath day: "And God blessed the seventh day and declared it holy, because on it God ceased from all the work of creation that God had done" (2:1-3). Note that the word *Shabbat*, as a noun, is not found in the Creation story. In Exodus 16:23-30 the people are told not to collect manna on the seventh day, because it is "a Shabbat unto the Lord." The Sacred Covenant of Sinai, the kernel of which is the Ten Commandments, establishes the Shabbat now as a permanent and regular weekly institution. It becomes a day to remember God's resting after having completed the Creation, and serves as a sacred, blessed time. Thus, the seventh day of the week, Shabbat, has become our re-enactment of God's resting after having completed the Creation in the first six days.

Nahum Sarna and others have insisted that there is no precedent for the Shabbat in any other religion or culture. The Babylonians had a day with a similar name (Shappatu), but of a different character. Israel's Shabbat has its own unique character and quality, and the Jewish people can take credit for having bequeathed this special day to its daughter religions and to the world.[1]

Sarna writes: "The Sabbath is the sole exception to the otherwise universal practice of basing all the major units of time — months and seasons, as well as years — on the phases of the moon and solar cycle. The Sabbath, in other words, is completed dissociated from the movement of celestial bodies. This singularity, together with the Creation as the basis for the institution, expressed the quintessential idea of Israel's monotheism: God is entirely outside of and sovereign over nature."[2]

Why Does the Torah Command Us to *Remember* the Sabbath Day?

The Ten Commandments appear twice in the Torah — here, and in Deuteronomy 5. There are some notable differences in the two versions, and one is that in Deuteronomy we are told to *observe* the Sabbath Day. The verb to "remember," — "*zakhor*" — begins with the seventh letter of the Hebrew alphabet, *zayin*. The Hebrew verb "*zakhor*" has a stronger sense than the English "remember," and implies being exceptionally mindful, with an action result. In addition, the infinitive command form here (*zakhor* instead of *zekhor*) is stronger, more long-lasting and continuous, than the normal imperative.[3]

The need to "remember" the day of Shabbat also implies that it is an eternal obligation of the community of Israel to know which of the days of the week is the seventh, there being no external way, such as the cycle of the moon, sun, etc. to know which day is Shabbat. From the time of the original command to the present day Israel has "remembered" which day is Shabbat throughout history, merely by a solemn commitment to observe it in the proper time and fashion.[4]

There are many traditional interpretations of the differences between the word used in our verse, "remember," and the one in Deuteronomy 5:12, "observe," or "keep" ("*shamor*"). For example:

- We *remember* the Shabbat several days *before* it arrives, by purchasing the best food, flowers, dressing nicely, and doing all kinds of preparations in the home. (The Talmud has a broadly applied aphorism: One who prepares for Shabbat, is able to celebrate Shabbat). We *keep* the Shabbat *after* it has departed by holding on to it with a *melaveh malkah*, post-Shabbat celebration Saturday after dark, and by holding on to the spirit of the day as long as possible.

- We light two candles on Shabbat eve, one for *Zakhor* and one for *Shamor*. Others suggest that two *hallot* are placed on the Shabbat table in honor of *Zakhor* and *Shamor* (among other reasons, such as the double portion of manna that fell on Friday).
- *Zakhor* refers to the *positive* commands connected to Shabbat—things we do to honor it and remember it. *Shamor* refers to the *negative* commands, prohibitions and restrictions that keep us from violating its sanctity. Keeping Shabbat implies both kinds of observance.[5]
- In mystical lore, *remember* refers to daytime, and *observe* refers to nighttime. Shabbat encompasses a full period of over 24 hours, from sundown Friday to sunset Saturday.

To explain how the Torah could have two different words in the two versions of the Shabbat command, *Zakhor* and *Shamor*, the Talmud states (Tractate *Shevu'ot* 20b, *Rosh Hashanah* 27a) that God uttered both words at the same time, two simultaneous utterances, from Mt. Sinai, giving them a magical quality—and equality. The Jerusalem Talmud (*Nedarim* 3:2) describes the miracle this way: "Both [*Zakhor* and *Shamor*] were stated in a single act of speech, which is not possible for a mortal mouth to speak or a mortal ear to hear. Thus Scripture says: 'One thing God has spoken; two things I have heard; this (unique) power belongs (only) to God' (Psalm 62:12)."

This explains, argues Nahmanides, how one book of the Torah (Exodus) interprets God's commands about Shabbat with *positive* commands, and another (Deuteronomy) with *negative* commands. There is no contradiction. We must do *both*. Shlomo HaLevi Alkabez (1505-1584), mystical Safed poet, enshrined this beautiful thought into his moving Shabbat hymn, *Lekha Dodi*, sung universally on Friday night to welcome Shabbat, "*Shamor* and *Zakhor* were recited in a single utterance."

The *Mekhilta* (midrashic collection edited around 400 C.E.) reminds us to *remember* Shabbat by calling each day of the week by a number, in relation to its position after Shabbat, rather than by a special name, as Shabbat is called. (Cultures with which we are familiar give each day a name, usually after some Greek god). In both biblical and modern Hebrew (to this very day in Israel) Sunday is called "*Yom Rishon*," or "the first day of the week"; Monday, "*Yom Sheni*", "the second day of the week," etc., until Friday, "*Yom Shishi*," "the sixth day of the week." All the six days revolve around Shabbat. That is one more way to *remember* Shabbat during the week, by referring to the secular days with reference to their position in relation to Shabbat.

What Is the Meaning of "*Lekadsho*," to Sanctify the Shabbat?

There are two basic elements in sanctifying Shabbat. First, by personal and communal behavior on that special day, in elevating our thoughts and actions to a higher spiritual level. And second, by publicly proclaiming it a holy day in a ritualized fashion. A very concrete way to sanctify Shabbat is by reciting the prayer that mentions the sanctity of Shabbat, the *kiddush*. The rabbis commanded that we do so over a cup of wine, the symbol of overflowing joy.[6]

A major, specific path of sanctifying Shabbat is by avoiding labor and commerce: "Six days you shall labor and do all your work, but the seventh day is a Shabbat of the Lord your God; you shall not do any work...." (Exodus 20:9-10). Rabbi Ovadiah Sforno writes that even though it is truly impossible to "do all your work in six days," one should create an attitude as if one's work had been completed. This permits you to put thoughts of work aside, and clear the mind for higher thoughts and experiences without the intrusion of daily, secular matters. This comment follows that of Rashi who echoes this same thought from earlier midrashic sources. A spiritual peace must reign in the soul, the home, and the community during Shabbat.

The Hafetz Haim (Rabbi Yisrael Meir HaKohen Kagan) made an illuminating comparison between the first and second halves of our verse. To *remember* and to *keep* Shabbat are the basic, lowest levels of observance. These can be performed almost by rote—avoiding the prohibitions, and performing some simple rituals. Going beyond these levels is a higher level—that is *lekadsho*—to sanctify Shabbat. This immersion in Shabbat's beauty and mystery must be done with sincerity, intention (*kavanah*), and the fullness of one's heart. It is much higher than the levels of merely observing some ritual details, and involves the body and soul of the Jew in one's relationship to God and God's special day.

The Midrash (*Exodus Rabbah* 25:12) informs us that the holiness of each Shabbat is so great that if the entire Jewish People observed one Shabbat, they would be credited by God as if they had fulfilled all the mitzvot in the Torah. Further, if all Israel kept one Shabbat fully, it would make them worthy of having the scion of David [the Messiah] appear.

Cessation from commerce, the preoccupation of most people on earth, is the first prerequisite for Shabbat observance. This frees up the human being from the absorption of one's time and energies that are devoted during most of one's life to making a living and providing the material necessities and luxuries of life. The second prerequisite is to take that time and use it for higher purposes, what is generally referred to as spiritual endeavors. In Judaism this means the study of the Torah and performance of its commands. In the broader sense, anything which enables a person to engage in non-materialistic pursuits, or more spiritual avenues, would fall in the category of Shabbat observance.

Traditionalists and moderns would differ here in terms of detailed rules to comply with Shabbat requirements. But in general the kind of activities which would be considered "holy" or "sanctified" include time with family and friends, prayer, study, appreciation of nature, intellectual and spiritual refreshment and stimulation, such as reading, discussion, leisurely thought and meditation, and physical rest (the body and soul are both important in Judaism). These are the things that do not provide basic material needs, but rather higher needs (what Abraham Maslow, late Brandeis University psychologist, called "Being" needs) — the spiritual values of life.

Rabbi Shimon bar Yochai (ca. 100 C.E.-160 C.E., Palestine) saw the word *lekadsho* as related to the same root as *kiddushin* — or the Jewish marriage ceremony. As if the Torah is saying: Remember the Shabbat, to be wedded to it (*lekadsho*). He then explains that each day of the week has a "mate" —Sunday/Monday; Tuesday/Wednesday; Thursday/Friday. But Shabbat seems to be without a mate. By fulfilling the fourth commandment literally, says Rabbi Shimon, Shabbat becomes the "bride" of the Jewish people (Genesis Rabbah 11:8).

Perhaps the most widely-quoted modern expositor of the value, beauty and significance of Shabbat, as the cornerstone of Judaism, the Jewish family and religion, is the late Rabbi Abraham Joshua Heschel, who writes: "The meaning of the Sabbath is to celebrate time rather than space. Six days a week we live under the tyranny of things of space; on the Sabbath we try to become attuned to holiness in time. It is a day of which we are called upon to share in what is eternal in time, to turn from the results of creation to the mystery of creation, from the world of creation to the creation of the world."[7]

Ahad Ha'Am (b. Kiev, Ukraine, 1856, d. Tel Aviv, 1927), pioneer Zionist thinker, also well summarized the power of Shabbat in his famous aphorism, in terms of what it has done for the unity of Jewry and the preservation of the Jewish People: "More than Israel has kept Shabbat, Shabbat has kept Israel."

Why is There a Strong Connection to God in the Shabbat Command?

Verse 10 states, as in many biblical passages, that Shabbat is *"Shabbat LAdonai,"* a Sabbath to the Lord. Why this constant association? Since the reason given in Exodus for the observance of Shabbat is that God rested on the seventh day, it is natural that the connection between God's Sabbath and the people's resting be clearly driven home through constant pedagogic repetition.

It is also important to remember, as Sarna teaches, that God is sovereign and transcendent over nature, which is the key distinction between polytheism and monotheism. In polytheism, the gods were part of nature, and subject to all the same forces of good and evil, human appetites, mortality, etc., that living beings were. The difference between monotheism and polytheism is not simply a reduction from three gods, to two gods, to one God. It is a difference in *kind* and *quality*. The one God of the universe, who created the entire world, is thus in charge of everything—all living creatures and the material world, with all its laws, which they inhabit.[8]

It is also important to note that the observance of Shabbat is not just a social institution for the betterment of humanity. It is a divine *command*, part of the larger system of Judaism which has created a broad pattern and structure of ethnic, cultural and spiritual rules, regulations, rituals and traditions which dictate the totality of one's life—all of which are considered to be part of God's plan for the universe. Shabbat in one's life is not merely the discovery by some ancient people that periodic rest for people, land and society is necessary for maximum effectiveness and productivity of the working days. The higher goals of Shabbat are the true goals of life for which all the rest is secondary. Insofar as the spiritual activities of Shabbat lend a more inspired tone to the rest of the days of the week, and to our physical and other labors during the six other days, Shabbat infuses our entire life with a higher quality, making it more commensurate with the divine purpose for which we have been placed on this earth.

The Midrash *Lekach Tov* (compiled by Rabbi Toviah ben Eliezer HaGadol, 1036-1108, Greece & Bulgaria) gives another reason for connecting Shabbat to God. Whoever observes Shabbat is a witness, he says, to God, an affirmation of God's creation of the world in six days and resting on the seventh. By calling the day "God's Shabbat," we also make it our own Shabbat by being witnesses to God's acts of creation and rest.

Why Is the Shabbat Sometimes Considered a Day of Prohibitions, Restrictions and Isolation?

The New Testament portrayal of Talmudic Judaism and its major sect, the Pharisees (the rabbis who created the Talmud and post-biblical Judaism—the core of Judaism that is observed to this day by traditional Jews), was a negative one. The early Christians rejected the detailed minutiae of Jewish law in favor of a more generalized theology of faith and love. Other groups since that time have also characterized Halakhic Judaism as legalistic, dry and confining.

The Midrash gives a different view. The Shabbat was created for higher spiritual purposes, and its laws and customs were designed to support the feeling of tranquility, warmth, community, and spiritual opportunity. The Midrash states that "The Shabbat is given to you, and not it to you [and you are not servants of the Shabbat]." When a similar statement is made in the Gospel of Mark (2:27) it is stated as derogatory toward the supposed rigidity of Shabbat restrictions: "The Sabbath was made for humans, and not humans for the Sabbath."[9]

Rabbi Joseph Hertz brings a fascinating admission by a modern Christian scholar that this negative characterization of Shabbat as over-formalized is inaccurate:

> ...a German Protestant theologian of anti-Semitic tendencies has recently confessed: "Anyone who has had the opportunity of knowing in our own day the inner life of Jewish families that observe the Law of the fathers with sincere piety and in all strictness, will have been astonished at the wealth of joyfulness, gratitude and sunshine, undreamt of by the outsider, which the Law animates in the Jewish home. The whole household rejoices on the Sabbath, which they celebrate with rare satisfaction not only as the day of rest, but rather as the day of rejoicing. Jewish prayers term the Sabbath a 'joy of the soul' to him who hallows it; *he* 'enjoys the abundance of Thy goodness.' Such expressions are not mere words; they are the outcome of pure and genuine happiness and enthusiasm (Kittel)."[10]

Notes

[1] Sarna, *Exodus* 111.
[2] Ibid.
[3] cf. Rashi: Commentary on Exodus 20:8.

[4] *Da'at Mikra*, on Ex 20:7 II/2, 383.

[5] Ramban: Commentary on Exodus 20:8.

[6] Maimonides, Mishneh Torah, Hilkhot Shabbat 29:1 and Joseph Karo, Shulkhan Arukh, Orat Haim 273.

[7] Abraham Joshua Heschel, *The Sabbath: Its Meaning for Modern Man* (New York: Farrar, Straus, & Giroux, 1951) 10.

[8] See Kaufmann, especially Part One, on the character of Israelite monotheism in comparison to contemporary paganism.

[9] Quoted by Plaut 551.

[10] Hertz 298. Rabbi Pinchas H. Peli, a student of Abraham Joshua Heschel, furthered Heschel's well-known, beautiful conception of Shabbat through his own book, which he considers an embellishment of Heschel's earlier work, *The Sabbath*. Peli's book, *Shabbat Shalom — A Renewed Encounter With The Sabbath* (Washington, DC: B'nai B'rith, 1988), is a beautiful description of the joy, harmony and spirituality of Shabbat as experienced by knowledgeable and committed Jews. There is a wealth of modern popular literature in English on the Jewish Sabbath. cf. Dov Peretz Elkins — *A Shabbat Reader: Universe of Cosmic Joy* (New York: UAHC, 1998) 219-226.

13

Exodus 22:20

וְגֵר לֹא תוֹנֶה וְלֹא תִלְחָצֶנּוּ כִּי גֵרִים הֱיִיתֶם בְּאֶרֶץ מִצְרָיִם.

JPS (1916) — "And a stranger thou shalt not wrong, neither shalt thou oppress him; for ye were strangers in the land of Egypt."

NJV (1962) — "You shall not wrong a stranger or oppress him, for you were strangers in the land of Egypt."

Following close upon several laws to avoid pagan ritual practices, we find seven verses dealing with the disadvantaged in society. This highlights the tremendous differentiation between Israel and its pagan neighbors, and emphasizes the humane nature of the God of Israel and the laws that this humane God dictates to the Treasured People.

How Do We Account for the Command in This Verse Being Both in the Singular and the Plural?

Nahum Sarna points out that the grammatical pattern in this Hebrew legal formulation is similar to that of the Decalogue, containing some words in the singular ("You shall not wrong a stranger or oppress him"), and some in the plural ("for *you* [plural] were strangers in the land of Egypt"). The implication is that all the laws contained in the sacred Covenant between God and Israel are applicable to both the individual and the community, who are equally responsible and accountable. "Social evil is thus a sin against humanity and God."[1] Rabbi Abraham Joshua Heschel stated this principle in modern times: "When evil occurs, some are guilty, all are responsible." No one can point a finger at another, for each member of society bears the burden of fulfillment of these indispensable laws of social justice. No society can be just unless each link in that society upholds its high ethical principles.

Furthermore, there is a dual motivation for the fulfillment of this *mitzvah*. First, it grows out of the historical experience of the Israelite people, who were enslaved in Egypt. Empathy is a cardinal principle in the Torah, and the basis for many of the customs in the Pesah Seder. In the Pesah Haggadah we are told to see ourselves as though we ourselves went out of Egypt. It is not an issue of reaching back into ancient history, but reliving the experience of being a stranger in a foreign land, as if we were in fact the slaves ourselves, in each generation.[2]

Secondly, as in much of the Torah's legal prescriptions — especially with regard to areas of social equality — such just laws are a reflection of the nature of the God Who commands these laws. To Nahmanides, God is a God of justice and caring, who hears all the cries of his creatures and, just as God delivered us from oppression, will deliver any who cry out to him, regardless of their status or position. This is emphasized a few verses later: "If you mistreat them (the stranger, the orphan, the widow, the poor) I will immediately heed their outcry, and My fury shall burn..." (22: 22-23).

What Is the Precise Status and Meaning of the Hebrew *Ger*?

The Protestant Bible (*New Revised Standard Version*) translates *ger* as a "resident alien." Rabbi Aryeh Kaplan, in his traditional translation/commentary *The Living Torah*, renders "foreigner," and adds in his commentary: "specifically, a proselyte."[3]

Sarna distinguishes between three classes of residents in a biblical community. The *ezrah* is the native-born citizen. The *nokhri* is one who comes from outside but is temporarily residing in Israel. *Ger* is a specific status ascribed to one who is a foreign-born permanent resident. Thus, "resident alien" is a more technically correct translation. Such a person is a sojourner. He/she is neither a native, nor one who has roots outside the community in his own clan or tribe. This in-between status makes such a person especially vulnerable to discrimination and exploitation. He/she especially needs the protection of the community in which he resides.[4]

This "sojourner's" helpless status fits into that of others whose protection is mandated in this cluster of verses (vv. 20-26): the stranger, the widow, the orphan and the poor. This hapless foursome is the target of unique protection in biblical law, and we find their categories repeated over and over again.[5] Another passage in the Torah spells out the right mandated in this verse in more detail:

> And when throughout the ages, a stranger who has taken up residence with you, or one who lives among you, would present an offering by fire of pleasing odor to the Lord — as you do, so shall it be done by the rest of the congregation. *There shall be one law for you and for the resident stranger*; it shall be a law for all time throughout the ages. You and the stranger shall be alike before the Lord; the same ritual and the same rule shall apply to you and to the stranger who resides among you. (Numbers 15:14-16).

That this custom was maintained in later, prophetic periods, is testified to in the Book of Ezekiel (6th century B.C.E.):

> This land you shall divide for yourselves among the tribes of Israel. You shall divide it as a heritage for yourselves and for the strangers who reside among you, who have born children among you. You shall treat them as Israelite citizens; they shall receive allotments along with you among the tribes of Israel. You shall give the stranger an allotment within the tribe where he resides — declares the Lord God (47:21-23).

In post-biblical Hebrew, the term *ger* took on a completely new and different meaning. Then it means one who was born into another faith and adopted Judaism through a process of study and acceptance of the "yoke of the kingdom of Heaven" (the performance of the mitzvot). Today we use the phrase "Jew-by-choice," in place of the less felicitous "convert." In biblical times one accepted the Jewish religion through territorial and cultural assimilation (remember Ruth, who stated, "Your people shall be my people, and your God, my God" [Ruth 1:16]). It was only in the days of the Second Temple that the institution of proselytism developed in its initial stages.[6]

Midrashic commentary on this verse combines thoughts about the biblical as well as the post-biblical meaning of the word *ger*. The rabbis encourage their contemporaries to treat Jews-by-choice with the same care, concern and love that the Torah commands for the sojourner.

What is the Meaning of the Words "Wrong" and "Oppress"?

The rabbis of the Talmud developed an entire section of Halakhah (Jewish law) based on the several places in the Torah where the word "to oppress" (*ona'ah*) is used (Exodus 22:20, Leviticus 19:33 and 25:14 & 17).

There are two levels of *ona'ah*. First is *ona'at mamon* — financial harm. Included in this category are such things as the seller asking more than a fair price, or the buyer paying more than a fair price. One may not sell an article with a defect without pointing it out to the buyer, even if it does not change the worth of the object. No one should victimize or defraud another.

The second level of wronging another is *ona'at devarim* — verbal harm. (Mishnah, Bava Metzia 4:10 — "Just as there is *ona'ah* [harming, overreaching, deception] in buying and selling, so is there in verbal matters"). This can include embarrassing another — by reminding one of an ancestor who was punished, for example. Neither may one remind a repentant person of an earlier sin by saying: Remember your former deeds (Bava Metzia 57b). One may not try to suggest to a suffering person that one's pain is caused by a sin of which he may be unaware (as in the case of Job's friends). *Ona'ah* may also include asking prices of merchandise that one has no interest in purchasing, lest one falsely raise the hopes of the merchant. Neither may one call a person by a nickname to cause embarrassment, or invite one to a meal, knowing that the person will not accept the invitation. Offers of any kind that are designed only to receive unmerited appreciation, are verbal deception.

Ona'at devarim is a more serious offense than *ona'at mamom* because it cannot be translated into dollars and cents, which can be replaced. The humiliation of another human being is beyond compensation. Through carelessness and spite we can bring enormous harm to our friends and neighbors, and thereby commit a major sin.

What is the Significance of the Concept of Empathy in Biblical and Post-biblical Tradition?

There is a level of treatment of the stranger described in the Bible that goes beyond formal recognition of his or her difficult plight. Suffused throughout the Bible is the sense that the experience of slavery, the ultimate degradation of the stranger's status, had such a powerful impact on ancient Israel that it informs every law, ritual, custom and, even more importantly, their historical and spiritual consciousness.

The key phrase describing the concept of true empathy (more than sympathy, which is caring *for* someone, empathy is caring *with* someone) appears in Exodus 23:9: "You shall not op-press a stranger, for you know the *heart ("nefesh")* of the stranger, since you yourselves were strangers in the land of Egypt." He-brew *nefesh* is translated in NJV as "heart," because in English it is the seat of one's deepest feelings. *Nefesh*, however, is more than heart, and more than feelings. It is the essence of the being of another human person. There is no exact English equivalent, because it is the sum of all the thoughts, feelings, experiences and values of the individual. Furthermore, the Hebrew *yada'* is an intense form of knowledge connoting more than the simple English "know." It is the same term used in the intimate experi-ence of sexual relations. Thus, when the Torah states that "you **know** the **nefesh** of the stranger," it conveys a sense of empathy beyond what any English translation can bring.

When we realize that the central historical holiday of Juda-ism revolves around freedom of the oppressed and enslaved He-brews, and that the entire Jewish calendar begins with the month (Nisan) in which this Festival of Freedom occurs, it is easy to see how the ideas of freedom and equality, the avoidance of oppres-sion, and empathy with the disenfranchised, would be a core idea in Jewish theology and morality. The historical experience of enslavement transformed the Jewish psyche for all time. The Pesah ritual of the recitation of the Haggadah, and all its varie-gated and multitudinous readings, rituals and pageantry, rein-force the notion that Freedom must ultimately become the lot of all God's children.

The well-known Jewish philosopher, Hermann Cohen (Berlin, 1842-1918), expressed well how the biblical concern for the alien impacted all of Judaism, in an indelible fashion: "This law of shielding the alien from all wrong is of vital significance in the history of religion. With it alone true Religion begins. The alien was to be protected, not because he was a member of one's fam-ily, clan, religious community, or people; but because he was a human being. *In the alien, therefore, man discovered the idea of hu-manity*" [italics original].[7]

So central was the passion for fair treatment of the stranger, that the Torah carried its ethical mandate even one step further. It commands its adherents to *love the stranger*. "You shall love him as yourself, for you were strangers in the land of Egypt: I the Lord am your God" (Leviticus 19:34). Recognizing that this may not be an emotionally simple task, to bring oneself to love a stranger, the Torah insists that this love be copied from no less a source than divine love. "God upholds the cause of the orphan and the widow, and loves the stranger, providing them with food and clothing. You too must love the stranger, for you were strangers in the land of Egypt" (Deuteronomy 10:18-19).

Notes

[1] Sarna, Exodus 137.
[2] Ibid.
[3] Kaplan 205.
[4] Sarna, Exodus 137-8.
[5] Compare Exodus 23:9; Lev. 19:33-34; Deut. 10:18-19; 24:14, 17-21; 27:19. And the Hebrew prophets: Isaiah 1:17, 23; 3:14-15; 10:2; Jeremiah 5:28; 7;6; Ezekiel 16:49; 18:17; 22:7, 29; Amos l8:4; Zechariah 7:10; Malachi 3:5; also Psalms 82:3; 94:6; 146:9.
[6] Cf. Kaufmann 300-1.
[7] quoted by Hertz 313.

14

Exodus 23:2

שמות כג,ב:

לֹא תִהְיֶה אַחֲרֵי רַבִּים לְרָעֹת וְלֹא תַעֲנֶה עַל רִב
לִנְטֹת אַחֲרֵי רַבִּים לְהַטֹּת.

*JPS (1916) – "Thou shalt not follow a multitude to do evil;
neither shalt thou bear witness in a cause to turn aside after
a multitude to pervert justice."*

*NJV (1962) – "You shall neither side with the mighty to do
wrong – you shall not give perverse testimony in a dispute
so as to pervert it in favor of the mighty."*

The first three verses of this chapter deal with *judicial integrity*. As Sarna explains, there are five prohibitions against actions
in a court of law that may pervert the impartiality of the judicial
process.[1] They relate, variously, to litigants, witnesses and the
judge. Verse one deals with unfounded rumors and fraudulent
testimony. Verse three deals with partiality towards the poor. It
is interesting that partiality toward the *poor* as well as the *rich* is
cited in several Torah passages (see also Leviticus 19:15 and Deuteronomy 1:17). The Torah so often demands compassion for the
poor that one may assume that they might be extended an extra
measure of mercy in a courtroom. However, this too is considered
a perversion of justice. Rich and poor are to be judged equally.

As we now examine verse two, the most complicated of the
three verses, we will see that the lack of vowel points in the text
allow a wide variety of translations, with an equally large number of interpretations. In the context of the first three verses of
chapter twenty-three, it is clear that the verse deals with some
kind of prohibition against perversion of justice. The questions
is: perversion in whose favor?

All traditional commentaries, and almost all modern translations and commentaries translate the verse to imply that one must not side with the *majority* (*rabim*). However, the NJV translation takes the Hebrew *rabim* to imply the *mighty*. This makes better sense as a balance to verse three, which prohibits favoritism for the poor. Verses two and three can then be seen as one idea: to favor neither those of high nor low station. In Leviticus 19:15, for example, the same prohibition mentions the poor and the *mighty* (here the Hebrew is *gadol*), rather than the rich and the *poor*. Likewise, in Deuteronomy 1:17, we are warned not to favor the "small" nor the "great." In other words, *great* and *mighty* seem to be the opposite of *poor* and *small*. The focus is not on the wealth amassed, but on the influence thereby attained.

There is also linguistic support for translating *rabim* in this verse as "mighty" instead of "majority," though either translation is linguistically valid. Compare Psalm 48:3, where the expression used is *melekh rav*, a mighty king. Thus the NJV translation makes perfect sense, and the warning not to favor the rich or the poor, the mighty or the weak, those of high or low station, is an appropriate and sensible warning in laying out the potential pitfalls in executing full justice.

What Happens to a Traditional Translation when we Discover it is Inaccurate?

While from a literary, linguistic and scientific point of view the newer translation makes perfect sense, for over two thousand years the tradition has built a case on the prior translation; i.e., do not favor the *majority*, a perfectly reasonable translation of Hebrew *rabim*. While this may or may not have been the original intention of the Author of this verse, its understanding in that vein by so many centuries of commentators, rabbis, judges and other biblical scholars and teachers, makes it imperative that we examine the implications drawn by them in interpreting the verse. The rabbis of the Talmud go into great detail in drawing out important implications for practicing true justice from this verse, according to the translation, of not favoring the *majority*.

Sometimes one translation, even though it may not be the literal, accurate one, takes on a life of its own. After new light from archeology, cognate Semitic languages, linguistic or literary analysis alters our understanding of a Hebrew word or phrase, or a historical event, the one that was understood by the rabbis of the Talmud, or the translation accepted by Jews and non-Jews for many centuries, becomes a living expression, and an idea *in its own right*, which often contributes significantly to the history of ideas.

The most obvious example is from the twenty-third Psalm. The classic expression, "Though I walk through the valley of the shadow of death," is now rendered "Though I walk through a valley of deepest darkness." The expression "shadow of death" is a misunderstanding and inaccurate translation. But the phrase has become so important a part of the English language, and has such rich, suggestive imagery and inspirational value, that it would be both foolhardy and impossible to ignore it completely.

In the case of our verse, it is thus necessary to examine the traditional commentaries based on the old translation, in order to understand the long history of rabbinic exegesis on the verse, and thus learn about the notion of justice as it was understood for centuries in the rabbinic mind.

What Possible Interpretations and Translations are Available for the Word Translated as "Dispute" *(riv)*?

Rashi quotes the rabbis as reading the Hebrew letters *resh bet* as *rav* instead of *riv*. Since there were no vowels in the ancient copies of the Torah, the vowels we now have are those of medieval Masoretes (sixth through tenth centuries), and thus are an interpretation of the text, not necessarily the original, authentic text. In our times, Dead Sea Scroll texts of the Bible often render different words by changes in spelling. Scribal errors have obviously entered the text over the past three thousand years. The Dead Sea Scrolls in general confirm the accuracy of the Masoretic text. The exceptions, however, are remarkably useful in helping us translate the biblical text more accurately.

Rashi's reading of the letters *resh bet* as *rav* instead of *riv*, i.e., the *chief* (judge), instead of the word *dispute,* would render the verse as follows: "You shall not speak against (disagree with) the chief judge." This would seem to suggest deference to the Presiding Judge, and doing the opposite of what is taught above — namely, not following the majority, or other opinions, blindly. In practice, however, this is how it worked, explains Rashi. The youngest judges would give their opinion first, so as to preclude the possibility that they might be influenced in favor of the opinion of the more senior judges.

Utilizing the same word *rav,* the Talmud (*Sanhedrin* 18b) warns that a decision may not be rendered when the King is present (*Rav,* or master, being interpreted as *king*), since the presence of royalty may influence the Judges, and thereby possibly distort true justice.

Another possible rendering of the Hebrew letters *resh bet* might be *rov*, or a "majority," in which case the phrase could be a repetition to emphasize the prohibition against following the majority. It also teaches that no court can have an even number of judges. Otherwise it would be impossible to have a majority if the court is evenly split. Thus a Bet-Din is usually made up of three judges, the local Sanhedrins of twenty-three judges, and the Great Sanhedrin had seventy-one judges.

One can see how difficult is the task of the modern translator, and why there are so many variations in translation among the modern editions of the Bible. Two simple Hebrew letters, *resh* and *bet*, can be read accurately, depending on what vowels one assumes (since no vowels were used in the original text), as meaning: quarrel — *riv*, chief (judge, or king) — *rav*, or majority — *rov*

How has Tradition and Halakhah Understood the Notion of Not Following the Majority?

Rabbi Moses Schreiber reads another interesting idea into the text. From the words "to turn aside after a multitude" he deduces that there are two kinds of decisions in Jewish law. The first is a case in which there is room for legitimate disagreement, when a ruling can be "turned" or viewed from various angles. However, in cases where the decision is clear and simple, a rabbi or judge must not be tempted to follow the custom of the majority, which may be to ignore or knowingly violate a Jewish custom or law. In other words, when the masses neglect matters of Jewish faith or religious observance, such is not sufficient cause for the leaders to follow them. The Torah's command to bend only applies in a case where there is room to bend.

Another remarkable case in which the will of the majority is ignored is when the Sanhedrin votes unanimously to condemn a person to death. In this Talmudic passage (*Sanhedrin* 17) it is assumed that if every single judge decided to convict a person, no one judge had the opportunity to be independent enough to dissent.

Rabbi Abraham ibn Ezra warns against following the majority in the case where your own knowledge of the situation is insufficient, and you rely on others for your opinion. Do not say to yourself in such a case, "How could so many people be wrong?" Do not, in that situation, follow the majority and cast your vote with them, assuming they are right and you are wrong. This is a warning not to side with the majority in the absence of a clear opinion of your own, or in the absence of sufficient data in your mind to make a proper decision.

Ibn Ezra's message is particularly relevant in today's world, with the coming of the Information Age, when one must master enormous amounts of facts and data to make a thoughtful decision. Demagogues in government often claim the right to decide for the masses, because they have "more information" than the average citizen. This is an easy path to dictatorship. In addition, it is easy to follow the sound bites of the media who research a complex issue, put out a one-paragraph summary to the public, and thus take control of the mind of the masses. It is the obligation of a responsible citizen in a democracy to be informed. Rabbinic Judaism always presumed an oligarchy of knowledge, not of power.

The Talmud (Sanhedrin 2a) interprets the verse to mean that in capital cases there must be a majority of two to convict, and a majority of only one to acquit. The interpretation was this: "Do not follow a *bare* majority for evil." (By implication, one *may* follow the majority to do good—to acquit). By not giving the accused person the death sentence on the basis of only one vote, the rabbis offer added protection against error in such a serious matter as the death penalty. In addition, no one judge alone will be required to bear the burden of a guilty conscience that it was his vote *alone* that sent someone to death. Eventually, the rabbis eliminated the death penalty completely. They placed so many restrictions on handing down a verdict of death that it was virtually impossible to render a guilty verdict to condemn someone to death.

Note

[1] Sarna, *Exodus* 142.

15

Exodus 25:8

שמות כה,ח:

וְעָשׂוּ לִי מִקְדָּשׁ וְשָׁכַנְתִּי בְּתוֹכָם.

JPS (1916) — "And let them make Me a sanctuary, that I may dwell among them."

NJV (1962) — "And let them make Me a sanctuary that I may dwell among them."

The he only difference between the two translations above is a single comma. This is a good example of how a tiny mark of punctuation can make a world of difference in a translation. Punctuation acts as a commentary, since it has a strong effect on how the reader understands the verse, and what the verse conveys to the reader.

The essential meaning of the verse is not affected by the comma, but the nuance of change, slight as it is, makes a difference. With the comma, you have two separate, though related thoughts. Thought one: Let the People of Israel build me a Sanctuary. Thought two: (By making me a Sanctuary) I may be enabled to dwell among them. Without the comma, the second clause is more dependent on the first, and there is less of a feeling that there are two separate thoughts. Clause two continues and interprets clause one. In modern English we would say: Let them build it *in order that* I may be a part of the community, and live with them. There is no break, or separation of thought. To paraphrase the words of a popular modern movie, "If they build it I will come." Absent the comma, the thought seems to be a more unified and direct statement.

As we proceed now to analyze this short but immensely important verse, we shall examine several important words, which, though only a few letters each, convey enormous religious and theological meaning, much as the comma (or absence of the comma) does in the translations. A perfect example is the word "me" (*li*). The verse could have said: Let them make a Sanctuary that I may dwell among them. The addition of the Hebrew word "*li*" must have a purpose. The *Stone Chumash* suggests that the word "*li*" —i.e., "for Me" (for God)—teaches the important lesson that the most lavish and luxurious synagogues have no true meaning unless they are built for the purpose of serving God.[1]

What is the Meaning of the Hebrew word *Mikdash*?

The meaning of the word *Mikdash* has occupied commentators of all religions, backgrounds, ideologies and centuries. Few subjects have received more attention. The word is also used in the "Song of the Reed Sea," (*Shirat HaYam*), Exodus 15:17, and in a different form in the same song in Exodus 15:13. Rabbi Abraham ibn Ezra connects both of these references in Exodus 15 to Mount Sinai, which is looked upon as a Sanctuary in Exodus 19 and 20.[2] Rabbi Benno Jacob (Germany, 1862-1945) comments as follows: "God, who on Sinai dwelt in a Sanctuary which God's hands have made, is now to dwell in a Sanctuary which Israel would make; and the Tabernacle would be a wandering Sinai."

A similar connection between Sinai and the *Mikdash* is made by Umberto Cassuto, an Italian Jewish commentator (1883-1951) who came to Israel in 1939 and was a professor of Bible at the Hebrew University in Jerusalem. Cassuto writes:

> In order to understand the significance and purpose of the Tabernacle, we must realize that the children of Israel, after they had been privileged to witness the Revelation of God on Mount Sinai, were about to journey from there and thus draw away from the site of the theophany. So long as they were encamped in the place, they were conscious of God's nearness; but once they set out on their journey, it seemed to them as though the link had been broken, unless there were in their midst a tangible symbol of God's presence among them. It was the function of the Tabernacle [literally, 'Dwelling'] to serve as such a symbol. Not without reason, therefore, does this section come immediately after the section that describes the making of the Covenant at Mount Sinai. The nexus between Israel and the Tabernacle is a perpetual extension of

the bond that was forged at Sinai between the people and their God. The children of Israel, dwelling in tribal order at every encampment, are able to see, from every side, the Tabernacle standing in the midst of the camp, and the visible presence of the Sanctuary proves to them just as the glory of the Lord dwelt on Mount Sinai, so does God dwell in their midst wherever they wander in the wilderness. This is the purpose of Scripture [Exodus 25:8] when it states: "And let them make Me a Sanctuary, that I may dwell in their midst."[3]

Rabbi Mortimer J. Cohen, an American Conservative rabbi (d. Philadelphia, 1972), inspired the world-renowned architect Frank Lloyd Wright to design a modern synagogue as a "traveling Mount Sinai."[4] Wright designed an almost completely glass synagogue, in the shape of a mountain, in Elkins Park, Pennsylvania, based on this idea. The ability of the worshippers to perceive God's presence both in the light of day and the dark of night through the mountain-shaped glass synagogue, helps create a sense of being in the Divine Presence. The notion of all sanctuaries as traveling Mount Sinai's is one that can infuse any house of worship with that unique and awesome feeling, based on this verse.

What is the Purpose of the *Mikdash*?

There are as many explanations for the building of the *Mikdash* (also known by several other names, as we shall see), as there are writers about it. One of the most well-known 19th century British Bible scholars, the Rev. S. R. Driver (1846-1914), presents this very lucid and informative explanation:

> The "Tabernacle,"...symbolizes directly, and gives visible expression to, various theological and religious truths. It must, however, be clearly understood that in the text itself no symbolism or significance whatever is attributed either to the Tabernacle or to any of its appurtenances; so that, if we go beyond what is suggested directly by the names or uses of the Tabernacle, or its parts, we are in danger of falling into what is arbitrary or baseless. Bearing this in our minds, we may however observe that by one of its principal names, the *mishkan*, or "Dwelling"..., the Tabernacle expresses in a sensible form the truth of God's presence in the midst of His people; by another of its principal names, the "Tent of Meeting" (27:21), it gives expression to the truth that God is not only present with His people, but that He reveals Himself to them; by its third name, the "Tent (*or* Dwelling) of the Witness *or*

Testimony," it reminded the Israelite that in the Decalogue, inscribed on the Tables in the Ark, it contained an ever-present witness to the claims of God and the duty of man. These three, especially the first, are the fundamental ideas symbolized by the Tabernacle.[5]

Rabbi Gunther Plaut illuminates the view of the well-known German-Jewish philosopher Franz Rosenzweig (1886-1929), to whom "the building of the Tabernacle was in fact the high point, even the goal and pinnacle of the Pentateuch; in Egyptian slavery Israel made buildings for the pharaohs, now they were privileged to expend their labor for God's sake. This more than anything else concretized their freedom. For even as God 'made' the world so Israel now 'makes' the sanctuary in a new act of creation, and the same words used in the opening chapters of Genesis characterize the creation of the Tabernacle."[6]

The *Da'at Mikra* connects the Hebrew root of the word *Mikdash* (kadosh, holy) to the idea that all acts of worship carried out in the Sanctuary should be done with holiness and purity.

What is the Meaning of the Word "veshakhanti", "That I May Dwell"?

Here again we find an age-old theological problem. Where does God dwell? Is the *Mishkan*, or *Mikdash*, God's house? If so, there are many anthropomorphic problems here for medieval and modern theologians.

Israel's late, preeminent Bible teacher, Nehama Leibowitz, quotes several medieval authorities on this question, which summarize the literature on the subject very well. First she brings the words of Don Isaac Abravanel: "Why did the Almighty command us regarding the construction of the Tabernacle saying 'I shall dwell among them' as if God were a circumscribed corporeal being limited in space when this is the opposite of the truth? For God is not corporeal, not a material force, and has no relation to place. Of God it is said in Isaiah 66:1: 'The heaven is My throne and the earth My footstool—where is the house that you may build for Me? and where the place of My rest?' Solomon likewise said regarding the building of the Temple: 'Behold, the heaven and the heaven of heavens cannot contain You; how much less this house that I have builded [sic]' (I Kings 8:27). These are evidently statements that contradict each other."[7]

Leibowitz then brings Abravanel's answer to his own question: "The Divine intention behind the construction of the Tabernacle was to combat the idea that God had forsaken the earth, and that God's throne was in heaven and remote from humankind. To disabuse them of this erroneous belief, God commanded them to make a Tabernacle, as if to imply that God dwelt in their midst, that they should believe that God lived in their midst and God's Providence was ever with them. This is the meaning of: 'And I shall dwell amidst the children of Israel,' .... It is all a parable and allegory representing the idea of *the immanence of God's Providence....* 'I do not need the Tabernacle for My dwelling place,... but I commanded these to be made in order to implant in their hearts My Providence (Isaiah 66:2)'."[8]

To further buttress the same point, Leibowitz quotes from *Sefer HaHinukh, The Book of Education* (an anonymous author of 13th century Spain, who comments on each of the 613 commandments) who makes a similar comment: "...the building of a house in God's name for us to perform therein acts of prayer and sacrifice was inspired by our needs, to put us in the right frame of mind to worship God, not because God needs to dwell among us. Were we to build it of cedars it would not suffice, for the heavens are God's...how much less a house built by mortals! Far be it... but it is the impact on ourselves which is important. Repeated actions make their impact on body and mind, purifying both. God wishes to promote the happiness of God's creatures. That is why God commanded us to set aside a place of the highest purity there to purify the thoughts of humans and refine their character."[9]

In the words of Shmuel David Luzzatto (Padua, Italy, 1800-1865) Leibowitz finds still another explanation: "After they had received the laws and observances of Judaism and God had become their Sovereign, it was fitting that they should make for God a Sanctuary, expressing the idea that their Ruler, as it were, dwelt among them. This would constitute an important factor in preserving the unity of the nation and promoting its loyalty to the Torah."[10]

Prof. Nahum Sarna pays special note to the use of the Hebrew verb *shakhan*, which he says connotes "the idea of temporary lodging in a tent and characterizes the nomadic style of life." He points out the connection between the verb *veshakhanti* ("that I may dwell") and the noun *mishkan* (Tabernacle) — see verse 9, for example. The Torah does not say that God will dwell "in it," but "in them" (i.e, in Israel). Thus, the *Mishkan*, or *Ohel*, is not meant literally to be God's home, as are temples in the pagan world, but to make God's Presence real and tangible to the people, a place toward which they can orient their heart and soul.[11]

In post-biblical literature, God's indwelling Presence is often referred to with the same verb (*shakhan* — to dwell) by referring to God as the *Shekhinah* (Indwelling Presence). In kabbalistic literature, the *Shekhinah* is the feminine side of God's nature (*Shekinah* being a feminine noun in Hebrew).

Rabbi Tarfon (46-117 C.E., one of the rabbis of the Mishnah) informs us that this verse offers proof that communication with God requires effort and work. God was not ready to repose the Divine Presence on Israel until they labored by building a Sanctuary. Only then was God ready to dwell among the People of Israel. First the verse says: "Let them make Me a Sanctuary." Following that it says: "And I shall dwell among them" (*Avot deRabbi Natan*, 11).

The famous Hasidic Rabbi Menahem Mendel of Kotzk, (Poland, 1787-1859) points out that the verse says that God will dwell "among them," i.e, among the People of Israel, and not "in it," in the *Mikdash*, to teach us that each human being must build the Sanctuary in his/her own heart, and only then will God dwell among them. If a person makes a Sanctuary in his/her heart, and fills it with love and awe of God, then "I will dwell among them" (literally *in them, betokham).*

Notes

[1] Scherman 445.

[2] Ibn Ezra: Commentary on Exodus 15:13.

[3] Umberto Cassuto *The Commentary on the Book of Exodus* (Jerusalem: Magnes Press, 1967) 319.

[4] As quoted in Richard Meier, "Synagogue: Contemporary Period" in *Encyclopaedia Judaica* XV, 626.

[5] Driver 260.

[6] Plaut 598.

[7] As quoted in Leibowitz, *Shemot* 471.

[8] Ibid. 472.

[9] Ibid. 482.

[10] Ibid. 483.

[11] Sarna, *Exodus* 158.

16

Exodus 34:6-7

שמות לד,ו-ז:

וַיַּעֲבֹר ה' עַל פָּנָיו וַיִּקְרָא ה' ה' אֵל רַחוּם וְחַנּוּן אֶרֶךְ אַפַּיִם
וְרַב חֶסֶד וֶאֱמֶת. נֹצֵר חֶסֶד לָאֲלָפִים נֹשֵׂא עָוֹן וָפֶשַׁע
וְחַטָּאָה וְנַקֵּה לֹא יְנַקֶּה פֹּקֵד עֲוֹן אָבוֹת עַל בָּנִים
וְעַל בְּנֵי בָנִים וְעַל שִׁלֵּשִׁים וְעַל רִבֵּעִים.

*JPS (1916) — "And the Lord passed by before him, and pro-
claimed: 'The Lord, the Lord God, merciful and gracious,
long-suffering, and abundant in goodness and truth; keeping mercy unto the thousandth generation, forgiving iniquity and transgression and sin; and that will by no means
clear the guilty; visiting the iniquity of the fathers upon the
children, and upon the children's children, unto the third
and unto the fourth generation.'"*

*NJV (1962) — "The Lord passed before him and proclaimed:
'The Lord! The Lord! a God compassionate and gracious,
slow to anger, abounding in kindness and faithfulness, extending kindness to the thousandth generation, forgiving
iniquity, transgression, and sin; yet He does not remit all
punishment, but visits the iniquity of parents upon children
and children's children, upon the third and fourth generations.'"*

Before Moses receives the second set of the Decalogue, God
presents him with a ritual teaching formula that may be invoked
at future occasions when God's anger might be aroused, so that
the situation may be prevented from escalating to tragic proportions. It is a ritual reminder to enable the Jewish People to learn
from God's qualities of Mercy.

These verses are known in Jewish Tradition as the "Thirteen
Attributes" of God's Mercy (*shelosh esrei middot*). There are ech-

oes to these Thirteen Attributes in various places in the Tanakh, such as Numbers 14:18, Jeremiah 32:18, Joel 2:13, Psalm 103:8, Nehemiah 9:17, etc. In Jewish Liturgy these Thirteen Attributes play a significant role and are repeated on important calendar occasions, including Yom Kippur (according to rabbinic tradition, the second set of Tablets of the Decalogue were given on Yom Kippur) and other festivals (when the Ark is opened prior to the Torah reading), fast days, and in times of threatened calamity. In the Sephardic ritual, the Thirteen Attributes are recited daily.

Rabbi Yohanan declares in the Talmud (*Rosh Hashanah* 17b) that God first recited these Attributes, draped in a prayer shawl (*tallit*), as the leader of the prayers, demonstrating to Moses how to recite this refrain, and telling him that "Whenever the People of Israel sins, let them recite before me this Section of Prayer, and I shall forgive them." In the Torah itself, Moses invokes the Thirteen Attributes after the sin of the twelve spies (Numbers 14:17-18), to "remind" God of these Attributes of Mercy. The frequent usage of this passage in the liturgy does *not* mean that the recitation by itself grants pardon for sin, but rather that the sincere recitation of the Thirteen Attributes moves the people to emulate God's moral qualities of compassion, forbearance, kindness and forgiveness.

A final note on the liturgical use of the *shelosh esrei midot*. For decades Christian polemicists have argued that the "Old Testament" portrayed God as vengeful and angry, and lacking in mercy and kindness. This ancient cultic confession invalidates that charge, as will an objective examination of the entire Tanakh. Conversely, as both mercy and justice are found throughout the Hebrew Scriptures, so are they in the New Testament, where one frequently finds threats of burning in hell for misdeeds, particularly in the book of Revelation's awful portents.[1] Furthermore, there is not a single word of commentary to be found on these verses in the standard, widely-used Christian commentary, the multi-volume *The Interpreter's Bible*.[2] In *The New Interpreter's Bible*, the updated version of the first, does comment on these verses, acknowledging that God in the Hebrew Scriptures is multifaceted. This reflects a welcome change in Christian scholarship over the past fifty years.[3]

Why Is the Lord's Name (*YHWH*) Repeated?

Among all the ancient, medieval and modern commentaries, the words of Rashi best summarize the Talmudic comments and captures the plain meaning and essence of the text, as well as the homiletical comments of the ancient rabbis. Much of the interpretation that follows on these verses is drawn from Rashi, the Prince of medieval commentators.

Regarding the repetition of God's Ineffable Name (recited only once a year, on Yom Kippur, in the Holy of Holies, in its pristine form), Rashi explains that it indicates that God is a merciful God both *before* and *after* one sins. The expectation is that the sinner will repent and change. God's mercy, however, is eternal, and does not alter in the face of potential or actual sin.

The two words for God's name are pronounced "Adonai," or "Lord," which is the name of God that reflects the merciful attribute displayed by God, rather than *Elohim*, which displays God's attribute of justice. The third attribute, *El*, according to Rashi, is specifically in the singular form, implying justice *and* mercy, instead of *Elohim* which might convey its normal meaning of strict justice — out of place in this collection of Attributes of Mercy.[4]

Grammatically, there are two ways to read this verse. 1) *Vayikra Adonai: Adonai;* And the Lord proclaimed: "The Lord God, merciful...." In this case the first use of the Name is the subject of the verb "called." Maimonides and others point out that in an invocation such as this, it is normal to repeat an important word or phrase. Thus, the other way to read the verse is, 2) *Vayikra: Adonai! Adonai!* And the Lord...proclaimed: "The Lord! The Lord!" For the standard counting of the Thirteen Attributes, each of the two repetitions is counted as one of the thirteen, since as pointed out above, according to Rashi each one conveys a slightly different context.

What are the Nuances of the Attributes of Compassionate, Gracious and Slow to Anger?

Rabbi Abraham ibn Ezra explains the attribute of *rahum*, or compassionate, with the analogy of a parent who wants to prevent her child from harm, and will thus go out of the way not to place the child in a position of difficult temptation.. Rabbi Ovadiah ben Yaakov Sforno suggests that when the sinner calls, the compassionate God will quickly lighten the punishment.

According to the Sforno, *hanun*, or God's graciousness, suggests that God rewards those who are not fully deserving of reward. The German-Jewish philosopher Moses Mendelssohn (1729-1786) points out the distinction between these two qualities (compassion and graciousness) in humans and in God. In humans the two qualities are ephemeral, whereas with God, compassion and grace are "permanent, inherent and necessary emanations" of God's nature. Thus it is possible to speak of God alone as *rahum ve'hanun*.

Erekh Apayim — slow to anger — according to Rashi, is the attribute that describes the desire to wait and give the sinner a chance to change before rushing to judgment and punishment. The Hebrew phrase means literally "one who is full-breathed." Anger was thought to shorten one's capacity for free, relaxed breathing. Note the subtle linguistic connection between the Jewish/biblical view of anger with the practice of Yoga, which brings relaxation and tranquility through slowing and focusing on one's breathing. Compare Proverbs 24:29, "One who is slow to anger (*erekh apayim*, or slow-breathed) brings much understanding; one who is quick to anger (*ketzar ru'ach*, short of breath) encourages folly."

It is interesting to note that the phrases "extending kindness to the thousandth generation" and "visits the iniquity of parents upon children until the third and forth generation" also appear in the Decalogue, but in the opposite order. There, in Exodus 20:5-6, God is described as a jealous God, visiting iniquity of the parents on the children to the third and fourth generation, and then showing mercy to the thousandth generation. In this collection, the order emphasizes God's compassion by mentioning that quality first, followed by the mention of punishment.

What is the Meaning of the Hebrew Word *Hesed*?

To understand the difficulty of translating this giant, often-repeated concept in the Tanakh, let's look at a few of the standard translations. Of course, the more translations there are, the more possibilities, interpretations, and difference of opinion, as well as the greater richness of the word, which cannot (like most important words in a language) be translated faithfully into another language. JPS translates *hesed* as goodness; NJV as kindness; Aryeh Kaplan as "tremendous [resources of] love;[5] New Revised Standard Version (NRSV — the modern Protestant translation) as steadfast love.

One of the reasons why the word *hesed* is difficult to translate is that it appears in a wide variety of contexts within different passages and books of the Bible itself, not to speak of post-biblical usage. It is one of the most important words in the Hebrew language, and in biblical theology. Many scholarly articles have attempted to analyze and dissect its components and contextual usages. As Sarna points out, it can sometimes imply an intimate relationship, as between God and Israel. In other passages it may reflect a moral-legal connotation, such as in a covenantal commitment. In still other uses, it connotes undeserved graciousness and kindness.[6]

The translation that seems to most precisely and eloquently capture the meaning of *hesed* is "steadfast love." There are other words in Hebrew for goodness, kindness, love, and all the other translations of *hesed*. But for the kind of love that is enduring and reflects an ongoing committed relationship, as in the Covenant between God and Israel, the adjective *steadfast*, added to the noun *love*, seem best to convey to the English reader the full richness of the Hebrew word *hesed*. Rabbi Abraham ibn Ezra's comment that God is steadfastly loving both to the righteous and the wicked, seems to exemplify the kind of love which is more than a passing fancy, however deep it appears.

Nahum Sarna points out that *hesed* often appears together with the next quality, *emet* (truth), and that the two of them complement each other and in appearing as a pair, offer mutual meanings which present a unified concept. This further reinforces the accuracy of the translation of "steadfast love."[7] Rabbi Joseph H. Hertz comments wisely that whenever *hesed* and *emet* are used together, which is frequently in the Bible, *hesed* always comes first, "as if to say, 'Speak the truth by all means; but be quite sure that you speak the truth *in love*.'"[8]

Rashi notes that even though God's *hesed* is already listed, the next attribute, *notzer hesed la'alafim*, refers to its longevity. In other words, God's steadfast love is extended beyond the person who deserves it, but even to those who descend from that person, as far as a thousand generations. Noting that the word *thousands* is in the Hebrew plural, Rashi comments that such kindness is bestowed on at least *two* thousand generations. The rabbinic phrase *zekhut avot*, the merit of the ancestors, is a value concept in Talmudic theology, which implies that the descendants of the patriarchs and matriarchs, and those who followed them, can be recipients of the merit stored up by their previous good deeds. We benefit from the positive behaviors of our Founding Ancestors, even when we do not deserve to. In Rashi's comment, this can be compared to God "banking" the early deeds of the saints and sages of the past for the benefit of those who follow. It is indeed an act of grace, compassion, and steadfast kindness on God's part.

The Midrash (*Mekhilta of Rabbi Yishmael*, redacted by the fourth century C.E., on Exodus 20:6) notes that God's rewards of kindness and love are boundless, while punishment is limited to four generations.

What Are the Three Kinds of Sins Which God Forgives (Verse 7)?

Hebrew *Avon*, *Pesha*, and *Hata'ah*, are three different types of sins, all of which are forgiven by God. *Avon* is from the Hebrew root meaning "to be twisted," or "crooked." It refers to the perverted nature of a human being who is led astray by a character flaw. *Pesha* (modern Hebrew for crime, violence) is the Biblical term for the kind of evil deeds that flow from one who does not recognize God or moral standards, and does not hold oneself accountable to others or to society. Right and wrong are terms used only to describe what this person desires for his/her own selfish desires. According to Rashi, acts of *pesha* emerge from rebelliousness and malice.

Hata'ah, according to halakhic and liturgical usage, is the weakest of the three terms, related to Hebrew *het*, used frequently in the High Holiday liturgy, and is from the root "to miss the mark." This occurs when one is careless about moral matters, no matter how inadvertent the sin may be. *Da'at Mikra* points out that even while in the liturgy *hata'ah* is the least serious of the sins, in biblical usage it is the most serious.[9] The order of severity in this version is ascending, with *avon* being the least serious, *pesha* next highest, and *hata'ah* the most serious.[10]

The Talmudic rabbis point out that there are three levels of sin listed here to remind us that sinning once, twice, even thrice, is forgivable; but as in the modern saying, "three strikes and you're out," there is a limit. (For the modern saying, the third is out. For the rabbis, the fourth is out.) In other words, after three sins, even God loses patience and ceases to forgive.[11]

What is the Difference between the Biblical and Rabbinic Interpretations of the Phrase *"Nakeh Lo Yenakeh?"*

The traditional commentators take advantage of the grammatical form of this phrase to add their own insights. Since the verb is repeated—first in infinitive form (*nakeh*), then in the imperfect tense (*lo yenakeh*)—for emphasis—the rabbis are able to interpret and soften the apparent intent of the verse.

The *peshat*, or simple interpretation, indicates that while God is merciful and compassionate, there is a limit to forgiveness. A system of justice would not be valid in which everyone was automatically and quickly forgiven with neither repentance nor accountability. The Talmud modifies the verse significantly by taking the two Hebrew verbs to refer to two separate cases (*Yoma* 86a). The first Hebrew phrase, *nakeh*, it states, means that God will cleanse and forgive the individual who repents (taking *nakeh* as an independent verb), but not (*lo yenakeh*) the one who does not repent. *Teshuvah*, repentance, a post-pentateuchal doctrine, is the key difference in the rabbinic Jewish theology of divine forgiveness. While this may not be the literal intent of our verse, it is very much in line with subsequent Jewish theology.

Rabbi Ovadiah Sforno presents a slightly different duality: God forgives the person who repents out of love of God, but does not forgive those who repent out of fear of punishment. Others point out that the punishment extended is "not vindictive but remedial." Still others note that "punishment" of following generations means that in the natural course of things children and grandchildren will inherit the consequences of the evil acts perpetrated by their family, not that God will intentionally focus on them for punishment.

In another attempt to mitigate the severity of the punishment, Sforno argues that God will punish the third generation only if the sins of the grandchild or his or her generation add on to the sins of the grandparents' and the fourth generation will be punished if the simply continue the sins of the previous generations and not add on to them. In the Decalogue, the phrase "to those who hate Me" is added to this sentence, which allows the rabbis (Talmud, *Berakhot* 7a) to interpret the punishment as referring only to cases in which the following generations *repeat* the sins of their ancestors.

While the Biblical commentators attempt to mitigate the severity of the punishment clause in a passage which is characterized by compassion and steadfast love, the Rabbis quote the *Shelosh Esrei Middot* in the Liturgy by actually truncating the verse — cutting everything that comes after the word "not." By doing this they include the notion that God will forgive repentant sinners, and omit the idea that God will not forgive unrepentant sinners. If one takes the biblical passage in its literal and full refrain, the way the Talmudic rabbis utilize the phrase in the liturgy is the direct *opposite* of what is intended — a rather brash use of Torah text. This is much more characteristic of the ancient rabbis than of modern interpreters, who apparently seem to feel more impelled to preserve the text in its literal meaning than their rabbinic ancestors.

Notes

[1] Jeffery Wigoder, et al., eds., *Illustrated Dictionary and Concordance of the Bible* (New York: Macmillan, 1986) s.v. "God," esp. 401.
[2] Buttrick I-IV.
[3] Leander E. Keck, et al., eds., The New Interpreter's Bible: General Articles & Introduction, Commentary, & Reflections for Each Book of the Bible (Nashville, Abingtion Press, 1998) I, 946-9.
[4] For more on this subject see Plaut 31.
[5] Kaplan 459.
[6] Sarna, *Exodus* 80.
[7] Ibid. 216.
[8] Hertz 365.
[9] *Da'at Mikra* II/2, 334.
[10] See Exodus 32:21 regarding the Golden Calf, "Moshe said to Aharon, 'What did this people do to you that you have brought such great sin (*hata'ah gedolah*) upon them?'"
[11] Tosefta *Yoma* 5:13 in *Humash Torah Shleimah* (Jerusalem: Beit Torah Sheleimah, 1992) XXII, 67.

17

Leviticus 19:2

ויקרא יט,ב:

דַּבֵּר אֶל כָּל עֲדַת בְּנֵי יִשְׂרָאֵל וְאָמַרְתָּ אֲלֵיהֶם
קְדֹשִׁים תִּהְיוּ כִּי קָדוֹשׁ אֲנִי ה' אֱלוֹהֵיכֶם.

JPS (1916) – "Speak unto all the congregation of the children of Israel, and say unto them: Ye shall be holy; for I the Lord your God am holy."

NJV (1962) – "Speak to the whole Israelite community and say to them: You shall be holy, for I, the Lord your God, am holy."

The several chapters preceding and following Leviticus 19 deal with matters of holiness, such as Kashrut (the Jewish Dietary Laws), unlawful marriages and sexual immorality. Chapters 20-26 cover the topics of idolatry, priestly purity, holiness of the sanctuary, holy days and festivals, the sabbatical and Jubilee years. The section of Leviticus 17 to 26 is often referred to as "The Holiness Code." In a general way all of the subjects in these chapters relate to the biblical notion of "holiness." Since the concept of *kedushah*, or holiness, covers such a broad spectrum of objects, events and people, it is difficult to find the common denominator in the one word "*kadosh*," or "holy." By looking at the various commentaries on this primary verse—the command to be holy, as God is holy—we will get a clearer picture of what the concept of holiness has encompassed from the days of the Torah until modern times.

Chapter 19 of Leviticus contains some of the most sublime ethical teachings of Judaism or any religious or legal system. The rabbis of the Midrash refer to this chapter as containing "*rov gufei Torah*," the primary principles of the Torah, or the essential body of the Torah and Judaism.[1] Even after we examine this introductory verse, our study of several other verses in Leviticus 19 will further clarify the meaning of this comprehensive rubric of "holiness."

What is the Significance of Adonai Commanding Moses to Speak to the Whole Community of Israel?

The Midrash pays special attention to this commandment for Moses to address the whole community. Several reasons are given in the midrashic collection of *Leviticus Rabbah* (Section 24). Rabbi Hiyya (third century C.E., in the Land of Israel) explains that the presence of the whole community is important because so much of what is contained in Leviticus 19 summarizes all of the Torah. Of course, the Torah is observed in all its completeness in community, so learning it and observing it in community go together.

A contemporary of Rabbi Hiyya, Rabbi Levi, goes further, and shows how the commands in Leviticus 19 parallel the Ten Commandments, also given to the whole congregation (some are parallel in direct, and others in more indirect ways). For example, Leviticus 19:3a refers to reverence for parents (the fifth commandment); 19:3b refers to the Shabbat (the fourth commandment); 19:4 prohibits idolatry (the second commandment); 19: 11, 13, 15 and 35, all relate to deceitful conduct (the eighth commandment); 19:16 prohibits dealing basely with others (the ninth commandment); 19:18 forbids bearing a grudge (the tenth commandment); 19:12 talks of false oaths (the third commandment); and 19:36 is similar in content to the first commandment.

A very significant point of comparison between Israel and other nations is that the basic and essential commands of the Covenant are directed toward the entire People of Israel, not to a small priestly or cultic caste. The Talmud explains that even in the case of other laws, when there was a progression of teaching by God, first to Moses, then to the priests, and afterward to the whole people, this particular supreme command of holiness is taught to the whole people, telescoping the normal sequence into one step so that everyone would hear it simultaneously (*Eruvin* 54b). The democratization of ethical, ritual and spiritual laws made Judaism a religion that had more staying power, empowering the entire people, and thus creating a stronger system of checks and balances.

Rabbi Hayyim Sofer, a nineteenth century Hungarian rabbi, fought against the Jewish reformers of his day who were not circumcising their children and moving away from certain rituals and practices he considered essential to traditional Judaism. He emphasized that being holy applied in private as well as in *the community*. During his tenure in various communities in Hungary, a phrase was circulating that encouraged Jews to keep Judaism within the privacy of their homes, but to be just like everyone else in the world at large. The phrase, "Be a Jew at home, and a human being outside," was objectionable to him because it meant denying a major part of one's total Jewish practice and value system. His reading of the command to the whole community to be holy was that it implied being a Jew both at home and outside. Wherever one found oneself, there should be no hesitation or embarrassment to be fully Jewish, in all its sanctity, in every way.

What is the Meaning of "You Shall Be holy?"

When we discussed Verse # 10 (Exodus 19:6), we elaborated on the biblical concept of holiness, particularly with regard to a holy nation. Many of those points are closely related to our verse, and studying each of them helps understand the other. In a sense, our verse, Leviticus 19:2, and the entire chapter in which it is found, is a further elaboration of the verse in Exodus 19:6, "You shall be to Me a Kingdom of Priests and a Holy Nation." The way Israel becomes a holy nation is through the acts elaborated upon in Leviticus 19. These acts are both ritual and ethical, and the two categories cannot be separated. Through the ritual and ethical acts enumerated in Leviticus 19, Israel, as a united community, has the possibility of becoming a holy nation.

Rabbi Ovadia Sforno points out that the laws in Leviticus 19 are not only repetitions of the Ten Commandments, but embellishments. For example, while we are commanded to observe the Shabbat in Exodus 20, in this chapter the laws of Shabbat are extended to the sabbatical year for fields and monetary loans. The prohibition there against idolatry is expanded here to include anything that lends credence or respect to idols.

A modern Protestant commentary on the Bible, *The Interpreter's Bible*, explains that the Hebrew "*kadosh*" conveys two senses: one of awe and reverence (Rudolph Otto's term *numinous*), as well as being ethically transcendent or on a higher ethical plane:

> The holiness of the God of Israel refers at once to his infinite majesty, his immeasurable power, and his perfect righteousness. "By terrible things in righteousness wilt thou answer

us, O God of our salvation," said the psalmist (Psalms 65:5). Holiness is therefore a wider concept than moral purity, but includes it. Thus Zion is a "holy hill" as the dwelling place of the Lord, and all that is included in the approach to him, the ritual, the utensils, the garments of the priests, are holy; and this includes moral purity. "Who shall dwell in thy holy hill? He that walketh uprightly, and worketh righteousness, and speaketh the truth in his heart." (Psalms 15:1-2).[2]

Rabbi Gunther Plaut writes that while Rudolph Otto's book, *The Idea of the Holy*, has had a strong impact on students of religion since it was written, it does not truly reflect the many strands of the Hebrew word "*kadosh*." Trying to overcome the liberal tendency to associate holiness with ethics alone, Otto added the dimension of mystery, emotion and awe. Explains Plaut:

> It is striking that Otto, a pious Lutheran, made no mention of this chapter of Leviticus in his book. He spoke only of holiness as an emotional experience, not of *kedushah* as aspiration and task to be approached through a disciplined life. In his zeal to give religion a unique character, Otto reduced the ethical component of holiness to a mere "extra." This is not the Jewish view of the subject, as is plain from the text before us, and also from the recurrent declaration in our prayers and benedictions that God "sanctifies us through His commandments." In Judaism, religion and ethics, though not identical, are inseparable.[3]

Rabbi Mordechai Finley, a contemporary Reform teacher, explains that ethics is an indispensable part of spirituality and holiness, but not synonymous with it. Ethics, he explains, is not the *telos*, or end goal, of religion. Rather, it is a response to the holy, as well as a strategy to achieve the holy. To him, holiness embodies many divine attributes, including love, justice, truth and beauty. Ethics is part of justice. Compassion to living creatures, and service to humanity and the planet, are part of love. Appreciation of esthetics is part of beauty. The endless quest for knowledge and the scientific search for understanding reality are part of the divine quality of truth. All of these together, explains Rabbi Finley, are part of God's nature, and constitute a more complete definition of holiness, *kedushah*. Our finite capacity to describe God forces us to use terms like holiness, which is a linguistic attempt to capture in the only way humans can what the essence of God may really be.

Why Do Some Commentaries Explain "Kedoshim" as Being Separate?

Rashi explains Hebrew "*kedoshim*" as "*perushim*," following the ancient rabbis (Leviticus Rabbah 24:6), and the Aramaic translation Targum Onkelos (c. 90 C.E.). This is the same word chosen by the major movement of rabbinic Judaism, called in English the Pharisees. Rashi specifically mentions being *separate* from violating forbidden sexual relations, being separate from sexual immorality, as listed in the prior chapter, Leviticus 18. But being "*perushim*" meant much more than that to the ancient rabbis. It meant that the Pharisees ("*perushim*") must be separate as a community in all matters of ritual purity, and that the Israelite people must be separate from other nations whose Code of Conduct does not measure up to the Torah. Separate means apart and higher than the normative standards of ethical behavior of other nations, and of ritual behavior of less observant Jews.

In the Talmud (Yevamot 20a) the famous scholar Rava goes further and adds that being holy means not only following the dictates of the Torah, but going beyond them, by not indulging in an excess of things which are permitted (for example, wine). His classic Hebrew phrase is "to sanctify oneself with that which is permitted to you" ("*kadesh atzmekha bemutar lakh*"), by accepting moderation in all acceptable deeds.

From biblical days to modern times the nations of the world have noticed the "apartness" of the People of Israel. Balaam, the Mesopotamian prophet, called Israel a people "that shall dwell apart/ And shall not be reckoned among the nations" (Numbers 23:9). So too did Haman accuse the Jews of Persia as being separate and apart, "certain people, scattered and dispersed among the other peoples of your realm, whose laws are different from those of any other people...."(Esther 3:8).

Is God "Holy"? How Can Israel Become Holy if We Don't Know What It Means for God to be Holy?

Prof. Baruch A. Levine explains that in Jewish tradition, Leviticus 19:2 does not intend to describe God's *essential nature*, but rather God's "active attributes," or as Levine calls them, God's "observable actions," "the ways in which He relates to man and to the universe."[4] In theological language, this is known as *imitatio dei*, or the imitation of God. It is easy to understand, therefore, why this verse is the introduction to chapter 19 of Leviticus, which describes ethical behaviors which are similar to the divine attributes of Exodus 34:5-6: compassion, grace, and mercy.

Martin Buber (b. 1878, Austria, d. 1965 in Israel) wrote a profound essay on this subject, in which he explains:

> To imitate God means...to cleave to His ways, to walk in His ways. By these are meant not the ways which God has commanded man as man to walk in, they are really God's own ways. But, yet again, the old question comes back in a new form: How can we walk in his ways? . . . What are the ways of God? Those which He himself proclaimed to Moses: "God, merciful, gracious, long-suffering, abundant in lovingkindness and faithfulness." (Sifre on Deut. 11:22). . . . Another saying (Talmud, Sota 14a) is still more explicit: "After the Lord your God shall ye walk" (Deuteronomy 13:5); how should man be able to walk in the footsteps of the Divine Presence? Is it not written (Deuteronomy 4:24): "The Lord thy God is a devouring fire"? But the meaning is: Follow after the *middot*, the "attributes," still better, the modes in which God works as far as these are made known to man. As he clothed the nakedness of the first human beings, as he visited the sick Abraham in the grove at Mamre (where according to tradition Abraham suffered the pangs of circumcision), as he comforted Isaac with his blessing after Abraham's death, until the last act of God in the Pentateuch, when he himself buried Moses — all these are enacted *middot*, visible patterns for man, and the *mitzvot*, the commandments, are *middot* made human. "My handicraft," as the Midrash has God say to Abraham, "is to do good — you have taken up my handicraft" (Genesis Rabbah on 23:19).[5]

Buber does not include the following rabbinic quotation, which also elucidates the mysterious ways in which we can emulate divine holiness, even while not understanding completely what God's holiness is: "If a person sanctifies oneself a little, it will be granted to that person to become greatly sanctified. If a person sanctifies oneself here on earth, such a one will be sanctified from above" (Talmud *Yoma* 39a).

A Hasidic sage, Rabbi Menahem Mendel of Vorka, sees the same paradox. How can humans become as holy as God? he asks. His answer: "All that God demands is that we attain the level of holiness of which we are capable. In other words, be holy in any way you can, wherever you find yourself, and rise one level at a time in your holiness."[6]

Notes

1 Rashi: Commentary on Leviticus 19:2, quoting *Sifra*.
2 Buttrick 88.
3 Plaut 890.
4 Baruch Levine, Leviticus: The Traditional Hebrew Text with New JPS Translation, The JPS Torah Commentary (Philadelphia: Jewish Publication Society 1989) 256-7.
5 Martin Buber, *Israel and the World: Essays in a Time of Crisis* (New York: Schocken, 1948) 66-77.
6 quoted in Aharon Yaakov Greenberg, *Torah Gems* (Tel Aviv: Yavneh Publishing House, 1992) 309.

18

Leviticus 19:9-10

ויקרא יט,ט-י:

וּבְקֻצְרְכֶם אֶת קְצִיר אַרְצְכֶם לֹא תְכַלֶּה פְּאַת שָׂדְךָ לִקְצֹר
וְלֶקֶט קְצִירְךָ לֹא תְלַקֵּט: וְכַרְמְךָ לֹא תְעוֹלֵל וּפֶרֶט כַּרְמְךָ
לֹא תְלַקֵּט לֶעָנִי וְלַגֵּר תַּעֲזֹב אֹתָם, אֲנִי ה' אֱלֹהֵיכֶם.

*JPS (1916) — "And when ye reap the harvest of your land,
thou shalt not wholly reap the corner of thy field, neither
shalt thou gather the gleaning of thy harvest. And thou
shalt not glean thy vineyard, neither shalt thou gather the
fallen fruit of thy vineyard; thou shalt leave them for the
poor and for the stranger; I am the Lord your God."*

*NJV (1962) — "When you reap the harvest of your land, you
shall not reap all the way to the edges of your field, or
gather the gleanings of your harvest. You shall not pick
your vineyard bare, or gather the fallen fruit of your vineyard; you shall leave them for the poor and the stranger: I
the LORD am your God."*

As part of this exceptionally rich chapter of ethical obligations of the Jewish People, verses 9 and 10 deal with special treatment of the poor. These commands are repeated in part in other
places, such as Leviticus 23:22, Deuteronomy 24:22.

All the commentaries emphasize that these verses establish
a basic philosophy of societal commitment to the poor. It is not an
act of charity or compassion, but an obligation of the land-owner,
and a right of the poor and the stranger, to find food through
these various methods, on which we shall elaborate below. Rabbi
Joseph Hertz compares these laws to the British statutes that
make demands on the harvest for the English poor. He makes
the distinction between the Torah's laws and Roman law. The

latter, he says, was primarily to protect the wealthy class from outsiders, whereas the Torah's laws are to protect the poor, who are considered as siblings, as "family." This biblical welfare system can be compared to a system of social security for the indigent, and to an "income tax" for the wealthy. The essential idea is that the Land is the property of God, and as responsible tenants, it is only fitting to share God's land with those less fortunate than we.[1]

The poor and the stranger are meant to be viewed as ones who should be treated with an open hand and an open heart. When Job makes his beautiful statement of self-defense, he protests (Job 31:17-19):

Never have I eaten my meals alone,
Without sharing it with the orphan.
Never have I seen an unclad wretch,
A needy person without clothing.
I warmed them with the shearings of my lambs,
And their loins did surely bless me.

The Talmud maintains that the Torah designed the law in such a way so that the owner of the field could not select which poor to contribute to. Any poor person could approach the corner of the field, or the dropped sheaves, etc., in order that the poor should not feel required to be grateful to anyone for selecting them. The poor had the *right* to come to any farm, at any time, and not feel obliged in any way. This was their due by law (*Hulin* 131a-b).

Rabbi Menachem M. Schneerson, the late Lubavitcher Rebbe (d. 1994), makes a very poignant observation in stating that by removing a portion of one's possessions for the poor, the remainder of one's property is thereby consecrated and sanctified. Thus, it is not only the portion that is given away which is important, but by giving some away, the balance of one's resources are also affected, and ennobled."[2]

Why Do the Verbs and Nouns in the First Verse Shift from Plural to Singular?

Verse 9 begins in the Hebrew plural—"*uvekutzrekhem*" and "*artzekhem*"—and then shifts to the singular—"*lo tekhaleh et pe'at sadkha.*" Why this change of number in the middle of a verse, which is highly irregular? Rabbi Haim ben Moshe Attar, in his commentary on the Torah, *Or HaHaim*, suggests that the command would normally be in the plural, because it included all Israelites. But it shifts to the singular to teach the lesson that no individual has the right to say that his/her contribution is so small that s/he won't bother giving. How can one small contribution solve the problem of societal poverty? The lesson is that everyone's small gift adds up to a very large contribution to remove poverty from our midst.

A second interpretation for shifting from plural to singular is that of Rabbi Samson Raphael Hirsch, who explains that the verbs in the plural refer to the nation as a whole, prior to the division of the Land to individual tribes and families. The singular verbs that follow imply that even after the conquest of the Land, and its division to individual ownership, each owner should feel a part of the whole nation. Furthermore, no one may eat of the fruits of the land before the portion is set aside for the poor, as this is a national obligation.[3]

What are the Four Categories of Laws Contained in These Verses?

We can categorize the different types of gifts of food to which the poor and stranger have a *right*, into two areas: harvest of the *field* and of the *vineyard*. There are two kinds within each category:

1) *Pe'ah* — "the corner," or "the edge." The Torah does not specify the size of the corner. Rabbinic Law established a minimum at one-sixtieth of the yield (Mishnah *Pe'ah*, 1:1-2). The suggestion is made to consider such factors as the amount of the yield, the general wealth of the owner, and the immediate needs of the poor.

2) *Leket* — "gleanings." The same tractate of the Mishnah (4:10) defines *leket* as the crops that fall to the ground during reaping. A farmer would cut the stalks of grain with one hand, and catch the falling sheaves with the other. Whatever fell uncaught is called *leket*, and the farmer could not recapture it. The biblical story of Ruth (chapter 2, verses 2-3, 7-9, 15-16) describes such gleaning by the poor in ancient times. We see here a picture of Ruth and other poor from Bethlehem following after the reapers among the rows of grain. Rashi quotes the Midrash (*Sifra*), noting that if one or two ears, or stalks, fall to the ground at any point during the harvest, these are in the category of *leket*, but if three or more ears fall simultaneously, the farmer may retrieve them (cf. *Pe'ah* 6:5). Placing a minimal limit made the law reasonable and more likely to be carried out.

3) *Olelot* — "unripe grape clusters." This and the next category are the parallel food from the vineyard, as opposed to the field. Mishnah *Pe'ah* (7:4) defines these as grapes that are

underdeveloped at time of general harvest at the top and bottom of the cluster. Such clusters must be left until they mature, at which time only the poor and stranger may pick them. Rashi describes *olelot* as single grapes that have not yet formed clusters. Others say: scattered unripened grapes that did not yet form a full cluster.

4) *Peret* — "fruit which falls to the ground in the picking process" (as defined in Mishnah *Pe'ah* 7:3). The farmer must leave these grapes ungathered. Here too there is a reasonable limit, defined in the Mishnah, as a few grapes, not more than two (Mishnah *Pe'ah* 6:5, 7:3).

The Hebrew word *peret* is one of some ninety words in the Bible that appear in only one place in the entire Tanakh, and are known as *hapax legomena* (Greek for "once said"). Their meaning thus cannot be derived, as in the case of most biblical words, by comparing the word to its appearance in other locations. One must derive its translation either from comparison with cognate Semitic languages (Aramaic, Ugaritic, Akkadian, Arabic, etc.), or from post-biblical words of similar root.

A fifth category is derived from Deuteronomy 24:19:

5) *Shikekhah* — "the forgotten." While gathering the harvest, if one left a sheaf in the field, it was not permitted to go back and fetch it. Deuteronomy 24:20 mentions not returning for remaining olives on a tree, whereby the rabbis extended the rule of not harvesting the "corner of the field" to apply to trees also (Mishnah *Pe'ah* 1:5).

What Other Provisions Did the Tanakh Make for the Poor?

The Torah, Prophets and Writings make many references to the status of the poor. Israelite judges were commanded to give the indigent full protection (Exodus 23:3; Deuteronomy 16:19, etc.). One could not exact interest from anyone, includung the poor (Exodus 22:24, Leviticus 25:36, Deuteronomy 23:20). The poor had first rights to the sabbatical fruits, which land-owners were not allowed to farm (Exodus 23:11, Leviticus 25:6). The tithe of the third year was for the benefit of the needy (Deuteronomy 14:28-29; 26:14). On major Festivals, poor persons could not be excluded (Deuteronomy 16:11-12). Poor people were permitted to bring inexpensive offerings to the Temple (Leviticus 12:8; 14:21; 27:8). Kings and other authorities were to be concerned with the welfare of the poor (Psalms 22:26; 72:4; Proverbs 29:14).

In moral literature as well as legal material, concern for the poor is shown. Honoring the poor was equated with honoring God (Psalm 41:1, Proverbs 14:21, 31; 29:7). Empathy for the poor was based on remembering the slave status of Israel's past (Deuteronomy 15:11; 16:12). God would not forget the poor (Psalms 9:12; 10:12; etc.). God pities, comforts, and cares for the poor (Psalm 34:6, 107:41; 132:15; Isaiah 49:13, Job 5:15, Jeremiah 20:13). The prophets announced God's concern for just treatment of the poor (II Samuel 22:28; Isaiah 25:4, Amos 2:6; 4:1, Isaiah 1:23, Ezekiel 22:7, Micah 2:2, Malachi 3:5).[4]

Were the Laws in These Verses Maintained in Post-Biblical Times?

The Talmud and post-Talmudic, medieval law codes, such as Maimonides' *Mishneh Torah*, devote a great deal of space to expanding on these laws for the poor.

The Mishnah devotes an entire tractate to the subject of treatment of the poor, known as *Pe'ah* ("Corner," from this verse, Leviticus 19:9). There we learn that not only did agricultural society benefit from these measures, but urban poor as well. Societal mechanisms, such as daily distribution of food to the poor, were established as need arose. Minimal taxation was demanded, and generous beneficence was encouraged, to alleviate poverty, always with concern for the dignity of the poor. Maimonides' golden ladder of eight stages of charity is well-known. It encourages anonymity as well as assistance in job training and accessibility.[5]

In one fascinating second-century debate, two scholars differed as to whether a vineyard that contained only unripe grape clusters ("*olelot*") belonged to the owner or the poor. Rabbi Eliezer argued that it belonged to the owner, but Rabbi Akiva demanded that it be given to the poor. The Halakhah (legal decision) followed the opinion of Rabbi Akiva (Mishnah *Pe'ah* 7:7, and the Midrash *Sifra* on this verse). In another passage the rabbis stated that *Tzedakah* (Charity) and *Gemilut Hasadim* (Acts of Kindness) are equal to all the *mitzvot* (commands) of the Torah combined (Tosefta *Pe'ah*, 4:19).

In discussing the definition of a "poor person" eligible to take advantage of these special provisions, the rabbis said the Torah means one who has less than two hundred *zuzim* (dinarim) cash — which would be enough to support oneself in food and clothing for a whole year! (Mishnah *Pe'ah* 8:8). The midrashic Rabbis defined a "stranger" as a convert to Judaism (*Sifra* on this verse). Maimonides included non-Jews as well.

The question also arose as to whether these laws apply to land owned by a Jew *outside* Eretz Yisrael, since the verse says: "When you reap the harvest of *your land*." The decision was that any Jewish land was subject to such laws (Jerusalem Talmud, *Pe'ah*, 2, 5). Later authorities such as Rabbi Moshe Isserles (1525-1572, Cracow, Poland) stated that by his time, the law no longer applied outside the Land of Israel.[6] More recent authorities have stated that even in Eretz Yisrael it is no longer fitting for the poor to obtain subsistence in this fashion.

Why Does Verse 10 End With the Phrase "I am the Lord, Your God"?

This phrase, repeated throughout chapter 19 of Leviticus, is its refrain. It adds a significant religious imperative and spiritual dimension to the social laws contained in the chapter. One is to be kind, generous, compassionate, honest, and humane, not just because it is the right thing to do, but because these are part of the covenanted demands of God. Whether they seem logical and sensible, and possible, at every moment of every day, or not, they must still be carried out in loyalty to the Tradition, and in obedience to God's will.

Furthermore, the use of the word Adonai in the verse is reminiscent of the Thirteen Attributes of God's Mercy (Exodus 34:6-7, Verse Number 15 in our study). As God is kind and compassionate, so must we, God's creatures and partners, emulate the qualities set forth in the Thirteen Attributes. Being Godly implies concern for the poor, and obedience to all the other commands listed in this chapter.

Notes

[1] Hertz 499; see also an excellent study comparing Hebrew Law with that of Greek and Roman society — Ken Spiro, *World Perfect: The Jewish Impact on Civilization* (Deerfield Beach: Simcha Press, 2002).
[2] "Torah Thoughts", on Kee Tavo in *B'nai B'rith Messenger*, 19 September 1986 Los Angeles, California.
[3] Hirsch, *Leviticus* (part 2) 505-506.
[4] Cf. article, "Poor," in George A. Buttrick, ed., *The Interpreter's Dictionary of the Bible: An Illustrated Encyclopedia* (New York: Abingdon Press, 1962) III, 843.
[5] Maimonides, Mishneh Torah: Hilkhot Tzedakah 10:7-14.
[6] Notes on *Shulkhan Arukh, Yoreh Deah*, paragraph 332:1.

19

Leviticus 19:14

ויקרא יט,יד:

לֹא תְקַלֵּל חֵרֵשׁ וְלִפְנֵי עִוֵּר לֹא תִתֵּן מִכְשֹׁל
וְיָרֵאתָ מֵּאֱלֹהֶיךָ, אֲנִי ה'.

*JPS (1916) – "Thou shalt not curse the deaf, nor put a
stumbling-block before the blind, but thou shalt fear thy
God: I am the LORD."*

*NJV (1962) – "You shall not insult the deaf, or place a
stumbling block before the blind. You shall fear your God: I
am the LORD."*

This verse illuminates yet another mitzvah regarding personal holiness, focusing on a specific aspect of ethical behavior.
As we will see, the verse has much figurative significance, in addition to its literal meaning. The very first phrase, "*Lo teklalal,*" is
a good example. The 1916 JPS translation of this word is "curse"
and the newer translation is "insult." What can we glean from
this difference in interpretation?

The Hebrew root of the verb is *kalal.* In Leviticus 24:14 the same
verb is used in the sense of "cursing God." The new JPS translation
(of 1962) sees the verb in our verse differently, from the root that
means "make light of" (the adjective, *kal,* means light). In Hebrew
that which is *heavy* is honored, and that which is *light* is dishon-
ored, or disparaged, or insulted. Thus, in the Ten Commandments the Hebrew word to "honor" one's parents is *kabed,* from
kaved, or heavy. Thus, the NJV translates "insult" instead of "curse."

Additionally, it is clear that the commandment is not meant
to apply only to those who are literally blind or deaf, but to anyone in a vulnerable position. As Maimonides writes, if cursing

one who cannot hear is forbidden, how much more so is it forbidden to curse, or insult, one who can hear, and thus feels the emotional pain of the insult, or curse. The simple meaning of the verse seems to be the opposite, that cursing a hearing person is permitted because at least the person is aware and able to defend himself. Both views have legitimacy by virtue of human logic, and thus we conclude that neither should be so offended. Rabbi Joseph H. Hertz laments that such a law needs to be declared altogether — it being necessary only because of human callousness and cruelty.[1]

What Is Meant by "Placing a Stumbling Block Before the Blind"?

In terms of parallelism, a popular literary form in the Tanakh (especially in Psalms), "cursing" is parallel to "placing a stumbling block," and "deaf" is parallel to "blind." A repeated, parallel clause is often brought to emphasize a point. In our verse we can derive a pattern from the two clauses. In both cases what is involved is: a) harming someone who is handicapped, and b) harming someone with impunity, since neither the deaf nor the blind person, in each case, is not fully aware of the harm being done to them because of their handicap. The prohibition thus relates to harming others secretly, away from the public domain, and, implied, with the assumption of not being caught committing the wrong.

Nahmanides states that unobserved crimes are likely to be committed more frequently, and thus the necessity of this prohibition. He also notes that the Torah forbids cursing rulers, princes and judges (Exodus 22:27), because people often curse their leaders and thereby demoralize their intimate circle, while, in fact, it is only due to such leaders that society is ruled through justice.

Rashi, commenting on the word "blind," says that this term refers to someone who is "blind about a particular matter" (*hasuma badavar*). For example, he says, do not give one advice that is not appropriate for him. In other words, Rashi is widening the meaning of "deaf" and "blind" to include people who are unaware — either literally by hearing or sight, or figuratively by ignorance, inexperience, immaturity, naiveté, etc. This broadens the prohibition considerably, and the rabbis of the Talmud gave further examples to exemplify the broadening, to show how it can apply to any unsuspecting individual.

To illustrate his point, Rashi gives the example of an individual who gives advice to another, unsuspecting individual, hoping to benefit himself from the acceptance of his advice. This would be like a jeweler who finalizes a deal with a customer who has little expertise in the area of precious gems and fails to get a second, unbiased opinion before making the purchase. We often, ironically, refer to such commodities as "blind" items, because the purchaser is "blind" to the value of the desired object. It is easy to defend oneself in these kinds of "blind" actions, because it is impossible to prove an unsavory or selfish motive.

The Talmud is filled with examples of the allegorical implications of putting a stumbling block before the "blind." One may not offer wine to a *nazir* (one who is pledged not to drink, cf. Numbers 6:6, *Pesahim* 22b), a weapon to a person who is prone to violence, or a garment containing *sha'atnez* (a garment combining linen and wool, forbidden by Deuteronomy 22:11) to an unsuspected purchaser. One may not provoke someone else to anger (*Pesahim* 22b). Similarly, one may not strike one's grown offspring, lest the person return the blow or speak disrespectfully to the parent, and violate the Torah's commandment to honor one's mother and father (*Mo'ed Katan* 17a). These are examples of taking advantage of or abusing one who is particularly vulnerable in certain situations.

The fact that the rabbis of the Talmud and Midrash elaborate at such length, giving so many examples of what allegorical implications the words "deaf" and "blind" may have, is a reflection on how seriously they took moral actions which are not given to easy detection. The Midrash supplies these further examples: "Do not say to someone: Go out early, because robbers might seize him. Do not say: Go out at noon, when it is possible to get sunstroke. Do not say to someone: Sell your field and buy a donkey with the money, and then through your deceptive remarks you become the buyer of the field!" (Midrash, *Sifra Kedoshim* 2). The above are paradigms of ways one could mislead unsuspecting people in different areas — i.e., matters of personal safety, accidents of nature, and careless financial loss.

What is Considered a Transgression of this Commandment?

In still another passage in the Talmud (*Bava Metzia* 75b) the rabbis accuse a person who is a lender, borrower or guarantor of a usurious transaction (cf. Exodus 22:24) as being guilty of violating this commandment. In the same passage they include one who lends money without having the transaction properly witnessed (which could easily lead to fraudulent results in collection, or possibly unwitting denial of a loan, and hence a biblical infraction).

In another example, perhaps more extreme, the rabbis state that when one does not mark a grave, (either by not placing a marker when the grave was dug, or by passing a nearby grave whose marker has been damaged or removed) and thus allows the possibility that a *kohen* (a man of the priestly caste who is not permitted to come near the dead, or a cemetery) might unknowingly walk on it and thus violate a command of the Torah, is guilty of "placing a stumbling block before the blind" (*Moed Katan* 5a). Israel's best-known Bible teacher, Nehama Leibowitz, of blessed memory, points out that this is an example of someone who is guilty merely by sitting in his home and doing nothing, instead of being alert to the problems and needs of society around him. Such a person did nothing intentional, fraudulent, deceitful or selfish, but merely ignored a problem in his neighborhood![2]

In a most interesting example, the rabbis declared that one may not even curse oneself, using the divine name (YHVH), thus extending the prohibition of cursing others even to include oneself, fortifying their doctrine with another biblical verse, Deuteronomy 4:9, "Take care to guard your soul scrupulously...." Maimonides goes even further and declares that one who does something like sell a person with a history of robbery a lethal weapon, such as a knife, or sharpen their spear, is considered guilty of being an accessory to the crime.[3] This idea further extends our responsibility by prohibiting us from assisting an evil person even when they are not "blind" or "deaf," but aware and knowledgeable regarding their crime. Their blindness in this case may be considered to be their moral flaw.

We thus see how far the rabbis extended the responsibility of human beings living in a community and dealing on a daily basis with other persons. Their reading of this verse expands its potential for heightening moral awareness and deepening ethical behavior in important and far-reaching ways, reflecting their own concern for living a morally conscious existence. At the same time, they based their moral judgments on Torah laws and principles, rather than merely pulling decisions "out of the air," or from their own personal experience. The use of the Torah as a Constitution of Moral Principles enabled Jewish Law and the Jewish community to continually grow in intellectual, emotional, spiritual and behavioral stature.

Nehama Leibowitz applies this teaching to modern times: "The arms merchant cannot extenuate his act, by claiming that he had not sold his death-dealing instruments for illicit uses, and that he left the decision on when to use them, to the discretion of the purchasers."[4] One is also "blind" whose greed, selfishness and moral callousness prevent him from doing what is just, she says.[5] Creative minds could extend this significant principle to any human interaction, family relationship, business dealing, or community matter, giving those who accept the strictures of Jewish legal principles strong moral guidelines for conducting their daily affairs.

What is the Significance of the Last Words of the Verse, "You shall fear your God: I am the Lord"?

As pointed out in our study of previous verses in this important chapter of Leviticus, the religious and spiritual dimension of following moral laws is added to their social import when the declaration of God's existence is appended to the command. In the case of this particular verse, the phrase is expanded, and the expression "fear your God" is especially relevant. The expression to "fear God" in the Tanakh means that one is a moral human being. For example, in the story of Shifrah and Puah, the midwives who saved Hebrew male babies from Pharaoh's command to kill them (Exodus 1:21) are said to have done so because they "feared God."

One of the paramount roles God plays in the Tanakh, and throughout Jewish history and theology, is protector of the weak, the poor, the widow and the orphan—namely, the defenseless. Those who are prone to take advantage of the defenseless are here reminded that God will take up their defense, and should be forewarned with "awe" or "fear" of the Ultimate Protector of human life and human values.

In dealing with crimes where there are no witnesses, the persons are thrown back on their own conscience. The question of how the conscience is trained is a complex one, wrestled with by philosophers, educators and theologians for centuries. The Torah's answer is simple, yet elegant. Having fear of God implies the knowledge of a Higher Judge, a Supreme Standard of morality and ethics that transcends human courts, which are particularly fallible in the absence of witnesses, and cannot offer demonstrable proof in matters of conscience.

Perhaps a more mature response to the matter of the development of the conscience is offered by the anonymous thirteenth century author of the widely studied collection of all of the 613 mitzvot (commandments) of the Torah, *Sefer HaHinukh*, the *Book of Education.* Here we find that the world is upheld on three pillars: truth, mutual confidence and mutual trust.[6] In other words, in matters of human discourse and intercourse, human beings must have a certain degree of trust in one another. This is a Divine Principle, built into the universe, which makes human society tenable. Once this fundamental sense of trust is lost, no society can survive. This is a Principle that goes beyond laws, courts, police and military surveillance and enforcement, which are only successful insofar as the members of society entrust their authority within them. The final arbiter of justice in society is the human conscience, which is beholden to its Creator Who established with creation the rules and standards by which we all live. This, in the broadest and deepest way, is the meaning, I believe, of "Fear your God."

Notes

[1] Hertz 500.
[2] Nehama Leibowitz, *Studies in Vayikra (Leviticus): In the Context of Ancient and Modern Jewish Bible Commentary* (Jerusalem: World Zionist Organization, Department for Torah Education and Culture, 1974) 177-178.
[3] Maimonides, *Mishneh Torah: Hilkhot Rotzei'ah Ushmirat HaNefesh* (Laws of Murder and Preserving Life) 12:14.
[4] Leibowitz, *Vayikra* 175.
[5] Ibid.
[6] cf. Abraham Chill, *The Mitzvot: The Commandments and Their Rationale* (Jerusalem: Keter Books, 1974) 225.

20

Leviticus 19:16

וַיִקְרֹא יט,טז:

לֹא תֵלֵךְ רָכִיל בְּעַמֶּיךָ לֹא תַעֲמֹד עַל דַּם רֵעֶךָ, אֲנִי ה'.

JPS (1916)--"Thou shalt not go up and down as a talebearer among thy people; neither shalt thou stand idly by the blood of thy neighbour; I am the LORD."

NJV (1962)--"Do not (a) deal basely with (a) your country-men. Do not (b) profit by (b) the blood of your fellow: I am the LORD." [a-a Others "go about as a talebearer among"; meaning of Heb. uncertain. b-b Lit. "stand upon"; precise meaning of Heb. phrase uncertain.]

Compare the number of verses selected from the entire books of Genesis and Exodus, with the number of verses from this Chapter Nineteen of Leviticus. This is, indeed, as the rabbis stated, *"gufa shel Torah,"* "the [ethical] body (essence) of the en-tire Torah." This particular verse is especially interesting be-cause of the history of its interpretation. It is a splendid example of how modern scholarship, especially philology (the study of language and words), can affect translations, and therefore, the meaning, of a biblical verse.

As with other verses in this section, verse 16 ends with the phrase "I am the LORD," closing a thematic cluster of verses (verses 15 and 16) dealing with the perversion of justice for per-sonal gain. In addition, the phrase reminds the reader/listener that the laws enumerated here are not just socially expedient and legally mandated, but take on the weight of religious import and divine significance.

What is the Meaning of the Hebrew Word *rakhil*?

The New Jewish Version of the Jewish Publication Society (1962) has two options for this phrase, showing us immediately that the high-powered scholarly committee who did the translation did not feel certain enough to settle on one unambiguous version, and thus presented the alternative in a footnote. This is a sure sign that we simply cannot know for sure which of the two major interpretations is the more precisely correct one. In his *Notes on the New Translation of the Torah* the late Prof. Harry Orlinsky admits that the expression *holekh rakhil* "is elusive." He points out that in other biblical verses that contain this expression, "the wickedness of the people is surely more grievous than that of tale-bearing."[1]

Thus, the difficulty presented by the traditional translation is that it does not fit with certain other appearances of the phrase in the rest of the Bible. Yet the traditional commentaries, as well as other biblical usages, make a good case for the well-known and often-quoted translation: tale-bearing, or gossip-mongering.

Let us examine the arguments for the modern translation, "deal basely with," and the traditional one, "tale-bearing."

In Jeremiah 6:28, the prophet chastises the people's sinful ways in harsh terms: "They are all grievous rebels, *holkhei rakhil*, they are copper and iron [stubborn], they all deal corruptly." In another verse, Ezekiel 22:9, we find a similar chastisement: "People of *rakhil* in your midst are intent on shedding blood; in you they have eaten up the mountains; and they have practiced depravity among you." The NJV bases its newer translation on these contexts, and thus translates "deal base with." Either the prophets considered slander and gossip so vile that they appended it to worse sins, or the word *rakhil* means something more heinous than spreading gossip; or perhaps the word has a variety of meanings, and is understood by the reader in different ways in different contexts.

As to the arguments for "tale-bearing," here too there is good biblical precedent. In I Kings 10:14-15, it is clear that a *rokhel* is a merchant, one who goes from place to place, from house to house, as would a gossip, "selling" one's "news" (related to *rogel*—one who travels a great deal by foot). The verses read: "The weight of the gold which Solomon received every year was 666 talents of gold, besides what came from traders, from the traffic of *harokhlim*, and from all the kings of Arabia and from the governors of the country." Further, in Ezekiel 27:12-13 we read: "Tarshish traded with you due to your wealth of many kinds of products; they bartered silver, iron, tin and lead for your goods. Javan, Tubal, and Meshech were *rokhla'yikh* (your *rokhlim*); they traded with you in humans and copper implements."

Rashi argues that since the phrase in our verse is *telekh rakhil*, i.e., *going around* tale-bearing, it has the implication of *spying*. He makes an interesting philological note that the Hebrew word *rakhal* is similar to *ragal*, to spy (one form of this verb, *leragel* appears in many places in the Bible in the sense of *spying*). Thus, to Rashi, "going around talebearing" implies "going around spying."

In post-biblical Hebrew the common usage of *rakhal* is "to slander." The meaning of *rakhal* in the sense of "slander" could come from a number of philological linkages. Rashi connects it to a passage from II Samuel 19:28: "He spied against your servant to my lord the King." Elaborating on this verse, Rashi explains: "He spied out with subtlety in order to speak evil about me to my lord, the King." Therefore *ragal*, to spy, implies speaking evil about someone. In Rashi's commentary he claims (correctly) that sounds which emanate from a similar part of the speech organs are often interchangeable — so that *ragal* and *rakhal* can mean the same thing — to spread slander (originally from spying, and then to slandering — related acts). Other commentaries, such as Ramban and Rashbam, also link *ragal* and *rakhal* — spying and slandering.

It seems that the history of the word began with traveling on foot, as a peddler, then a spy, and finally a gossiper. From these various meanings of the word *rakhal*, the most common usage in post-biblical times of the word *rakhil* came to be that of "gossip and slander," and it is probably in this sense that it is used in our verse.

How Seriously do the Rabbis take the Sin of Gossip?

The rabbis of the Talmud were rather prolific in their condemnation about gossip and slander, and they perceived it as a wicked instrument of selfish and heinous design with grave consequences. It is not unusual, therefore, for it to be used in the Tanakh in these various contexts — as base acts, spying, and slandering. They are often intertwined and equal in potential damage. So, at least, the rabbis considered them. The rabbis condemned not only those who spread false rumors, but even those who repeat *accurate* information that may cause harm to others (*Sanhedrin* 31a). In the Yom Kippur Confessional (*Al Het*), one fourth of the sins listed have to do with sins of speech.[2]

A novel midrashic (homiletical) twist on this verse is offered by the rabbis, making a play on words with the Hebrew *rakhil* (talebearer) and *rakh* (soft, easy). As in all good midrash, the rabbis saw a connection even where there was no valid etymological connection. Their comment: "Do not go as a *rakhil*, is a charge to a Court not to be soft (*rakh*) with one defendant, and hard with another."[3]

Likewise, the Baal Shem Tov, Founder of Hasidism in the 18th century, takes the phrase not to tale-bear "among" your people, to mean "against" your people (the preposition, *al*, can mean either). A Jew must not do or say anything that will cause even inadvertent harm to the Jewish People.

Rabbi Yisrael Meir HaKohen Kagan of Radin, who became famous for his book on gossip and slander, and was known by the title of his book, *Hafetz Hayim*, told people that if he would ever by chance indulge in gossip, he would then be cheating those who bought his book on the subject, and from the sin of gossip, his sin would turn into theft.

What is the Connection Between the First Half of the Verse, the Prohibition Against Slander (or Being Base), and the Second Half, About Permitting Bloodshed?

Maimonides makes the following connection between the first and second parts of this complex verse:

> Whoever acts like a spy against another person violates a prohibition, as it is written (in the Torah): "You shall not go about speaking slander among your people" (Leviticus 19:16). ...This is a major offense that has brought about the death of many Jews. Because of this, we link these two ideas in the same verse: "You shall not stand idly by the blood of your neighbor." Consider for example, what happened because of Doeg the Edomite. (For details of this story, see I Samuel 22:6-19).[4]

Thus Maimonides connects gossip and slander with the possibility of bloodshed. The two ideas of gossip and slander are also mentioned in the same context in a verse from Ezekiel (22:9), "Gossipers in your midst were intent on spilling blood". Other medieval commentaries connect slander and murder by saying that slandering an individual can bring harm as serious as murder, and the concomitant obligation to prevent such pillorying devolves upon a person in the same way as preventing a murder.[5]

The Talmudic rabbis connected gossip with murder by saying that gossip was even worse than murder. The murderer destroys only one person, while whoever indulges in slander kills three people: the teller, the listener, and the one about whom the slander is said.[6]

What is the Source of the Differences in Translations of the "lo ta'amod al"?

This important, oft-quoted, and morally powerful verse is unfortunately the source of much difference of opinion, confusion, and lack of clarity. The essential meaning of the second half of the verse, however, remains the same — do not be passive or active in preserving your own self-interest, and thereby harm another. The problem revolves around the precise meaning of the Hebrew phrase "lo ta'amod al."

Considering the literal translation of the verb "la'amod" as "to stand," one can see how the phrase, used idiomatically, can be given to many different translations. In English we have the expression "to stand by one's convictions," and "to stand over someone," "to stand on ceremony," etc. Likewise, the Hebrew preposition al can be translated as "on," "over," "near," etc., and translated idiomatically with the verb amad, to stand, can mean many different things in biblical Hebrew.

The three major possibilities in our verse are conveniently laid out by Prof. Baruch Levine as follows:

First, the historically accepted understanding of the phrase is: "do not stand by passively when the life of a neighbor is in danger." The Midrash (Sifra), Rashi, and others support this traditional translation.[7] As it is written in Targum Yerushalmi: "Do not be silent concerning the 'blood' of your comrade when you know the truth in a legal case."

Secondly is the slightly different rendering of "to conspire against." Levine quotes Targum Onkelos (an interpretive Aramaic translation of the Bible written around the year 90 C.E.): "Do not rise up against the life of your comrade." Ibn Ezra's comment is similar: "One must not conspire with murderers." Other biblical books (though they are possibly some 1000 years after our verse) may preserve this sense of the phrase amad al. In Daniel 8:25 we find: "...He will rise up against the chief of chiefs...." (ve'al sar hasarim ya'amod); for similar usage cf. Daniel 11:14. In I Chronicles 21:1 we find: "Satan arose against Israel (Vaya'amod Satan al Yisrael) and incited David...."[8]

Thirdly, the twentieth century Jewish Bible scholar, Arnold Ehrlich (1848-1919, Russia, Germany, United States), has translated the phrase as: "to survive by means of, to rely on."[9] Ehrlich, in a clever comparison of biblical verses, looks at Ezekiel 33:26 —

"amadeta al harbekha" — "You have relied upon your sword for
survival," and also at Genesis 27:40: *"al harbekha tihyeh,"* — "By
your sword you shall live."[10] In other words, the preposition *al*,
together with the Hebrew verb *amad*, to stand, implies "subsist
by, or by means of." In other words, do not find your own way in
life at the expense of another person's welfare. Baruch Levine
prefers the third of these possibilities, as do the 1962 JPS translators, who give us "Do not profit by the blood of your fellow."[11]

What Are Some of the Implications of Not Saving Others' Lives While Protecting Yourself?

The standard Code of Jewish Law, the *Shulhan Arukh*, written by
Rabbi Yosef Karo (Spain and Safed, 1488-1575) is that one should
watch out for one's neighbor's welfare, while neither being required to endanger one's own life, nor being overly cautious for
the safety of oneself (*Hosen Mishpat* 426:2).

The ancient rabbis give three other useful examples to flesh
out the implications of this clause with practical situations:

First, if someone is trying to kill another person, it is permitted to kill the attacker, since otherwise one would be accused of
standing idly by the blood of a neighbor (Talmud *Sanhedrin* 73a).
The most notable case in modern times of passivity and insouci-
ance is the case of Kitty Genovese, a twenty-eight-year-old woman
murdered in New York City in 1964, when thirty-eight New
Yorkers watched and heard a screaming woman being attacked
and yelling, "Please help me!" for over a half hour, and did nothing because they were afraid to get involved? Rabbi Joseph
Telushkin points out that in American law no obligation exists to
rescue a nearby person in distress.[12] Such a non-biblical point of
view permits subjects of American law, as well as those living
during the time of the Holocaust, to escape such moral obligations with impunity.

Interestingly, the rabbis of the Talmud also utilize this verse
in defending the right of one who would bring about an abortion
if it is clear that the fetus might endanger the life of the mother.
The fetus in this case would be considered a "pursuer" and it is
therefore permitted to take its life to protect the mother. The
verse would mean: Do not stand by idly when the life of the
mother is endangered by its unborn child (*Sanhedrin* 72a).

A second example is seeing someone drowning in the sea
[read: a swimming pool or lake], or being dragged by an animal,
or being captured by robbers (we are frequently being warned in

these days, alas, to be wary of strangers who may kidnap young-sters). The rabbis derive the law that one is obligated to extend oneself for such individuals by referring to our verse (*Sanhedrin* 73a).

Finally, the Talmud states that if one has information that may lead to the exoneration of an accused person, it is incumbent upon such an individual to come forth, and not to remain silent (*Sifra*). In a poetic passage, in contrast to our verse that has the force of law, the Psalmist complains: "My friends and compan-ions distance themselves from my affliction; even my relatives stand far away" (Psalms 38:12).

Notes

[1] Orlinsky 217.
[2] Cf. Dov Peretz Elkins, *Moments of Transcendence: Inspirational Readings for Yom Kippur* (Northvale: Jason Aronson, 1992) 28, 33-36.
[3] Boruch Halevi Epstein, *The Essential Torah Temimah* (New York and Je-rusalem: Feldheim Publishers, 1989) II, 327.
[4] Maimonides, *Mishneh Torah: Hilkhot De'ot* (Ethical Ideas) 7:1.
[5] Ibn Ezra and Hizzekuni in Chill 228.
[6] *Midrash Tehillim*, Buber edition 284.
[7] Levine 129.
[8] This interpretation is the one supported by Buttrick, *The Interpreter's Bible* II, 96, which points to Exodus 23:7 to explain its rendering to seek to have someone put to death ("Keep far from a false charge; do not bring death to those who are innocent...for I will not let the criminal go free").
[9] A. B. Ehrlich, *Mikra Kifeshuto*, quoted by Levine 129.
[10] Ibid.
[11] Levine 129.
[12] Joseph Telushkin, *Jewish Wisdom: Ethical, Spiritual, and Historical Les-sons from the Great Works and Thinkers* (NewYork: William Morrow & Co, 1994) 34.

21

Leviticus 19:17

ויקרא יט,יז:

לֹא תִשְׂנָא אֶת אָחִיךָ בִּלְבָבֶךָ, הוֹכֵחַ תּוֹכִיחַ אֶת עֲמִיתֶךָ
וְלֹא תִשָּׂא עָלָיו חֵטְא.

*JPS (1916) – "Thou shalt not hate thy brother in thy heart;
thou shalt surely rebuke thy neighbour, and not bear sin because of him."*

*NJV (1962) – "You shall not hate your kinsfolk in your
heart. Reprove your kinsman but incur no guilt because of
him."*

Verses 17 and 18 of Leviticus 19 have to do with mature
emotions, and the self-destructive nature of hatred, vengeance
and the proper attitude toward others and self. We shall deal
with each verse individually. These two verses are millennia
ahead of their time if we compare them with the psychological
and spiritual wisdom of writers who followed, even up to modern times. They are as contemporary as the teachings of the most
modern doctrines of psychology.

Why Does the Torah Use the Expression "In Your Heart"?

A standard principle of biblical exegesis is the assumption that
anything that can be expressed in fewer words should be. The
Torah could have simply stated: "You shall not hate your kinsfolk," without adding "in your heart." If the latter expression is
added, there must be a reason. Traditionalists consider the Torah
to have been written by God, who would never use a superfluous word or expression. What, then, does "in your heart" add?

Hatred can be manifest in actions and in attitudes. The Torah includes both, since it specifically adds "in your heart." Modern educational theorists encourage teachers and parents to transmit values of behavior and attitude, action and emotion. This verse encompasses the morality of both.

Modern psychologists affirm the long-range dangers of harboring negative emotions, including hatred and anger. Storing such feelings "in the heart" instead of dealing with them constructively spreads poison in the person who holds them, and between the two people involved in the dispute. It is a poor model for transmitting positive emotional health to children and others.

Rabbi Elazar ben Judah ben Kalonymuus of Worms (1165-1230), who lost both his wife and children in the Crusades, taught that "the most beautiful thing a person can do is to forgive".[1] Not bearing a grudge is applicable not only in the personal realm, but also the national. Bearing grudges keep hostilities fresh, baring the way to peace and reconciliation. In Deuteronomy 23:8, the Torah teaches this lesson: "You shall not hate an Edomite, for he is your brother. You shall not hate an Egyptian for you were a stranger in his land," even though both nations wronged the Israelites.

Rabbi Samson Raphael Hirsch points out the similarity between the Hebrew roots of *sana* (*samekh nun aleph*), to hate, and *seneh* (*samekh nun heh*), a bush, or thorn, suggesting that when we hate another, it causes us to avoid that person like a bristle, and brings a distancing process between two persons who, if not perhaps for a certain bristling issue, may be good friends.[2]

Why Does the Torah Use the Expression "Your Brother" (or, NJV: "Your Kinsfolk")?

Rabbi Hirsch, quoted above, pays special attention to the use of the additional phrase "your kinsfolk." When someone commits an evil act toward us, and forfeits any rights of being called a friend, there is still one title the person can never lose, that of "family." Says Hirsch: "This he remains by the common thread of Divine descent...joined in kinship to us in God, and through God. We remain kin, children of the same familial House. And for the sake of our common Parent, Who still recognizes us as God's child, and Who still grants us a place next to us in the Divine House—and in the Divine heart—*sinah* must not arise with us."[3]

Rabbi Hayim ben Attar wonders whether it is possible to be free of all hatred. He answers that if we consider all humans our "brothers" (and sisters), it will be easier to destroy the hatred in our heart, and replace it with feelings of love (cf. v. 19, "Love your neighbor...."). It makes sense that the closer the relationship, the more sincere the rebuke will be, and the more openly will it be heard and accepted. If one considers the other a "brother," then the criticism has a better chance to be treated with appreciation, as a sign of love and affection.

Why Must the Jewish People Remain Particularly Sensitive to Hatred of Others?

Rabbi Hertz reminds us that most hatred in the world is baseless, using the Hebrew expression *sinat hinam* (causeless hatred). The Talmud tells us (*Yoma* 9b) that the Second Temple was destroyed (by the Romans in 70 C.E.) because of *sinat hinam*. Even though the people of that period performed many wonderful deeds and good works, this sin alone caused the holy Temple to be destroyed. No people, says Rabbi Hertz, has suffered more from causeless hatred than has the Jewish People. Thus should we be even more sensitive than others not to commit this terrible violation of the Torah's moral demands.[4]

In a different Talmudic passage (*Shabbat* 119b) we learn that Rabbi Haninah claimed that Jerusalem was destroyed because no one reprimanded anyone else! In other words, apathy about the other's behavior, and the lack of caring for one another — to the point of never reproving one another (as commanded in the next part of the verse), made a condition of society so lackadaisical that Jerusalem became vulnerable and was destroyed.

Rabbi Abraham ibn Ezra notes that the various commands in this section all relate to matters of the heart and spirit. By living a noble spiritual life, Israel will be privileged to remain in their Land. By implication, Ibn Ezra quotes from the Talmud to note that inner spiritual decay, including causeless hatred and lack of caring for the community, is a major cause of a people's exile.

How Does the Tradition Define "Rebuking" or "Reproving" Your Neighbor?

The Talmud warns (*Shabbat* 54b — 55a) that it is incumbent upon us to share helpful warnings to others, and that whoever can prevent one's household or community from sinning, and does not do so, is held responsible for their sin. Nahmanides (Spain 1194-1270) points out that the entire community benefits when we help straighten out a wayward soul. Part of the Dead Sea Scrolls, the *Damascus Covenant*, commands that its adherents report misdeeds to a special "examiner,"[5] not unlike the code of military academies in the United States.

Nahmanides suggests that if we rebuke our neighbor, he may admit to his fault, and ask your pardon, whereupon you can forgive him easily, and not "hate him in your heart." Rebuke is the natural corollary to assist in not "hating one's kinsfolk in your heart," and logically follows it in the verse. In the biblical Book of Proverbs (9:8) we read: "Reprove not a scorner, lest he hate you; reprove a wise person and he will love you."

All the commentators point out that openness in a relationship is a prerequisite for a healthy, mature and successful friendship. Only in modern times have we begun to use terms about relationships such as "open," "authentic," "real," etc. All the self-help books in the bookstores today start with the premise that honesty, directness and appropriate ventilation of grievances are prerequisites for maintaining and sustaining a close relationship. When one party holds back from sharing an annoyance or bitterness, the result will be a souring of the relationship, and unfair prevention of the other party from either telling his/her side, recognizing the mistake, apologizing, or regretting the hurt that was caused.

The Baal Shem Tov (Israel ben Eliezer, Carpathian Mountains, Podolia, 1698-1760) emphasizes the word "neighbor," arguing that criticism is more sincere and welcome it if is offered by and to one who is considered a neighbor and a friend. Rabbi Menahem ben Binyamin Recanati points out that the Jewish People has survived because they have been open and critical with one another, thus utilizing every possible opportunity and resource in the community to strengthen the community as a whole. This mutual openness and community responsibility enabled Jews to withstand the onslaughts of centuries of anti-Semitism by banding together in mutual protectiveness.

How Do the Commentators Regard the Repetition of the Hebrew *"hokhe'ah tokhiah"* ("surely rebuke" or "rebuke, rebuke")?

As pointed out above, any seeming repetition cries out for explanation by the traditional commentators. In biblical Hebrew the use of the infinitive form of the verb preceding the command is an indication of emphasis. But the rabbis took it as an implication of other hidden meanings.

One rabbi suggests that the first "reprove" means that it is a mitzvah to chastise those who are interested in listening; the second "reprove" is to teach us that it is also a mitzvah *not* to reprove those who are likely to ignore what we offer (Talmud *Yevamot* 65b). In modern parlance, we would say that criticism is only useful when the listener is "psychologically ready" to hear it.

Another teacher says that the first "reprove" implies that a teacher may criticize a student; but the second "reprove" allows a student to [politely] critique a teacher (*Bava Metzia* 31a). Still another suggestion is that the repetition is a sign that one must continue repeating the criticism even up to one hundred times, until listeners changes their ways (*Ibid*).

In the Talmud, Rabbi Tarfon taught that receiving criticism was so difficult that he knew almost no one in his generation who could offer it tactfully. Rabbi Elazar argued that no one in his generation could receive it easily. Therefore one should persist with criticism until the recalcitrant sinner gets angry enough to hit you. For Rabbi Joshua, who is a bit more lenient, it is enough if one curses you. Ben Azzai is gentlest of all, and says that the criticism should cease when one insults you (*Arakhin* 16b). All three scholars in this debate apparently consider the obligation to help a friend so important that they should be prepared to receive some form of abuse in return. That is apparently a sign that the message has hit the target.

Maimonides presents a hierarchical system of steps which are necessary to challenge another's behavior, from mild to harsh. If the violation is against God, and the sinner persists in refusing to listen, Maimonides goes so far as to demand that it is necessary to embarrass the guilty party and publicize the sin, just as the biblical prophets did (*Mishneh Torah: Hilchot De'ot* 6:5-8).

Rabbi Simhah Zissel of Kelm comments on the Talmudic demand to criticize up to one hundred times, saying that this means in some cases it is necessary to take critical words and break them up into one hundred small parts, delivering them one at a time, making it easier for the listener to absorb the painful message.

The Baal Shem Tov analyzes the verse in a way that is remarkably similar to specialists in modern marriage counseling. The first "reprove," he says, is for oneself. No one is permitted to offer criticism to others before criticizing oneself. By thus showing the ability to empathize, and be self-critical, one earns the right to criticize others. A marriage counselor once suggested that every word of criticism one offers to another should be couched in these terms: For example—"As an expert in laziness, I would like to suggest that you try to wake up earlier in the morning." Critics thus "credentialize" themselves, and own their own projections, instead of always putting the full blame on another person. This is another example of how our ancestors, especially the Hasidic masters, anticipated the most modern and sophisticated psychological concepts through their native intuition and deep wisdom about human growth and development.

What Is the Meaning of the Last Clause in the Verse—"Bear No Sin Because of Him"?

There are several plausible translations and explanations of this clause. NJV notes that the meaning of the Hebrew conjunction *"ve"* is "uncertain." In different contexts it can mean such things as "and," "but," "or," "however," etc. The most logical way to view it here is to connect it to the preceding clause, this clause functioning as a dependent or consequent phrase. Following are several suggestions:

1) Rabbi Abraham ibn Ezra says that if you don't reprimand others, and give them an opportunity to explain, deny or apologize, you will be unnecessarily suspicious, and then hate them "in your heart," thus bringing sin upon yourself.

2) If you don't correct the behavior of your peers, you will be influenced by them, and hence cause yourself ultimately to indulge in the very same sin.

3) By being angry at someone, and hating them, you may come to punish and harm them, thereby committing a sin.

4) Nahmanides says that whoever does not reprove a neighbor is divorcing oneself from the community and its responsibility, and thus acts sinfully to the community.

5) The Talmud states that by rebuking someone too harshly, or in a hurtful, insensitive way, one will come to bring sin on oneself (*Arakhin* 16b). The rabbis use the expression *"malbin panav barabim"* — to cause one's face to flush and pale from shame in public, which they consider equivalent to murder, or shedding blood (since blood rushes from the face in the paling stage). Their hyperbolic rhetoric is designed to avoid shaming a person in public, a humiliating and unacceptable act.

6) A Hasidic master, Reb Aryeh Yehudah Leib (the Mokhiakh [Reprover] of Polonnoye, d. 1770) offers a novel interpretation. He links the three parts of the verse in this way: Make sure you do not hold a grudge against your kinfolk before you allow yourself to reprove them, because that

would be what is called in modern psychology "displaced anger" — and you would then be sinning by getting angry at something, when what you are really angry at is an old matter about which you are holding a grudge (and thus violating verse 19).[6]

7) In *Havot Yair* by Rabbi Yair Hayim Bacharach (Frankfort, 1638-1702) the author connects the third clause with the first part of the verse — i.e., If you rebuke someone, think of the person as a neighbor, a friend, and an equal; do not place sin on them, do not treat them like a sinner, or they will not listen to you, and you will have achieved nothing.

Notes

[1] Eleazar ben Judah of Worms, *Sefer HaRoke'ah* (Lemberg: Shalom Tsverling, 1910) 13c.
[2] Hirsch III/2, 522.
[3] Ibid.
[4] Hertz 501.
[5] Levine 130.
[6] quoted in *Iturei Torah*.

22

Leviticus 19:18

ויקרא יט,יח:

לֹא תִקֹּם וְלֹא תִטֹּר אֶת בְּנֵי עַמֶּךָ, וְאָהַבְתָּ לְרֵעֲךָ כָּמוֹךָ,
אֲנִי ה'.

*JPS (1916) — "Thou shalt not take vengeance, nor bear any
grudge against the children of thy people, but thou shalt
love thy neighbour as thyself: I am the LORD."*

*NJV (1962) — "You shall not take vengeance or bear a
grudge against your countrymen. Love your fellow as yourself: I am the LORD."*

This verse completes a group of verses which deal with human relations and high standards of treatment of others, and
seals the section with the religious formula we have seen several
times before — "I am the LORD," establishing God as the source
of human morality. There is a religious implication here that
whoever treats humans poorly is expressing a low level of faith
in the Creator of all of God's children as equal before their
Maker.

Rabbi Yehudah Leib Alter remarks that since to love your
neighbor as yourself is such a difficult command, you should know
that God stands ready to help you if you sincerely wish to do it!

What Is the Meaning of "Vengeance" and "Bearing a Grudge"?

The general idea of retaliation in personal relationships is repug-
nant to the Torah. Although one may immediately connect this
vocabulary to military action, the bulk of the commentary focus

on inter-personal action. The general idea is similar to verse 17, namely, that licking our wounds is neither ethically sound nor psychologically healthy.

The classic distinction between "vengeance" and "bearing a grudge" is given in the Talmud and Midrash (*Yoma* 23a; *Sifra* 4:10-11), and is quoted by Rashi: To illustrate vengeance in a hypothetical case, the rabbis pose the following situation: A says to B: Lend me your sickle, and B answers: No. The next day B in turn asks to borrow a hatchet. A replies: No! Just as you did not lend me your sickle, so I will not lend you my hatchet. That, say the rabbis, is vengeance. They then turn to a second hypothetical case to illustrate "bearing a grudge." A says to B: Please lend me your hatchet, and B replies No. The next day B asks: Please lend me your sickle. A replies: I will lend you the sickle, even though you did not lend me your hatchet! That is bearing a grudge. Even though there is no *revenge* in the second case, the person still holds in his heart the negative feelings, and this is *bearing a grudge*. In short, we can consider "vengeance" to imply action, and "bearing a grudge" to imply only thought. Another, different, way to distinguish between the two acts is that bearing a grudge can be defined as postponed vengeance.

The Palestinian Talmud, (also known as the *Yerushalmi*, or the Jerusalem Talmud), in *Nedarim* 9:4, offers this advice: "How is it possible to avoid vengeance and bearing a grudge? The answer: If one were cutting food and by accident cut oneself, would the injured hand wreak vengeance by cutting the other hand?" In English we have the expression "cutting off our nose to spite our face." The assumption is that if we regard all humanity as children of God, and one united family, it would be just as foolish to hurt another as it would be to hurt oneself.

Rabbi Joseph Hertz gives two splendid examples to show that throughout history Jews have avoided mean-spirited vengeance and retaliation. One is of Samuel ibn Nagrela, an eleventh-century Spanish-Jewish poet, who was vizier to the King of Granada. Once when Samuel was cursed in the presence of the King, the monarch commanded Samuel to cut out the curser's tongue. Samuel disobeyed, and treated the man kindly, thus receiving blessings from him. The next time the King saw the offender he noticed that the punishment had not been carried out, and asked Samuel why. "Samuel replied, 'I have torn out his angry tongue, and given him instead a kind one.'"[1]

The other story told by Hertz comes from an older source, perhaps the second century B.C.E., from a book called *The Testaments of the Twelve Patriarchs*, in which it is related: "Love one another from the heart. If one sins against you, expunge the poison of hate and speak in a warm manner to the person. If the person admits the fault and is regretful, forgive him. But even if the person shamefully repeats the ugly act, forgive him from the heart, and leave to God any vengeance. Beware of hatred; it brings lawlessness even against God. Hatred denies the divine command to love one's neighbor. Love brings even the dead back to life, and restores to life even those condemned to die. Hatred, on the other hand, kills the living."[2]

Is It Truly Possible to "Love Your Neighbor as Yourself"?

Rabbi Pinchas Peli points out that it is easier to love the whole world than to love one's neighbor, the real, live people with whom we interact on a daily basis. He also asks whether love, being a strong emotion, is something that can be commanded. He quotes two biblical verses to make his point: "Love the Lord your God with all your heart, with all your might and with all your soul" (Deuteronomy 5:5), and "Love is strong as death; many waters cannot extinguish love" (Song of Songs 8:6-7). Rabbi Peli notes that the Torah's command is simply a powerful and innovative idea that means what it says: that we must love everyone, for altruistic reasons, not for the sake of being loved in return. Love of other humans, and the human race, is part of the divine plan. Thus, the verse concludes, "I am the LORD."[3]

In arguing about the question: What is the most important verse in the Torah?, Rabbi Akiva (2nd century C.E.) quotes our verse. His colleague, ben Azzai, prefers Genesis 5:1-2, that humans were created in the image of God. Ben Azzai sees love of others dependent on the fact that all of us are created by the same God, in God's image, and that alone makes us loveable and worthy (Yerushalmi *Nedarim* 9:4; *Sifra* 4:12).

Nahmanides claims that the Torah is teaching by exaggeration, and that it is really not possible to love others the same way one loves oneself. Nahmanides agrees with the sage who preceded him, Maimonides (Egypt, 1135-1204) who wrote: "One is to speak in praise of one's neighbor, and be as careful of one's neighbor's property as one is of own's own."[4] Nahmanides stresses the *action* component of loving behavior in interpreting this verse. He bases his idea on the fact that the Torah uses the preposition l*erayekha* — to, or *for*, your neighbor, but not the direct object sign, *et*. Grammatically, Nahmanides is wrong, because in Hebrew *ahav le* takes the direct object. He further argues that if the Torah had used the Hebrew *et* instead of *le*, it would have implied that a person should love his neighbor completely, and without reservations and limitations. He cites the love of Jonathan for David as an example of such love, about whom the Bible says: "He loved him as he loved his own soul" (I Samuel 20:17).

What Implications Do the Rabbis See in the Command to "Love Thy Neighbor"?

"Love Your Neighbor as Yourself," explains the Talmud (*Ketubot* 37b, *Sanhedrin* 45a) means that in capital punishment the least painful death must be used. (Note: capital punishment was ultimately eliminated in Talmudic times by creating an impossible number of restrictions required to convict someone to death). In other passages (*Kiddushin* 41a, *Niddah* 17a) the Talmud demands that a husband may not put his wife in situations which may make her distasteful to him, such as marrying someone without meeting her first (and then possibly growing to resent her), basing its rule on this same verse. At a later date, Rabbi Jacob ben Asher, known as the "*Baal HaTurim*," (Germany and Spain, 14th century) adds that one should always be sensitive to the needs of others. He then gives the example of a husband having sexual relations with his wife. One should not, based on this verse, think of another woman at such an intimate moment.

Being a pragmatist, the sage Hillel (Jerusalem, 70 B.C.E.-10 C.E.) summarized the whole Torah by saying: "What is hateful to you, do not do to your neighbor. The rest is commentary" (*Shabbat* 31a). This negative formulation made it both clearer and more possible to fulfill the law of loving one's neighbor. Polemical theologians have criticized Hillel for this negative formulation, but when one considers that he was replying to a cynical and defiant pagan who demanded to have Hillel summarize everything about Judaism "while he stands on one foot," it is understandable that Hillel was searching for a simplified version of the Golden Rule. In other passages Hillel tells us to "love humanity" (*Pirke Avot* 1:12). The great teacher and pioneer of rabbinic Judaism did not truly distinguish between the positive and negative formulations, but merely considered one to be an elaboration, or simplification, of the other, and perhaps a more down-to-earth formula for an uneducated person to begin with.

Rabbi Joseph Hertz points out correctly that Hebrew *reiya* (neighbor) refers to Israelites and non-Israelites in the Torah. For example, in Exodus 11:2 the word refers to Egyptians, and in Leviticus 19:34 we are commanded to love strangers.[5] The spiritual wisdom of this verse is similar to the talmudic statement (*Gittin*

36b): "Be among those who accept insult but do not inflict it; who listen to reproach but do not [lower themselves to] reply; who act out of love and accept pain with equanimity. About them the Scriptures say: 'Those who love are like the sun rising in might' (Judges 5:31)."

The Hasidic master Rabbi Moshe Leib of Sassov went so far as to report that he learned the true meaning of loving one's neighbor from an intoxicated Russian peasant. Sitting at a bar, the drunkard asked his friend, "Ivan, do you love me?" "Of course I love you," answered Ivan. "Then," continued the peasant, "what hurts me?" "How do I know?" replied the friend. "Well if you don't know what hurts me," said the drunkard, "then how can you say that you truly love me." To Rabbi Moshe Leib, love meant caring deeply about another's welfare, and obviously he was not embarrassed to learn an important lesson from anyone who could teach him something in a deep and striking fashion.

What Is Implied in the Expression "Love Your Neighbor *As Yourself*"?

The conventional interpretation of loving one's neighbor as oneself is to endow the concept of love in general with the most natural and innate kind of human love—love of self. Jewish Tradition sees love of self as positive, healthy, normative, and necessary to foster love of others. It is not selfish, but humane, because it does not stop with love of self; it enables love of others.

Hillel summarizes priorities well in *Pirke Avot, Ethics of the Fathers,* 1:14: "If I am not for myself, who will be? But if I am for myself alone, what am I? And if not now, when?" In a debate with a certain ben Petura, Rabbi Akiva argued that "your life precedes the life of another" (Talmud, *Bava Metzia* 62a).

The Hasidic sage, the Alter of Slobodka, explained that if you love others as you love yourself, you will love them without conditions and reasons, just instinctively and normally. This is what is called in modern psychology "unconditional love."

Ralph Waldo Emerson agreed with the Torah when he said, "By trusting your own heart, you shall gain more confidence in others." And in George Bernard Shaw's words, "One's interest in the world is only the overflow of one's interest in self." Conversely, the Baal Shem Tov warned that those who hate themselves will ultimately hate others even more so. The modern well-known pioneer psychiatrist, Harry Stack Sullivan wrote that "As you love yourself, so shall you love others. Strange, but true, and with no exceptions."[6]

Notes

[1] Hertz 501-502.

[2] as quoted by Hertz 502.

[3] Pinchas Peli, *Torah Today: A Renewed Encounters With Scriptures* (Washington, DC: B'nai B'rith Books, 1987) 138-9.

[4] Maimonides, Mishneh Torah: Hilchot Mada 6:3.

[5] Hertz's essay on this verse in an excursus on pages 563-4, makes fascinating reading. Written in the 1930s, it is a polemic against anti-Semitic interpretations of our verse which tried to imply that Jews were narrowly concerned only with their own, and that this verse proved it! The late Rabbi Bernard J. Bamberger, a distinguished Reform Rabbi, makes a similar point in his essay on this verse. See "The Golden Rule," in Plaut 892-3.

[6] Cf. Dov Peretz Elkins, *Glad To Be Me: Building Self-Esteem in Yourself and Others* (Princeton: Growth Associates, 1989) 105.

23

Leviticus 22:32

ויקרא כב,לב:

וְלֹא תְחַלְּלוּ אֶת שֵׁם קָדְשִׁי וְנִקְדַּשְׁתִּי בְּתוֹךְ בְּנֵי יִשְׂרָאֵל,
אֲנִי ה' מְקַדִּשְׁכֶם.

*JPS (1916) – "And ye shall not profane My holy name; but
I will be hallowed among the children of Israel: I am the
LORD who hallow you,"*

*NJV (1962) – "You shall not profane My holy name, that I
may be sanctified in the midst of the Israelite people – I the
LORD who sanctify you,"*

The context of this verse is the profanation of God's name
through ritual impurity, as the command is given to the priestly
class, or the *kohanim*. Its simple meaning is to respect God through
proper behavior toward the sanctuary and the priesthood. Treating that which is sacred in God's house (the Tabernacle and later
the Temple) as ordinary desecrates (or profanes) God's name,
causing *Hillul HaShem*.

The general understanding of *Hillul HaShem*, profanation of
God's name, in traditional sources, is to sully God's reputation
among the nations of the world. In short, to rob God of respect
and dignity by one of God's creatures acting in such a way to
bring shame and dishonor to what God has taught. Every Jew
must act in such a way that God's prestige and honor must be
upheld. Every action of every Jew must reflect glory and dignity
on the name and Torah of God. When one does the opposite, and
brings public disgrace upon the Jewish People, it sullies God's
teachings and God's chosen people, and thus profanes the divine name.

Conversely, any action that brings honor and glory to Judaism reflects honor and sanctification on God's name and reputation, and is known as *Kiddush HaShem*. *Kiddush HaShem* has come to connote the standard of ethical behavior expected of all worthy Jews. The theological notion of sanctifying God's name has become so pervasive in Jewish law and liturgy that it begins the ubiquitous kaddish prayer, "*Yitgadal veyitkadash shemei rabba*," "May God's Great Name become magnified and sanctified...."

As to why both profaning and sanctifying God's name are mentioned in the same verse, Rabbi Bahya ben Asher gives a logical explanation. Whenever one profanes God's name, one should make up for it by doing the counterpart action of sanctifying God's name. For example, he writes, if one utters slander, one should speak words of Torah. If one's eyes see forbidden things, one should weep. If one commits a cluster of sins, one should then carry out a cluster of mitzvot (divine commandments).

How Do We Understand Hillul Hashem and Kiddush Hashem Today?

The shift of the meaning of *Hillul HaShem*, from profaning the sanctuary to mistreating other humans, appears in some passages in the biblical prophets. For example, Jeremiah calls the inhuman treatment of slaves *Hillul HaShem* (34:16), and Amos uses the expression to condemn oppression and sexual immorality (2:7). In Isaiah (49:3) God says of those who obey the Torah and thus bring credit to the Jewish People: "You are My servants, O Israel, in whom I take pride."

There is an important distinction drawn between public and private sinning, since a public violation not only brings Judaism and its God into disrepute, but may also lead other Jews to a similar violation and have a negative "mob psychology" effect. The Talmud goes so far as to say: "If you must sin, do so privately, but refrain from profaning the divine name publicly" (*Kiddushin* 40a).

In short, when a Jew, through her/his behavior, performs an act of goodness, kindness, justice and truth, and a Jew or Gentile observes or hears about such an act, and remarks: "What a wonderful religion that person lives by!" — then an act of *Kiddush HaShem* has been performed. When one performs a shameful deed, and others see it, and say: "What kind of religion does this person live by?" — then an act of *Hillul HaShem* has been perpetrated.

Maimonides classifies *Hillul HaShem* under three separate categories:

1) When a Jew is told to violate a Torah command under penalty of death, it is permitted to commit the violation, rather than submit to death. There are, however, three exceptions to this rule: idolatry, sexual immorality, or murder [cf. Babylonian Talmud, Sanhedrin 74a]. If a Jew violates one of these three "never-violate" rules, he is committing a *Hillul HaShem*.

2) If a Jew, without force, willfully violates the Torah in defiance of God's will, this is the second type of *Hillul HaShem*.

3) If a person who is otherwise of impeccable character lapses into a one-time failure of unethical behavior, bringing special embarrassment to his people and faith, this is the third type of *Hillul HaShem*.[1]

One may logically ask how it is possible for a mortal person, made of dust and ashes, to profane the Holiness of God? Nehama Leibowitz raises and answers this question as follows: The Torah does not say to sanctify or profane God, but *God's name*! She explains that the command is to propagate human acknowledgment and recognition of God and God's holiness, as the verse states, "in the midst of the children of Israel." Furthermore, this paradox of the slave crowning, as it were, the Ruler of Rulers, and a transitory being admonished to magnify the eternal name of God, is also dealt with in another passage. In Isaiah 43:10, "You are My witnesses, says Adonai..." is explained by the rabbis to mean that when we are God's witnesses, then God is God, and when we are not God's witnesses, then God is, as it were, not God (*Pesikta deRav Kahana*). In other words, knowledge, awareness and obedience to God, not God's existence, is in the hands of God's creatures. We sanctify God through our daily lives, and sometimes, when necessary, through our death.[2]

How Did *Kiddush HaShem* Become Associated with Martyrdom?

The British scholar Hyam Maccoby, of London's Leo Baeck College, traces the history of the concept of *Kiddush HaShem* and posits that any right action constitutes uplifting the reputation of God. He writes:

> This concept must be distinguished sharply from heteronomy, a moral system in which an action is right only because it has been decreed by God. On the contrary, while heteronomy reduces all virtues to one, obedience, the concept of *kiddush ha-Shem* raises the value of moral actions to cosmic

proportions and enhances the status of man by identifying love of one's fellowman with love of God.... The most extreme of such situations is that in which the right action can be performed only at the cost of one's life. In such a situation, all the self-seeking motivations that are ordinarily mixed with even the most altruistic act are absent, and only the motive of *kiddush ha-Shem*, the honoring of God, remains. It is this most extreme situation that represents the prime example of *kiddush ha-Shem*.[3]

Maccoby notes that in Judaism martyrdom is not a desideratum, but an "occasionally unavoidable necessity,"[4] not a duty or a sacrament. He notes that in the Holocaust the truest act of *Kiddush HaShem* was to save lives, not sacrifice them. He also emphasizes that while the term *Kiddush HaShem* has come to connote martyrdom, it is truly an idea that is supposed to pervade the way a Jew lives even more than the way a Jew dies.[5]

The expression *Kiddush HaShem* has been associated with martyrdom throughout Jewish history. While suicide is frowned upon in *Halakhah* (Jewish law), Jews always took pride in those brave souls who were prepared to give up their life rather than violate the primary principles of their faith. In Jewish literature martyrs are known as *"kedoshim,"* those who are sanctified, or sanctifiers (of God's Name). Death was to be chosen above public apostasy, which became formally forbidden in Jewish Law (*Shulhan Arukh, Yore De'ah*, Section 157). In reconciling two outwardly contradictory verses: (1) Leviticus 18:5 – "You shall live by them [the commandments]" – to which the rabbis add: "and not die by them"; and (2) our verse, not to profane God's name (even if it means dying to do so), the rabbis state: "Live by them" – *in private*; "Do not desecrate My holy name" – (even if one must die) – *in public*. To the rabbis this meant that one might violate a divine command in private, and not incur death, but when ten or more Jews were watching, this does incur the death penalty (Talmud, *Avodah Zarah* 54a). (However, idolatry, sexual immorality and murder are under no circumstances sanctioned, in private or public).

The multitude of stories of Jewish martyrdom include that of Hannah and her seven sons in the days of the Maccabees, in the second century B.C.E.; and the famous ten martyred rabbis, at least some of whom died under Hadrianic persecution in Eretz Yisrael in the second century C.E., to whom an entire section is devoted in the Yom Kippur liturgy ("*Eleh Ezkerah....*" – "These Will I Remember" -also known as the "Martyrology"). In the Middle Ages there were mass suicides during the Crusades.

The Jews of Nordhausen, on their way to be burned alive during the Black Death, employed musicians to play while they marched to their end, accepting their inevitable fate with an inner spiritual joy.[6] The story of the Akedah, the Binding of Isaac (Genesis 22), became a model for medieval Jewish communities to sacrifice their own children rather than permit them to be raised forcibly as Christians.

How Did the Rabbis of the Talmud Interpret *Kiddush HaShem*?

The classic story associated with the concept of *Kiddush HaShem* is that of Rabbi Shimon ben Shetah, Nasi (President) of the Sanhedrin in the early part of the first century. Rabbi Shimon was a flax trader whose disciples asked him to give up his trade in favor of receiving a donkey which they would buy him to make his life easier. They purchased a donkey from an Ishmaelite, and as fortune would have it, the donkey had a valuable pearl in its fur. His overjoyed students told him the good news, and encouraged him to sell the pearl and live comfortably from then on. Rabbi Shimon asked his disciples if the Ishmaelite knew about the valuable pearl, and they had to say, "No." His students became pedantic and argued that since the object was lost, he had no obligation to return it. Shimon became angry and asked them: "Do you think Shimon ben Shetah is a barbarian? Shimon ben Shetah would rather hear 'Blessed be the God of the Jews' than reap any financial gain in the entire world" (Yerushalmi, *Bava Metzia* 2:5, 8c). In a parallel version (*Deuteronomy Rabbah* 3:3), the Ishmaelite is quoted as saying "Blessed be the God of Shimon ben Shetach!"

The Palestinian Talmud (*Bava Metzia* 2:5) tells a similar story. Rabbi Shmuel went to Rome at the time when the Empress lost her bracelet, and was fortunate enough to find it. A proclamation was issued that whoever found the bracelet could return in within thirty days and receive a reward. On the other hand, if it were returned after thirty days, the finder would lose his head. Rabbi Shmuel decided intentionally to return it *after* the thirty days. When the Empress asked him why, he replied: "I did not want anyone to think that I returned the bracelet out of fear of you, because in truth I returned it out of awe of the All-Merciful One." Whereupon the Empress declared: "Blessed be the God of the Jews!"

In another Talmudic passage (*Sotah* 36b) the rabbis extol the praises of Joseph who resisted the sexual advances of Potiphar's wife (Genesis 39) and consider him the paradigm of *Kiddush HaShem*. On a far more mundane level, the rabbis teach that in a

place where it is customary to pay the butcher in cash, it is a
Hillul HaShem not to do so (*Yoma* 86a).

In a most striking passage, the rabbis describe Abraham as
instructing God that the destruction of the evil cities of Sodom
and Gomorrah would be viewed by the world as a *Hillul Ha-
Shem*, since God's moral behavior might be blemished by not distin-
guishing between the guilty and the innocent (*Genesis Rabbah* 49:9).

What is the Significance of the Phrase "In the Midst of the People of Israel"?

The Talmudic rabbis frequently utilized proximity of phrases as
the basis for interpretation. The biblical charge to bring sanctification in the midst of the people meant to them that prayers in
which God's name was sanctified, such as the *kaddish* and the
kedushah, required a quorum of ten males (*Berakhot* 21b).

As we discussed above, the rabbis distinguished between
public and private violations of the Torah in deciding whether it
was permissible to violate a law to save one's life, or to die rather
than do so. The criterion which sometimes distinguishes between public and private violations is whether there is a "quorum" of ten Israelites present; i.e., if it is "in the midst of the
People of Israel." Rashi explains that one might think that based
on this verse one must die rather than violate a Torah law, even
in the presence of a single individual. Thus the verse states: "in
the midst...." to teach us that the presence of many witnesses is
the major criterion, so that God's name not be profaned in public,
and many people derive the false lesson that the absence of a
community of witnesses it is permissible to violate the Torah and
profane God's name.

Rashi further points out in his comment on this verse, that
when one does voluntarily submit one's life to die rather than
transgress the Law, it must not be on the assumption that God
will have mercy and miraculously save them. He points out the
example of Hananiah, Mishael and Azariah (Daniel 3:17-18),
who refused to bow down to idols and gold images, and told
Babylonian King Nebuchadnezzar that God may save them from
the fiery furnace, "but even if God does not, you should know, O
Sovereign, that we will not serve your god...."

Notes

1 Maimonides, Mishneh Torah: Hilkhot Yesodei Torah 5.
2 Lebowitz, *Vayikra* 13ff.

[3] Hyam Maccoby, "Sanctification of the Name," in Cohen and Mendes-Flohr 852.

[4] Ibid. 853.

[5] Ibid. 853-4.

[6] Rabbi Alan Unterman, *Dictionary of Jewish Lore and Legend* (New York: Thames & Hudson, 1991) 129.

24

Leviticus 25:10

וִיקרא כה,י:

וְקִדַּשְׁתֶּם אֵת שְׁנַת הַחֲמִשִּׁים שָׁנָה וּקְרָאתֶם דְּרוֹר בָּאָרֶץ
לְכָל יֹשְׁבֶיהָ, יוֹבֵל הִוא תִּהְיֶה לָכֶם וְשַׁבְתֶּם אִישׁ אֶל
אֲחֻזָּתוֹ וְאִישׁ אֶל מִשְׁפַּחְתּוֹ תָּשֻׁבוּ.

JPS (1916) — "And ye shall hallow the fiftieth year, and pro-claim liberty throughout the land unto all the inhabitants thereof; it shall be a jubilee unto you; and ye shall return every man unto his possession, and ye shall return every man unto his family."

NJV (1962) — "and you shall hallow the fiftieth year. You shall proclaim release [others: liberty] throughout the land for all its inhabitants. It shall be a jubilee [Heb. yobel, "ram" or "ram's horn."] for you: each of you shall return to his holding and each of you shall return to his family."

In various places in the Torah law, the seventh year finds pride of place. There are several provisions for the seventh year (called in Talmudic times the *Shemitah* year, from the word "to drop," referring to cancellation of debts). We find several similarities as well as differences between the Sabbatical (seventh) year, and the Jubilee Year.

In the Seventh, sabbatical year, Deuteronomy 15:1-10 refers to nullification of debts, an economic measure which prevented perennial poverty for those who could not dig their way out of a financial hole. This may be compared to modern bankruptcy laws, though it is automatic, whereas in bankruptcy one must apply for debt cancellation. In post-biblical times when lending money became a vital aspect of economic life, and there was a fear of lending money which might not be repaid, the famous sage Hillel established a legal fiction called *prosbul*, by which the Court collected debts, thus circumventing the Torah law and saving the economic system. We also learn that in the Sabbatical year the land must lie fallow, and whatever produce grows of itself becomes available to the poor (Exodus 23:10f. and Leviticus 25:2-7).

By comparison, in the Jubilee Year, the following rules obtain: The land is to lie fallow (Leviticus 25:8ff.); Landed property must revert to its original occupant (those who received it when the land was divided up under Joshua, according to Joshua, chapters 13-21) (Leviticus 25:10); Hebrew slaves, who serve normally for a period of six years, are released on the seventh year. In the law of Exodus 21:2, a Hebrew slave is freed in the seventh year of his slavery, but this apparently did not correspond to the "sabbatical year." In the Jubilee Year, all such slaves were free, regardless of their stage in the slavery cycle.

What is the Meaning of the Word "Jubilee"?

As the new JPS translation (NJV) points out, Jubilee is a Hebrew word (*Yovel*) which means both a ram, and, in abbreviated form, a ram's horn. It was the blasting of the ram's horn at the outset of the fiftieth year that began the Jubilee Year. The Talmud debates whether it began on Rosh Hashanah or Yom Kippur (*Rosh Hashanah* 8b). Leviticus 25:9 makes it clear that Yom Kippur was the actual starting point — either of the Jubilee, or certainly of the enactments attached to it. Rashi also points out that this is a unique year in that it is given a special name, Jubilee Year, in contrast to the sabbatical year, which is called "sabbatical" but does not have a formal name.

Nahmanides sees a different etymology, and connects *yovel* with Hebrew *lehovil* — as in Isaiah 23:7 — where the meaning is to "carry" or "cause to travel." In other words, the *Yovel* is the time when people traveled, or were brought back to their ancestral homeland and native clan. It is also possible that a more ancient word, from the root *yaval*, connotes the person who moved, or directed the flock of rams (connected the words for movement and a herd of rams [male sheep]).

The English form of *Yovel*, Jubilee, is one of hundreds of Hebrew words which have entered the English language, many of which are legal or liturgical, such as amen, hallelujah, cherub, satan, kabbalah, paradise, Sabbath, rabbi, kosher, etc.[1]

When Did the Jubilee Year Arrive?

The verse clearly states that the Jubilee Year occurred every fiftieth year. The problem presents itself, however, that if the fiftieth
year is so designated because it follows seven periods of seven
years, then the fiftieth year would follow a sabbatical year (the
forty-ninth year, the seventh year of the seven seven-year cycles).
In effect, there would be two consecutive sabbatical years. While
the scope of release in the Jubilee Year is broader than the seven-
year-cycle Sabbatical Year, they are nevertheless very similar—
i.e., slaves and debts are freed. Some scholars believe that the seventh year of enslavement corresponded to the Sabbatical Year.[2]

Rabbi Joseph Hertz seems to suggest, without extensive explanation, that the Jubilee Year is indeed on the *forty-ninth* year.
He brings as evidence other languages, such as French, which
uses the term "*quinze jours*" (fifteen days) to refer to two weeks.
Perhaps he is suggesting that the fiftieth year means the end of
the forty-ninth year. Or, the beginning of the fiftieth year; i.e., the
forty-ninth year.[3] Other more recent scholars also claim that the
year intended is the forty-ninth, presumably because two consecutive years without farming would be an economic disaster.[4]

What is the Meaning of the Hebrew Word
for *Release (dror)*?

The translation of the Hebrew word *dror* presents a lovely example of the history of translations; of how the creative minds of
translators and interpreters, and our recent enhanced understanding of ancient Semitic languages, have evolved over the
years, in part due to recent archeological discoveries.

The classic eleventh century commentator, Rashi, quotes
midrashic sources (*Rosh Hashanah* 9b and *Sifra Behar* 2:2) wherein
Rabbi Yehudah says that the word *dror* connotes freedom of
movement, namely, a person who lives in one place but does his
trading throughout a wider area, traveling to and fro without
limitation. This means, explains Rashi, that *dror* comes from the
Hebrew root *dur*, to live, and refers to one who lives wherever he
wishes, at home or away, without external control.

Rabbi Abraham Ibn Ezra gives a slightly different explanation. The word *dror* already appears in the Bible (though very
infrequently) with the meaning of a *swallow*. Ibn Ezra quotes
Proverbs 26:2, "as a swallow flies." He says that this small bird
sings when it is free, but when under the control of others, the
swallow will starve itself to death. *Dror*, therefore, to Ibn Ezra,
means freedom, as a swallow is free to fly wherever it wants.

Modern scholars have discovered that the Hebrew *dror* has a much older history than previously known. In fact, it goes back to a pre-biblical Babylonian legal institution in which amnesty was granted on special occasions, such as the ascension of a new monarch, and is related to the Akkadian word *duraru* which variously implied freeing slaves, the return of confiscated land, or the nullification of debts.[5] According to this pre-biblical definition, slaves were permitted more freedom of movement when *duraru* was announced. This sheds light on several other biblical passages, such as Jeremiah 34:15, in which we read of a war proclamation of King Zedekiah granting *dror*, or release, to indentured servants. Another example is found in Isaiah 61:1 which describes the end of the captivity of the exiled Hebrews in Babylonia.[6]

Who Was Affected by the Jubilee Year?

Our verse clearly states that the release applies "to all the inhabitants" of the Land, or Hebrew slaves exclusively. In a lengthy discussion on slavery in the biblical world, Rabbi Joseph H. Hertz shows how the institution of slavery in ancient Israel was considerably less onerous than in other nations, and in many ways rather humanitarian.[7] Rabbi Bernard Bamberger also discusses the various complexities related to defining the different categories of slavery in biblical times, and how Hebrew slaves were treated much more humanely.[8]

Rashi claims that any Hebrew slave is freed when the Jubilee Year is proclaimed, regardless of when in the previous seven-year cycle he was enslaved. It also applies, says Rashi, to the servant who voluntarily waived his freedom during the sabbatical year and had his ear bored according to the provisions of Exodus 21:5-6.

Scholars have pointed out that the pre-biblical institution of *duraru*, in contrast to the biblical release (*dror*), was purely an economic measure to relieve the misery of the poor. In ancient Israel it was also a social step, which preserved the clan structure through restoration of land to its previous owners.

A commentary titled *Penai Yehoshua* explains that the phrase "for all its inhabitants" suggests that freedom must be the lot of *all* the inhabitants, or else it belongs to none of them. Where even a small number of people are enslaved, the spirit of slavery infects all the inhabitants, and hence unless there is freedom for everyone, no one is truly free. Thus say our sages: "Whoever acquires a slave acquires a master for oneself."[9]

What is the Economic and Social Philosophy of the Jubilee Year?[10]

From a technical point of view, land was temporarily transferred when a family was evicted from their home and farm due to foreclosure. At the time of the proclamation of the Jubilee Year, such families could return and reclaim their property, and their indebtedness and temporary displacement was terminated. This had the social and economic benefit of preventing a society broken into landed gentry and poor workers. We can refer to this radical and ingenious economic innovation as the biblical "War on Poverty," one of the earliest pieces of socialist, anti-poverty legislation in ancient history. The wealthy class had time limits placed on its capacity to amass property, and the poor had an opportunity to begin again. It created a single class of people in an economy built on fairness and justice.

Verse 23 in this chapter is the key to understanding the "theory of land tenure" underlying the philosophy of chapter 25. Verse 23 states that "the land is Mine," i.e., God's. All land belongs to the Creator who brought it into being, and anyone occupying it must be considered a tenant, or guest. "Ownership" of land is a tentative and temporary category, since the ultimate and final owner of all property is God. Thus, by obeying the fair distribution laws of the Israelite community, those who occupy the land could never consider themselves permanent landlords. They were always subject to the authority of the Permanent Landlord, God. The biblical philosophy of stewardship made it possible for this humane social and economic legislation of the Jubilee Year to establish the fundamental principles of land and property use.

Maimonides taught that "All the laws of the Sabbatical Year and the Jubilee Year were enacted to teach the Jewish People compassion, charity and justice."[11] The anonymous author of the thirteenth century *Sefer HaHinukh* (*The Book of Education*), writes in similar vein:

> The Blessed Holy One wished to impress on our people that everything belongs to God, and that ultimately everything will revert to whom God wanted to give it originally. The obligation to count toward the Jubilee Year will deter people from stealing their neighbor's land, since they know that everything must return to whomever God so wills it. This idea brings to mind the custom of temporal rulers who appropriate from time to time the lands that belong to their barons around their castles in order to assert royal authority. Mortal rulers assert ownership over many lands to intimidate oth-

ers, but the Blessed Holy One does so to promote welfare and increase the merit of God's people.

Because of the lofty ideals embedded in this exceptional legal concept, this verse, "Proclaim liberty throughout the land unto all the inhabitants thereof," was chosen for inscription on the famous American Liberty Bell, a historic relic near Philadelphia's Independence Hall. The Liberty Bell, first hung in 1753, was appropriately rung in July 1776, proclaiming the Declaration of Independence. (The bell was cracked in 1835 when it tolled the death of John Marshall).

The prevention of permanent slavery and permanent loss of property both hark back to the fact that we humans are servants to one Master, and not, as the rabbis put it, "servants of servants." The theological doctrine of Divine Ownership creates a foundation of humane legislation that avoided the problems of other societies wherein humans considered themselves the final arbiters of economic policy, and all the inequities that follow in the train of such a fallible system.

Were the Laws of the Jubilee Ever Followed?

Rabbi Bernard Bamberger argues that although the laws of returning property, the unique aspect of the Jubilee Year, were high ethical ideals, they were never really carried out. Laws of the Sabbatical Year, regarding freedom of slaves, canceling debts, and letting the land lie fallow, undoubtedly were followed for many centuries. In modern Eretz Yisrael the laws of letting the Land lie fallow is circumvented by a legal fiction of selling the land to gentiles.[12]

"Many modern critics," writes Bamberger, "have...concluded that the jubilee law was the proposal of a high-minded theorist whose notions were admirable, but impracticable. And in fact the Torah includes a number of provisions that have an air of unreality about them; concerning several of them the Rabbis state that they never have been operative and never will be."[13] He refers to such laws, nullified by the Talmud, as destroying an idolatrous city (Deuteronomy 13:13ff.), the death penalty for obstreperous teenagers (Deuteronomy 1:18ff.), etc.[14]

Even those who believe that the laws of returning land to original owners were carried out acknowledge that after the period of the first temple, they certainly had no potency. Royally imposed slavery, expropriation of land, and other measures made knowledge of original ownership impossible to determine.

Bamberger points out that even though the high ideals of the Jubilee Year may never have been carried out exactly as laid out in the Torah, their influence on later economic and moral history has been profound.[15] For example, through the creation of the Jewish National Fund (JNF), or in Hebrew, *Keren Kayemet LeYisrael*, the Jewish People as a whole, since the birth of the Zionist Movement in the nineteenth century, has come to realize the dream of shared land. Through contributions from Jews all over the world, JNF has purchased land in Israel that is the collective property of the Jewish People. Such lands are used for farming and communal living, but not for profit. JNF land may not be sold, but must be used for farming, public building and industrial development, as well as infrastructure for the absorption of immigrants from the former Soviet Union, Eastern Europe, Ethiopia, Yemen, Syria, Argentina, etc. In its enormously significant work, the JNF has conserved the soil and protected the resources and environment of Eretz Yisrael, keeping its ultimate deed in the hands of the corporate Household of Israel and its God, as laid out in the laws of the Jubilee Year. Israel, to this day, in many ways, is still imbued with the spirit of public responsibility inspired by the Torah in Leviticus chapter 25.

Notes

[1] See Dov Peretz Elkins, "The Influence on Hebrew on the English Language," unpublished paper.

[2] cf. Christopher J. H. Wright, "Sabbatical Year," in *The Anchor Bible Dictionary*, ed. by David Noel Freedman (New York: Doubleday, 1992) V, 859.

[3] Cf. Hertz on Leviticus 25:10 and on Jeremiah 35:14, 323.

[4] See Shemuel E. Lunshtam, "Yovel," in *Entziklopediah Mikra'it*, ed. by Shemu'el Ahitov (Jerusalem, Mosad Bialik 1958) III, 578-9.

[5] Wayne Meeks and Jouette Bassler, eds., *The HarperCollins Study Bible: New Revised Standard Version, with the Apocraphal/Deuterocanonical Books* (New York: HarperCollins Publishers, 1993) 192.

[6] Cf. also Levine 171-2.

[7] cf. on Leviticus 25:46, 537-8.

[8] Plaut 570-1, 945.

[9] quoted in *Torah Gems II*, 334.

[10] Professor Baruch A. Levine of New York University, in *Leviticus* 172, discusses extensively the social and economic philosophy behind the Jubilee Year (see also 270-4).

[11] as quoted by Chill 300.

[12] Plaut 942.

[13] as quoted in Plaut 942.

[14] Ibid. 942-3.

[15] Ibid.

25

Numbers 6:23-27

במדבר: ו,כג-כז:

דַּבֵּר אֶל אַהֲרֹן וְאֶל בָּנָיו לֵאמֹר,
כֹּה תְבָרְכוּ אֶת בְּנֵי יִשְׂרָאֵל אָמוֹר לָהֶם:
יְבָרֶכְךָ ה' וְיִשְׁמְרֶךָ: יָאֵר ה' פָּנָיו אֵלֶיךָ וִיחֻנֶּךָ:
יִשָּׂא ה' פָּנָיו אֵלֶיךָ וְיָשֵׂם לְךָ שָׁלוֹם:
וְשָׂמוּ אֶת שְׁמִי עַל בְּנֵי יִשְׂרָאֵל וַאֲנִי אֲבָרֲכֵם.

*JPS (1916) – "Speak unto Aaron and unto his sons, saying:
On this wise ye shall bless the children of Israel; ye shall say
unto them: The LORD bless thee, and keep thee; The LORD
make His face to shine upon thee, and be gracious unto thee;
The LORD lift up His countenance upon thee, and give
thee peace. So shall they put My name upon the children of
Israel, and I will bless them."*

*NJV (1962) – "Speak to Aaron and his sons: Thus shall you
bless the people of Israel. Say to them:*
  The LORD bless you and protect you!
  *The LORD deal kindly and graciously with you! [Oth-
  ers: "make His face to shine upon thee and be gracious
  to thee."]*
  *The LORD bestow His favor [Others "lift up His
  countenance."] upon you and grant you peace! [Or
  "friendship."]*
  *Thus they shall link My name with the people of Israel,
  and I will bless them."*

This ancient, beautiful and oft-quoted blessing is known as
the *Birkat Kohanim*, the Priestly Blessing. In three short verses, the
kohen would bless worshippers who came to the altar with their
sincere sacrifices. Rabbi Abraham ibn Ezra says that the Karaites'

view was that the blessing was presented to each worshipper individually, while ibn Ezra himself follows the rabbinic view (*Sifrei Bamidbar* 39) that the blessing was offered to the entire community of Israel jointly. Plaut believes that in the times of the First Temple, the blessing was to the individual worshipper, and later to the people as a whole. He notes that modern rabbis have reverted to the earlier custom of using the blessing for individuals (such as at a birth, Bar/Bat Mitzvah, Confirmation, wedding or wedding anniversary, etc.)[1].

The *Birkat Kohanim* was an important part of the ancient Temple worship, morning and afternoon, both in the Temple in Jerusalem, and in its successor, the Synagogue. Agreeing with Plaut, then in the Temple the priests would bless each pilgrim at the altar at the conclusion of his sacrifice. As we read in Deuteronomy 21:5, "The *kohanim*, of the Tribe of Levi, have been chosen by the LORD your God to...pronounce blessings in the name of the LORD...." It was also said that when Aaron and his sons were consecrated as *kohanim*, the *Birkat Kohanim* was recited. The verse, Leviticus 9:22, reads, "Aaron lifted his hands toward the people and blessed them...." The rabbis (*Sifra*, Shmini 30) say that this blessing was the *Birkat Kohanim*, although that is not specified in the text.

Dramatic evidence of the antiquity and popularity of the *Birkat Kohanim* came to light with the discovery in 1979 of two cigarette-sized, rolled-up silver plaques from the seventh century B.C.E., unearthed by archeologists in the tomb of a wealthy family just outside biblical Jerusalem on the western hill of the Hinnom Valley, below St. Andrew's church, opposite Mt. Zion. These silver scrolls of the *Birkat Kohanim* had escaped the hands of tomb robbers for over 2600 years. This copy of the biblical text is four hundred years older than the Dead Scrolls, making it by far the oldest copy of a biblical text known today. The archeologist who discovered these tiny silver plaques grew up in a Jerusalem home less than a mile from the discovery, and was familiar with the text from his childhood, when his father would place his hands on his head and recite the blessing over his children on Shabbat eve. Anyone who goes to the Israel National Museum in Jerusalem can now see this remarkable discovery proudly displayed in a well-protected case.

From the time of the Protestant Reformation, this blessing has been recited in churches in every country and in every century. Rabbis, priests and ministers use it today to bless their congregants at special occasions, and to close the worship service with a biblical benediction.

The Three Parts of the Priestly Blessing

Most commentators, following the Midrash *Sifrei*, agree that the Blessing is divided into three parts. The first part, "May the LORD bless you and keep you," clearly refers to material blessings, prosperity (Rashi) and long life (Abraham ibn Ezra). The second part, "May God's Presence enlighten you," refers to spiritual blessings, such as Torah knowledge and inspiration. The third part, "May God's Providence be directed toward you," [translation adapted from Aryeh Kaplan][2], refers to an unearned spiritual benefit of God's eternal compassion. Nehama Leibowitz sees the third part as combining both material and spiritual blessings.[3]

From a strictly literary point of view, the Blessing is couched in poetic and inspiring language. The first stich is comprised of three words; the second of five words; the third of seven words, building toward a crescendo of the highest blessing: Shalom. Besides rising in length, each phrase also rises in spirituality, the cap of the blessing being the wholeness and integration of all blessings, which is the true meaning of *shalom*. As Rabbi Hertz says, the words of the blessing "are clothed in a rhythmic form of great beauty, and they fall with majestic solemnity upon the ear of the worshipper."[4]

Prof. Jacob Milgrom points out that "God initiates six actions: bless *and* protect; shine *and* be gracious; bestow *and* grant peace. However, the transitional *and* may indicate consequence: blessing results in protection; God's shining face results in grace; the bestowal of God's favor results in peace. Thus the Priestly Blessing may actually express three actions."[5] Each of the three parts of the blessing, and each word within each line, requires detailed analysis, which we begin now.

(1) "May the LORD Bless and Protect You"

Volumes could be written on the simple, elegant Hebrew word *berakhah*, blessing. It is used in a wide variety of ways in modern parlance, but as one modern commentator points out, its essential meaning is that of a "gift."[6] Very often in the Bible blessings are given by God—gifts of material wealth (Genesis 24:1: "The Lord blessed Abraham with all things"), of a prolific family (Genesis 1:28: "God blessed them, saying, 'Be fertile and increase.'"), of fertility (Genesis 24:60—Rebekah's family blessed her saying "May you grow into thousands of myriads...."). When Jacob returns after twenty years of separation and alienation from his twin brother Esau, Jacob sends ahead servants with herds of animals and various lavish gifts, and when the two meet, Jacob says to Esau: "Please accept my blessing (*berakhah*) which has been brought to you, for God has favored me and I have plenty" (Genesis 33:11).

The Midrash (*Sifrei Bemidbar* 40) makes it clear that in the Bible *berakhah* generally refers to material possessions. While Rashi stresses the material possessions in this blessing, ibn Ezra emphasizes long life. Rabbi Ovadiah Sforno explains that the blessing of material wealth is designed to enable its recipient to find time to devote to Torah study. The fullest list of material blessings in the Torah is found in Deuteronomy 28:1-14.

Milgrom explains that bestowing a blessing is a hope, or prayer, that God will fulfill that wish. The blessing (or curse) has no inherent powers of fulfillment itself. The efficacy of this gift depends entirely on the will of God.[7] On other occasions, humans bless God, as in the standard statutory blessing of Jewish liturgy: "Blessed are You, Ruler of the Universe...." What gifts can humans grant to God? The gift of our words of praise, thanksgiving and commitment.

Unlike blessing, the traditional commentators (Rashi, ibn Ezra, Sforno) suggest that protection is a natural corollary of ownership. Material possessions are open to robbery, and the prayer/blessing is that once one is blessed with prosperity, it will not be removed from the owner. A Hasidic comment on this verse by the Tzechiver Rabbi makes the interesting observation that often physical possessions bring problems and evil in their train, so that the blessing would then be to protect us from our own possessions. Or, to protect us from having our possessions possess us![8]

(2) "The LORD Deal Kindly and Graciously with You"

The translations of this phrase differ. Literally the Hebrew text asks that God's face shine upon the recipient. This is an anthropomorphism, with metaphoric overtones. A shining face usually signals a warm, friendly concern. Rabbi Aryeh Kaplan's translation is felicitous: "May God make His presence enlighten you."[9] This rendering sees the word "shine" in the sense of "light" or "enlighten", as with knowledge. Thus, many commentaries interpret the expression to mean that the recipient be blessed with Torah knowledge and inspiration. Light and knowledge are often connected in the Bible and Talmud (as in the English word "enlightened"), thus Midrash *Bemidbar Rabbah* 11:6 comments:

"'May the Lord's face shine upon you....' This is the light of Torah that God should enlighten your eyes and heart in Torah, and
grant you children learned in Torah, as it is written in Proverbs
6:23: 'For the commandment is a lamp, the teaching is a light'."

Ibn Ezra interprets the notion of God's face shining on someone as: May God answer your prayers and fulfill your requests.

The Hebrew word for Grace in the Bible (*hen*) is related to
the adjective *hanun*, gracious, which always refers to God's forgiveness, tempering justice with mercy. Rashi, quoting *Sifrei
Bemidbar* 41, says: May God grant you grace (*hen*), i.e., be kind to
you. Others render: May God make you gracious (reading the
verb in the causative form). Midrash *Sifrei* paraphrases: May
God cause you to find favor (*hen*) in the eyes of others, and use
the blessings listed above wisely. Nahmanides modifies this by
rendering: May you find favor in God's eyes.

(3) "The LORD Bestow Favor upon You and Grant You Peace"

Rabbi Aryeh Kaplan translates: "May God direct His providence
toward you."[10] Ibn Ezra renders: May God always be favorably
disposed to you. The Midrash *Sifrei* explains: God's favor implies God's compassion—above and beyond what one deserves,
such as forgiveness of sin and the blessings of peace. Rashi interprets: God will not punish you harshly for your sins.

The Hebrew expression, "to lift up one's face," is a metaphor for one's attitude. Turning one's face toward you means to
look favorably, or smile on you; while turning one's face away
from you (e.g., Deuteronomy 31:17, "May [God's] anger will
arise toward them, and I will abandon them, and hide my face
from them") implies looking unfavorably to you, or treating you
with disfavor. Targum Yonatan (an Aramaic translation and interpretation of the Torah, written some time in the first centuries
of the Common Era) explains that God will answer the peti-
tioner's prayer.

The Hebrew phrase *shalom* is far greater than English "peace."
It is one of the most important and comprehensive phrases in the
Hebrew language, and has become the international word for total and universal peace. It implies far more than the greeting people extend to one another upon meeting or parting. Its true
meaning cannot be expressed in one English word. Shalom implies wholeness, integration, fulfillment, completion and unity.[11]

Midrash *Sifrei* states that *shalom* is the climax of the *Birkat
Kohanim* because all other blessings count for naught without the

blessing of *shalom*. At the very end of the sixty-three tractates of the Mishnah, we find in Tractate *Uktzin* (3:12) these words: "The Blessed Holy One could find no vessel that would contain Israel's blessings as well as peace, as it is written (Psalms 29:ll): "Adonai will give strength to the People of Israel, Adonai will bless the People with peace (*shalom*)."

Rabbi Ovadiah Sforno writes that *shalom* in this blessing refers to the everlasting peace of the world to come. Milgrom brings various biblical verses to show that *shalom* can mean a wide variety of positive concepts, including "prosperity (Deuteronomy 23:7); good health (Psalm 38:4); friendship (Jeremiah 20:10 and 38:22); and general well-being (I Samuel 16:4f. and II Samuel 18:28)."[12]

What Is the Meaning of the Verse That Follows the *Birkat Kohanim*?

To understand Numbers 6:27, let's re-read it. The JPS translation of 1916 states: "So shall they [the *kohanim*] put My name upon the children of Israel, and I will bless them." The newer translation (NJV) renders the Hebrew in more poetic terms: "Thus they shall link My name with the people of Israel, and I will bless them."

The newer translation implies that the Hebrew words *vesamu et Shemi* — to *put* My name — on the People of Israel, are to be read metaphorically, not literally. By pronouncing God's name, it ties, binds, or "links" the name of God, and all the blessings connected to it, with the Israelite People. However, with the discovery of the ancient silver amulets apparently worn on the neck, perhaps on a string, or metal chain, we realized that the blessing was actually placed on the *body* of the Israelites. In our day, this may be compared with the practice of many Jews to place the mezuzah (containing scriptural passages, and meant to be affixed to the right doorpost of doorways in the home) on necklaces, worn as a sign of pride in one's Jewishness. Perhaps the priestly blessing was also worn in biblical times, as a good-luck charm, with some unexpressed magical overtones in mind. Now that we know of the wearing of the Priestly Blessing on the body, we may interpret this verse either figuratively *or* literally — that the blessing is *put on* the Israelite People.

Rabbi Abraham ibn Ezra notes that the phrase "and I will bless them" may refer to the *kohanim*, after they bless the people, as well as to the Israelite People themselves.

Does a *Kohen* have the Authority to Bless People, or is that the Sole Prerogative of God?

Many commentators have discussed whether it is the *kohen* who blesses the worshippers, or if he merely invokes the blessing of God. In short, can a mortal human bestow divine blessings, or is this left only to God? In the latter case, what is the role of the *kohen*?

Our text contradicts itself, and begs for interpretation. In verse 23 we read: "Speak to Aaron and his sons: Thus shall you bless the people of Israel." This would seem to imply that it is the *kohanim* who bless. Yet, in verse 27, we read "and I [God] will bless them." Various midrashim stress the fact that the role of the *kohanim* is merely to be God's vehicle in the blessing process, but it is only God who can truly bestow the all-encompassing gifts of the *Birkat Kohanim*. In other cases of biblical blessings, people are known to bless one another, and even bless God ("And David blessed the LORD in front of the entire community, saying, Blessed are You, LORD, God of Israel our father, from eternity to eternity" (I Chronicles 29:10). But when the *kohen* stands at the altar invoking *God's* blessing, he is doing precisely that — invoking, not blessing.

Midrash *Tanhuma* (a collection attributed to Rabbi Tanhum bar Abba, Palestine, fourth century C.E.) states: "Said the People of Israel to the Blessed Holy One: Lord of the Universe, why do You order the *kohanim* to bless us, when we want only Your blessing? The Blessed Holy One replied: Though I commanded the *kohanim* to bless you, I stand with them together and bless you." Rabbi Moshe Alshekh adds that it was the special role of the *Kohanim* to set the proper religious tone to this sacred moment of receiving God's blessing.

The fact that God's ineffable name (the Tetragrammaton) was used in the *Birkat Kohanim* in each of the three parts, is further evidence that it is indeed God who is blessing the people, and the *kohanim* are merely invoking the blessing of God.

The Custom of *Kohanim* Blessing the People Today

While the *kohanim* have not blessed worshippers bringing sacrifices to the Temple since its destruction by the Romans in 70 C.E., there remains today a vestige of this practice in synagogues throughout the world. The ritual is known in Yiddish as "*duchanen*" from the Hebrew word *duhan*, the wooden platform on which the *kohanim* stand in the synagogue to pronounce the *Birkat Kohanim*. This custom is considered by many Jews to be one of the most dramatic and inspiring moments in the Jewish worship service, and it is being reintroduced even in very liberal synagogues today.

In modern traditional synagogues, towards the end of the repetition of the Amidah prayer, the *kohanim* step out of the sanctuary, wash themselves for special spiritual purification, and then stand in front of the congregation and recite the *Birkat Kohanim*, preceded by a special Hebrew blessing. The *kohanim* place their *tallitot* (prayer shawls) over their heads, raise their hands, their fingers forming the Hebrew letter *shin*, the first letter of Hebrew *Shaddai*, Almighty, and chant the blessing in an eerie and mystical melody. Congregants are not supposed to look at the *kohanim*, because the moment is too fraught with mystical transcendence (cf. *Shulchan Arukh*, Orah Hayim 128). This custom is practiced in the Diaspora only on Festivals, while in Israel it is done every Shabbat, and in Jerusalem every day.

The Mishnah (*Tamid* 7:2) describes this custom in biblical days. In the Temple in Jerusalem God's sacred name, the Tetragrammaton, was used, while outside Jerusalem they used the word Adonai (the Lord). In the Temple the *kohanim* raised their hands above their heads, but outside the Temple they raised their hands only as high as their shoulders. This is only one example of how the Tradition made distinctions between practices in the Temple and outside of it. Some other examples include the permission to light the fire on the altar on Shabbat in the Temple, while no fire was permitted to be kindled outside the Temple. In Temple days, the Shofar was blown on Rosh Hashanah even on Shabbat; whereas after the destruction of the Temple, it was forbidden to be blown on Shabbat. In Temple days musical instruments accompanied Shabbat and Festival worship (see Psalm 150), and after the destruction, musical instrumentation was no longer permitted (though many modern synagogues today have re-introduced musical instruments, in an effort to enhance the beauty of Jewish worship comparable to Temple times).

The simple two-letter Hebrew word *ko*, or "thus," in Numbers 6:23, was interpreted by the rabbis to mean that the blessing was to be recited as it was at the dedication of the *Mishkan* (Tabernacle). At that sacred moment in Israel's history, we read (Leviticus 9:22) "Aaron lifted his hands toward the people and blessed them." The Talmudic rabbis deduced three specific regulations in this regard: 1) that the *kohanim* shall stand during the recitation, 2) that their hands shall be raised, and 3) that the blessing must be recited in its original, in Hebrew (*Sifrei Bamidbar* 39).

Notes

[1] Plaut 1065.

[2] Kaplan 691.

[3] Nehama Leibowitz, *Studies in Bamidbar (Numbers): In the Context of Ancient and Modern Jewish Bible Commentary* (Jerusalem: World Zionist Organization, Department for Torah Education and Culture, 1980) 66-67.

[4] Hertz 594.

[5] Jacob Milgrom, Numbers: The Traditional Hebrew Text with New JPS Translation, The JPS Torah Commentary (Philadelphia: Jewish Publication Society 1990) 51.

[6] "Parashat Vayishlach," Reflections 2 November 1991: 3.

[7] Milgrom 360ff.

[8] Louis I. Newman, The Hasidic Anthology: Tales and Teachings of the Hasidim (New York: Bloch, 1934) 359.

[9] Kaplan 691.

[10] Ibid.

[11] Dov Peretz Elkins, *Humanizing Jewish Life* (South Brunswick: A.S. Barnes, 1976) 203-209.

[12] Milgrom 52.

26

Numbers 10:35-36

במדבר י,לה-לו:

וַיְהִי בִּנְסֹעַ הָאָרֹן וַיֹּאמֶר מֹשֶׁה, קוּמָה ה' וְיָפֻצוּ אֹיְבֶיךָ
וְיָנֻסוּ מְשַׂנְאֶיךָ מִפָּנֶיךָ:
וּבְנֻחֹה יֹאמַר שׁוּבָה ה' רִבְבוֹת אַלְפֵי יִשְׂרָאֵל.

*JPS (1916) – "And it came to pass, when the ark set for-
ward, that Moses said: 'Rise up, O LORD, and let Thine
enemies be scattered and let them that hate Thee flee before
Thee.' And when it rested, he said: 'Return, O LORD, unto
the ten thousands of the families of Israel.'"*

*NJV (1962) – "When the Ark was to set out, Moses would
say:*

> *Advance, O LORD!*
> *May Your enemies be scattered,*
> *And may Your foes flee before You!*
> *And when it halted, he would say:*
> *Return, O LORD,*
> *You who are Israel's myriads of thousands!" [Others:*
> *"Return, O LORD, unto the ten thousands of the fam-
> ilies of Israel!"]*

The Israelite People is about to leave Mount Sinai for the first
time, on the twentieth day of the second month of the second
year after leaving Egypt (Numbers 10:11). Their first journey, of
three days duration (v. 33), took them from Egypt to Mt. Sinai
(Exodus 3:18). Numbers 2:17 describes the *Ohel Moed* (Tent of
Meeting) in the Center of the traveling camp, with the Levites
surrounding it, and the tribes around them. Here, we find the
Ark in *front* of the camp, leading it forward. The Midrash sug-

gests that there were two arks (*Sifre Bamidbar* 82), one made by Moshe when he first received the Two Tablets, which was always in front of the Camp, and the second ark made later with the Mishkan by Bezalel, in the middle of the Camp, held by the Levites, which contained the new tablets. Rabbi Shmuel David Luzzatto (ShaDaL; Padua, Italy, 1800-1865) understands the placement metaphorically — meaning that the Ark was actually in the Center of the Camp, but its spirit led the People, and was thus, in a way, "out front."

Rabbi Hertz describes the drama of the Holy Ark being lifted and carried into battle with the Israelites in the wilderness: "...We still feel the thrill of sacred enthusiasm that animated the men of old on hearing them."[1] This "Song of the Ark," as the two verses are known, is the same Song whose words are used when the ark is opened and closed in the Synagogue today.

Why Are There Two Brackets Surrounding These Two Verses?

Our verses are surrounded by special "brackets," which set them apart from the balance of the text. There are several reasons offered as to why the section is distinguished with special marks, sometimes referred to as an inverted form of the Hebrew letter *nun*, or *nun hafucha*; and sometimes as *simaniyot* (*Shabbat* 115b), or inverted commas. The only other place in the Tanakh with such brackets is Psalm 107.

The first explanation for the brackets is that the verses seem to be out of place. The rabbis (*Shabbat* 116a, *Sifre Bemidbar* 83) saw a more logical place for these verses in the beginning of the Book of *Bemidbar* (Numbers) in the description of the configuration of the tribal locations (2:17).

Secondly, as Rabbi Yehudah HaNasi, President of the Sanhedrin and editor of the Mishnah (ca. 200 C.E.), suggests (*Sifre Bemidbar* 84) these verses form a separate book of the Torah. In other words, the Torah book which we call *Bemidbar* (Numbers), is in fact three separate books: 1) Numbers 1:1 to 10:34, 2) Numbers 10:35-36; 3) Numbers 11-36. This theory is supported by the Mishnah (*Yadayim* 3:5), which states that any biblical scroll which contains 85 letters, such as Numbers 10:35-36, "defiles the hands." When touching a book that was holy, or divine, and which was to be included in the biblical canon, one had to wash one's hands to purify them. Thus, a divine book "defiled the hands." Rabbi Yehudah HaNasi further suggests that when the biblical Book of Proverbs speaks (9:1) of Wisdom hewing out her seven pillars, the verse is referring to the *seven* books of the Torah (*Sifre Bemidbar* 84).[2]

The third explanation for the brackets is that these two verses are transplanted here from an outside source, not of the Torah. One must remember that the biblical texts and apocrypha (non-canonical literature of biblical age, rejected by the rabbinic sages) which are in our possession today constitute only a small fragment of the literature written in ancient times. The rabbis suggest that these two verses originate from some work that even in their day no longer existed.

Several sources from which these verses may have been taken are suggested. One is an unknown Book of the Wars of the Lord (alluded to in Numbers 21:14). Prof. Jacob Milgrom refers to an eleventh century manuscript pointing to another source, a book called "The Prophecy of Eldad and Medad" (assistants of Joshua, mentioned in Numbers 11). He connects this medieval source with a Talmudic statement of Rabbi Yehudah that these two verses come from an independent book that was *nignaz*, or suppressed.[3] Milgrom then makes this remarkable and astute observation about the process of the canonization of the Tanakh, and the implications it has for the issue of divine revelation: "The attribution of the verses to Eldad and Medad...not only represents a rare medieval instance of denial of Mosaic authorship to a part of the Torah but also indicates that there was continuous awareness in traditional sources that the process of the canonization of Scripture was a highly selective one: Much was 'suppressed,' that is, rejected."[4]

Finally, the theory exists that these two verses are separated from the rest of the Book of Numbers to distinguish them from two episodes of sinning by the Israelites. In the verse preceding these two, we find that the Israelites ran away from Mt. Sinai. The Midrash describes this event as a child running away from a teacher, who might impose still more rules (in addition to the Ten Commandments). Then, in Numbers 11, we read about the murmuring of the people.

What Is the Function of the *Aron* in This "Song of the Ark"?

The fact that this song is quoted elsewhere in the Tanakh is evidence that this Song of the Ark was used on many occasions of battle. God's Presence has the capacity to make followers rejoice and feel at ease, while enemies are punished. In Psalm 68:2-3 we read: "God will arise, Adonai's enemies shall be scattered; foes shall flee before God. Disperse them as smoke is dispersed; as wax melts at fire, so the wicked shall perish before God. But the righteous shall rejoice; they shall exult in the presence of God; they shall be especially joyous." In Psalm 132:8, we find a similar phrase: "Arise, O LORD, to Your resting-place; You and Your powerful Ark!"

From Numbers 14:44 we can infer that the Ark was a popular symbol of God's Presence in battle. Disobeying God's instructions not to enter the Land, one group "dared to climb up to the top of the mountain, even without the Ark of the Covenant of the Lord. Moshe, however, remained in the camp. The Amalekites and Canaanites then smote them and defeated them."

It is clear that in the ancient world, the Ark and other polytheistic symbols and images of gods were identified with the god itself. In one battle in which King David defeats the Philistines, we read that "The Philistines abandoned their idols there, and David and his soldiers carried them away" (II Samuel 5:21). On another occasion, the Philistines become exceedingly frightened when they hear that their Israelite enemies are bringing the Ark into battle at Aphek: "When they learned that the Ark of the Lord had come into the camp, the Philistines were frightened, and they said: 'God has entered the camp;' and they cried out: 'Woe to us! Who will save us from this powerful God?'" (I Samuel 4:6-8).

As we have pointed out on other occasions, throughout the entire Bible and later Jewish tradition, we find countless instances of borrowing of *forms* from other peoples, cultures and religions. What is always unique in the biblical presentation are the modifications and "monotheisation" of the physical forms, rituals, myths, institutions, symbols, language and other borrowings. The major thesis of Prof. Yehezkel Kaufmann is that while Israel may have borrowed much from the surrounding world, the ideas or institutions borrowed are invariably colored by its own monotheistic viewpoint.[5]

Milgrom offers a similar point, arguing that the Ark is not a representation of God, but only Adonai's footstool, or throne. In the battle of Aphek mentioned above, we read of God referred to as "YHVH of Hosts enthroned on the Cherubim" (II Samuel 6:2). As he notes, "The image of God resuming His place on His throne after vanquishing His enemies (originally pagan nature gods) is found in Psalms 29 and 89:16-19...and was probably modeled after Canaanite prototypes that describe the march of the divine warrior god into battle and his enthronement as king of the gods upon his victorious return."[6] Thus, God's association with the Ark is temporary, and symbolic. God's glory appears in the Tabernacle when God wishes to address Moses, but does not permanently reside there. In Exodus 17:7, when the people were thirsty, they complained and argued among themselves, asking "Is the LORD present among us or not?" Only with divine will did God descend from the cloud-pillar above and assume the divine position on the Throne in the Holy of Holies inside the Mishkan. Further evidence that although God's dominion is the entire world, only personal desire prompts the Deity descend into the Tent and communicate with Moses is found in Exodus 33:9: "When Moses entered the Tent, the pillar of cloud would descend and stand at the entrance of the Tent, while God spoke with Moses."[7]

In another passage it is crystal clear that it is God alone who decides when the Ark shall arise, and when it shall rest, when the people shall travel, and when they shall encamp (Number 9:18ff.): "At the command of the LORD they encamped; they remained encamped as long as the cloud remained over the Mishkan. When the cloud lingered over the Mishkan for a long time, the Israelites kept the LORD's command and did not journey on. But when the cloud remained over the Mishkan only for a short time at the command of the LORD, they broke camp as soon as the cloud lifted. Day or night, whenever the cloud lifted, they would break camp and travel on....On a *sign from the LORD* they made camp and on a *sign from the LORD* they broke camp."

Thus, in biblical theology, the presence of the Ark in times of battle, the Place of Meeting with Moses, was the Israelites' assurance that God would be there to give them courage and hope when they prayed for divine assistance, and that their answer would be positive.

Rabbi Samson Raphael Hirsch interprets the calling of the Aron into battle as symbolic of the Presence of God and Jewish Values, Torah, in the ever-present war for justice, truth and peace. Enemies of God, he argues, are enemies of Torah and Torah values, foes of the final victory of God's eternal Sovereignty on earth. Rabbi Hirsch sees these two verses as summarizing the history of Israel's ongoing battle to vanquish evil and accomplish the divine mission. Thus, these two verses well deserve to constitute their own Book of the Torah.[8]

What Is the Meaning of the Expression *"rivvot alfei Yisrael"*?

The expression is awkward, and both its meaning and intent are unclear. We can see this from the difference between the 1916 JPS translation, "Return, O LORD, unto the ten thousands of the families of Israel," and the NJV which brings: "Return, O LORD, You who are Israel's myriads of thousands."

Rabbi Hertz quotes an old tradition that the Hebrew *elef* does not always mean "thousand," but can also mean "families" or "clans."[9] It makes more sense that the number of people who left Egypt was not six hundred thousand, as the text implies, but six hundred families. Six hundred thousand males over the age of twenty would bring the total Hebrew population to millions. With such a presence, the Israelites would have been able to overtake Egypt and liberate themselves from oppression.

Besides the awkward phraseology, "myriads of thousands," the question is: "What is the connection between *returning* or *resting* and the astronomical numbers of Israelites?" The large number is intended to indicate a huge mass. The new JPS translation of 1962 (NJV) sees the last phrase, Israel's myriads of thousands, as being in apposition to *shuvah*. In other words, it is a phrase that describes God, the one who is "Israel's myriads of thousands." Arnold B. Ehrlich (Russian-American, 1848-1920) understood the phrase that way, and this is the basis of the NJV translation. Rabbi Ovadiah Sforno understood it to mean: "Return, LORD of the hosts of the myriads of Israel."

Milgrom notes that in pre-biblical Egyptian writings the gods are thought to be worth more than all the millions of foot soldiers who fought in the war. Thus, if the Torah is borrowing from ancient Near East literary usage, this phrase may be referring to a God who is greater than all the hordes of the armies of Israel. In a later biblical passage, the prophet Elijah, ascending to Heaven in a whirlwind, is referred to as "Israel's chariots and horsemen" (II Kings 2:12). In the frequent expression "The Lord of Hosts," there is an implication that God's heavenly armies make war on the side of Israel. So here, we may have a reference to the hosts in Heaven fighting along with Israel's hosts on earth.[10]

Notes

[1] Hertz 613.
[2] Milgrom 375.
[3] Ibid 375-6.
[4] Ibid. 376.
[5] Kaufman.
[6] Milgrom 374.
[7] Ibid. 373-5.
[8] Hirsch 169-170.
[9] Hertz 613.
[10] Milgrom 81.

27

Numbers 11:29

במדבר יא,כט:

וַיֹּאמֶר לוֹ מֹשֶׁה הַמְקַנֵּא אַתָּה לִי וּמִי יִתֵּן כָּל עַם ה׳
נְבִיאִים כִּי יִתֵּן ה׳ אֶת רוּחוֹ עֲלֵיהֶם.

*JPS (1916) – "And Moses said unto him: 'Art thou jealous
for my sake? would that all the LORD's people were prophets, that the LORD would put His spirit upon them!'"*

*NJV (1962) – "But Moses said to him, 'Are you wrought up
on my account? Would that all the LORD's people were
prophets, that the LORD put His spirit upon them!'"*

After some time in the desert, the people are becoming rebellious, pining for the "easy" life they had in Egypt, where food
was plentiful and life was simple. Their slave mentality caused
them to selectively recall the secure part of their former life,
thereby idealizing it. There was food (though certainly not plentiful or fancy), and the routine of slave life, as harsh as it may
have been, without the vicissitudes of desert existence, suddenly
seemed appealing to them in retrospect.

God thus tells Moses to appoint seventy elders upon whom
God would place the Divine spirit upon them, to assist Moses in
his burdensome tasks of leadership, to handle the extra burdens
of dissatisfaction. When the spirit descended on them, they began to "prophesy," a term which had retained in Torah times an
earlier Semitic connotation of charismatic religious frenzy, often
through dance and song, to reach a deeper spiritual consciousness.

At the same time, two of the elders, Eldad and Medad, who
had remained in the camp, also prophesized. Joshua, Moses'
trusted and loyal assistant, rushes to his master and pleads with

him to restrain them from their prophesy, fearing that Moses' authority would be challenged or diminished. Moses, on the other hand, is confident of his own authority, and reacts with aplomb. It is interesting to distinguish between the response of a self-confident leader and one who is not. The answer of Moses constitutes the verse we now examine.

What is the *"Navi,"* or "Prophet" in the Tanakh?

The notion of prophetic calling evolved in the biblical period. In its early stages, in the biblical books known as Early Prophets (*Nevi'im Rishonim*), the prophet is referred to as: a) *mitnabe*, (an ecstatic, frenzied person, usually found in a group, who brings on the spirit of God through music, dance and sometimes musical instruments, from the reflexive form of the verb "to prophesy"); b) *hozeh* (seers); and c) *ro'eh* (clairvoyants). The notion of the *navi* as moral teacher became more common in the period of the great classical prophets, the *Nevi'im Aharonim*.[1]

The early *mitnab'im*, such as the Seventy Elders including Eldad and Medad, induce their ecstatic state through unusual behavior, such as a trance. One of the best descriptions of this kind of early prophecy is found in I Samuel 10:5ff, where a band of prophets is accompanied by lyres, timbrels, flutes and harps, and the prophet Samuel tells Saul that "the spirit of the Lord will grip you, and you will speak in ecstasy along with them, and you will become a different person."

Sometimes, as in the case of Deborah the prophetess, the trance state is utilized to arouse soldiers into the proper mood to fight a battle without inhibitions. As a military chaplain in the U.S. Army in the 1960s, at the beginning of the Vietnam War, I recall going out in my jeep to the basic training fields, and watching young 18-year-olds learning to thrust their bayonet into a straw "enemy" figure, screaming "kill!" in order to help them overcome their fear of killing. The ancient methods of prophecy were useful, in part, in helping soldiers overcome their natural inhibitions through a flourish of ecstatic moods, and throw caution to the wind.[2]

The early connotation of "clairvoyant" was replaced in the days of Isaiah, Jeremiah, Micah, Amos and Hosea, with the idea of prophetic moral teaching, the notion now associated with the great biblical prophets of the classic prophetic period (8th to 6th century B.C.E.). Rabbi Abraham Joshua Heschel discusses the differences between ecstasy and prophecy:

The ecstatic is moved by a will to experience ecstasies. He is in quest of what is not promised and what does not spontaneously communicate itself, and he must ever anew strive to attain his goal by means of various stimulants. Dramatic gestures, dance, music, alcohol, opium, hashish, the drinking of water of a sacred well, or of the blood of an animal, induce the state of rapture, which enables man to transcend the barriers of self. The prophet, on the other hand, is not moved by a will to experience prophecy. What he achieves comes against his will. He does not pant for illumination. He does not call for it; he is called upon. God comes upon the prophet before the prophet seeks the coming of God. . . . Ecstasy is motivated by man's concern for God, by his will to be illumined. Prophecy, to the prophet's mind, is motivated by God's concern for man, by God's will that the prophet illumine his people.[3]

What Does Moses' Response Tell Us About His Character and Personality?

When Moses remains unbothered by the prophesying of Eldad and Medad, he implies that in his ideal world, *all* of God's children would become prophets, contrary to Joshua's impulse. Not only is Moses not jealous of Eldad and Medad, but he would not even be jealous if *all* God's people possessed the spirit of prophecy! He is prepared to forgo the honor of being alone in his prophetic ability, and would gladly step aside and defer to others. Moses' humility is evidenced in several passages in the Torah (cf. Numbers 12:3). After all, prophecy is assigned to him; he did not seek it (Exodus 3:11).

The Hebrew verb *"kana"* comes from a Semitic root, similar in Arabic and Syriac, which means to become red in the face, angry, impassioned. Later connotations include expanded meanings, such as being "jealous" and "emotionally involved," or "wrought up."[4] The nuances of the JPS and the NJV translations are different, but the sense is similar. Dr. Yechiel Zvi Moskowitz makes the interesting observation that Moses' tart reply to Joshua is perhaps his way of recognizing that Joshua is the one who is jealous, since he is not included in the Seventy Elders, and is displacing his jealousy onto Moses, something which Moses quickly recognizes and points out to his disciple. This is the mark of an honest and devoted teacher![5]

Rabbi Yitzhak ben Moses Arama (Spain, 1420-1494) notes in *Akedat Yitzhak,* his commentary on the Torah, that Moses fails the first test of patience with the people in verses 11-15, begging to die rather than to witness his own failure. But by the end of the chapter, Moses rises to the occasion, and prays that the entire people become prophets! Arama stresses Moses' humility:

> In my view the words of Moses constitute a remarkable example of humility. Aside from not being envious of his disciples, those whom he appointed and trained, as the Talmud notes (Sanhedrin 105b): 'Humans envy everyone except one's own child and disciple', Moses sincerely desires that all the people of God should be prophets and that the Creator should bestow the Divine Spirit upon them directly, without Moses' intervention. While this would be something all others would be jealous of, Moses did not evidence jealousy!

What is the Nature of Moses' Wish for the People?

Moses' response to Joshua is a remarkable example not only of the Prophet/Teacher's humility, but also of his understanding of the relationship between God and all human beings. Moses does not see the need for an intermediary between the Creator and the Creatures. He is indeed a teacher and prophet, but Moses sees this status as achievable by all human beings. It is a meritocracy, not a status bestowed by virtue of cast or special status.

Martin Buber points out incisively that the verb used in connection with the seventy elders is *mitnabim*; while what Moses asks is that the people become *nevi'im*:

> It is worthy of remark that he does not make use of the verb employed in the previous account, and stating that those possessed by the Spirit 'behaved themselves like prophets', that is, expressed themselves in ecstatic fashion like the bands of *nebiim*: but instead he employs the substantive itself. Hence what he means is not a transitory state but the summons in virtue of which a man has immediate contact with Godhead and receives its behest directly.... For when the whole people have become *nebiim*, in direct contact with God, it would no longer be necessary for somebody to be charged by God with the function of bearing them on his bosom like an infant.[6]

Rabbi Samson Raphael Hirsch gives Moses the highest credit for this remarkable response, and sees it as a premonition of the democracy of learning that ultimately won out among the Jewish People. This biblical episode:

> proclaims that by the appointment of the highest intellectual and spiritual authority in Israel, no monopoly in intellectual-

ity or spirituality is to be formed, that the spiritual gifts of God are in no way dependent on office or profession, and that the lowest in the nation could be considered as equally worthy of the spirit of God as the first official in the highest office. But Moses' answer to Joshua remains for all teachers and leaders as the brilliant example they should keep before their eyes as the highest ideal aim of their work, viz., to make themselves superfluous, that the people of all classes and ranks reach such a spiritual level that they no longer require teachers and leaders. And indeed the successors of these 'elders' have well inherited the spirit of their Moses, have recognized their highest mission to be *leharbitz Torah be-Yisrael* (to make the knowledge of the Torah the broadest foundation of life in the people), and have proclaimed *ve-ha-ameedu talmidim harbeh* (establish many students) [*Pirke Avot*, chapter 1] as the first maxim for all spiritual leaders of their people. With his 'Are you jealous for me?' our Moses has broken down the dividing wall between 'intellectuals' and the 'lower classes,' between clergy and laity, forever in Israel.[7]

Da'at Mikra notices an interesting yet subtle nuance, in pointing out that in verse 25 God announces that the Seventy Elders will be given some of the prophetic spirit previously given to Moses. Now Moses, in response to Joshua, asks that any Israelite can have the prophetic Divine spirit, even without being given to the individual by God. It is thus the wish of Moses that God's spirit rest on all, even without specific assignment or appointment, a yet further dramatic reaction that we might not have anticipated from Moses.[8]

What Moses asks for is repeated by a later classical prophet (Joel 3:1), who envisions a future (messianic) age in which:

It shall come to pass that
I will pour out My spirit upon all flesh;
And your sons and your daughters shall prophesy;
Your old shall dream dreams,
And your young shall see visions.

Notes

[1] For the history of the institution of prophecy, see Milgrom, Excursus 25, "Ecstatic Prophecy in Israel and the Ancient Near East," 380-383, and Excursus 26, "Prophecy in Israel and the Ancient Near East," 383-384.

[2] Cf. Orlinsky 230, "the *hithpael* form of *nb'* is usually employed for ecstatic utterances....".

[3] Abraham Joshua Heschel, *The Prophets* (Philadelphia: Jewish Publication Society, 1962) 358.

[4] Cf. Milgrom 216, on Numbers 25:11,13; and Orlinsky 175, on Exodus 20:5.

[5] *Da'at Mikra* IV, 130.

[6] Buber, *Moses* 167.

[7] Hirsch IV, 185.

[8] *Da'at Mikra* IV, 130.

28

Numbers 12:3

במדבר יב,ג:

וְהָאִישׁ מֹשֶׁה עָנָו מְאֹד מִכֹּל הָאָדָם אֲשֶׁר עַל פְּנֵי הָאֲדָמָה.

JPS (1916) – "Now the man Moses was very meek, above all the men that were upon the face of the earth."

NJV (1962) – "Now Moses was a very humble man, more so than any other man on earth."

The high status of Moses as God's leading prophet is the envy of other members of his family. In this chapter it is Aaron and Miriam who are jealous. A few chapters later (16) we find Moses' cousin, Korah, rebelling against his authority. Those who challenge his leadership claim that they too are prophets of God, and seem to want to elevate their own prophetic status. The pretext of the complaint by Moses' siblings is that he married a Cushite woman (a foreigner). The real complaint of Aaron and Miriam, however, is one of (prophetic) authority and power. The response to their complaint is the statement about Moses' humility in our verse.

Rabbi Hertz points to several other verses in the Torah where Moses is described as having sinned, claiming that this is evidence of Moses' humility and devoutness (presuming that Moses wrote the Torah, and admits his own guilt). In Numbers 20:12 ff, we read of Moses' punishment by God for disobeying Adonai's command, thus denying him the privilege of entering the Promised Land. In Exodus 4:24 we find that Adonai wants to punish Moses for not circumcising his son at the proper time, on the eighth day, as is commanded to Abraham. Finally, in Deuteronomy 1:37, in Moses' final speeches in the last weeks of his life, he recounts the history of his relationship with God and the Israelite people, and includes the episode of God's anger towards him regarding the incident of striking the rock at Merivah ("Strife").[1]

How Can Moses, Author of the Torah, Call Himself "More Humble Than Any Other Man on Earth"?

If we are to credit Moses with co-authorship of the Torah, then we have the problem of how Moses is able to call himself "the most humble man on earth." Rabbi Hertz argues that in biblical times it was not unusual for someone to call himself an "*anav*," or humble. He points to Psalms 10:17 and 22:27 for evidence of authors who refer to themselves in such a way. The same issue arises when we read, toward the very end of the Torah (Deuteronomy 34:10) that "Never again arose in Israel a prophet like Moses."[2]

For those who believe that God handed Moses the entire Torah, all five books as one complete unit in the exact form in which we have it today, this is no problem. They can simply reply by saying that Moses was merely the "scribe" who wrote at God's command, and had no editorial participation.

Those who accept the Documentary Theory, on the other hand, have little difficulty explaining that a Redactor (editor, or in Franz Rosenzweig's phrase, the "R" contributor to the Torah, or the "Rebbe") skillfully weaved together various documents that ultimately became part of the Torah. In accomplishing the task of editing, the Redactor felt no qualms in making editorial comments about matters discussed in the Torah. Such comments give the Torah a clarity and smoothness without which the several authors and strands would appear disjointed and uncertain in meaning.

That said, how do we understand the unusual construction "*Ha'Ish Moshe*" — "The man Moses"? Rarely does the Torah refer to Moses as "the man Moses." The same expression is used in Exodus 11:3, where Moses appears great in the eyes of the Egyptians, but not necessarily in his own eyes. In English we might have a parallel in the phrase "This guy Moses," used when we may want to emphasize something special about someone. Another possibility is that the Torah wants to emphasize that while Moses was a most humble person, he was still an "*ish*" — a mortal, a human being, just a man like all other men.

Finally, if this phrase were written in a modern English text, it would be placed in parentheses, since it is clearly an editorial gloss placed here to explain why Moses does not respond to the charge of Aaron and Miriam. But why does Moses find no need or reason to defend himself? Ibn Ezra states that it is unthinkable to accuse Moses of placing himself over other prophets. The Midrash (*Sifrei Bemidbar* 100) points out that Moses paid no attention to the slander and gossip of his siblings, though God took up the cause of his servant. Likewise, the Natziv notes that God is not defending Moses because Moses asked him to, or because Moses felt the sting of the insult. Moses himself felt no pain; it was God's decision not to let Aaron and Miriam defame the great Prophet. This further emphasizes Moses' humility.

What is the Meaning of the Hebrew Word "Anav"?

Previous Christian translations, including the most prominent King James Version (KJV) and the modern Revised Standard Version (RSV), as well as the 1916 Jewish Publication Society version (JPS), render the Hebrew "anav" as "meek." The 1962 Jewish translation (NJV) is closer to the original Hebrew, with "humble."

While our verse is the only one in the Bible that uses the word "anav" in the singular, it does appear in the plural elsewhere (for example, Zephaniah 2:3). The clearest and easiest way to determine the meaning of a Hebrew word in the Bible is to find a place in which it appears in a poetic verse with a parallel verse following. In Psalm 22:27 we find this parallel construction: "Let the anavim eat and be satisfied / Let all who seek Adonai praise God." In this couplet the word "anavim" is parallel, and therefore synonymous with (at least similar to) those "who seek Adonai." Its connotation is thus of one who is devout and trusting of God, not smug and arrogant; aware of one's limitations and of God's awesome power.[3]

Yeshayahu Leibowitz makes this interesting observation about our verse:

> Nowhere does the Torah state explicitly that Moses was wiser, or more righteous, or heroic, than any man, although we can deduce from the events that he was wise, with great insight, and that he was righteous and heroic. But the Torah finds it proper, or necessary, to stress only one thing: that he was more humble than any other man.... In which way was Moses 'humble'? He was the man who attained the highest comprehension of God that man is able to attain. One might then imagine that for a person who had reached that high a level, it would be psychologically impossible not to be conscious of his superiority. We even find one of the great prophets in Israel, many centuries after Moses, warning—at God's command—that no man should boast of his wisdom, his might or his wealth, but explicitly allowing a man 'to boast of this, that he understands and knows Me, that I am God' (Jere-

miah 9:22). Yet Moses attained a comprehension of God that was superior to that of any of the prophets. The Talmud states in Tractate Yevamot: 'All the prophets looked [on God] through a murky glass; our master Moses looked [on God] through a clear glass.'[4]

Leibowitz then concludes that it was Moses' ability to realize that humans can never completely understand God — "that God is beyond human comprehension" — which made him the prophet with the truest and deepest humility.

It is clear, then, that the Hebrew *anav* does not mean "meek." Nowhere in the Torah's description of Moses do we find him acting meekly. Even when God calls him to become a prophet, and he expresses reluctance, humility, and reservations, still he answers *"Hineni,"* "Here I am" (Exodus 3:4). As the Torah depicts the leadership of Moses, facing both Pharaoh and the Israelite People, the prophet shows himself to be assertive, strong, confrontational and even argumentative with God. He does not court popularity or avoid danger. He is a true leader and prophet; humble, but not meek.

Another modern scholar, Rabbi Zvi Yehuda, makes an interesting comment on the concept of humility: "The '*anav*' is modest, not meek; humble, not timid, a person who does not lack in self-esteem, but neither lusts for self-glorification. Being confident and assertive, not shy or diffident, the '*anav*' is a person without arrogance; well aware of his worth and virtues, he has no need to boast."[5] Rabbi Yehuda then quotes from Pirke Avot (Ethics of the Fathers) 2:9: "If you have learned much Torah, do not pride yourself; for this purpose you have been created."[6]

What Embellishments Did the Midrash Offer on the Humility of Moses?

The rabbis of the Midrash offer many comments and stories to illustrate the humility of Moses, mostly from their imaginative capacity to read between the lines of biblical stories. We shall bring just two examples here.

In the first of the two midrashim we will quote, we find Moses descending Mt. Sinai, and Satan asks God: "Where is the Torah?" God replies: "Go ask the son of Amram (i.e., Moses)." Satan asks Moses: "Where is the Torah which the Blessed Holy One gave you?" Moses replies: "Who am I that the Blessed Holy One should entrust to me such a sacred book filled with important secrets?" Whereupon God turns to Moses and calls him a liar. Moses replies to God: "Master of the Universe, You have a precious treasure filled with holy secrets in which You take great pleasure every day. Shall I take credit for it?" The Holy Blessed One replies to Moses: "Since you minimized your own role in writing the Torah, it will forever be called by your name." Thus it is written (Malachi 3:22) "Remember the Torah of Moses My servant" (Talmud, *Shabbat* 89a).

In another Midrash we find Moses confronted by the five daughters of Zelophehad (Numbers 27). Perplexed by the question of female inheritance in a case where a man died and had no sons to inherit his land, Moses turns to God for advice. The Midrash then embellishes the Torah story by putting this thought into the mouth of Moses: "If I were to answer them directly, without consulting God, I would diminish their pride." (The daughters would presumably be much more honored to think of the decision in their favor as a divine one). Thus, Moses turns to God for advice, and by doing so admits that there is a greater Judge than he. Both before the daughters of Zelophehad and before God, Moses evinced deep humility (Midrash *Tanhuma*, *Pinchas* 9).

How Do Hasidic and Other More Recent Masters Interpret the Phrase "Humble"?

Rabbi Aharon Yaakov Greenberg brings several interpretations from Hasidic and other pietistic literature, from which we shall quote three. Among teachers for whom piety was such a high priority, humility was naturally a very highly prized trait. Thus the following comments on this verse are of special interest.

Rabbi Moses of Kobrin focuses on the phrase "[*Now the man Moses was very meek, above all the men that were upon*] the face of the earth." Rabbi Moses points out, as Rabbi Zvi Yehuda did above, that humility does not consist of being obsequious and turning one's head down to the earth, and yet having an arrogant thought about being superior to others. Moses recognized the need to be the leader of B'nai Yisrael, and even in this position of strength and assertiveness was more humble than those who keep their heads bowed down toward the earth (i.e., more than all the humble people whose faces were turned toward "the face of the earth").

Second, Greenberg notes that the founder of Hasidism, the Baal Shem Tov, was known to teach that real humility is not what a person displays on the outside, but rather that which is felt in the heart. The story is then told of a king who insisted on walking behind his empty carriage. He was reprimanded for trying to appear humble by publicizing his action. A truly humble person would have ridden in the carriage and still have been able to remain humble.

Third, a comment from Rabbi Israel Salanter, founder of the nineteenth century Mussar (Ethics) Movement in Lithuania, who points out that this praise of Moses' humility is enunciated (by God) at the height of Moses' powers, not at the end of his life. In the case of another person, such praise might have made the person into a conceited individual. Moses, however, remained humble until his death, many years after it was said about him by God that he was the most humble person on earth. Rabbi Salanter notes that such an accomplishment made Moses able to reach a level of humility unattainable by anyone else in the world.[7]

Notes

[1] Hertz 618.

[2] Ibid.

[3] Robert Alter, *The Art of Biblical Poetry* (New York: Basic Books, 1985) 3ff.

[4] Yeshayahu Leibowitz in *The Jerusalem Report*, 2 June 1994: 56.

[5] Rabbi Zvi Yehuda in *Cleveland Jewish News*, 12 June 1987: 42.

[6] Ibid.

[7] Greenberg III, 53-56. For an interesting scholarly study on this subject see Rabbi Sol Roth, "Towards A Definition of Humility," *Tradition* Spring-Summer 1973: 5-21. Cf. also Rabbi Mordecai M. Kaplan, *The Future of the American Jew* (New York: Macmillan Co., 1948) 274-283.

29

Numbers 20:12

במדבר כ,יב:

וַיֹּאמֶר ה' אֶל מֹשֶׁה וְאֶל אַהֲרֹן יַעַן לֹא הֶאֱמַנְתֶּם בִּי
לְהַקְדִּישֵׁנִי לְעֵינֵי בְּנֵי יִשְׂרָאֵל לָכֵן לֹא תָבִיאוּ
אֶת הַקָּהָל הַזֶּה אֶל הָאָרֶץ אֲשֶׁר נָתַתִּי לָהֶם.

*JPS (1916) — "And the LORD said unto Moses and Aaron:
'Because ye believed not in Me, to sanctify Me in the eyes of
the children of Israel, therefore ye shall not bring this assembly into the land which I have given them.'"*

*NJV (1962) — "But the LORD said to Moses and Aaron,
'Because you did not trust me enough to affirm My sanctity
in the sight of the Israelite people, therefore you shall not
lead this congregation into the land that I have given them.'"*

The sin of Moses, which caused God to deny to him (and
Aaron) the privilege of entering the Promised Land, is one of the
most confusing episodes in the entire Torah. It is a subject that
has occupied scholars and commentators in countless writings
from earliest times to the present, more than almost any other
biblical story. From the staunch traditional commentators to the
most modern and scientifically oriented authorities, there is a
candid admission of confusion and puzzlement.

Plaut, in words that gives voice to so many other commentaries, writes: "None of these explanations...satisfies the question of how a minor transgression committed in frustration and
justifiable anger would wipe out a life-time of merit and service.
Seen as an isolated incident, the punishment does not fit the
crime."[1] Nahmanides confesses similar confusion, but expresses
his inability to interpret the story in theological terms. In his

words: "The matter is a great secret of the mysteries of the Torah."

In lieu of our normal format, the best way to handle the diverse and confusing explanations for this verse, none of which is completely satisfactory, is merely to list them seriatim, with their pluses and minuses.[2]

Explanations Unrelated to the *Merivah* (Striking the Rock) Incident

Since the conventional explanations seem so unacceptable to commentators, some modern scholars (for example, Ehrlich and Gray) suggest that the real sin of Moses and Aaron was edited out of the Torah text to preserve their reputation. This is incompatible with the Torah's style of presenting the bad as well as the good qualities and deeds of the greatest heroes of the Bible. A cognate, but more traditional expression of such a view is expressed by Chief Rabbi Hertz who says that the Torah may have intentionally omitted the true reason for the punishment. Just as the grave of Moses will never be known, so too his uncharacteristic sin which caused him to be buried on the eastern side of the Jordan, will also never be known.[3]

The *Da'at Mikra* argues similarly that it was not the specific sin that the Torah wanted to convey, but rather the notion that even the greatest heroes of the Torah, Moses and Aaron, were merely human, and were capable of sin and punishment. The commentator (following Hertz) points to both Abraham and Job as individuals in the Bible who reached the highest levels of divine revelation, and yet, with it all, remained merely creatures of flesh and blood. In this view this is the important spiritual lesson of the episode.[4]

A related interpretation comes from the late Rabbi Morris Adler, prominent Conservative Rabbi of Detroit's Shaarey Zedek congregation, who suggests that the Torah is intentionally vague, and wants "to teach us by indirection, as it so often does, the great truth that the sins of leaders are not necessarily overt, blatant, obvious; that the important failings of great leaders could be subtle yet deep, unclear yet destructive." The sins of political leaders are that they cater to the crowd instead of standing on firm principles of justice. "So the Torah does not spell out the sins of the leader...but is purposely vague and uncertain. Maybe there was a moment of pride...of anger...a careless word.... Maybe he [Moses] failed to apply the wisdom of his mind to today and was satisfied with repetitions of insight taken from remote yesterdays." So is it with most leaders and most people. They don't commit the grand obvious crimes in the public eye, but rather "the subtle and intangible and impalpable corrosions" that block the gate to the Promised Land.[5]

Some midrashim suggest that the incident of striking the rock was the occasion for announcing the punishment of Moses and Aaron, but not the reason, which lies in previous actions of the brothers. Some of the suggestions include Aaron's behavior with the golden calf; Moses' involvement with the spies, or in killing the taskmaster in Egypt. There is simply no evidence of this, and the proximity of the *Merivah* incident is too obvious to ignore it.[6]

Explanations Related to the *Merivah* Incident

These interpretations are all based on some behavior perpetrated by Moses in dealing with the rebellion of the Israelite people. We are now in the 38th year since the Exodus. A new generation has been born, which is coming toward the end of the forty-year trek from Egyptian slavery to the Land of Israel. The people are hungry, thirsty, frustrated, and unaware of the horrors of life of their parents in Egypt—which they now imagine must have been better than their arduous desert life. Miriam has died, and her two brothers, harried and impatient, proceed to the Tent of Meeting to consult with God. They are instructed to speak to the rock, and then water will emerge. Moses and Aaron are old and tired, and Moses' temper is clearly short. Psalm 106:32-33 reminds us: "They (the Israelite nation) provoked wrath at the waters of *Merivah* and Moses suffered on their account, because they rebelled against God and Moses spoke angrily."

Most of the more popular commentaries, such as Rashi and Rashbam, and the weight of the many subsequent Jewish expositors who follow their line of thinking, take the text at face value and accuse Moses of striking the rock instead of speaking to it. Ramban wonders why it would make any difference whether Moses spoke to or struck the rock. It is the water coming from the rock that proves God's miraculous salvation. Since when are such instructions so inviolable that one must distinguish between speaking and striking? Furthermore, part of God's own instruction to Moses was to "take the rod" (verse 7). In most cases where the rod is used, using it to strike is either specified or implied (see, for example, Exodus 7:17, 20; 8:12; 17:5-6). Especially interesting is the parallel story (perhaps this incident is a retelling of it) in Exodus 17:5-7, in which Moses is commanded

"Take the rod.... Strike the rock and water will come forth from it." In sum, striking the rock just does not add up to the magnitude of a sin that would bring such severe consequences.

Rabbi Don Isaac ben Judah Abravanel argues that it would have been unfair for the generation of the wilderness, who sinned in the episode of the spies by agreeing with the ten who demoralized the people, to be denied entry into the Land, while Moses and Aaron were permitted, especially since it was Moses who dispatched the spies. Thus, when God found a reasonable justification, God declared that Moses and Aaron should be included in the prohibition. The flaw in this argument is that God could have included Moses and Aaron in the original punishment of the Wilderness Generation, since they were part of it. Why view God as waiting, and acting capriciously, seeking an "excuse" to even things out?

Ibn Ezra believes that the act of striking the rock twice instead of once was the rebellious act of Moses that failed to sanctify God by adherence to divine instructions. Alas, the great medieval sage brings no evidence from the text that this was a matter of import to God.

The idea does, however, make for a good midrashic text. The Hasidic Rabbi Yisrael of Rozhin uses the example of Moses as a paradigm for anger. Getting angry (striking the rock) once is normal, but not stopping the anger (striking the rock *twice*) is not forgivable. Rabbi Yisrael quotes the Talmud, which teaches that even God gets angry every day, but only for an instant ("God's anger is but an instant" — Psalm 30:6). It is important to know when and how to stop one's anger. Moses was punished not because he became angry, but because he lost control over his passions.

Maimonides points to a fatal flaw in the character of Moses, his volatile temper. Instead of dealing with the people, as a good parent, teacher or leader might, with patience and maturity, Moses lets go and screams at his flock, calling them names (*Hamorim*, which may mean either fools or rebels), insulting them and failing to sanctify God through the example of seasoned prophetic leadership. Flying into a blind rage and shattering the rock which will quench the people's thirst is hardly leadership behavior.[7]

Rabbi Samson Raphael Hirsch argues along the same lines. He conjectures that Moses was forced to pick up the rod, which had lain in the Sanctuary for almost 40 years, and was exceedingly disappointed to think that after four decades he still had not instilled confidence by the people in his leadership. In his bitter frustration he forgot the details of the divine command, screamed at the people, and in the heat of passion raised his hand and struck the rock.[8]

A third proponent of this theory is the great 17th century Hasidic master, Rabbi Levi Yitzhak of Berditchev, well known for his advocacy of the good nature of the average Jew. Levi Yitzchak sees God as being very disappointed at Moses for treating them with scorn and loss of temper. "There are two types of criticism," argues Reb Levi Yitzchak. "One makes use of kind, understanding words, uplifting others by reminding them that they are created in God's image and that their good deeds bring God much pleasure.... When criticism is then given, it does not tear a person down but strengthens the will of the person to accept and fulfill the commandments of Torah." Moses and Aaron are guilty of using the second kind of criticism, which is harsh, demeans people, lowers their self-esteem, and uses shame as a tool to accomplish God's will.[9]

It is Nahmanides, however, who refutes the words of Maimonides. A careful reading of the text shows that God condemns Moses because "You did not trust Me...You disobeyed My command" (20:12, 24). There is no reference in God's charge to Moses' anger, only his disobedience. Furthermore, in the case of the *Merivah* incident Moses is angry at the people of Israel. On other occasions Moses gets angry even at God and does not receive any punishment (see Numbers 11:11-22).

In refuting Maimonides' argument that it was Moses' temper that was his sin, Nahmanides substitutes his own logic. He claims that it was Moses and Aaron's doubt of God that constituted their sin. In verse 10, Moses asks the people, "Shall we get water for you from this rock?" He might rather have said "Shall God bring water for you from this rock?" Instead, by couching their challenge in these words, Moses and Aaron display a lack of trust in God, and also take credit for themselves instead of attributing the miracle to God. Thus they "failed to sanctify God in the eyes of Israel."[10]

Prof. Jacob Milgrom elaborates on this argument. He looks at the religious context of ancient Israel, and sees Moses as rebelling against God differently. Citing several medieval and modern sources, Milgrom concludes that one of the primary tasks of Moses was to wean the people away from idolatrous Egyptian notions of the gods, and teach them to accept Adonai as the one God. In ancient Egypt magicians and miracle workers performed their divine magic with verbal commands, while with a monotheistic God such acts were done in silence. Moses not only announced in advance that he would perform a miracle, but took full credit for it for himself.[11] Says Milgrom, "The ideal prophet in Israel, as exemplified by Moses, was constrained to speechlessness during the performance of a miracle, a practice that contrasted sharply — deliberately so — with the wonder-workers of other nations."[12] The flaw in Milgrom's argument, however, is that it is based on a reading of the text which claims that God commanded Moses to speak *at* (a valid use of Hebrew *el* in other biblical citations) the rock, and not *to* the rock, and it is difficult to read Numbers 20:8 in this way.

The late Rabbi Pinchas Peli, former professor of Bible at Ben Gurion University of Beer-Sheva, Israel, makes the case that Aaron was punished along with his brother because he did nothing to stop Moses, in his anger, from acting out of pique instead of common sense. The passive stance of the spectator brings the guilt of the accomplice.[13]

After analyzing many possible interpretations, the obvious one still seems cogent. Dr. Julius H. Greenstone, late professor of Bible at Gratz College, Philadelphia, summarizes the explanation this way: "A large rock or hill may have springs of water within it, which, however, may be clogged by stones or earth. If Moses had spoken to the rock, as he was ordered to do, and the water had come forth, the miracle would have been quite patent and the name of God would have been sanctified thereby. In obtaining water by striking the rock, Moses failed to sanctify the name of God, because the people might say that there was nothing miraculous about it, as the obstruction was removed when the rock was struck and the water came forth in a natural way."[14]

Rabbi Shmuel David Luzzatto insists that we must return to the simple explanation accepted by every initiate in Bible study: that Moses is punished because he hit the rock instead of speaking to it. In Luzzatto's words: "Moses our teacher committed one sin, but our teachers through the ages have piled upon him thirteen or more, each scholar having invented a fresh one.... I have therefore refrained from delving further into the problem for fear of attributing to Moses a new sin!"

Notes

[1] Plaut 1155.

[2] The student who wishes to delve more deeply into the sources for the list of possible interpretations itemized below can turn to several excellent summaries. First is Plaut's brief discussion in *The Torah* ("The Sin" 1155-6). Another modern summation of the problem and some potential solutions can be found in Fields III, 60-64. Schreiber (*The Stone Chumash*) 844-5 also provides a brief, detailed list of explanations by

traditional Jewish commentators. A much more comprehensive discussion is found in Excursus 50 in Milgrom 448-456.

3 Hertz 657.

4 *Da'at Mikra* IV, 229ff.

5 Morris Adler, *The Voice Still Speaks* (New York: Bloch Publishers, 1996) 341-5.

6 cf. Plaut 1155.

7 Maimonides, *Shemonah Perakim: Hakdamah le'Avot* (Introduction to Pirke Avot) 4.

8 Hirsch IV, 368-9.

9 David Blumenthal, *God at the Center: Meditations on Jewish Spirituality* (San Francisco: Harper & Row, 1988) 118-119.

10 Nahmanides: Commentary on Numbers 20:10.

11 Milgrom 456.

12 Ibid.

13 Peli 179.

14 Julius H. Greenstone, *Numbers with Commentary* (Philadelpia: Jewish Publication Society of America, 1939) 213-214.

30

Numbers 23:9b

במדבר כג,ט:

הֶן עָם לְבָדָד יִשְׁכֹּן וּבַגּוֹיִם לֹא יִתְחַשָּׁב.

JPS (1916) – *"Lo, it is a people that shall dwell alone,*
And shall not be reckoned among the nations."

NJV (1962) – *"There is a people that dwells apart,*
Not reckoned among the nations,"

During the final years of the Israelites' wandering in the desert they passed through the territory of Moab (part of the present Kingdom of Jordan) on the east bank of the Jordan River. Balak, King of Moab, has heard of the military strength and skill of the Israelites, and fearing their power, calls upon a Mesopotamian prophet (magician-sorcerer), Balaam, to curse the Israelite people. Being (or becoming) a true prophet of God, Balaam finds that he cannot curse those whom God blesses, and he ends by heaping upon Israel one of the most beautiful paeans of praise found anywhere in world literature. What a great irony that this prophet, commissioned by Israel's enemy, eventually comes to write a song of praise now used as the introduction to Jewish worship services ("How beautiful are your tents, People of Jacob, Your dwelling places, descendants of Israel!"). Our verse comes from the first of three poems of prophetic praise Balaam utters upon Israel.

What Is The Meaning of the Phrase "Shall Dwell Alone"?

Rashi sees the word "alone" as a special compliment, stating that it is because they follow the traditions of their ancestors that they remain separate and apart from other peoples. Rabbi Hertz finds two separate definitions for a people who is "alone," or "distinct." First, they are isolated and distinguished by their religious and moral laws, and second, they are chosen as an instrument of a Divine purpose.[1]

Jacob Milgrom points out that the Hebrew *badad* (alone) is attributed to God (Deuteronomy 32:12). In several other passages in the Tanakh the same phrase is also attributed to the Israelite people (Deuteronomy 33:28, Jeremiah 49:31 and Psalms 4:9).[2] In all these cases, involving both God and Israel, the phrase *badad* is parallel to and synonymous with *secure*. Balaam is clearly giving Israel a compliment and is uttering an expression of high praise. From these parallel verses it seems clear that Balaam's intent was to praise Israel's strength and ability to be secure and safe. However, as we shall see below, medieval commentators stressed the "aloneness" and "separateness" of Israel, maintaining their own separate identity even while living as a minority among gentiles in the Diaspora.[3]

In Midrash *Shemot Rabbah* 15:7 we find a fanciful, yet serious, interpretation based on the first Hebrew word of this phrase, "*hen*." The 1916 JPS translation renders this word "Lo, it is...." The NJV says "There is...." Hebrew *hen* is similar to *ken*, meaning "thus," or "so it is," similar to modern Hebrew "yes," or "indeed it is." The Midrash, however, for its own clever and imaginative purposes, uses the word to corroborate the balance of the verse regarding Israel's uniqueness. First it claims that in Greek the word "*hen*" means one (special, unique). Second it uses some clever numerology to prove the uniqueness of the two Hebrew letters that make up the Hebrew *hen*, "*heh*" and "*nun*." Both are middle numbers in the decimal system. In Hebrew numerology, *gematria*, *heh* is five and *nun* is fifty. In their own ten-group each of these letters is the only one without a partner. In other words, counting from one to ten each letter has a partner, except five: 1+9=10. 2+8=10. 3+7=10. 4+6=10. Only five, or *heh*, stands alone. The same with *nun* (which equals 50 in *gematria*). 10+90=100. 20+80=100. 30+70=100. 40+60=100. Only 50 (*nun*) stands alone. Concludes the Midrash: "Said the Blessed Holy One: Just as these two Hebrew letters do not mix with other letters, thus Israel does not assimilate with the nations of the world."

Another clever play on words is discovered by the Natziv. When the Jewish People are apart (*levadad*), separate, and do not intermingle and assimilate with the surrounding peoples in the Diaspora communities among whom they live, they will then dwell (*yishkon*) in peace and in honor. However, if they want to assimilate and mix with the nations (*uvagoyim*), then they will not be considered—i.e., they will not be thought of by other nations as worthy of being given any consideration or honor. In short, he translates the verse as follows: "Yes, when the people are alone (separate), they will dwell; but when they are among the nations, they will not be considered."

Hertz's Commentary On This Verse

Rabbi Hertz's explanation of 23:9b is an interesting example of how a commentary is used for the commentator's own purposes. The verse states that the people of Israel "shall not be reckoned among the nations." The Hebrew verb *hashav*, in the reflexive (*hitpa'el*) form of the verb, appears only here in the entire Tanakh. This unique appearance of the verb in the reflexive opens the door for Rabbi Hertz to find a new interpretation in place of the traditional translation "shall not be reckoned." He finds a rendering that means "to conspire."[4] The translation Hertz gives is thus that Israel does not conspire against the nations. He supports this translation by the logic of the context, namely, that if Israel is not a belligerent, war-prone people, why should the prophet Balaam curse them? The translation fits nicely.

From the studies of Prof. Harvey Meirovitch of Jerusalem, we know that Hertz's commentary is usually directed polemically in refutation of the attacks against the Bible and the Jewish People by nineteenth and early twentieth century German Christian commentators who wish to detract from its uniqueness and find fault with the Jewish People and its claim to Scriptural authority. Among the popular charges against Jews by nineteenth century critics was the claim that they considered themselves superior to other nations, as God's "chosen people." By using Jastrow's translation, Rabbi Hertz is able to refute this charge. The Jews, say both Balaam and Jastrow, do not, in fact, conspire against other nations.

Some Other Explanations of the Phrase "Not Reckoned Among the Nations"/The Chosen People

Rashi explains (following other ancient translations such as Targum Yonatan) that the Israelite nation will not be exterminated along with the other nations. Rashi quotes Jeremiah (30:11), for example, to prove his point: "I will make an end of all the nations among whom I have scattered you; but I will not make an end of you." Thus, says Rashi, the verse means that the nation of Israel will not be reckoned (punished) in the same fashion that the other nations will. They will, instead, thrive and prosper.

Nahmanides interprets Balaam's blessing that Israel will not be like the other nations to mean that just as the Jewish People is now living separately, so will they continue to live in safety and will never become assimilated into the other nations among whom they may dwell.

Rabbi Samson Raphael Hirsch explains that Israel will not have much intercourse with other nations, but will be more concerned with its own internal mission as a people appointed by God to be a light unto the nations. Its personal mission of ethical monotheism will steer it away from competition with other nations, and as a people it will not be interested in impressing other nations with its national power.[5]

Rabbi Gunther Plaut takes up the subject of Jewish distinctiveness in his comments on our verse. Plaut points out that while setting Jews apart has historically led to anti-Semitism, ghettoization, disenfranchisement, and ultimately the Holocaust, it has also brought a unified mission of commitment to God and Torah, and the attempt to hasten the reign of God on earth. Balaam's prophecy, says Rabbi Plaut, has become Jewish doctrine. Separateness has become the vehicle through which Jews have maintained their identity and pursued their dream of a better world.[6] He writes:

> The Jew will be what he was. For his anchor-point is the awesome, hidden Other One who Himself dwells alone. Aloneness is the existential burden of the Jew. He is, as tradition and meaning convey, *kadosh*, holy and separate at once. . . Separateness is the yoke of the Jew. It demands a heavy price; it demands it of all and of each. It tears the soul with longing for the embracing friendship of the nations, and it drives us back to the lonely post of waiting. It aims its beam into the heart of every Jew, searing some and illuminating others. Our psyche is burned by desire and rejection, by forgetting and remembering, by openness and withdrawal.[7]

The Talmud On Israel's Relationship With Other Nations

In one passage in the Talmud (*Sanhedrin* 39a-b), a heretic comes to challenge the notion that the people of Israel is special and different. He quotes the Bible: "Who is like Your people, Israel, a unique nation in the land?" (II Samuel 7:23). Continues the heretic, your prophet Isaiah (40:17) says that "*All* the nations are as nothing before God" (meaning that all nations are equal — in this case equally evil — before God). Rabbi Avina answered the challenge: A gentile, one of your own [Balaam], testified to the contrary; i.e., that the Israelite people *is* different. Balaam, the Mesopotamian prophet, said: "Among the nations Israel shall not be reckoned."

From Balaam's blessing that the Israelite People will remain differentiated from the other nations of the world, we can infer his intended curse; namely, that Israel would become assimilated among the nations and end up without a religious identity of their own (compare Talmud, *Sanhedrin* 105b).

Notes

[1] Hertz 674.
[2] Milgrom 197.
[3] See Menahem Haran, *Olam HaTanakh* (Tel Aviv: Davidzon-Iti, 1993) III, 145.
[4] Marcus Jastrow, *Talmudic Dictionary*, quoted by Hertz 674.
[5] Hirsch IV, 407.
[6] Plaut 1183.
[7] Gunther W. Plaut, *The Case for the Chosen People* (Garden City: Doubleday, 1965) 150.

31

Numbers 25:11-12

במדבר כה,יא-יב:

פִּינְחָס בֶּן אֶלְעָזָר בֶּן אַהֲרֹן הַכֹּהֵן הֵשִׁיב אֶת חֲמָתִי מֵעַל
בְּנֵי יִשְׂרָאֵל בְּקַנְאוֹ אֶת קִנְאָתִי בְּתוֹכָם: וְלֹא כִלִּיתִי אֶת
בְּנֵי יִשְׂרָאֵל בְּקִנְאָתִי לָכֵן אֱמֹר הִנְנִי נוֹתֵן לוֹ
אֶת בְּרִיתִי שָׁלוֹם.

JPS (1916) – "'*Phinehas, the son of Eleazar, the son of Aaron the priest, hath turned My wrath away from the children of Israel, in that he was very jealous for My sake among them, so that I consumed not the children of Israel in My jealousy. Wherefore say: Behold, I give unto him My covenant of peace;....'*"

NJV (1962) – "'*Phinehas, son of Eleazar son of Aaron the priest, has turned back My wrath from the Israelites by displaying among them his passion for Me, so that I did not wipe out the Israelite people in My passion. Say, therefore, 'I grant him My pact of friendship....'*'"

Close to the time when Israel would enter the Promised Land, they continue to be unfaithful to Adonai. Many Israelite men are enticed by Moabite harlots to commit idolatrous worship of Baal Peor, involving immoral and licentious acts on the pagan altar. God's wrath is kindled and thus God commands that the Israelite leaders be condemned to death. The episode of "The Sin of *Baal-Peor*" culminates in a flagrant act of betrayal of God when a prince of the Israelite tribe of Simeon, Zimri ben Salu, brought a Midianite woman, Cozbi bat Tzur, the daughter of a royal Midianite family (the Midianites were close allies of the Moabites), in front of the mourning Israelite camp and in front of

Moses himself, and engaged in further immoral sexual acts. To put an end to the divinely caused plague which had already decimated 24,000 Israelites, Phinehas leaps forward and thrusts Zimri and Cozbi with his sword, putting an end to their lives, and to the ravaging plague which was taking countless Israelite lives.

The Hasidic master Rabbi Yitzhak Vorker (Poland, 1779-1848) pays special attention to the fact that even though Phinehas distinguished himself from the more passive leaders of the people through his zealous act, he nevertheless remained one of them (*betokham*). The *Stone Chumash* adds to this the comment that even zealots must be a part of their people and act "out of love rather than anger and hatred."[1] Perhaps a good definition of a praiseworthy zealot, as opposed to a fanatic, is one who is absent of hatred and anger.

What Is The Meaning Of The Biblical Term *kin'ah*?

The act of Phinehas was, in the Torah's words, *bekane'o et kinati* (v. 11). The JPS versions translate "was jealous for My sake" and "displaying...his passion for Me." Milgrom translates literally "in his becoming impassioned with My passion."[2] The Hebrew verb *kana* connotes jealousy, zealousness, vengeance, and passion — all connected to an intense feeling and action to protect the welfare and/or reputation of a cause, ideology, or deity. (Its etymology is from a more ancient Semitic word meaning to "become very red," referring to an angry face). The Hebrew expression "*El Kana*," a jealous God, is used in the Torah exclusively in connection with acts of idolatry.

As we will see below, later biblical interpreters had mixed feelings toward the impassioned zeal of Phinehas. From the Torah itself, however, there is little doubt that what Phinehas did was praiseworthy and necessary. The question is whether the reward Phinehas received (*briti shalom*) was for slaying the offending couple, or for saving thousands of Israelite lives. It is more likely the latter, and thus in the Torah's view the reward is clearly deserved.

As Milgrom points out, Phinehas was Chief of the Tabernacle Guards, and it was his duty to protect the purity of the Mishkan (portable Tabernacle). Numbers 25:13 clearly points out that through his daring act Phinehas "made atonement" for the Israelites.[3] This brought an end to the plague that God brought to punish the people for their idolatrous orgy. Earlier in the Book of Numbers we find that part of the task of the *kohanim* was to serve the Tent of Meeting (used interchangeably with Mishkan, Tabernacle) and "to make expiation for the Israelites so that no plague may afflict them" for violating the Sanctuary and its official rules.

As Rabbi Gunther Plaut correctly notes, "we must remember that the Moabite fertility cult was to the Israelites the incarnation of evil and the mortal enemy of their religion. At a crucial moment in its formative history, Israel's very purpose and existence were challenged. The strict moral code of a new nation was put to its first public test."[4]

Some commentators see in Phinehas' action a rebuke of Moses who should have risen immediately to the challenge of the Sinai Covenant he himself brought to them. Moses is now close to death, and perhaps has lost some of the youthful zeal that prompted him to kill an Egyptian taskmaster in a similar fit of passionate idealism (Exodus 2:12).[5] In Midrash *Bamidbar Rabbah* (20:24) we find that Moses was punished for his lack of zeal by not letting anyone know the site of his grave, to pay him proper honor. In the absence of other official leadership, Phinehas could prove himself and earn his right to dynastic priesthood.

What Other Biblical Events Are Reminiscent Of The Incident of *Baal-Peor*?

Milgrom notes that the idolatry and expiation at *Baal-Peor* resembles the incident of the Golden Calf (Exodus 32) in that both involve worship of other gods and appeasing God's anger by the slaughter of the perpetrators. Further, the heroes of the two stories are both rewarded with promises of sacred service in the Sanctuary. The Levites' election to divine service followed the Golden Calf story, as does that of Phinehas' election to permanent priestly duty.[6] A similar incident of rebellion is that of the Twelve Spies, in which, again, two individuals (Caleb and Joshua) distinguish themselves for loyalty, opposing the majority and acting on behalf of God (Numbers 14:6-10). The rest of the people are punished while the two heroes are rewarded with entry into the Promised Land.

Since the incident at *Baal-Peor* is so similar in content to the stories of the Golden Calf and the Twelve Spies, it would seem that the action of Phinehas should not be singled out for special condemnation. Yet, because in this case alone the punishment comes at the hand of a human, rather than God, some later commentators felt justified in criticizing Phinehas.

In a later biblical period the prophet Elijah also states his passionate defense of God in terms similar to those of Phinehas: "I am passionately zealous (*kano kinayti*) for Adonai, the God of hosts...." (I Kings 19:14). Elijah is also associated in Jewish tradition with being the harbinger of the Messiah, who will usher in the era of *shalom*. Rabbinic tradition, interestingly, identifies Phinehas as the very same person who was later reincarnated as Elijah.

What Is The Nature Of The Reward Bestowed Upon Phinehas?

The Torah tells us that Phinehas, for his act of brave passion to expiate the sin of the

Baal-Peor, received God's *brit shalom*. Avraham ibn Ezra, who was not only a Bible commentator but also a Hebrew grammarian, explains this unusual Hebrew grammatical construction (*briti shalom*) as an elliptical form of *briti, brit shalom*, "My covenant, the covenant of peace." The same form is found in Leviticus 26:42, *briti Yaakov...briti Yitzhak...briti Avraham*—"My pact with Jacob...my pact with Isaac...my pact with Abraham."

Rashi writes that the meaning of the *brit shalom* is that Phinehas will now be assured of a friendly attitude by God, even in the face of initial public criticism by the people for killing a prince of Israel. Rashi further explains (based on the Talmud, *Zevahim* 101b) that it was because of this incident, in killing Zimri, that Phinehas attained the status of priesthood.[7] Even though we read in the Torah (Exodus 28:40-41 and Leviticus 8-10) that Aaron's sons were also made kohanim and consecrated with him, including their sons after them, Phinehas had already been born and was thus not a beneficiary of this consecration. Thus the priesthood of Phinehas began at this moment as his reward for his zealotry for God.[8] The rabbis' forced logic is necessitated by verse 13, which seems to make the "everlasting priesthood" the reward of Phinehas, even though this does not match the previous Torah accounts of the consecration of Aaron's descendants.

Later biblical passages show that it was the through the line of Phinehas that high priests were descended (I Chronicles 5:30-40, 6:34-38). Even though the evidence shows that it was the descendants of Phinehas who served in the priesthood, Jacob Milgrom believes that the promise (*brit*) to Phinehas was for *all* descendants of Aaron. He deduces this from the prophet Malachi (2:4-7; 3:3) where mention is made of God's covenant with Levi (connoting *all* the descendants of Aaron). Malachi, the last of the prophets of the Hebrew Bible, is presumed to have lived in the fifth century, during the period of the second temple. Several centuries after Phinehas, his descendant Zadok became the parent of the Zadokite line of priests to whom the priesthood was confined (Ezra 7:1-6 and Ezekiel 40:45-46; 44:15-16). Thus Phinehas did become the ancestor of the main group of *kohanim* in the Temple service.[9]

Ibn Ezra argues that Phinehas' reward was that he was to be protected from the family of the slain Zimri, who were powerful princes capable of damaging revenge. The Netziv writes that the promise of God's Covenant was not the reward of Phinehas, but rather the cure for his over-zealousness, and a protection from the inevitable inner guilt and demoralization for killing a human being without due process of law.[10]

Milgrom lists five separate covenants granted by God in the Torah: the promise to Noah that the world will never again be destroyed by flood; the promise of land and progeny to Abraham; the covenant of the Torah with Moses and the Israelite people at Sinai; and with Phinehas and David who would be assured of a continuing dynasty of, respectively, the *kehunah* (priesthood) and the kingship.[11]

What Is The Attitude Of Later Generations Toward Phinehas?

By the time of the Psalmist, the *Baal-Peor* incident had enshrined Phinehas as a great biblical hero:

> They attached themselves to Baal-Peor and ate pagan sacrifices.
> They aroused (God's) anger by their actions, bringing on a plague.
> Phinehas stepped forward and intervened, and the plague ceased.
> It was counted to his merit for all eternity. (Psalm 106:28-31)

In the apocryphal (non-canonical) book I Maccabees we read of Mattathias, father of the five brave sons who comprised the Hasmonean family, heroes of the Festival of Hanukkah: "When a Jew came forward in the sight of all to offer a sacrifice on the pagan altar in Modin, Mattathias saw it and burned with zeal. He gave vent to righteous wrath, ran and killed the man on the altar. He also killed the (Hellenistic) officer who forced the pagan sacrifice and tore down the altar. He burned with zeal for the Torah, just as Phinehas did against Zimri ben Salu" (I Maccabees 2:23-26). Later, at the time of Mattathias' last days, he gave his children this charge: "My children, show zeal for the Torah, and sacrifice your lives for the covenant of our ancestors. Remember the deeds of our ancestors, such as Abraham, Joseph, and Phinehas, who was deeply zealous and thus received the covenant of everlasting priesthood" (I Maccabees 2:51-54).

Rabbinic authorities were not as kind to Phinehas. The two prominent third-century founders of the Babylonian academies at Sura and Nehardea, Rav and Shmuel, held opposing views on most issues, including the nature of Phinehas' action. Rav condemns Phinehas, claiming that he should have left judgment to God. While recognizing Phinehas' action as legal, he faults him for taking matters into his own hands.[12]

We read in the Jerusalem Talmud of Rabbi Yuda bar Pazzi who says that just as the court and community were ready to condemn and excommunicate Phinehas, God intervened and declared Phinehas' action praiseworthy, declaring him to be the recipient of the *brit shalom*. This sage would have preferred to see Phinehas go through proper legal process instead of taking the law into his own hands (Jerusalem Talmud, *Sanhedrin* 9:7). Samuel, on the other hand, glorifies the action of Phinehas, seeing in him a model of the opponent of idolatry and lascivious violations of God's commands.

Maimonides writes in his Code of Jewish Law (*Mishneh Torah*: Laws of Illicit Relations 124-5) that a zealous Jew may kill one caught in the act of sexual intercourse with a prostitute, giving Phinehas as his example. Short of catching the culprit in the act, there may not be such harsh punishment. Jewish law provides for the necessity of warnings to potential offenders before stern punishment is exacted. Most reasonable authorities note that even when a severe punishment is legal, it is not always considered expedient or reasonable.[13]

Another interesting point of view is offered by Rabbi Moshe ben Hayim Alshekh who writes that Phinehas was acting in a self-aggrandizing way, promoting his own claim to priesthood. His action had ulterior motives, and was not based totally on pure zealotry on God's behalf (commentary on Numbers 25:1).

A positive, yet cautionary view of Phinehas' actions is taken by Rabbi Y. L. Maimon, who distinguishes between one who holds passionate views of his own (i.e. "fire in his belly") regarding some evil committed, and one who is fired up by others — even his rabbi. A true zealot, he explains, does not wait to be led on by some other firebrand. He has the ethical fire in his own soul. Thus, he concludes, most significantly, if one *asks* whether it is permissible to commit an act such as that of Phinehas, he should be told not to do so. Such a question would, apparently, put the person in a different category from Phinehas, who acted in the heat of passion. While Maimon's caution in not granting permission to others to act as Phinehas did is commendable, the suggestion that an act of rash and passionate zeal without consulting carries its own dangers.[14]

An eighteenth century Torah commentator named Rabbi Meir Ashkenazi of Eisenstadt, in his book, *Kosnot Or*, points out the irony that zeal is in fact the opposite of peace, and more often connotes disharmony rather than *shalom*. The Torah comes to teach us that *honest zeal* in the cause of a sacred goal often leads to *shalom*, to peace.

Notes

[1] Scherman 876-6.

[2] Milgrom 216.

[3] Ibid. 467-468.

[4] Plaut, *The Torah* 1195.

[5] See Milgrom 478, and Torye-kval, *Wellsprings of Torah: An Anthology of Biblical Commentaries* (New York: Judaica Press, 1969) II, 335.

[6] Milgrom 21 6, 478.

[7] Rashi: Commentary on Numbers 25:13.

[8] Ibid.

[9] Milgrom 216-217.

[10] *Torat Elohim: Hamisha Humshe Torah im Perush Ha-Amek Davar* (Jerusalem: Yeshivat Valozin, 1998) III, on Numbers 25:11-12.

[11] Milgrom 217.

[12] Fields III, 76-7.

[13] J. David Bleich, *Contemporary Halakhic Problems* (New York: Ktav, 1983) II, 273-4.

[14] quoted in Greenberg III, 133.

32

Deuteronomy 5:3

דברים ה,ג:

לֹא אָת אֲבוֹתֵינוּ כָּרַת ה' אָת הַבְּרִית הַזֹּאת כִּי אִתָּנוּ
אֲנַחְנוּ אֵלָה פֹה הַיּוֹם כֻּלָּנוּ חַיִּים.

JPS (1916) — "The LORD made not this covenant with our fathers, but with us, even us, who are all of us here alive this day."

NJV (1962) — "It was not with our fathers that the LORD made this covenant, but with us, the living, every one of us who is here today."

The Book of Deuteronomy, as its Greek name implies, is the repetition of the Torah, or the Law. In it Moses, during the last month of his life, delivers three long speeches reviewing the events of the forty years of wandering in the Sinai Desert. He sums up his life, God's teaching, and the historical events that led to the point of entry into the Promised Land. The covenant at Horeb (Sinai), to which this verse refers, is the mutually binding contract between God and Israel that the people would show loyalty through following God's Torah, and God would protect and care about the special people chosen to observe the Torah and carry forward its moral teachings. The embodiment of the covenant is the Ten Commandments, which follows our verse (5:6-18).

With Whom Was the Sinai Covenant Made, and Are Jews Today Free to Ignore It?

Nehama Leibowitz, treats this issue by examining the writings of one leading medieval commentator, Don Isaac ben Yehudah

Abravanel, who was a giant in his day in Portugal, Spain and Italy. Abravanel wrote his commentary after the expulsion from Spain in 1492, and his writings reflect the bitter experience of his own age. He makes the point that many in his generation tried to assimilate and accept forced Christianity, and even that did not save them. Their denial of the notion of covenantal obligation, i.e., that the Sinai Covenant was binding on them as it was meant to be for all future generations, did not save them from their murderers. Abravanel's discussion is extraordinarily contemporary, a point not lost by Nehama Leibowitz. Her comments, and her quotations from the Abravanel and other sources, are worth studying in full:[1]

WE WERE ALL AT SINAI

Neither with you only do I make this covenant and this oath; but with those who stand here with us this day before Adonai our God, and also with those who are not here with us this day [Deuteronomy 29:13-14]

The above verses confront us with a difficult question. How could a covenant contracted in those far-off days be capable of obligating all the generations to come? Abravanel tells us in his commentary to the Torah how he fought with the Sages of his generation in the kingdom of Aragon regarding this covenant and this text that we have quoted. Citing the sages of Aragon, Abravanel formulates the question as follows:

Who gave the generation of the wilderness which stood at the foot of Mt. Sinai the power of obligating all those who would arise after them to accept the implications of their statement "we shall do and hearken!" They bound them by all the words of the Torah and the covenant and the penalties for violating their contents, as we see from this text and wherever the Sages in the Talmud employ the phrase "but surely he is *a priori* bound by the Sinaitic revelation!?" This is surely not a legitimate obligation.[2]

Abravanel replies to this question by arguing that receipt of the Torah can be compared to the receipt of a loan. The obligation to repay the loan falls on the descendants of those who took the loan. Children must pay their parents' debts, even if they were not alive when the debt came into being.

In the same way, when God gave us the gift of the Torah, we became indebted to God to repay it. After all, was it not God who brought us out of Egyptian slavery? Do we owe God nothing for this precious gift of freedom? One can argue that God "owns" our bodies, for granting us this freedom, and by the same token,

God owns our souls. When God gave us the Torah, we achieved a certain spiritual perfection. This is the meaning of the Covenant.

When the people of Israel received the Torah, and entered into the Covenant, they promised God "We shall surely obey this Covenant" (Na'aseh venishma). This surely implies that we pledged to God to be God's children, God's servants, forever.

When we entered this first Covenant, we also entered another Covenant, somewhat later — that of receiving the Land of Israel (Eretz Yisael). Receiving the Land meant that we were God's permanent tenants, as the Torah tells us, (Leviticus 25:22): "and the land shall not be sold in perpetuity, for the land is Mine." Receiving the Torah and the Land bound our People to God in a permanent way.

Abravanel continues: "To this our Sages certainly referred in the Midrash Tanhuma...when they stated that the souls of the whole nation were present at the time of the covenant, since the covenant included all those destined to be born in the future generations."[3]

Abravanel's view is buttressed by Yehudah HaLevi who points out that the Ten Commandments begin not with a description of God who created heaven and earth, but rather with the statement, "I am the Lord thy God Who brought you out of the land of Egypt from the house of bondage."[4]

Leibowitz further argues that there is even more proof in our tradition that the Covenant with God at Sinai is permanent, as she quotes the Midrash on two verses in Ezekiel, 20:32-33: "And that which comes into your mind shall not be at all; in that you say: We will be as the nations, as the families of the countries, to serve wood and stone. As I live, says the Lord God, surely with a mighty hand, and with an outstretched arm, and with fury poured out, will I be Ruler over you."[5]

On this verse in Ezekiel, the Midrash Tanhuma comments:

And so you find that when Israel sought to free itself from the yoke of its oath in the days of Ezekiel — what is stated there (Ezekiel 20:1)? There came men of the elders of Israel to seek Adonai. They said to him, If a priest purchases a slave, may the latter partake of terumah? He replied, He may. Thereupon they asked, If the priest sold him back again to an Israelite, has he thenceforth left the priest's domain? He said to them, He has. Thereupon they said, So it is with us; we have already left God's domain and we shall be like the heathen nations. Ezekiel replied to them: "And that which comes into your mind shall not be at all: in that you say: we will be as the nations, as the families of the countries...as I live, says the Lord God, surely with a mighty hand and with an outstretched arm, and with fury poured out, will I be Ruler over you," for you are still under oath to serve Me. For this reason it is stated "that God may establish you this day for a people, and that God may be unto you a God, as the Divine spoke to you, and as God swore unto your ancestors...neither with you only do I make this covenant...but with those who stand here with us this day...and also with those who are not here with us this day."[6]

Abravanel continues in his commentary by arguing that the passage in Ezekiel makes it crystal clear that the obligation of the people of Israel to keep God's covenant is a permanent one, flowing from the Covenant at Sinai. He takes a leap by pointing out that his own generation was suffering a bitter exile, have forsaken the traditions of their ancestors because of the persecution they suffer, and want to be like the other nations of the world, trying to avoid the harassment and anti-Semitism they constantly face. By assimilating into the other nations, they would take themselves out from the obligation of following God's Torah, and dissolving the Covenant of Sinai. But Ezekiel's prediction, says Abravanel, came true, that "with fury poured out will I be Ruler over you." In other words, no matter how hard the people of his generation try, they will never succeed in divesting themselves of the Covenant obligations. To the contrary, no one will ever forget that they are Jews, and in fact they may be burned at the stake, as many were in the Spanish Inquisition, because they will be accused of hiding their Jewishness, and practicing it in secret. Even though only some did, they would also suffer in one way or another – be exiled or be burned at the stake.[7]

Are We Bound to God's Covenant in the Twenty-First Century, and if so, How?

Living in contemporary America, with the notion that we are all free individuals, and accepting the Torah's view of free will, it is hard to justify the full meaning of this verse philosophically not to mention legally. Each human being is free to accept or reject her past. And those who accept it are free to accept it in part or in whole. To say that we are bound to the Covenant at Sinai is not an argument that holds much water from these points of view. How then can we understand this seminal verse?

In my view, there is no coercion from a philosophic or legal point of view, but rather a moral and spiritual obligation one can feel, and voluntarily accept. This is the difference between Orthodox and non-Orthodox Judaism. A traditional Jew will read the words of Abravanel, Yehudah HaLevi, and other ancient and medieval commentators, and say — "Aha! Here is proof that we are all bound to the Covenant at Sinai!" Even Hitler, may his name be blotted out, agreed with this Torah concept! No one could escape their Judaism, no matter how hard they tried, no matter to what degree they assimilated into European Aryan society. If a person was found to have had one Jewish grandparent, she was considered Jewish by the Nazis, and was not permitted to assimilate into German, Austrian, or other Western societies.

The modernist can only say that one can voluntarily accept the Covenant, and feel morally and spiritually connected to one's people, and the agreement our ancestors made millennia ago in the Sinai desert under the leadership of Moses (approximately in the thirteen century B.C.E.). In fact, in light of the severe punishment the Jewish People has endured for the three millennia since the time of Moses, it would be hard to understand why someone might choose such a covenant. In Jewish Law, rabbis are obliged to discourage anyone who wants to convert to the Jewish faith by reminding them of all the duties, obligations, and discrimination one must face if Judaism is truly accepted.

But for the enlightened, modern Jew, who chooses to accept the Covenant voluntarily, the rewards are more than ample. The connection to a rich and ennobling ethical tradition that has enhanced the quality of the intellectual, spiritual and moral life of millions of people from the time of Moses to now, is incomparable. The high and noble ideals, the extraordinary individual and societal norms laid out in the Torah, Talmud and Judaism's subsequent teachings, the values of a close-knit family, passionate pursuit of knowledge for its own sake, and the remarkable contributions the Jewish People has made to every land, culture and civilization of which they have been a part, makes it a privilege and a blessing to be part of this People. As God promised to Abraham, (Genesis 12:3), "All the families of the earth shall be blessed through you."

The verses which we have chosen to highlight in this book, the forceful, eloquent and ardent ethical demands advocated by the classical biblical prophets, and the witness of thousands of years of history, is evidence too clear and manifest to be denied. In sum, while the Torah's claim that the Covenant made between Israel and God at Sinai is permanent and irrevocable it is not one that every Jew today accepts. It is also one that no Jew can cavalierly dismiss absent serious confrontation with its historical, moral and spiritual implications.

Notes

[1] Nehama Leibowitz, *Studies in Devarim (Deuteronomy): In the Context of Ancient and Modern Jewish Bible Commentary* (Jerusalem: World Zionist Organization, Department for Torah Education and Culture 1980) 298-302.
[2] As quoted by Ibid. 298.
[3] Ibid. 299.
[4] Ibid. 300.
[5] Ibid. 300-301.
[6] Ibid. 301.
[7] Ibid. 302.

33

Deuteronomy 6:4

דברים ו,ד:

שְׁמַע יִשְׂרָאֵל, ה' אֱלֹהֵינוּ ה' אֶחָד.

*JPS (1916) – "HEAR, O ISRAEL: THE LORD OUR
GOD, THE LORD IS ONE."*

*NJV (1962) – "Hear, O Israel! The LORD is our God, the
LORD alone."*

The *"Shema"* is the cornerstone of Jewish liturgy and theology. It is the pristine statement of ethical monotheism. As the verses in the text which follow indicate, this verse is to be recited twice daily, "when you rise up and when you go to sleep." Its centrality in Jewish worship and thought has never been challenged. Its implications are central for any understanding of Judaism, past or present. It is the first prayer a child learns, and the last words a Jew recites on the deathbed. There is no credo comparable to it in all of Jewish literature. Its words are etched on every Jewish doorpost, and in the boxes (*tefillin*) that are wrapped on the arm of the Jewish worshipper each morning.

This one verse was selected from the Torah's 5,845 verses as the eternal watchword of the Jewish Faith. In six short words we find the "battle cry" of the Jewish People, the basic truth of Judaism. Since it originates in the Torah, it is one of the oldest prayers in the Siddur.

What Is the Correct Translation of this Verse?

There are two important words for God in this verse, and in the Torah generally. YHVH, sometimes called the Tetragrammaton (the holy word of four letters), is interpreted by tradition (in its pronunciation of Adonai) to refer to God's quality of mercy and compassion. Furthermore, YHVH is considered to be more of a "name" (even though in its present pronunciation, a substitute for the original name, which we no longer know how to pronounce, it means, technically, "our Lord"), rather than a generic term for a divine being. The original sound of YHVH was pronounced only by the *Kohen Gadol* (High Priest) after emerging from the Holy of Holies on Yom Kippur during the Avodah Service. Some believe YHVH is related to the Hebrew verb "*hayah*," "to be," and that its meaning is "I am."

God's other important name, Elohim, generally refers to God's quality of judgment.

Thus, some translate this verse as follows: "Listen (or, Understand), People of Israel, YHVH is our God, YHVH is the Only One."

What Is The Meaning of the Word *"Shema"*?

Shema means hear, listen, or understand. Since this verse appears in Deuteronomy 6, following the Ten Commandments (in Deuteronomy 5), it can be interpreted as follows. Those who were present to experience God, or "see" God, at Sinai, have a direct message from Adonai. Those who followed the generation of Sinai can only "hear" the message, and accept God indirectly from the evidence of a previous generation. Thus, if we recite the *Shema* twice daily we hear the voice of God from Mt. Sinai, albeit indirectly.

The 20th century German-Israeli philosopher Martin Buber was once asked what was the most important message he could impart to American Jewry. He answered by saying that if people would truly listen, as the *Shema* commands, the world would be a different place. Listening to God is our primary command, as an "I" to a "Thou." By this Buber meant to be with God existentially in a direct, intentional and intense way. Then, listening to one another as children of God, we emulate the intense I-Thou relationship, the paradigm of all relationships. Such focused listening is the true way to "be" with another human being. Buber's thought teaches that we find God in the bridge between human beings who communicate intensely, sincerely, and totally.

Who Is Yisrael?

Yisrael is, of course, the name of the Jewish People. It was the name given to Jacob at the ford of Yabok when he wrestled with the angel of God (Genesis 32). Since we are the descendants of Jacob (Yisrael), we are known as the children, or descendants, of Yisrael (*benei Yisrael*), or simply "Yisrael."

It is interesting to note that while the *Shema* is the central prayer of Judaism, it is not addressed to God, but to the Jewish People, and reads as one Jew addressing another. A novel interpretation by Rabbi Dov Baer of Lubavitch (1774-1827) suggests that in reciting the *Shema* each Jew addresses himself, or the "Israel" part of his soul. In other words, the worshipper speaks to the highest within him or herself. Prayer thus means telling yourself something important.

A famous legend in the Talmud (*Pesahim* 56a) identifies the "Yisrael" in the *Shema* with Jacob himself. According to this midrash, when Jacob was dying in Egypt he gathered his twelve sons around his bed, and charged them to maintain their faith in the unity of Adonai. He asked his sons if there were any among them who could not accept the God of his fathers, Abraham and Isaac. In one voice all twelve sons answered: "Hear, O Yisrael (Jacob), Adonai is our God, Adonai is one!" The legend then continues by saying that Jacob answered his sons with the sentence that we recite (silently) following the *Shema*: "Blessed be the name of God's glorious sovereignty forever and ever." The essence of the legend in the Talmud is that each time we recite the *Shema* we are repeating to our ancestor Jacob that we have kept faith with his teachings.

Still another explanation, found in the medieval mystical book, *The Zohar*, is that Yisrael is one of God's names. The word Yisrael, in this interpretation, means "God is right" (*Yashar El*). Thus, the prayer is an expression to God of the worshiper's confidence that Adonai is God and that God is one.

What Is The Meaning Of The Word "*Ehad*" (One)?

Perhaps the word "one" is the key to the entire biblical verse. Some translate the word as "unique," "singular," or "alone." The prophet Malachi (2:10) emphasized the unity of humanity that is an indispensable corollary of the unity of God in these famous words:

> Have we not all one Father?
> Has not one God created us?
> Why then do we deal treacherously
> Each against our neighbor?

Scholars point out that the selection of the *Shema* verse out of the entire Torah may have been meant to draw attention to Judaism's opposition to other non-monotheistic theologies. It is a clear statement of opposition against "polytheism and pagan ethics, to the dualism of the Zoroastrians, the pantheism of the Greeks, and the trinitarianism of the Christians."[1]

In Maimonides' Thirteen Principles of the Faith, the unity of God is foremost. Says the great medieval sage: "I believe with perfect faith that the Creator, Whose Name is blessed, is One only and that there is no unity in any manner like God's, and that Adonai alone is our God, who was, is, and will be."

God's unity, as expressed in the *Shema* verse, is captured eloquently by the twentieth century's greatest scientist and humanist, Albert Einstein, who wrote:

A human being is a part of the whole called by us universe, a part limited in time and space. He experiences himself, his thoughts and feelings as something separated from the rest, a kind of optical delusion of his consciousness. This delusion is a kind of prison for us, restricting us to our personal desires and to affection for a few persons nearest to us. Our task must be to free ourselves from this prison by widening our circle of compassion to embrace all living creatures and the whole of nature in its beauty.

Clearly, the affirmation of one God as Parent to all humanity is the basis of Judaism's gift to all major world religions: ethical monotheism.

How Is The *Shema* Used in Jewish Liturgy?[2]

As pointed out above, the paragraph which follows the *Shema* verse requires Jews to recite the words of this biblical sentence when one arises in the morning and when one goes to sleep at night. The *Shema* verse, together with the three paragraphs which follow it in the liturgy (Deut. 6:5-9, 11:13-21; and Numbers 15:37-41) are known in Talmudic terms as *Keriyat Shema*, or the Recitation of the *Shema*. Traditional Jews recite the *Shema* in the evening both during the Maariv (evening) service, as well as at bedtime (*Keriyat Shema Al HaMitah*).

The *Shema* is part of the very early morning prayers in the Siddur to ensure that the person who prays recites the verse within the prescribed early morning period. When the Torah Scroll is read in public on Shabbat and festivals, the *Shema* verse is chanted after removing the Torah from the ark. It is also recited as part of the Shabbat and Festival Musaf (additional) service during the *Kedushah* (holiness) section. In addition, it is recited at the conclusion of Yom Kippur. Some scholars believe that at times when it was forbidden to recite the *Shema* by an unfriendly gentile government, the verse was squeezed into later locations in the hope that no one would notice, or that it would be chanted after government officials had departed.

There is one other important time when the *Shema* is recited: at the approach of death. Anyone who knows that death is near is directed by Jewish Tradition to recite the *Shema* as a way of proclaiming one's faith in God even at a moment of supreme emotional difficulty. It may also offer comfort at such a time for the dying person to know that God is by his/her side. Since the *Shema* is customarily recited when one is near death, it became a sign of heroism for a person about to be killed for being Jewish to proclaim faith in God even when being Jewish is the cause of losing one's life. This is the supreme act of faith and trust in God and God's universe. In Hebrew the act of martyrdom is known as *Kiddush Hashem*, or Sanctification of God's Holy Name. It is thus appropriate to recite the *Shema* at such a time of sanctification.

This use of the *Shema* during experiences of martyrdom is most frequently associated with the death of the famous second century sage, Rabbi Akiva, who rebelled against the conquering armies of Rome. Akiva refused to obey the Roman laws prohibiting study and practice of Judaism. He preferred death to living without God and Torah, providing a heroic example for future martyrs throughout the ages. The Talmud (*Berakhot* 61b) provides this touching story about Akiva's martyrdom:

> When the saintly sage was taken out to be killed by the Romans it was time for the reading of the *Shema*. The Roman soldiers flayed his flesh with iron combs. Nevertheless Akiva accepted upon himself the yoke of the sovereignty of Heaven (recited the *Shema*). His loyal disciples, shocked at the treatment of their master, and also at his incredible ability to withstand the pain and still recite *Shema* and affirm God's sovereignty, asked him: Master, even at a moment like this you are still faithful? Rabbi Akiva answered: The *Shema* tells us to love Adonai our God "with all our heart, with all our might, and with all our soul." My whole life I could not understand what it means to love God "with all your soul." Now I understand. It means that even when God takes away your soul, you must still love God. Now that it is in my power to fulfill this command, shall I not do it?" As Akiva was dying he recited *Shema*, and when he came to the last word, "*Ehad*," ("One"), he prolonged the word until his soul left him. A Voice came forth from Heaven

and said: "Fortunate are you, Rabbi Akiva, that your spirit
has left you at '*Ehad*.'"

How Do The Talmudic Rabbis Refer To This Verse?

In rabbinic parlance this verse is called "*Kabbalat Ol Malkhut
Shamayim*," or "Acceptance of the Obligation of the Sovereignty
of Heaven." Very simply, this means that whoever recites this
biblical verse in a prayerful way is accepting upon him/herself
the obligations of God's covenant. The *Shema* verse thus becomes
the declaration of faith of Judaism. It implies that one accepts the
one God of Israel, and is willing to bear the burdens and responsibilities of carrying out the Covenant that Israel made with God
at Sinai. Remember that the *Shema* follows the Ten Commandments in the preceding chapter of Deuteronomy, and thus af-
firms one's belief in God and one's willingness to carry out the
laws, traditions, customs, rituals, and ethical demands of the
Torah.

In the actual Torah Scroll, two letters of the *Shema* verse are
enlarged, the third letter of the first word (*ayin*), and the last letter of the last (sixth) word (*dalet*). These two letters, placed together, spell the Hebrew word *ed*, or "witness". Some explain the
enlargement of these letters to mean that whoever pronounces
the *Shema* is a witness to God's unity, another way to proclaim
the "*Kabbalat Ol Malchut Shamayim*" (Abudarham, 14th century,
Spain).

In Psalm 81:9 we see the connection between hearing and
bearing witness: "Hear, my people, and I will give testimony. . .
you shall have no foreign god." When the prophet Isaiah says in
God's name (43: 12), "You are My witnesses," the Midrash
(*Yalkut Shimoni, Yitro* 271, *Sifrei Devarim* 346, *Pesikta deRav Kahana*
Parashah 12:6 (Ed. Mandelboim), *Midrash Tehillim* 123:2, Ed.
Buber) says: "If you are My witnesses, then I am God. But if you
are not My witnesses, then I am not God." This daring statement
of the rabbis suggests that without an army of loyal devotees to
the doctrine of ethical monotheism, God's presence in the world
cannot be felt or recognized.

How Did Jewish Mystics Use The *Shema* Verse?

As far back as the 2nd century we find that Rabbi Shimon in the
Mishnah (*Pirke Avot* 2:18) warns: "Be careful in reciting the

Shema.... When you pray do not make your prayer a rote matter, but rather a plea for mercy and grace before Adonai...." Saying the *Shema* was not merely reading a verse from Scripture. It had mystical connotations. Commenting on the Mishnah just quoted, Rav Chaim Heikel of Amdor comments that the Hebrew word for "be careful" (*zahir*) also means "shining" or "glowing." He states that "one should shine after reciting the *Shema* and praying. The Holy Creator will then shower upon us radiance and light."[3]

There is clear evidence from ancient times that the *Shema* was used as one might use a *mantra* in modern meditation. The Jerusalem Talmud (*Berakhot* 1:1, 2d) suggests that it is desirable to continue reciting the *Shema* over and over again when going to sleep, until sleep overtakes the person saying it. Further, because a bridegroom could not achieve total concentration in reciting the *Shema*, he was exempt from reciting it (*Tur, Orah Haim*, 70) on his wedding night.

Rabbi Aryeh Kaplan describes the following pattern of using the *Shema* as a meditation:

> The *Shema* can be said as a prayer or a declaration of faith, and it is said as such by Jews all over the world. But if the words are said very slowly, and if a person prepares himself mentally, the *Shema* can be an extremely powerful meditation. Indeed, the Torah itself prescribes that the *Shema* be said twice daily, and it seems highly probable that this was originally prescribed as a short daily meditation for all Israel. . . The technique consists in saying the words very slowly, in a manner very similar to that of using the *Amidah* for a meditation. In the *Amidah*. . . the prescribed rate was approximately one word every seven seconds. The *Shema* can be said even more slowly. You can dwell on each word for as long as fifteen or twenty seconds, or with experience, even longer. During the silences between words, let the meaning of each word penetrate your innermost being. . . . It is easier to use the *Shema* as a meditation than the *Amidah*, since the main portion of the *Shema* consists of only six words, which are easy to memorize. Before you can use these words as a meditation, you must know them well and by heart. You should be seated while saying the *Shema* and keep your eyes closed. Strive to be perfectly still, with no body motion whatsoever.[4]

It is customary today for the worshiper to cover one's eyes with the Tallit in the morning service while reciting *Keriyat Shema*, or with one's hand during the evening service. This is to shut out all external sensory interference so that one can concentrate and focus one's total attention on the words and their deepest meaning, and contemplate the true feelings of God's unity in the world.

Notes

[1] Plaut, *The Torah* 1369.

[2] For a fuller discussion of the usage of the *Shema* in the liturgy see Mary Nulman, *The Encyclopedia of Jewish Prayer: Ashkenazic and Sephardic Rites* (Northvale: Jason Aronson, 1993) 294-298. There is also an extensive treatment of the *Shema* and the history of its usage in *The Authorized Daily Prayer Book* by Rabbi Joseph Hertz (New York: Bloch Publishing Co., 1975) 263-269. See also Norman Lamm, *The Shema: Spirituality and Law in Judaism* (Philadelphia: Jewish Publication Society, 1998).

[3] Tuvia Kaplan, *Fathers and Sons: The Chassidic Masters on Pirkei Avos* (Southfield: Targum Press, 1992) 53.

[4] Aryeh Kaplan, *Jewish Meditation: A Practical Guide* (New York: Schocken Books, 1985) 127-128.

34

Deuteronomy 6:5

דברים ו,ה:

וְאָהַבְתָּ אֵת ה' אֱלֹהֶיךָ בְּכָל לְבָבְךָ
וּבְכָל נַפְשְׁךָ וּבְכָל מְאֹדֶךָ.

*JPS (1916) – "And thou shalt love the LORD thy God with
all thy heart, and with all thy soul, and with all thy might."*

*NJV (1962) – "You shall love the LORD your God with all
your heart and with all your soul and with all your might."*

Thus **begins the first** of three paragraphs which follow the
"*Shema*" verse in the liturgy, and instructs the Israelite people to
love God in all ways and at all times, and to continue to rehearse
and transmit this teaching to the people of Israel for all times. It is
important to understand each part of this essential verse.

"With all your heart." In the Tanakh, the seats of intellect
and emotions are a level lower physiologically than in modern
times. The heart, not the brain, is the seat of the intellect. The kid-
neys, not the heart, are the seat of the emotions. Thus, to love
God with all one's heart means to do so with one's *mind*. The rabbis noticed that the Hebrew word used for heart is "*levav*," instead of the more common "*lev*." The double use of the Hebrew
letter *bet* is the source of their idea that one should love God with
both human instincts (i.e., both parts of our heart), our positive as
well as our negative inclinations and passions, our *Yetzer HaTov*
and our *Yetzer HaRa* (Talmud, *Berakhot* 54a). In other words,
serve God even with our most terrestrial ambitions. Let our libido be channeled into positive directions.

"With all your soul." One must serve God with all one's
soul, even if it means, as it did in the case of Rabbi Akiva, that

God takes away one's very soul (*Berakhot* 54a). This is the height of devotion to God's service.

"With all your might." The Talmud's view is that the Hebrew "*me'od*" refers to one's property (*Berakhot 54a*). One must not permit financial or material considerations enter into a decision to perform the will of God. Surely the rabbis would consider some limits to this command, but in general it is a worthy goal to place our spiritual goals on a higher level than our material comforts. Abraham ibn Ezra claims that this phrase commands us to serve God and love God to the utmost in our power.

Can One *Demand* the Love of God?

Ancient and modern commentators struggled with this difficult commandment, whose complexity involves a variety of interwoven questions.

Rabbi Eliyahu ben Avraham Mizrahi, rabbi of Constantinople and Chief Rabbi of the Turkish Empire (1450-1526), asks a basic question: "How can a human be commanded to love a Being one has never even seen?" Rabbi Yitzhak ben Moshe Arama wonders how it is possible for the Torah to command something such as an emotion, which is not in our control?

A homiletical answer is given by Rabbi Yehudah Leib Alter, who says that every person has a love of God embedded in his or her heart. The command to love God means to consciously open the heart and permit this internal love to the fore. A less possible answer is offered by Shmuel David Luzzatto, who suggests that the expression to "love" God is an anthropomorphism. Whoever follows the verse in Psalms to "place Adonai before him always" and is exclusively concerned with doing God's pleasure, will be known as "the friend" (or "beloved") of God. Thus, he explains, the love of God is *not a separate commandment*, but an underlying principle of *all* the commandments. Luzzatto argues that "The love itself cannot be the subject of a command."[1]

Maimonides who, despite being a neo-Aristotelian rationalist, had distinctly mystical strains in his writings, states that love of God is a command second only to belief in the Supreme Being. "We are to dwell upon and contemplate God's mitzvot, words and deeds, so that we may come closer to understanding God and thus reach absolute joy and love of God.... In other words, through the act of contemplation of God we come closer to understanding Adonai, and attain the exalted stage of joy in which love of God must naturally follow. By doing so we shall bring others to serve and to believe in God." In short, Maimonides stresses contemplation and study as pathways to learning to love God. Both of these acts are, naturally, within our ability and willpower to achieve.

In yet another book of Maimonides we see the emotional component of loving God: "One should become enraptured by God, as one who is lovesick does not cease to languish after his beloved on whom he always dotes, whether sitting or rising, eating or drinking. This love is like the love expressed in the biblical book, Songs of Songs, as King Shlomo says allegorically 'For I am lovesick.' Thus we should become versed in science and arts in order best to know God, each according to capacity."[2] As Nehama Leibowitz explains, Maimonides stresses a two-fold approach to learning to love God: through performance of God's commands (*mitzvot*), and through learning more about the physical world and nature through which we come to appreciate God's creation.[3]

A third path to love of God, far less normative in Judaism, but by no means outside the pale of the wide range of Jewish thinkers, is the view of Bahya ibn Pakuda, a popular Spanish philosopher. Bahya's mystical view is that quiet, isolated, mystical contemplation is the best path to learning to truly love God: "Of what does the love of God consist? It is the soul's total surrender of its own will to the Creator, to cleave to God's supernal light.... One should be totally engulfed with God's service and have no room for any other thought.... One should walk, move and speak only in order to be conscious of God and praise God out of love of and longing for Adonai"[4] The love relationship between God and the people of Israel is one that is a frequent theme in later biblical literature. In Plaut's felicitous expression, God and Israel in the Tanakh are in a "quasi-conjugal relationship,"[5] and the loyalty and devotion of husband and wife are often the test of Israel's success or failure in its service to the Creator.

This third and most emotionally laden path to of loving God is the favorite of the medieval mystics, the kabbalists, found in the famous mystical treatise, *The Zohar*, as well as in the writings of the Safed school of kabbalists of the sixteenth century. In some of their writings the erotic imagery is extraordinarily explicit.[6] To the devotees of the mystical path in Jewish religious practice, pure love of God is the highest goal. *The Zohar* explains our verse in these terms: "It is required for one to be attached to God with a most elevated love. All of one's worship of the Blessed Holy One should be with love. No form of worship can be compared to the love of the Blessed Holy One. Nothing is as precious to the Blessed Holy One as the person who loves God with a pure love. Such a one is surrounded by lovingkindness from all sides as the person performs acts of lovingkindness to all, having no regard for one's own property or person. We know this from Abraham who, because of his love for the Blessed Holy One, had no regard for his own heart, his own soul and his own property."

A fourth method of learning to love God is explicated in a rabbinic midrash, *Tanna debei Eliyahu* (a midrashic collection compiled in Eretz Yisrael around the tenth century C.E.). This midrash explains that the true path to loving God is to bring others to love God by way of moral exemplary behavior. A person devoted to Torah study, ethical actions in the world of business, and through generally high moral comportment, will cause others to comment on the person's relationship to God, and will in turn come to love God oneself.

Modern Interpretations of the Commandment to Love

The modern psychoanalyst, Erich Fromm, in his popular book, *The Art of Loving,* agrees that actions are the producer and product of true love. To Fromm love is "an activity, not a passive affect; it is a 'standing in,' not a 'falling for.'" Fromm writes that "the active character of love can be described by stating that love is primarily *giving*, not receiving. . . . Giving is the highest expression of potency. In the very act of giving, I experience my strength, my wealth, my power. This experience of heightened vitality and potency fills me with joy. I experience myself as overflowing, spending, alive. . . Giving is more joyous than receiving, not because it is a deprivation, but because in the act of giving lies the expression of my aliveness."[7]

Rabbi Harvey J. Fields, a rabbi in California, suggests that the struggle to explain the command to love God by all the many commentators throughout the centuries falls short in one respect:

> They fail to recognize that love is not static, but dynamic. It evolves, grows, matures. The love expressed by a child is not the same as that felt by a young adult or that achieved by an elderly person who has a life filled with experience. Love is a construct of many feelings: respect, knowledge, loyalty, caring, mercy. It is expressed in uplifting the needy, in the pursuit of justice, in the nurturing of others, in the warmth of an embrace, and in the passion shared by two human beings. . . Perhaps Moses, the wise and aged leader of the Israelites, understood that love is not a single expression but rather a mysterious and wonderful gift evolving from human beings and expressed in a variety of ways. That understanding may account for his command: "You shall love *Adonai* your God

with all your heart, with all your soul, and with all your might." Moses may have meant that the love of God is achieved only when we develop our emerging powers of mind (heart), spirit (soul), and physical strength (might). Love of God grows, changes, and ripens. As with love among human beings, it is the achievement of a lifetime, not of a moment. For that reason, Moses commands that its cultivation be given the highest priority in every aspect of our lives.[8]

Rabbi Louis Jacobs, a contemporary British theologian and distinguished scholar and writer, divides all approaches to God into those who show love of God through religious acts, and those who exhibit intense mystical longing for the nearness of God and for communion with God:

> [Even the mystics] emphasize the great difficulties in the way of attainment of their ideal and teach that in its highest reaches it is only for a very few rare souls. The contemporary Jew will hardly wish to eliminate this mystical approach from his own religious strivings and he will have some appreciation of its tremendous power. The late Rabbi Kook used to say that man is by nature a mystic. But the contemporary Jew, the heir to both trends, will rightly be more than a little suspicious of the more bizarre, and especially erotic, fancies with which the concept is at times attended. If he is wise he will avoid self-delusion and he will not aim too high. He will fall back on the moral force of the first tendency in which to love God is to do His will.[9]

What is the Difference Between the Love of God and the Fear of God?

According to many ancients and moderns, love of God is preferable to fear of God. Rashi says that one who serves God out of love is superior to one who serves out of fear, for one who serves out of fear, when tested, will lose his fear and break off the relationship, whereas one who serves out of love will be more likely to sustain the relationship, and find more fulfillment in it.

Louis Jacobs notes that in many ways both love and fear of God are similar, in that both reflect an intense relationship with God, and both are connected with high standards of ethical conduct. The phrase "*yirei shamayim*," one who fears God, is a biblical description of one who is noted for a high degree of piety and moral worth. Job, for example, is known for his "*yirat shamayim*," fear of Heaven. Job was "whole-hearted and upright; he feared God and shunned evil" (Job 1:1).[10]

Rabbi Avraham ibn David of Posquieres, (France, 1125-1198) suggests that there are two kinds of fear of God. The first, presumably on a lower level, is "*Yirat Ha'Onesh*," fear of punishment, or fear of the consequences of sin. A higher level of fear of God is "*Yirat HaRomemut*," fear of being in the presence of the exalted majesty of God. This second level of fear is perhaps better translated as *awe* or, to use Abraham Joshua Heschel's phrase, "radical amazement." The modern Christian theologian, Rudolph Otto, refers to this as the sense of the numinous (from the Latin for "spirit"). This is what is called in theology the *mysterium tremendum*, the sense of enormous mystery and inspiration. It is a non-rational, mystical appreciation, just as one would have for awe-inspiring music. The classic biblical phrase in this regard is from Psalms (111:10): "The fear [awe] of Adonai is the beginning of wisdom."

Rabbi Louis Finkelstein, late distinguished Chancellor of the Jewish Theological Seminary, writes about the rabbinic difference of opinion as to whether fear or love of God is greater. The School of Hillel preferred love of God to fear of God, since the mitzvot are designed to help humans develop their love of other humans. Fearing God might not necessarily lead to loving humans, and is thus not considered sufficient. To Hillel the Torah is a symbolic system expressing the basic principle that all humans must love one another. To Shammai, devotion to and fear of God and God's mitzvot are primary, because the aim of existence is to observe the mitzvot. Love of God is not sufficient, since the Torah is a symbolic system expressing the idea that God must be obeyed. Finkelstein notes that "the anthropocentricism of Hillelite theology, and the theocentricism of Shammaitic theology, both have the same purpose — the raising of the standards of human conduct, in which the glory of God becomes most clearly manifest on earth."[11]

Notes

[1] Cf. Leibowitz, *Devarim* 65.

[2] Maimonides, Mishneh Torah, Hilkhot Teshuvah 10:3, 6.

[3] Leibowitz, *Devarim* 65-68.

[4] Bahyah ibn Pakudah, *Duties of the Heart* (NewYork: Feldheim, 1978).

[5] Plaut, *The Torah* 1370.

[6] Cf. for example, Isaiah Tishby and Fischel Lachower, *The Wisdom of the Zohar: An Anthology of Texts* (Oxford, New York: Oxford University Press, 1989).

[7] Erich Fromm, *The Art of Loving* in Fields III, 113.

[8] Fields III, 115-116.

[9] Louis Jacobs, *A Jewish Theology* (New York: Behrman House, Inc., 1973) 173. See also chapters 11 and 12.

[10] Ibid. 174.

[11] Louis Finkelstein, "Judaism As a System of Symbols" in the *Mordecai M. Kaplan Jubilee Volume,* ed. by Moshe Davis (New York: Jewish Theological Seminary of America, 1953) 225-244, especially 240.

35

Deuteronomy 6:7-9

דברים ו, ז-ט:

וְשִׁנַּנְתָּם לְבָנֶיךָ וְדִבַּרְתָּ בָּם בְּשִׁבְתְּךָ בְּבֵיתֶךָ וּבְלֶכְתְּךָ בַדֶּרֶךְ
וּבְשָׁכְבְּךָ וּבְקוּמֶךָ: וּקְשַׁרְתָּם לְאוֹת עַל יָדֶךָ וְהָיוּ לְטֹטָפֹת
בֵּין עֵינֶיךָ: וּכְתַבְתָּם עַל מְזוּזֹת בֵּיתֶךָ וּבִשְׁעָרֶיךָ.

JPS (1916) — "and thou shalt teach them diligently unto thy children, and shalt talk of them when thou sittest in thy house, and when thou walkest by the way, and when thou liest down, and when thou risest up. And thou shalt bind them for a sign upon thy hand, and they shall be for frontlets between thine eyes. And thou shalt write them upon the door-posts of thy house, and upon thy gates."

NJV (1962) — "Impress them upon your children. Recite them when you stay at home and when you are away, when you lie down and when you get up. Bind them as a sign on your hand and let them serve as a symbol on your forehead; inscribe them on the doorposts of your house and on your gates."

These three verses are in essence one long sentence. They are all elaborations on one simple theme: the spreading of the doctrine of the *Shema*. These remaining verses of the first paragraph of the *Shema* all revolve around a variety of methods with which to transmit the important teaching of ethical monotheism: through our children, our homes, and our individual person at all times and in all ways. These verses can be compared to a teacher's lesson plan on how to make sure that the teaching of God's unity, loving God, and Israel's Covenant with God is propagated throughout the community for all time.

Hertz comments that the Hebrew verb "*Veshinantam*" (and you shall teach them) means literally "to prick them in." The verb connotes something stronger than merely to teach. Its sense is to teach with intensity, thoroughness, and completeness, as the following verses make clear. Plaut suggests two possible Hebrew roots: a) *shanan,* to sharpen, as making an incision. That is, "dig them into" your children's minds and hearts. Or, b) from *shana,* to repeat,[1] in which case the meaning is to review again and again until they are an integral part of the child's value system (Abravanel).

What is the Importance of Imparting Torah to the Young?

The duty to transmit the teachings of the Torah is found first in the Five Books of Moses, but continues to be a resounding theme throughout all subsequent Jewish literature. The transmission of the knowledge of the Torah and its succeeding books is the highest religious duty. The Talmud tells us that "*Talmud Torah Keneged Kulam,*" "The study (teaching) of Torah is equal to all the other mitzvot combined" (*Shabbat* 127a). So important is study and knowledge that the Talmud declares that a learned *mamzer* (bastard, one born of a biblically illegal marriage) takes precedence over an ignorant Kohen Gadol (Mishnah *Horayot* 3:8, Midrash *Bemidbar Rabbah* 6:1).

While in many societies the obligation to teach the heritage and culture of a people devolves upon the community, in this verse it clearly falls on the parent. Jewish tradition teaches that as soon as a child can speak, the child should learn to recite by heart the Torah verse (Deuteronomy 33:4) "The Torah which Moses commanded us is the inheritance of congregation of Jacob."

In *Pirke Avot* (Ethics of the Fathers) 2:5 we learn: "Hillel taught: An ignoramus cannot be a pious person." When it became customary for a system of schools to supplement the education given at home the Talmud declared it forbidden for one to live in a community without a school. Around the twelfth century a pious Jewish woman on her deathbed in Egypt wrote to her sister: "If the Lord on High should decree my death, my greatest wish is that you should take care of my little daughter and make an effort for her to study. Indeed, I know that I am imposing a heavy burden on you. For we do not have the wherewithal for her upkeep, let alone the cost of tuition. But we have an example from our mother and teacher, the servant of the Lord."[2] In this impecunious family two generations of learned women succeeded in passing on to the next generation the importance of Jewish learning.[3]

The House of Study (*Beit HaMidrash*) has been the central institution in any Jewish community. In modern parlance the synagogue is often called a *shul*, Yiddish for school, because the most important function of a synagogue is its role as the seat of education and Torah learning.[4]

Often when I am giving lectures, or leading seminars and workshops in different cities throughout the world, I will ask people to name the highest value of Judaism. People's typical responses include: a strong sense of family, a clear sense of history, a commitment to other Jews, and the importance of education. Rashi explains "teach them to your children" to imply not just your own children, but to all children, since anyone we teach is compared to our child in a cultural/intellectual sense. "Child" is a metaphor for one to whom one gives intellectual birth. Rashi points out several passages throughout the Tanakh where "child" is understood figuratively rather than literally, for example, II Kings 2:3, "the children (students) of the prophets."

Teaching These Words "at Home and Away, Lying Down and Getting Up"

"At home and away" is the Bible's way of saying "in all places, everywhere you may find yourself." The technical term for this is "merismus," a rhetorical figure by which totality is expressed by listing the two extremes of a class (ex.: small and large cattle).[5] While the next phrase, "lying down and getting up" similarly means *at all times*, and has been interpreted literally by the rabbis. Lying down precedes getting up because the Jewish day begins with sundown. The Talmudic rabbis derived from this verse the ritual obligation to recite the *Keriyat Shema* twice daily, evening and morning. Since the *Shema* is the cornerstone of the prayer services, this command also implied reciting *Ma'ariv* (evening) services and *Shaharit* (morning) services, based around the *Shema* and the *Amidah*.

In Rabbi Hertz's words, "To fill one's mind with high and noble thoughts is a wise preparation for the hours of darkness."[6] He then quotes the Talmud, which advises, "The *Shema* is a double-edged sword against all the terrors and temptations of the night."[7] Rather than explain this as a magical incantation which wards off demons, it would seem more acceptable to moderns to understand this Talmudic dictum as implying that deep faith and trust in God and the unity of God's creation will stand us in good stead against the fears and anxieties which darkness often brings. The Talmud records a debate as to whether lying down and rising up refers to the *position of the body*, or to *the time of day* (*Berakhot* 10b), and concludes that the latter is what is intended.

The Natziv, in his commentary *Ha'Amek Davar*, says that one should study Torah at all times, but the command to recite the *Shema* twice daily sets the basic minimum for a committed Jew.

What Are the Sign and Symbol on the Hand and Forehead?

Rashi explains that this is to be taken literally and not figuratively, and thus refers to wearing the *Tefillin* on the arm and forehead. Each of the two boxes of the *Tefillin* contains the *Shema* sentence, the paragraph that follows in the Torah, and three other Torah paragraphs which refer to these same symbols on the arm and forehead (Deuteronomy 11:13-21, Exodus 13:1-10, 11-16).

The Hebrew expression *ot* (sign, or symbol of God's relationship to Israel) also refers to two other mitzvot: Shabbat and circumcision. These three mitzvot are essential symbols in Jewish practice. *Tefillin*, *Shabbat*, and *Brit Milah* are three of the core mitzvot of Judaism. Since both *Tefillin* and *Shabbat* are referred to as *ot*, it is not necessary, according to *Halakhah* (Jewish Law), to repeat the use of the symbol on Shabbat. Thus, *Tefillin* are not worn on Shabbat.

The two locations on the body where the *Tefillin* are worn, head and hand, represent the power of our intellect and our actions in bringing us closer to the Sovereignty of God. Others claim that the *Tefilah* — singular for *Tefillin* — on the arm, since it is close to the heart, reminds us of our emotional attachment to God. The *Tefilah* on the head is called *totafot*, variously translated as *emblem*[8] or *ornament*[9]. It is worn above the hairline midway between the eyes.

Tefillin were worn during daylight hours in Talmudic times, and only during *Shaharit* worship in modern days (and during *Minhah* on *Tisha BeAv*). (thus its name, *Tefillin*, prayers, plural for Hebrew *Tefilah*). Such prominent display of the *Tefillin* on the arm and head is a typical example of Judaism's graphic attempt to concretize its teachings in a dramatic way, rather than leave them to abstract intellectual ideas.[10]

Maimonides (*Mishne Torah: Hilkhot Tefilah* 4:25) delineates the objective of the *Tefillin* in these words: "The sanctity of the

Tefillin is very great. As long as they are on one's body, one feels humble and is God-fearing. Thus one will not be drawn to laughter and idle gossip, nor will evil thoughts enter one's mind. One will rather turn the heart to words of truth and righteousness."

After the Lubavitcher Rebbe, Rabbi Menachem Schneerson, persuaded the famous sculptor Jacques Lipchitz to begin using *Tefillin* and reciting prayers each morning, the artist described his experience in these words: "I *daven* [pray] every morning. It is of great help to me. First of all, it puts me together with all my people. I am with them. And I am near to the Lord, the Almighty. I speak with God. I cannot make my prayers individual, but I speak to God. God gives me strength for the day. . . . I could not live anymore without it."[11]

What Is The Meaning of Placing The *Shema* On The Doorpost?

Verse 9 refers to the well-known custom of placing the first *Shema* sentence and the first paragraph which follows it in a small case (made of metal, wood, ceramic, glass or any other material) on the right side of the doorway as one enters the house or any room in it. (The rule of *mezuzah* applies to a room in which one *lives*, excluding, therefore, a bathroom, closet or garage). The mezuzah must be placed at the beginning of the upper third of the doorpost (Talmud, *Menahot* 33a). According to the *Encyclopaedia Judaica*, "The custom has become widespread and almost universal at the present day to affix the *mezuzah* to the entrance to public buildings (including all government offices in Israel) and synagogues. [However] there is no authority for this. . . ."[12] Some pious Jews kiss the *mezuzah* when entering or leaving the house, or touch it and kiss their fingers.

In the Torah the word *mezuzah* means the actual doorpost, but in later times it came to mean, by transference, the container affixed to the doorpost enclosing the hand-written parchment with the *Shema* contained in it. Before Second Temple times the words were apparently inscribed on the stone doorpost itself.[13]

As the *tzitzit* (fringes on the *Tallit*), and the *Tefillin*, the *mezuzah* is another reminder of God's eternal Presence, in this case in the Jewish home and all of its rooms. Upon entering and leaving the home, or any room therein, the Jew is reminded of the potential for sanctity in all aspects of life, and of the relationship one must have with God to achieve a saintly life. In that way the love of God and the positive consequences of our relationship with God will be our central interest and goal in life.

Notes

1 Plaut, *The Torah* 1366.

2 Joseph Telushkin, Jewish Literacy: The Most Important Things to Know About the Jewish Religion, its People, and its History (New York: William Morrow & Co., 1991) 556.

3 Ibid.

4 On the importance of Torah study see also Louis Jacobs, *Jewish Values* (Hartford: Hartmore House, 1969) 11-30.

5 Cf. Moshe Weinfeld, *The Anchor Bible: Deuteronomy 1-11* (New York: Doubleday, 1991) 333.

6 Hertz 771.

7 as quoted by Ibid.

8 Kaplan 901.

9 Plaut, *The Torah* 1367.

10 For a fuller treatment of the subject of the *Tefillin* see Jeffrey M. Cohen, *Blessed Are You: A Comprehensive Guide To Jewish Prayer* (Northvale: Jason Aronson, 1993) 268-275.

11 William Berkowitz, "Jacques Lipchitz: An Interview" in *Reconstructionist*, February 1974: 20-1.

12 Louis Isaac Rabinowitz, "Mezuzah," *Encyclopaedia Judaica*, 1972

13 Weinfeld, *Anchor Bible* 343.

36

Deuteronomy 8:3

דברים ח,ג:

וַיְעַנְּךָ וַיַּרְעִבֶךָ וַיַּאֲכִלְךָ אֶת הַמָּן אֲשֶׁר לֹא יָדַעְתָּ וְלֹא יָדְעוּן
אֲבֹתֶיךָ לְמַעַן הוֹדִיעֲךָ כִּי לֹא עַל הַלֶּחֶם לְבַדּוֹ יִחְיֶה הָאָדָם
כִּי עַל כָּל מוֹצָא פִי ה' יִחְיֶה הָאָדָם.

JPS (1916) — "And He afflicted thee, and suffered thee to hunger, and fed thee with manna, which thou knewest not, neither did thy fathers know; that He might make thee know that man doth not live by bread only, but by every thing that proceedeth out of the mouth of the LORD doth man live."

NJV (1967) — "He subjected you to the hardship of hunger and then gave you manna to eat, which neither you nor your fathers had ever known, in order to teach that man does not live on bread alone, but that man may live on anything that the Lord decrees."

As the saying goes, "We do not live on bread alone." There is a wonderful irony to the popularity of this phrase in modern language. It is a common epithet, used to justify people's attachment to any number of worldly pursuits. However, in its context, it is meant quite specifically to warn against ignoring one's spiritual needs.

Physical food and sustenance are, of course, requisite for human life. However, we risk becoming mere machines if we run our lives simply by working in order to eat, and then in turn eating in order to work. Spiritual well-being is just as important as physical well-being, and so the verse goes on to state: "humans may live on anything that Adonai decrees." In fact, in the literal Hebrew, that phrase is "a human may live on anything which goes out from God's mouth." In the Creation story in Genesis, the world came into existence through God's word. Here too, in the wilderness, God's word creates our world, our reality, and provides all that we need for spiritual as well as physical sustenance.[1]

The *New Interpreter's Bible* puts it quite nicely: "Whereas most people spend their lives seeking to secure themselves from famine by ensuring a plentiful food supply and from cold and destitution by surrounding themselves with fine and warm clothing, they fail to see that the most basic of all essentials for life is to be found in the Word of God. Real poverty is poverty of the spirit, and even those who feel secure because they have no fear of hunger and destitution may fail to see this."[2]

What is Manna?

"We do not live on bread alone," and in fact, in the wilderness, the people of Israel did not even live on bread. They lived on manna, a mysterious food unknown to the Israelites before their journey and unknown to the world ever since.

There are several theories as to what exactly this mystery food was. The Israelites themselves begin this search for identification, when they ask in Exodus 16:15—"*Man hu?*" meaning, "What is it?" This "*man*," (midrashic form of Hebrew "*mah*" — or "what?") rendered in English "manna," became the food's official name. In its very name, then, is embedded its mysterious nature.

In Arabic, "*man*" means honeydew, or the insects that produce a sticky secretion. Modern scholars believe that manna was in fact some sort of insect secretion, which tended to crystallize and then fall to the ground as sticky solids. However, this secretion is found only in certain parts of the Sinai, and only during the months of June and July; and so the mystery seems far from solved. As the JPS Commentary suggests, if the secretion theory is correct, then it was indeed miraculous that an entire people could have been sustained by it, finding it year round in all parts of the Sinai during their journey. [3]

According to Jewish tradition, manna contained the ingredients of every delicious food, and tasted good to each person who ate it. And so we get a highly symbolic picture of God's gift of sustenance to the Israelites in the wilderness. First, God provided for them daily; second, each person was given something of which he or she liked the taste, that is, something each person could live from; and third, no generation beyond the one who experienced God's manna could know what it was like. As Rabbi Hirsch teaches, the Torah's lesson in this verse is that each individual should form her own convictions, based on her own experiences in life.

The Test of the Manna

There is more to be said regarding the fact that no generation before or after Moses' knew manna. God could have fed the Israelites anything during their journey. However, God purposely chose to sustain them on an unknown food, one with which neither they nor their ancestors were familiar. Thus the Israelites were taught to depend entirely on God and trust that God would provide them with their daily sustenance. Moreover, they were to learn that humans live from whatever God decides is nourishing. We are to recognize that we can live off whatever God grants us in life, no matter how unusual, unknown, or challenging; we are to trust God and know that God will provide us with sustenance and guidance in life.

The verse preceding ours poses an interesting question regarding manna. Deuteronomy 8:2 reads: "Remember the long way that the Lord your God has made you travel in the wilderness these past forty years, that God might test you by hardships to learn what was in your hearts: whether you would keep God's commandments or not." This, directly preceding as it does our verse, led the Rabbis to combine the two and understand that the manna itself was a kind of test. What, then, was the test of the manna? The Rabbis have come up with very different answers to this question.

Rashi wrote that the test was whether the Israelites would keep the *mitzvot* connected with the manna, namely, not to store the manna overnight and not to collect any on Shabbat.[4]

Ibn Ezra suggested that the test was the giving of manna itself, since there was only just enough for each person to eat each day and no more. Thus the manna was a "light form of diet." As David Lieberman puts it in *Eternal Torah,* the Israelites' hunger in the wilderness was designed to teach them (and us) to limit their needs as they ate just as much as was granted them and no more. The test was whether they would be able to limit their physical needs even as they heightened their spiritual goals.[5]

Nahmanides felt that the test was in the larger picture of the manna. God gave the Israelites an unknown food, which was not given in abundance, and could not be stored: would Israel trust in God's guidance and providence, or be filled with daily anxiety?

Sforno focused on the opposite aspect of manna, that it symbolized abundance and prosperity, since the Israelites did not have to work for it and could be assured of its coming. In this interpretation, the test was whether Israel would love God and keep God's commandments in times of prosperity — that is, when food was given to all and without work or competition.

With these four differing and even opposing positions, we see the depth of the text and the meaning it holds. We also see the fundamentals of Rabbinic commentary and argumentation: for thousands of years Jews have been interpreting and re-interpreting the Torah, both respecting those who have come before them and yet wrestling with the text to draw their own conclusions and lessons from it.

Why does God Choose to Subject the Israelite People to Hunger?

This verse comes at a very specific point in Moses' first sermon to the Israelites, just before a description of the Promised Land, of its fertility and abundant food. It also comes just before the injunction to thank God for the food of the Land once they arrive there and eat of it. It is no accident that this verse, warning that "man does not live on bread alone" but also must nourish his relationship with God, comes where it does.

Rabbi Hirsch points out that the root *l'h'm*, (known most popularly in its noun form as *lehem*, meaning bread) means in its verbal form both "to eat" and "to wage war." Humans compete for food and livelihood, these homonyms suggest, and this competition is the root of wars and other social evils.[6] Bread is a product of nature and human labor; it symbolizes human control over nature, human mastery over the earth. In granting the Israelite nation manna, and specifically not bread, God is in a sense robbing them of their control over nature. God is reminding them that their ability to yield bread from the earth is God's doing and not their own.[7]

Placed where it is, this verse also comes to remind us that we often cannot fully appreciate what we have until we lack it. The memory of the years of hunger and want, God hopes, will induce the Israelite people into full gratitude when they arrive in the land and eat of its wonderful abundant foods. God's manna lasts only as long as the journey; with their entry into the Promised Land they are left once again to their own devices to feed themselves. God can only hope that they will remember who gave them the land and its foods, and so impresses on their memory the pangs of hunger and the ensuing God-given manna.

The verse states that God purposefully afflicted the Israelite nation. Their suffering during their forty-year journey — the hunger, the thirst, etc. — was somehow part of God's plan for them; God was at the root of it. What does it mean to have a God who afflicts the chosen people, or any people for that matter? What does it mean to have a God who is described as One who instigates human suffering? Can we believe in such a God?

Traditionally, this passage is seen as part of a broader theology presented in the Torah, the theology of God as the "loving Father." Like any father who loves his children and wants the best for them, God must sometimes scold them, chastise them. God does this not out of selfishness or meanness, but rather out of love, out of a divine hope that through their hardship they will learn right from wrong. As Plaut suggests, God may weep over the effects of chastisement, at the suffering God has caused; but God knows it must done in order that God's children develop properly.[8]

This theology seemed to work well for Jews during Biblical, post-Biblical, and even early Medieval times. In the Tanakh itself we have evidence of the popularity of such theology, for example in Psalm 94:12-13: "Happy is the one whom You discipline, Adonai/the one You instruct in Your teaching/to give her tranquility in times of misfortune..." Also Psalm 119:71: "It was good for me that I was humbled/so that I might learn Your laws." Even Job, famous for his questioning of God's judgment and justice, ultimately surrenders to the knowledge that God's wisdom is far superior to a human's imperfect understanding of the world. For many centuries, then, Israel's status as God's chosen people meant enduring special hardships. The theology of God as loving Father was a source of comfort, as Jews held onto the idea that their suffering was for some higher purpose, some higher end of spiritual perfection.

The Mishnah wrestles with the image of God as loving Father weeping over the children who were divinely punished. *Sanhedrin* 6:5 states: "Rabbi Meir said: When one is grieved, with what words does the Divine Presence (*shekhinah*) speak? As it were, 'I am lighter than my head, I am lighter than my arm.' If the Ominpresent is grieved over the blood of the wicked that is shed, how much more so over the blood of the righteous." Kahati elucidates this passage as meaning, when one is punished for sins, with what words does God complain and express grief? God complains, "My head and heart are heavy."[9] God indeed punishes us, but does not like it and is in fact deeply grieved to witness our suffering — especially when the righteous suffer.

During the Middle Ages, this theology was challenged. Maimonides, for one, came up with three categories of suffering: suffering because the human body degenerates (this includes injury from natural disasters, such as earthquakes or floods); suffering due to social corruption; and finally self-inflicted suffering. Thus no human suffering comes directly from God. Social corruption and self-induced problems are human responsibility, not divine and suffering from natural disasters is a byproduct of being human and living in this world. God, in the loving Father's role, is therefore dramatically reduced and limited.[10]

In our post-Holocaust world, the theology of God the loving Father, who both suffers with and afflicts us, cannot stand. It is inconceivable that God would inflict such radical and terrible punishment on so many innocent, righteous people. The moral lesson is too hard to find in that experience, and a theology which insists there is any reason behind the Holocaust falls apart on itself. As Plaut so eloquently puts it: "In the Torah's telling [of this verse], Moses believed God to have been a disciplining Father to Israel, an interpretation which we today need not find compelling. This theology, cogent for many centuries, will hardly convince the modern reader whose concept of God differs from the Bible's...."[11] It is up to us to create our own theology. As Rabbi Hirsch taught, we must each form our own theological convictions from the personal experiences we endure.

Notes

[1] Cf Hertz 782, Plaut, *The Torah* 1390.
[2] Keck II, 357.
[3] Jeffery H. Tigay, *Deuteronomy: The Traditional Hebrew Text with New JPS Translation, The JPS Torah Commentary* (Philadelphia: Jewish Publication Society, 1996) 93.
[4] Rashi: Commentary on Exodus 16:4
[5] David Lieberman, *The Eternal Torah: A New Commentary Utilizing Ancient and Modern Sources in a Grammatical, Historical, and Traditional Explanation of the Text* (River Vale: Twin Pines Press, 1979) I, 457.
[6] Hirsch II, 226-7.
[7] Ibid. V, 138-9.
[8] Plaut, *The Torah* 1390.
[9] *The Mishnah: A New Translation with a Commentary by Rabbi Pinhas Kehati* (Jerusalem: Eliner Library, Dept. for Torah Education and Culture in the Diaspora, 1987) 80-81.
[10] Maimonides, *Guide of the Perplexed* III:11-12.
[11] Plaut, *The Torah* 1391.

37

Deuteronomy 8:10

דברים ח,י:

וְאָכַלְתָּ וְשָׂבָעְתָּ וּבֵרַכְתָּ אֶת ה' אֱלֹהֶיךָ
עַל הָאָרֶץ הַטֹּבָה אֲשֶׁר נָתַן לָךְ.

*JPS (1916) – "And thou shalt eat and be satisfied, and bless
the LORD thy God for the good land which He hath given
thee."*

*JPS (1962) – "When you have eaten your fill, give thanks to
the LORD your God for the good land which He has given
you."*

In the course of describing the many wonderful features of the
Promised Land, *Eretz Yisrael*, a commandment is included to enjoy the land to its fullest and be certain to bless God for its
bounty, alerting the people to the hazards of complacency.

According to Halakhah, every Jew who eats bread is obligated to recite *Birkat HaMazon*, the Grace After Meals, including
women, servants and minors. These are the three categories of
people generally exempt from most mitzvot. Women are connected to servants and minors only since these three groups are
all normally exempt from the performance of positive mitzvot.
(Cf. Talmud Yerushalmi, *Berakhot* 1:1 and 3:3). The rabbis interpret the Torah's use of the word "bless" to mean "in any language you choose to bless" (Babylonian Talmud, *Sotah* 33a).

What Is The Meaning of "And You Shall Eat and Be Satisfied?"

When the Israelite people enter the Promised Land, and the
Land yields its bountiful blessings so that each person can eat to

his/her heart's desire, the people are taught to recognize that the Land is God's gift, as is all the food that emerges from it. In general, the commands around eating are part of Judaism's recognition that material benefits are blessings bestowed by God which should be enjoyed. Rabbi Ovadia Sforno states that this verse comes to teach us that everything comes from God, and that nothing is to be taken for granted, even the simple necessities of life such as daily food.

In contemporary Jewish practice, the rabbinic influence of hallowing every daily act has made the entire experience at the table one of holiness. The Jewish table is considered to be an altar of God, the meal a part of the sacrificial service similar to the food offered in the holy temple in Jerusalem, and the people seated at the table are compared to *kohanim* at the altar. In general the Jewish home is called a *"mikdash me'at,"* a miniature (traveling) sanctuary. In the words of Rabbi Shlomo Riskin, "to fathom what makes a holy nation holy, don't look at its people when they fast or pray; look at them when they eat."[1]

Having a sufficient daily ration of food was an unusual experience for those who had been slaves just a generation before. Nahmanides explains that when the people arrive in the Land and find ample sustenance, they should be especially grateful for their daily bread.

Is it necessary to eat to satiety in order to be grateful to God? The Talmud explains: "Rabbi Avira taught: the Ministering Angels challenged God with the following question. How is it proper for God to show favoritism to the Israelite people? God replied: 'Should I not show favoritism? I commanded them to recite *Birkat HaMazon* only when they are satisfied, but they choose to bless Me even if they eat only a piece of bread as small as an egg or an olive.'" (Talmud *Berakhot* 20b).

A Hasidic master, Rabbi Shlomo of Karlin (Lithuania, 1738-1792) taught that by blessing God one becomes "satisfied." Another comment from the "Ner LaMaor," suggests that the meaning of this verse is that one must bless especially when full, i.e., when things are going well, not only when hungry. In other words, prayer should not be reserved for those in need, but also for those who have had their needs filled. Too often prayers come to mind only when one is hungry, and not when one is satisfied.[2]

What Jewish Laws Result From the Phrase "Give Thanks to Adonai Your God?"

As we shall explain below, the entire *Birkat HaMazon* is based on this verse (Talmud *Berakhot* 21a, 48b). Judaism considers it sacrilegious to enjoy gifts of this world without reciting a blessing as an act of thanksgiving (*Berakhot* 35a). By committing such a sin one not only robs the Blessed Holy One but the human community as well (Ibid. 35b). It is a sin to God for not showing gratitude, and to the community for not establishing the ethical norm of thankfulness.

The importance of reciting a blessing over everything placed into the mouth as food was brought home to me powerfully when, as a rabbinical student, a colleague and I entered the liturgy class of the late Rabbi Louis Finkelstein, Chancellor of the Jewish Theological Seminary. My classmate was carrying a cup of coffee in his hand, and before he sat down for the lecture, asked Prof. Finkelstein if it were permissible to drink coffee during class. Rabbi Finkelstein's immediate answer, without a second of thought, was: Of course, as long as you make a *berakhah*.

The act of reciting *berakhot* before eating, and other acts which require appreciation for the blessings of God's world, is characteristically Jewish. The recitation of the blessing prior to an act, such as eating, studying, putting on a new garment, or even when using the bathroom, endows all human acts with sanctity. One Talmudic passage suggests that each Jew recite at least one hundred *berakhot* every single day! (*Menahot* 43b).[3]

The Talmud relates the importance of reciting blessings before eating as a sign of gratitude and appreciation with the following explanation. There are two biblical verses, both from the Book of Psalms, which seem to contradict one another. One verse states that "The earth belongs to Adonai and the fullness thereof" (Psalm 24:1). The other verse states that "The heavens are the heavens of Adonai, but the earth God has given to mortal humans" (Psalm 115:16). How do we reconcile this seeming contradiction that says in one place that the earth belongs to Adonai, and in another place that God has given the earth to humans? The Talmudic answer is elegantly simple: "There is no contradiction! One case ('The earth belongs to Adonai') refers to a situation before a blessing has been said, and the other case ('The earth God has given to humans') refers to a situation after the blessing has been recited" (*Berakhot* 35 a-b).

What Is The Origin of the *Birkat HaMazon*?

The Talmud has a tendency to ascribe rabbinic prayers to early biblical authorship. This gives such prayers added authority and significance, even when it is not entirely accurate from a historical point of view. It is likely that the rabbis understood that their statements were hyperbolic, rather than literally correct, and their intention is, it seems, to point to the true idea that the basic kernel and motivation of the prayers have early origins.

Thus we find in Tractate *Berakhot* (48b) that Moses instituted the first blessing of *Birkat HaMazon* when the manna descended for the Israelite nation. Joshua instituted the second blessing, for the land, upon entry into Eretz Yisrael. David and Solomon instituted the third benediction, about Zion, Jerusalem, when Jerusalem was captured from the Jebusites and the temple constructed, and about the restoration of the Davidic line in the time of the Messiah.

Originally there were only these three blessings, but later a fourth was added, "Who is good and bestows good" (*HaTov VeHamayteev*). This was instituted (or, perhaps historically more correct, redefined) in Yavneh in the year 135 C.E., when the Bar Kokhba rebellion failed, and the last stronghold of Betar fell. This was the final hope for Jewish independence after the Romans destroyed Jerusalem and sent the people into exile. Under the Roman Emperor Hadrian, the leading rabbis of the generation were brutally and mercilessly tortured. At the failure of the rebellion the people were despondent, but refused to lose faith and courage, even when it seemed as if there were no hope. The Talmud explains that God was "good" (*"hayteev"*) because the bodies of the soldiers at Betar did not putrefy, and "bestows good" (*"mayteev"*) because they were allowed to bury their dead.

Rabbi Emanuel Rackman makes a telling comment on the Talmudic explanation about the privilege of burying the dead. He notes that during the Holocaust we were not privileged to bury our six million dead, and thus can appreciate how our ancestors felt when Betar fell and they were initially unable to inter their martyrs in proper dignified fashion. He points out that this is a magnificent daily reminder to count our blessings, even little ones, even "the thinnest silver lining to the thickest cloud." He then continues: "Who knows but that the survival of our people may have been due to this very capacity to make the best of the worst possible situation. Having lost everything, Jews at least gave thanks for the privilege of being able to bury their dead."[4]

A Summary of The Content of The *Birkat HaMazon*

Let us look at each section of the Grace After Meals.

The first paragraph is called *"HaZan"* (The One Who Provides), and concludes *"HaZan et hakol,"* "Who provides food for all." It is noteworthy that the Hebrew word *"kol"* (all) is repeated six times in this section. We are thankful, as God's creatures, for all the bounties of this world. We view God as a universal, all-embracing, merciful, loving Ruler. The word *"olam,"* (world) is repeated four times, but there is not a single mention of Jews. We are part of the all-embracing humanity, children of a God Who feeds and sustains all. The fact that so much hunger exists in today's world is not a contradiction of the words of this prayer, that God is "Sustainer of all," but rather an indictment of humankind who cannot manage, with all our modern technology, to marshal the resources and willpower to distribute food equally and properly. As God blesses us with ample food, so must we feel a concomitant obligation to feed others as an act of imitation of God (*Imitatio Dei*).

The second blessing (*"Ha'Aretz"*) deals with the Land, from which food derives. As Jews we also thank God for the events of Jewish history, which brought us into our Land: our redemption from Egyptian bondage, our Covenant with God at Sinai, and the gift of our Torah by whose rules we live in our Land. It is a special privilege for a people to be able to eat the food of its own Land, a privilege denied to Jews for a large part of its history. In this paragraph we quote our Torah verse (Deuteronomy 8:10), which is the biblical source for the entire *Birkat HaMazon*. (In the middle of this section we add a special prayer, **"Al HaNissim"** on Purim, Israeli Independence Day and Hanukkah).

The third paragraph (*"Bonei Yerushalayim"*) expresses gratitude for the realization of the pinnacle of religious aspirations, the dream of restoration of our highest moments of national glory, when Jerusalem will be rebuilt as a City of Peace, and when all cities will be rebuilt, like Jerusalem, in peace. (In the middle of this paragraph, when it is Shabbat or Yom Tov, we add special prayers: *"Retzeh"* for Shabbat, and *"Ya'aleh VeYavo"* for Festivals, both of which refer to Jerusalem and are thus appropriately placed). By adding a prayer for the restoration of Jerusalem and the Temple (the *Beit HaMikdash*), we assert the indispensable nature of the sacred dimension of living in the Land.

At the end of the third blessing, for Jerusalem and world peace, we say "Amen," something that is usually done only when answering a *berakhah* recited by someone else. Two reasons are offered for this unusual occurrence. First, that this "Amen" separates the first three biblical blessings from the fourth, rabbinical blessing. Second, "Amen" originated as the initial end of the Grace, before the fourth blessing was added (Berakhot 45a).

Rabbi Avraham Yitzchak HaKohen Kook sees a progression in the three original blessings. First, the prayer for food thanks God for personal physical sustenance. Second, the prayer for the well-being of the Land offers thanksgiving to God for the blessings of the entire nation. Third, the blessing for Jerusalem gives thanks for the spiritual life of the people. We move thus from the personal, to the national, to the spiritual.

We have already examined the origins of the fourth, additional, blessing, above. In the words of Rabbi Pinchas Peli, "together, the four *berakhot* convey the promise, reaffirmed after every meal, of a good and precious land, which proclaims freedom from bondage, freedom from hunger, both physical and spiritual starvation, and freedom from fear that what went wrong in this world will go uncorrected."[5]

In the course of time, when people felt additional reasons for thanking God at the table, other sections were added. These include:

- The *Mezuman*, the introduction used when three adults are present (like the "*Barkhu*" during *Shaharit* and *Ma'ariv* services) to invite others at the table to join in the Grace.
- Psalm 126 ("*Shir HaMa'alot*" has been chanted on Shabbat and Festivals since the sixteenth century, stressing once again the memory of Zion.
- The *HaRahaman* litany, each of which begins with the phrase "May the All-Merciful. . . ." The Ashkenazic liturgy has nine standard blessings in this rubric, and the Sephardic liturgy has seventeen! Maimonides, on the other hand, mentions only three. Additional ones have been added in recent times for the State of Israel and its Defense Forces, for oppressed Jews, and other personal occasions. The medieval authority on liturgy, David ben Yosef Abudraham (14th century, Spain), rules that these additions are personal, private prayers which may be used as the occasion demands, such as honoring special guests at the table, a special birthday or anniversary, etc.
- Ending verses from the Tanakh — *Magdeel yeshu'ot* (*Migdol* on Shabbat and Festivals) — giving an opportunity to employ both versions of an (almost-) identical verse found in Psalm 18:5 and First Samuel 22:51; and *Oseh Shalom*, ending on a note of peace (as we do also at the end of the Amidah and of the kaddish). There are many abbreviated versions of the *Birkat HaMazon*, but none of them omits this final prayer for peace, shalom.

Notes

1 Shlomo Riskin, *Jerusalem Post* 10 August 1990.
2 As quoted by Greenberg 210.
3 See Pinchas Peli, "Blessing — The Gateway to Prayer," *Tradition* Fall, 1973, and Max Kadushin, *Worship And Ethics* (Chicago: Northwestern University Press, 1964), and the notion of "normal mysticism."
4 Emanuel Rackman, *American Examiner-Jewish Week* 10 February 1972: 11.
5 Pinchas Peli, *Jerusalem Post* 17 August 1985.

38

Deuteronomy 11:13-17

דברים יא,יג-יז:

וְהָיָה אִם שָׁמֹעַ תִּשְׁמְעוּ אֶל מִצְוֹתַי אֲנֹכִי מְצַוֶּה אֶתְכֶם
הַיּוֹם לְאַהֲבָה אֶת ה' אֱלוֹהֵיכֶם וּלְעָבְדוֹ בְּכָל לְבַבְכֶם וּבְכָל
נַפְשְׁכֶם: וְנָתַתִּי מְטַר אַרְצְכֶם בְּעִתּוֹ יוֹרֶה וּמַלְקוֹשׁ וְאָסַפְתָּ
דְגָנֶךָ וְתִירֹשְׁךָ וְיִצְהָרֶךָ:
וְנָתַתִּי עֵשֶׂב בְּשָׂדְךָ לִבְהֶמְתֶּךָ וְאָכַלְתָּ וְשָׂבָעְתָּ:
הִשָּׁמְרוּ לָכֶם פֶּן יִפְתֶּה לְבַבְכֶם וְסַרְתֶּם וַעֲבַדְתֶּם אֱלוֹהִים
אֲחֵרִים וְהִשְׁתַּחֲוִיתֶם לָהֶם: וְחָרָה אַף ה' בָּכֶם וְעָצַר אֶת
הַשָּׁמַיִם וְלֹא יִהְיֶה מָטָר וְהָאֲדָמָה לֹא תִתֵּן אֶת יְבוּלָהּ
וַאֲבַדְתֶּם מְהֵרָה מֵעַל הָאָרֶץ הַטֹּבָה אֲשֶׁר ה' נֹתֵן לָכֶם.

JPS (1916) – "And it shall come to pass, if ye shall hearken diligently unto My commandments which I command you this day, to love the LORD your God, and to serve Him with all your heart and with all your soul, that I will give the rain of your land in its season, the former rain and the latter rain, that thou mayest gather in thy corn, and thy wine, and thine oil. And I will give grass in thy fields for thy cattle, and thou shalt eat and be satisfied. Take heed to yourselves, lest your heart be deceived, and ye turn aside, and serve other gods, and worship them; and the anger of the LORD be kindled against you, and He shut up the heaven, so that there shall be no rain, and the ground shall not yield her fruit; and ye perish quickly from off the good land which the LORD giveth you."

NJV (1962) – "If, then, you obey the commandments that I enjoin upon you this day, loving the LORD your God and serving Him with all your heart and soul, I will grant the rain for your land in season, the early rain and the late: you shall gather in your new grain and wine and oil, and I will provide grass in the fields for your cattle; thus you shall eat your fill. Take care not to be lured away to serve other gods and bow to them. For the LORD's anger will flare up

*against you, and He will shut up the skies so that there will
be no rain and the ground will not yield its produce; and
you will soon perish from the good land that the LORD is
giving you."*

These verses form the beginning of the middle paragraph of
the Shema Yisrael prayer. In the Torah, they come toward the
end of Moses' first speech to the Israelites, and introduce a new
theological idea: Divine reward and punishment.

As they appear in the Siddur, the first and second paragraphs
of the Shema seem to have somewhat overlapping themes. Both
include injunctions to wear *tefillin*, post *mezuzot* on our door-
frames, and teach our children (The verses we've quoted above
stop just short of these commandments, which are given in
11:18-21, and form the end of the middle paragraph of the *Shema
Yisrael* prayer). Both demand that we love God and serve God
"with all your heart and soul." Why so many redundancies?

In order to answer that question, we must turn back to the
Torah, and put these passages back in their original context. The
first two paragraphs of the Shema actually form the beginning
and end of Moses' first speech to the Israelite people. "Hear O Israel, the Lord our God, the Lord is One" — With these words Moses began his first discourse, his first attempt to convey how he
hoped the Israelite people would behave after his death. The apparent redundancy is therefore a literary device, a stylized and
purposeful repetition of the key elements of Moses' speech as he
drew to a close.

Of course, for all of the redundancies there are also some major differences between the two passages and their messages. One
of the most noted differences is the change from singular in the
first passage to plural in the second. This grammatical change is
difficult to notice in the English translation, since in English the
word "you" is used to address both one person alone and a
group of people. However, in Hebrew, there are two forms of the
word "you" — one used to address one person alone, and another used to address two or more. In the Hebrew, then, it is obvious that the first paragraph of the Shema ("And you shall love
the Lord your God with all your heart, with all your soul, and
with all your might") is in the singular, addressing one person
alone; whereas the second passage, ("If, then, you obey the com-

mandments that I enjoin upon you this day, loving the LORD your God and serving Him with all your heart and soul") is in the plural, addressing a group of people.

Rashi and other commentators notice this grammatical change and see in it a significant teaching. The first passage, he notes, teaches each of us to love and worship God as individuals. The second passage teaches that we must also love and worship God as a community. Each message is of vital importance, and so both must be included in the seminal prayer. Moreover, the passages are ordered as they are — with the singular coming first, followed by the plural — in order to teach that we cannot form a meaningful community unless each of us has already undertaken personally to love God and make Judaism a significant part of our lives.

Some Bible scholars see something else in the change between singular and plural verb forms. They take this change to be evidence of multiple authors of the Bible, or at least multiple versions of the text which were later edited together to form a cohesive book. Others, however, argue that the grammatical change is simply an attempt at literary variation, possibly even done in hopes of appealing to both individual readers and groups.

What Does it Mean to "Serve God with All Your Heart"?

In the first paragraph of the Shema, we are commanded to "love God with all your heart." Here, the command is phrased slightly differently: we are to "serve" God will all our heart. We have already discussed the idea of loving God with all one's heart . What does the rephrased commandment mean?

The rabbis interpreted "serving God with all one's heart" to mean prayer. Strangely, there is no more explicit command to pray found in the Torah. In a deeply spiritual religion which demands that its adherents pray three times a day every day, and which boasts such a rich liturgy, one would expect that the injunction to pray would be obvious and unambiguous. Surprisingly, it is not — and so the rabbis felt that this verse was a less-explicit command to pray to God. In fact, prayer is often referred to in Hebrew as "service of the heart."

In fact, it is quite natural that the command to pray is not more explicitly worded in the Torah. While there are several instances of prayer found in Torah and in the Bible — most famously, Hannah's prayer to God that she be granted a child, for example — the main form of worship in Biblical times was animal sacrifice. Large sections of the Torah are devoted to describing and prescribing the sacrificial rites. Eventually the Temple was built in Jerusalem to centralize the daily offerings. It was only after the Temple was destroyed in 70 C.E. and animal sacrifice was no longer possible that prayer became an increasingly important mode of Jewish worship. Hence it is not suprising that the Torah does not explicitly command prayer — it was written in a time and place that emphasized another form of worhsip and so it too focused on that form. Only later, when prayer was an intergral part of Jewish worship, was "serving God with all one's heart" understood to be a source requiring Jewish prayer.[1]

Why are God's Promises to the People Tied to Agriculture?

Given that Israel's journey to the Promised Land is the central plotline of the Torah, it is not surprising that the reward-and-punishment system put forth in 11:13-17 is agriculturally based. The entire story centers on the land, and so it is only fitting that God expresses the promise of protection through it. In fact, the verses directly preceding these proclaim the goodness of the land they are about to enter in highly charged theological terms: "For the land that you are about to enter and possess is not like the land of Egypt from which you have come. There the grain you sowed had to be watered by your own labors, like a vegetable garden; but the land you are about to cross into and possess, a land of hills and valleys, soaks up its water from the rains of heaven. It is a land which the Lord your God looks after, on which the Lord your God always keeps his eye, from year's beginning to year's end."

Thus the Promised Land is spiritualized. It is not like any other land the Israelites have known, and not like any other land on earth — it is watered and protected by God. The Land itself is filled with God's presence, and thus serves as a reminder of the Covenant into which the Israelite nation has entered. As Rabbi Hirsch teaches, the flourishing and prosperity of this truly Holy Land depend on our moral behavior, our behavior toward God.

Beyond the spiritualization of the Promised Land which takes place in connecting God's promise and Israel's obedience to the Law, there is also the practical reality that in the desert that is the Middle East, prosperous farms and rain are not taken for granted. Judaism was not the first religion in that region to connect people's behavior to agricultural prosperity. The Canaanites worshipped Ba'al, their male god of life and fertility. Ba'al

was thought to be the lord of thunder, storms, and rain. His female partner, Anat, was in charge of yielding fruit on earth. Jewish monotheism did away with the theology of gods running
different subdivisions of nature; the Israelite's God was an all-
powerful Master of the entire earth and of all of nature. In fact,
the verses quoted above regarding God's watering the Land may
in fact be a reference to and denial of Ba'al's supposed role as
rain-giver.[2]

In the millenia before modern irrigation systems were invented, rain was even more important in Israel than it is today.
Our verses speak of granting "the rain for your land in season,
the early rain and the late." The timing of the rains in Israel, even
today, are crucial—both the winter and spring rains must come
on time and in the right amounts of water, not too much or too
little, or the crops will be ruined. Rashi understood the phrase
"in season" to mean that the rains would come at night, when it
would least bother the inhabitants of the land; or perhaps that it
would come on Friday night, when everyone was already home
celebrating Shabbat. Whether we understand the phrase literally
or figuratively, the spiritual message seems to be clear, that God
will send the Israelite people what they need, when they need it,
if they obey the commandments to love and serve the Holy One.

What is the Jewish View of Divine Reward and Punishment?

The concept of Divine reward and punishment is one of the most
deeply contested in all religion. If God is just, the argument goes,
than the righteous should be rewarded and live good, easy lives,
while the wicked should be punished. Unfortunately, we know
all too well that that is not the way of the world. Still, our sense of
justice mandates that if there is a God, the world should be a
place where everyone gets their due.

One of the main characteristics of the Book of Deuteronomy
is its "if-then" clause. IF you obey God, THEN God will reward
you. Here, in Deuteronomy 11:13-17, the reward is rain and
prosperity in the Promised Land. Elsewhere it is abundant children, or conquest of the Promised Land. What is interesting is
that Moses' speeches alternate between using this

if-then, reward-and-punishment scheme, and ignoring it.
Rabbi Hertz describes this alternating as Moses' own way of impressing upon the people the importance of obeying God's commandments. Moses, he suggests, hoped that the people would
love God of their own free will, and obey the commandments ac-

cordingly. Knowing as he did, however, that not everyone is as spiritually strong as he, he used the concept of reward and punishment as an alternate inducement.[3]

In contrast to Deuteronomy's oft-repeated reward-and-punishment scheme, many of the Prophets and Writings despair over the injustice evident in this world. Job, Jeremiah, Ecclesiastes, Habakkuk, and the Psalmist all wrestle with the presence of evil and God's seeming unwillingness to intervene to right the wrongs of this world. Thus, even the Bible itself is uncertain what to make of the concept. In more recent times, the Holocaust has forced Jews to rethink our concept of justice and Divine reward and punishment more than any other event in history.

There are two main attitudes toward this issue. The first is that God does reward the righteous and punish the wicked, in which case evidence of this reward-and-punishment must be supplied. The second approach is more agnostic: it doesn't matter, because if you love God that should be enough. We will examine both of these attitudes below.

To many of those who insist that God rewards good and punishes evil comes the concept of *Olam HaBa*—The World to Come. As Joseph Telushkin writes: "If one believes in a God who is all-powerful and all-just, one cannot believe that this world, in which evil far too often triumphs, is the only arena in which human life exists. For if this existence were the final word, and God permits evil to win, then it cannot be that God is good. Thus, when someone says he or she believes in God but not in afterlife, it would seem that either they have not thought the issue through, or that they don't believe in God, or the divine being in whom they believe is amoral or immoral."[4] The Talmud states that "There is no reward for performing mitzvot in this world" (*Kiddushin* 39b)—meaning, of course, that reward awaits in the World to Come. For many, the idea of a World to Come in which God distributes the justice which is so lacking in this world is the only comforting answer to Deuteronomy's reward-and-punishment scheme.

Nahmanides, on the other hand, insists that Divine reward and punishment exist in this world, but are discernible only in extreme cases. For most people who are neither extremely righteous nor extremely wicked, "God bestows good and bad in a natural manner," that is, in a manner which is largely unobservable to people used to the ups and downs of life. Thus the highs and lows of normal living can be seen as a form of Divine reward and punishment. The birth of a healthy new baby, for example, might be seen as a reward for the goodness one has done, whereas illness or financial trouble might be seen as some sort of punishment for transgressions committed. In extreme cases, however, God's responses would be obvious to all. While this answer is comforting in its treatment of the "average Joe" and the ups and downs of life, in this post-Holocaust, post A-bomb world it seems inadequate to explain the torture and death of so many millions of innocent people. The Holocaust, one would expect, would be an extreme case in which, if Nahmanides were correct, God's punishment of the perpetrators would be obviously observable.

Another answer for those who insist that reward and punishment is a very real part of God's relationship with the Jewish people is *"sekhar mitzvah mitzvah"* — a mitzvah is its own reward (*Pirke Avot – Ethics of the Sages*). By this logic, transgressing God's commandments is "punished" by the fact that one has "missed out" on performing that commandment; the converse for the reward. In fact, the *Mekhilta Beshalah* (as cited in *Torah Temimah*) cites 11:13 as a source for this outlook. In the Hebrew, the beginning of verse 11:13 literally reads: "If you obey, you will obey" — a common Hebrew literary structure of doubling the verb for emphasis. The *Mekhilta Beshalah* asks, why this doubling here? What is the extra "obey" coming to teach us? It comes to teach that when you perform one mitzvah, God helps you to do another. Thus, God rewards you with the joy and satisfaction that comes from living an observant Jewish life.

The second approach acknowledges that reward and punishment exists, but sees it as an imperfect form of faith to make it a major part of one's theology. Maimonides, for example, sees the idea of reward and punishment as a sort of spiritual crutch, to be used by people as they strive for spiritual perfection. As Rabbi Hertz states, Let one serve God at first for a reward; afterward such an individual will end by serving God without any motive.[5] Or, as stated in *Ethics of the Fathers*: "Be not like servants who serve their master for the sake of a reward; rather be like servants who serve their master without the condition of a reward, and let the fear of Heaven be upon you." For many Jews, this is the easiest answer to swallow: the Torah tells us that Divine reward and punishment exist, and so it does; but that is not why we believe in God or, really, how we believe in God.

As the Hasidic teacher, the Alter of Novardhok taught, the weekly Torah portion following this one, *Re'eh*, opens with God's presenting the children of Israel with a blessing and a curse. A blessing if one chooses to obey God's commandments, and a curse if one does not. We make our own choices in life, and we know before we act what is right and what is wrong in God's eyes. The basic idea behind the concept of Divine reward and punishment as that we as humans are free to do whatever we choose in this life, free to ignore God or love God. In a sense, then, the point of the Deuteronomic IF-THEN theology is not so much to teach us about God, but to encourage us to make sound moral and behavioral choices.

Notes

[1] For a full discussion on the development of prayer and the liturgy, see Abraham Millgram, *Jewish Worship* (Jewish Publication Society, Philadelphia, 1971).
[2] Keck II, 374.
[3] Hertz 925.
[4] Telushkin, *Literacy* 548.
[5] Hertz 925.

39

Deuteronomy 11:26

דברים יא-כו:

רְאֵה אָנֹכִי נֹתֵן לִפְנֵיכֶם הַיּוֹם בְּרָכָה וּקְלָלָה.

JPS (1916) – "Behold, I set before you this day a blessing and a curse."

NJV (1961) – "See, this day I set before you blessing and curse."

As the Israelite people prepare to cross the border into the Promised Land, Moses delivers a series of speeches designed to instill faith in and obedience to God. In the verses that follow 11:26, the Israelites are given a choice between a life of morality and obedience to God, resulting in "blessing," or a life of corruption and transgression, leading to "curse." This verse, introducing the "blessing versus curse" theme which is carried throughout the rest of Deuteronomy, proposes the concept of human free will.

Does Judaism Believe in Free Will?

It is no wonder that the free will versus pre-destination debate has been at the core of religious philosophy for so many centuries. The dilemma arises out of the Torah itself, which seems to offer conflicting visions. On the one hand, God is all-powerful, all-knowing, and sovereign. This is the God who hardens Pharoah's heart so that he refuses to let the Israelite slaves leave the country (Exodus 10:1), for example, or the God who prevents Abimelech, king of Gerar, to cohabit with Sarah (Genesis 20:6). On the other hand, there is the God of our verse, who presents the Israelite people with the liberty to choose for themselves the sort of lives they want to lead. This is the God of Deuteronomy 30:19: "I have put before you life and death, blessing and curse. Choose life...."

David Winston argues that Judaism has synthesized these two seemingly antithetical theologies into a unified philosophy. The Jewish concept of free will is not absolute. Rather, Judaism believes in relative free will: "...the concept of relative freedom found in classical Jewish sources fully acknowledges that all free human action is ultimately atributable to the efficacy of the Divine causality,"[1] he writes. In other words, free will exists, but at the root of all human action is the hand of God.

Examples of this belief in relative free will abound in rabbinic literature. In Mishnah Avot 3:15, for instance, Rabbi Akiva states: "Everything is foreseen by God, but humans have the capacity to choose freely." Rabbi Hanina ben Hama states in the Talmud (*Berakhot* 33b): "Everything is in the hand of Heaven except for the fear of Heaven." This comment is referred to again in the Talmud, in Tractate *Niddah* 16b, where God is confronted with a drop of sperm, and must decide its fate: "Master of the Universe, what will be the fate of this drop? Shall it produce a strong man or a weak man, a wise man or a fool, a rich man or a poor man?" The Talmud continues: "The terms 'wicked' or 'righteous' are not mentioned, as Rabbi Hanina ben Hama taught, 'Everything is in the hand of Heaven except for the fear of Heaven.'"

The Midrash tells a provocative story about Cain. Responding to God's accusations of guilt following the murder of his brother Abel, Cain replies to God: "Master of the World, if I have killed [Abel], it is You who has created in me the *yetzer hara*, the evil inclination. It is You who killed him." (*Tanhuma* Gen. 9b)[2]. In this story, Cain admits to the possibility that he voluntarily killed Abel, but also holds God responsible as his Creator and the Creator of the free will which led to Abel's death.

Relative free will can be understood another way as well. While we have free choice, we are limited in any decision by our circumstances, over which we generally have no control. This is perhaps the "bottom line" of relative free will. God controls the universe, not humans. People are born into social, economic, family, and physical conditions over which they have no control. People can, however, choose how they respond to their circumstances, and how they behave within their destined situation. Rabbi Hirsch teaches a wonderful parable on this theme:

> Mount Gerizim and Mount Ebal are two peaks of the Ephraim range of mounatins which still show a striking contrast in their appearance. Gerizim, to the south of the valley of She-

chem, presents a smiling green slope rising in fruit-covered terraces to its summit. Ebal, on the north side, is steep, barren and bleak, slightly higher than Gerizim. The two mounts lying next to each other form accordingly a most telling instructive picture of blessing and curse. They both rise on one and the same soil, both are watered by one and the same fall of rain and dew, the same air breathes over both of them, the same pollen wafts over both of them, yet Ebal remains in barren bleakness while Gerizim is clad to its summit in embellishments of vegetation. In the same way, blessing and curse are not conditional on external circumstances but on our own inner receptivity for the one or the other, on our behavior toward that which is to bring blessing.[3]

Our free will is often a matter of our attitude toward the situation in which we find ourselves. Or, put differently, it is a matter of seeing the glass half-empty or half-full: is my life full of blessing or full of curse? As Josephus put it: "To act rightly or not rests for the most part with us, but in each action Fate cooperates." Fate, or God, deals us the cards we play in the game of life; but how we play them is up to us.

This belief in relative free will is beautifully reflected in the blessings we recite every morning at the beginning of the morning prayers. The opening blessing of the morning prayer service is: "Blessed are You, Adonai our God, Ruler of the Universe, Who grants to the rooster understanding with which to distinguish between day and night." Rabbi Yehudah Leib Alter teaches that this blessing refers to our free will. The "understanding with which to distinguish between day and night" is our God-given capacity to see blessing or curse in our lives, to choose how we want to live. We recite this blessing first thing every morning in thanks to God for our liberty and also as a reminder that every day we are in a position to choose evil or good. Immediately following this blessing, however, come a series of blessings for things over which we have no control: for being Jewish, for not being slaves, and for being a man or a woman. Thus every morning, we begin by thanking God for our free will, and then we go on to acknowledge that this free will is constrained by our circumstances. Still, all are phrased as blessings. We begin every morning by asserting this relative free will, this partnership with God to find and create blessing in our lives. We thank God every morning for both our freedom and our limitations, and try the rest of the day to live up to the moral challenge this relative free will presents.

Theological Implications of God Being the Source of Both Blessing and Curse

One of the main thrusts of our verse is to underscore that God is in the Source of both blessing and curse. In Judaism there is no devil-type in charge of evil, while God handles goodness. Rather, there is One God in charge of all aspects of life. This raises an important question about the existence of evil and suffering. If God is the Creator and Source of everything, then God must be the Creator and Source of evil and suffering. How does Judaism handle this difficult theological question?

In one sense, Judaism hedges its bets. Religions which insist on absolute free will deduce from this belief that evil in the world is the direct result of human sin. Judaism, with its philosophy of relative free will, walks a slightly different path, placing the blame for evil and suffering on the shoulders of both God and humans. In fact, the long-standing Jewish tradition of arguing with God, of complaining to God about Jewish suffering and hardship, is derived from this philosophy. As much as Jews try to redeem ourselves and improve our lot in life, we hold God responsible and shake our fingers at Heaven, wondering, in the words of Rebbe Moshe Leib of Sasov, "Dear God, How long are you going to let us suffer in the dark exile? We can't stand it any more!"[4]

Thus in Judaism God and human beings are partners, sharing the responsibility for both goodness and evil in the world. The Midrash says that the "sword and the Book came down together…If people observe what is in the Book, then they will be saved from the sword." God grants us the choice between blessing and curse; but it takes human decision and action to actually incur the curse, the suffering. In fact, rabbinic literature tends to insist that God's plan is for the world to be full of goodness and blessing. It is people that force God into inflicting suffering and pain on the world. The Natziv teaches that God provides creatures with one single good, before they do anything, to encourage them toward the good. After that, they are on their own to choose.[5] Similarly, Rashi writes that blessing is granted to a person even before one proves him or herself to be good. Curse, however, comes only after one has sinned. He quotes Psalm 104 (verse 24): "How many are the things You have made, Adonai/ You have made them all with wisdom" as proof that the world is fundamentally good. From this point of view, God is responsible for the *existence* of evil in the world; however, it is humankind that is responsible for the actual *presence* of evil in the world.

As the *New Interpreter's Bible* writes, blessing and curse may easily be seen as human doing. Deuteronomy comes therefore to teach that God is the Creator and the arbitrator of such matters. The bottom line is that there must be a "tight integration of spiritual, ethical, and political authority"[6] in order for goodness and justice to prevail in the world.[7]

What Does it Mean to "See" the Blessing and the Curse?

In discussing the verse, "Hear O Israel, The Lord is our God, the Lord alone" (Deutereonomy 6:4), we looked into what it means to hear a commandment, to hear the voice of God or of another human being. This verse commands us not to *hear* the blessing and curse, but to *see* it. What exactly does it mean to see such a thing?

Obviously, the act of seeing is very different from the act of hearing. In hearing, we are listening to something happening externally to us. We are seeking to connect to someone else, to someone communicating to us. The act of seeing, however, can also be internal. In order to fully understand the choice between blessing and curse, in order to fully appreciate the gift and power of free will, one must be able to see clearly into his or her own conscience. Only then can a person be truly free to act as he or she sees fit.

In fact, while this verse is in the plural ("I set before you blessing and curse" — the word "you" is in its Hebrew plural form), the initial word, "see," is in the singular. The rabbis noted that this was to teach the distinction between community and individual responsibility. Although the whole community is responsible for determining its ethical behavior, each of us as individuals must "see" into our hearts and decide whether to obey or disobey Judaism's ethical code.[8]

Sforno focuses on the fact that the blessing and curse are set "before" us. They are nearby, visible, and in a place where we cannot help but see them: directly in front of us. The Torah is trying to teach us that the ethical choices we confront in our lives are manageable, attainable. They are right before us, so that we cannot move forward from one day to the next without considering the morality Judaism requires of us.

Notes

[1] David Winston "Free Will," in Cohen and Mendes-Flohr 273.
[2] Ibid.
[3] Hirsch V, 197.

4 Martin Buber, *Tales of the Hasidim* (New York: Schocken Books, 1948) 85.
5 Quoted by Leibowitz, *Devarim* 121.
6 Keck II, 375.
7 Ibid.
8 Rabbi Bahya ben Asher as quoted by Plaut, *The Torah* 1418.

40

Deuteronomy 16:20

דברים טז,כ:

צֶדֶק צֶדֶק תִּרְדֹּף לְמַעַן תִּחְיֶה וְיָרַשְׁתָּ אֶת הָאָרֶץ
אֲשֶׁר ה' אֱלֹהֶיךָ נֹתֵן לָךְ.

*JPS (1916) – "Justice, justice shalt thou follow, that thou
mayest live, and inherit the land which the LORD thy God
giveth thee."*

*NJV (1961) – "Justice, justice shall you pursue, that you
may thrive and occupy the land that the LORD is giving
you."*

According to rabbinic thought, no word — indeed, no letter — of the Torah is accidental. Every word is written to teach
something. So why, the rabbis ask, is the word "justice" repeated
at the beginning of this sentence? This question really served as
an entry-way for the rabbis to examine what it means to pursue
justice, and how one goes about pursuing justice.

The Talmud explains that the first "justice" is to teach regarding judgments, and that the second "justice" is to teach regarding compromises. The Talmud (*Sanhedrin* 32b) gives the
example of two ships trying to pass through a narrow strait at
the same time. If both insist on sailing ahead first, both will sink.
If, however, they agree on a system in which one waits for the
other, they will both arrive safely to the opposite shore. Sometimes compromise is the best way of "pursuing justice," and so
the word is doubled in order to remind us that our compromises,
like our judgments, must be fair.

Bahya ibn Asher taught that the word is repeated to teach
"justice under any circumstance, whether to your profit or loss,
whether in word or action, whether to Jew or non-Jew. It also

means: Do not use unjust means to secure justice."[1] According to Ibn Ezra, the doubling of the word "justice" teaches that one must pursue justice whether it is to one's advantage or loss.

What is the Jewish Sense of Justice?

"Justice, justice shall you pursue" has been the battle cry for generations of Jews and Christians in their fight for social justice and human rights. The notion of justice in Judaism is much broader than it is in Western culture. It is comprised of both legal justice, and compassion. In Western culture, these values often work alone: the legal system is supposed to be fair but not necessarily compassionate, and individuals are supposed to be compassionate even at the expense of dispensing justice. In Judaism, however, the two values must always be practiced together. To act justly is to act with both compassion and a sense of fairness.

A good example of this difference in attitude is found in the giving of charity. In English, the word "charity" comes from the Latin *caritas*, meaning "from the heart." Charity in Western culture is thus conceived of as something nice, voluntary, and emotionally-driven. It has nothing to do with legal obligation or a rendering of justice. The Jewish tradition approaches charity very differently. The Hebrew word for charity is *tzedakah*, which comes from the same linguistic root as *tzedek*, meaning justice (the first words of our verse, "Justice, justice shall you pursue" are in Hebrew, "*tzedek, tzedek tirdof*"). In the Jewish tradition, charity, *tzedakah*, is related to justice, to what is fair and legally-bound. Justice, *tzedek*, is about more than just legal rights. It is about compassion and humanity as well. In fact, the word *tzedek* is often translated as "righteousness," in an attempt to capture the full essence of the word.

Pursuing justice is a positive commandment, requiring positive action. It is not enough to refrain from doing harm or wronging others. Rather, God commands us to actively pursue justice, to engage in social work, to give charity, to go out of our way to help those in our communities. As Rabbi Elie Munk notes, there are only two commands given in the Torah regarding our personal character: pursuing justice, given here, and distancing ourselves from lies and falsehood (Exodus 23:7).[2] It is not enough that we value justice in some general way; we are commanded to make the pursuit of justice a paramount factor in our lives.

Because justice is not limited to the legal sphere, it affects how we interact with our fellow human beings on a daily basis. Rabbi Hertz explains that this conception of justice is the foundation of democracy in Judaism. Human beings are created in the

image of God, and there is a spark of the Divine in each of us —
therefore human life is sacred, and each human being must be
valued, loved, and respected as much as The Holy One. The Torah's legal code reflects this demand, for example, in Deuteronomy 25:3: "He [the one convicted of a crime] may be given up to
forty lashes, but not more, lest being flogged further, to excess,
your brother be degraded before your eyes."[3] This theme is
taken up also in the Mishnah: "Yehudah ben Tabbai says: When
serving as a judge, do not act as a lawyer. When the litigants
stand before you, consider them both as guilty; but when they
are dismissed from you, consider them both as innocent, provided they have accepted the judgment." (*Ethics of the Fathers*
1:8). It is just as important that a person — even one convicted of a
crime meriting punishment — be respected, as it is that he or she
be punished according to the law.

That legal fairness and compassion are two elements of the
Jewish notion of justice is reflected in God's names. The Torah
uses two names to refer to God: *Elohim* and *Adonai*. The tradition
teaches that each name is associated with a different aspect of
God. The name *Adonai* represents God's loving, compassionate
aspect. *Elohim*, in contrast, is associated with justice. The moral
of the two names is that, just as God is One and so manages to
combine both love and justice, so too we need both love and
justice to sustain the world.

How is Justice Perceived by the Prophets?

The Prophets are most famous for their insistence on the pursuit
of justice. One of the most-quoted lines of the Prophetic writings
is Amos 5:24: "Let justice roll down as waters, righteousness as a
mighty stream." In fact, examples of Prophetic writing on justice
can be taken from nearly any of the Prophetic Books, as it forms
one of the main themes of nearly all of them.

The chief concern of the Prophets was, in fact, to convince a
morally corrupt people to change their ways, to return to the
path of justice laid forth for them in the Torah. Whereas the Five
Books of Moses are concerned with both human morality and religious law, the Prophets focus largely on the former. As Frank S.
Frick writes, the importance of the Prophetic writings is "seen to
lie largely in the fact that they transformed the religion of ritual
to a religion of morality. Their contribution to humanity's spiritual growth was what was called 'ethical monotheism' ....The
popular image of the prophets [is] that of preachers of morals
and spiritual religion as opposed to ceremonialism and ritual."[4]
The Prophets focused on the message of justice given in Deuter-

onomy 16:20 and used that as the basis for their religious message. "He has told you, O man, what is good, and what the Lord requires of you: only to do justice and to love goodness, and to walk modestly with your God." (Micah 6:8)

Rabbi Abraham Joshua Heschel, in his classic work, *The Prophet*, questions this view of the Prophetic message. He argues that "ethical monotheism" emerged long before the time of the Prophets.[5] Moreover, the Prophets' main point was not "justice for justice's sake," but rather was to infuse the secular—and largely unheeded—idea of justice with the Toraitic belief in God's involvement in history. Because God is a God who acts in human history, we too must act, and act according to God's will—pursuing justice and a compassionate humanity. Rabbi Heschel thus sees the Prophets as proclaiming "God's pathos, speaking not for the idea of justice, but for the God of justice, for God's concern for justice."[6]

In fact, God is bound by the same requirement to pursue justice as Jews are. In the episode of Sodom and Gemorrah relayed in Genesis 18, God tells Abraham of his intention to destroy the cities because of their wickedness. Abraham responds passionately (Genesis 18:25), "Far be it from You to do such a thing, to bring death upon the innocent as well as the guilty, so that innocent and guilty fare alike. Far be it from you! Shall not the Judge of all the earth deal justly?" This belief in the God of Justice is at the root of the Prophet's insistence on justice, even as it lies at the root of the Torah's laws commanding human obedience to the pursuit of justice. As Isaiah wrote (5:16), "The Holy God is proved Holy through justice."

What is the Connection between the Pursuit of Justice and Jewish Legalism?

The development of law and a system of justice was one of the major contributions the ancient Near East made to modern Western culture. In examining our verse, we must understand that the larger context in which it lies is a legal one. At this point, God is giving directions (still through Moses) for the court system. Its features included a system of local courts, fair judges who were to judge without partiality, and an absolute ban on bribes. While today, these elements seem the most basic components of a legal system, in the ancient Near East they were revolutionary. Society was based on kinship ties, on clans and tribes. Legal disputes were generally settled by the eldest male of the household or tribe, and inter-tribal disputes often resulted in bloody feuds. The legal system prescribed in Deuteronomy was revolutionary in removing justice from the home and the tribe, and transforming it into an impartial institution available to all members of society.[7]

Jewish law is known as *halakhah,* or literally, "the way to go." Law is perceived as "the way to go" to satisfy God's will. According to Rabbi Gunther Plaut:

> Giving meticulous attention to [the law's] minutiae was to be doing His will, and, while in time this preoccupation often became extreme, its ultimate purpose was never in question: it was and remained to carry out Israel's obligation under the covenant to perfect the kingdom of the Almighty. Conversely, to act with lovingkindness was to act justly, for such was one's obligation.[8]

The Jewish love of law, love of justice, is thus rooted in love of God. As noted earlier, the pursuit of justice does not exist for its own sake, but rather stems from love of God and of the Law God commanded.

In fact, several of the rabbis have interpreted our verse in purely legalistic terms. Rashi, quoting Midrash *Sifrei Devarim* 144, interprets "justice, justice shall you pursue" as a commandment to search for a reliable, fair court. Sforno teaches this verse as applying to the appointment of judges: judges must be chosen according to their capacity to judge fairly, even if they lack other qualities generally associated with being a judge (for example, an imposing appearance or dignified manner). The Talmud interprets this verse as teaching that a *beit-din* (religious court) must seek defenses for the accused in a capital case (Talmud Yerushalmi, *Sanhedrin* 5:2). Resh Lakish, (Babylonian Talmud, *Sanhedrin* 32b), explains that the word "justice" is repeated in order to teach that caution, or "extra justice," must be used in cases in which deception or falsehood is suspected.

The Jewish preoccupation with *halakhah* and law in general is thus rooted in the Torah, in this very verse. It is based on an early concern for justice, and stems from a theology which holds that God acts justly. God is the ultimate Judge and Source of justice, and has given us laws designed to help us enact justice on earth. The love of law reflected in Deuteronomy 16:20 is a reflection of our love of the God of justice, and the desire to see all human beings treated fairly in the societies which we create and uphold.

What is the Connection Between the Pursuit of Justice and Living in the Promised Land?

In setting forth the pursuit of justice as a condition for happy settlement in the Promised Land, the Torah is making an important statement. Justice, it claims, is at the heart of any secure society. On one level, the verse implies a threat, that God will not allow the Israelites to live in the Land if they do not pursue justice. On another level, it is simply forewarning: without justice, you will not be able to thrive or securely occupy the Land I have promised to give you; it will simply be impossible for you to exist there. As Rabbi Hertz points out, corruption is the "most alarming sign of national decay"[9] in any society. Our verse comes to remind the Israelites of exactly that as they prepare to build a new society in Eretz Yisrael, the Land of Israel.

The pursuit of justice is just that — a pursuit, a constant questioning and search. Rabbi Elie Munk quotes the *Hiddushei HaRim* (Rabbi Yitzhak Meir Rothenberg Alter, 19th century Polish found of Ger hasidic dynasty) as teaching that righteousness — justice — is never fully attainable in this world. We must always pursue it, with the hope of ultimately finding it in the World to Come.[10] Nachmanides also interpreted the phrase "that you may live" as suggesting the World to Come; for how can we ever achieve perfect justice on earth? Still, the challenge has been given in the form of a command: Pursue justice, that you may live. As is stated in *Ethics of the Fathers* (2:21): "You are not obligated to complete the work, but you are not free to withdraw from it.... Your Employer can be relied upon to pay you the wages for your work, but be aware that the reward of the righteous (*tzadikim*) will be given in the World to Come."

Notes

[1] as quoted in Plaut, *The Torah* 1462.
[2] Elie Munk, *The Call of the Torah: An Anthology of Interpretation and Commentary on the Five Books of Moses* (Brooklyn: Mesorah Publications, Ltd., 1995) V, 176
[3] Hertz 821.
[4] Frank S. Frick, *A Journey Through the Hebrew Scriptures* (Harcourt Brace College Publishers, 1995) 388. Frick acknowledges that he is drawing on the writings of Abraham Joshua Heschel.
[5] Heschel, *Prophets* 218.
[6] Ibid. 219.
[7] Keck II, 416-7.
[8] Plaut, *The Torah* 1461.
[9] Hertz 821.
[10] Munk V,176.

41

Deuteronomy 19:14

דברים יט,יד:

לֹא תַסִּיג גְּבוּל רֵעֲךָ אֲשֶׁר גָּבְלוּ רִאשֹׁנִים בְּנַחֲלָתְךָ
אֲשֶׁר תִּנְחַל בָּאָרֶץ אֲשֶׁר ה' אֱלֹהֶיךָ נֹתֵן לְךָ לְרִשְׁתָּהּ.

*JPS (1916) – "Thou shalt not remove thy neighbour's land-
mark, which they of old time have set, in thine inheritance
which thou shalt inherit in the land that the LORD they
God giveth thee to possess it."*

*NJV (1961) – "You shall not move your countryman's
landmarks, set up by previous generations, in the property
that will be allotted to you in the land that the LORD your
God is giving you to possess."*

The law of *hasagat gevul* — moving a neighbor's landmark —
lies at the heart of Jewish ethics. It forms the basis of many Jewish
laws regarding property ownership, business practices, and copyrights. In its context in Deuteronomy, this commandment is included in a section dealing with criminal law, in a larger section
pertaining to justice and law in general. Literally it intends to impose a respect for landmarks, or boundary stones — an especially
important law for a people about to enter a new Land and divide
it according to tribe and family. However as the rabbinic tradition expanded the Biblical laws and sought to apply them to new
socio-economic conditions developing over many centuries and
in many different places, *hasagat gevul* became the cornerstone
on which to build laws regarding free trade, monopolies, intellectual property, and tenants' rights. It is therefore an important
verse to study, as it opens the door not only to many specific
laws governing diverse areas of life, but also as it demonstrates

the development of *halakhah*, the transformation of a Biblical law into a rabbinic precept.

How is This Commandment Different from "You Shall Not Steal?"

In an agricultural society, moving a neighbor's landmark, or boundary stone, was the equivalent of theft. Ancient societies lacked maps and regulated systems of land-measurement. Landmarks were thus considered sacrosanct, and tampering with them deeply threatening to a peaceful and honest society. Moving a neighbor's landmark was threatening because it could easily be done without witnesses, and without maps or land-measurement systems it would be virtually impossible to prove the crime. In fact, that may be why this law is listed immediately before laws regulating witnesses of a crime: to emphasize the fact that in the case of moving a neighbor's landmark witnesses were generally of no help in proving wrongdoing and the act could easily go unproven, and therefore unpunished.

Of course, if moving a neighbor's landmark was tantamount to theft, then there seems to be no need for a law specifying against theft of land in particular. The eighth commandment given at Mount Sinai (Exodus 20:13) is "You shall not steal," and the injunction is repeated in slightly different terms in Leviticus 19:13: "You shall not commit robbery." Restating the law in terms of moving a neighbor's landmark seems unwarranted in the face of such explicit injunctions against the taking of another person's property.

The Midrash addresses this problem directly. "Why is the law necessary when we are already commanded, 'you shall not steal'?" it asks. The answer the Midrash gives provides an insight into the way this law was, early on, treated as a jumping-off point from which new laws were created: "In order to make clear that any infringement of a neighbor's rights is included. The law also prohibits selling one's family graves, even those as yet unoccupied; and it forbids changing the words of a teacher which are pronounced in his name."[1] Far from being redundant, the Midrash sees the law as expanding the commandment against theft beyond one's property, and applies it to both intellectual property and the property of the dead.

The Talmud is somewhat less creative with Deuteronomy 19:14 than the Midrash. There the law is taken literally, as applying specifically to landowners. In particular, the law was seen as regulating landowners in Israel itself. Rashi, quoting the *Sifre*, in-

terprets this verse in a similar vein. He writes that the law of
hasagat gevul comes to teach that in Israel, the land is guarded not
only by the law "you shall not steal," but also by a second law,
"you shall not move your neighbor's landmark." The Land of Israel is more holy than the lands of the rest of the earth, and so
must be regulated more stringently, treated with more respect
and care. Thus a second law was given regarding stealing the
Land of Israel itself, to teach that it is a very different offense than
any other sort of theft.

What is the Significance of Landmarks "Set up by Previous Generations?"

In rabbinic literature, much attention is paid to the mention of
"previous generations" in this verse. A law against moving a
neighbor's landmark is understandable, but why specify that the
landmark in question is one set up by previous generations?
Moreover, the word translated by JPS first as "they of old time"
and later (NJV) as "previous generations" is vague. In Hebrew it
is "*rishonim*," from the root "*rosh*" meaning head or beginning.
Different commentators interpret *rishonim* differently. Rabbi
Hertz teaches that it is a general reference to "those of a former
age."[2] The *Soncino Chumash* takes a somewhat different tack and
explains that the *rishonim* were those who originally divided up
the land of Israel.[3] Numbers 34 gives the precise divisions of the
Land, to be made after conquest under the supervision of the
High Priest Eleazar, the military leader/prophet Joshua, and one
prince from each of the 12 tribes. The *Soncino Chumash* argues
that *rishonim* is a reference to these original land-dividers, appointed by God.

The question of what exactly is meant by *rishonim* and who
precisely they were, however, misses the significance of the
phrase itself, from which several ethical precepts can be drawn.
First, as Jeffrey Tigay notes, the fact that the landmarks or boundaries were set up by previous generations transforms the law
from one of simple property theft into one involving inviolable
emotional attachments to inherited traditions. As such, *hasagat
gevul* means more than simply moving boundary stones or even
encroaching on another's livelihood: it demands a sensitivity to
the emotional ties people have with their inherited lands and traditions, and a respect for those lands and traditions as handed
down to our contemporaries.[4]

Nahmanides taught that the reason for the *hasagat gevul* law
is to prevent not only theft of a neighbor's land, but also coveting

it. No one should think that his or her portion of land is not big enough, that the dividers erred in giving a neighbor too much and oneself too little. Rabbi Bahya taught that "a disgruntled Jew who is convinced that his family was treated unfairly in the division casts aspersions on the integrity of those 'early ones,' and even more so on the Divine nature of the lots by means of which the properties were divided."[5] The inclusion of the word "*rishonim*" thus comes to teach the very important lesson that one should be content with one's lot in life — even if that lot is smaller than that of one's neighbor.

The main point, then, of the verse's emphasizing that the landmarks had been set up by previous generations is to teach respect. Respect for tradition, and respect for the decisions made by one's ancestors. The verse seems to admonish us to be careful with what we have inherited, to tread lightly in changing what has been established by those who came before us. In commanding us not to move the landmarks set up by our ancestors, it reminds us to treasure what we have inherited, and to uphold the boundaries and landmarks past generations felt were important to hand down to us.

The Ethical Implications of *Hasagat Gevul*

The precept of *hasagat gevul*, moving a boundary stone, was expanded in the Talmud and post-Talmudic literature beyond its literal meaning. Over the centuries, it came to be an ethical value, admonishing against the unfair encroachment on another's livelihood, honor, or rights. The basic idea of moving a landmark was expanded from a purely agriculturally-based law into a general ideal of not pursuing one's own interests at the expense of one's neighbor's.

In his *Encyclopaedia Judaica* article on *hasagat gevul*, Menachem Elon observes that *hasagat gevul* is used as a base on which the rabbis over the centuries built laws during later socio-economic conditions, covering areas and situations which had not been otherwise provided for. For example, the prohibition on withholding the gleanings of one's field from the poor is based on *hasagat gevul* (Mishnah, *Peah* 5:6). Also several seemingly modern problems are regulated by *hasagat gevul*, including issues of tenants' rights, free trade, and intellectual property.[6] We will examine each of these in turn.

Tenants' Rights

As early as the 10th century, the concept of *hasagat gevul* was used to bar the eviction of tenants and to prevent unfair pricing of leases and rents. Because Jews were restricted as to the neighborhoods in which they could live, the Jewish quarters were often overpopulated and housing shortages were common. Jews were therefore in competition with one another for housing. *Hasagat gevul* was invoked to stop the inflation of rental prices, and to bar the eviction of tenants upon the termination of a lease. In 13th century Crete, for example, a *takanah* (rabbinic ordinance) was issued stating that "a person shall not encroach on his neighbor's boundaries by evicting him from his home…from today onward, no Jew shall be permitted…to offer excessive payment or rental to any landlord in order to gain occupation of his house…and thereby cause him to evict the existing Jewish tenant, for this is a transgression against 'cursed be one who moves one's neighbor's landmark.'"[7] Moreover, the offender was fined and no one was allowed to rent the residence in question for a period of one year from the date of its vacation.[8] The basic principle of *hasagat gevul* was thus extended to apply to the "new" problem of tenants' rights and housing shortages, and used to ensure honest dealing and fair practices within the Jewish community.

Monopolies

The rabbis of the Mishnaic period (ca. 70 C.E.-200 C.E.) generally supported free trade and competition. Few laws regulating or limiting business practices arose in this period. However, the Amora'im (rabbis of the period ca. 200-600 C.E.) began to grow somewhat uncomfortable with the status quo. Rav Huna, for example, states that a resident of a particular alley who earns his livelihood by operating a handmill may legally prevent another person from opening a handmill shop in that alley, as it would hurt his livelihood. Rav Huna's statement is not made into *halakhah* (law), but it does represent a strong voice against free trade (Talmud *Bava Batra* 21b).[9]

In the Middle Ages, Jews were restricted in the types of occupations they could hold. This led to fierce competition among Jews within these limited occupations. By the 10th century, the question of monopolies was of paramount concern. If one has a monopoly in a certain field, and his livelihood is based on the success of that monopoly, then may another Jew go into competition against him? Given how few fields of business were open to Jews, the question was of great practical, as well as ethical, import. The generally held opinion was negative, that a Jew did not have the right to threaten another's Jew's livelihood. However, there was never one hundred percent agreement regarding the issue. The question was applied to all sorts of occupations. Can a teacher steal the pupils of another teacher? What about the *shohet*, the ritual slaughterer, or the ubiquitous Jewish tax-collectors of Poland?[10]

The question was also asked about rabbis—could a rabbi have a "monopoly" in a given town, or was it permissible for another rabbi to set himself up "in competition" with the first? Originally, competition among rabbis was generally permitted, on the grounds that accepting payment for such services as weddings and funerals was not easily *halakhically* justifiable. However, as the role of rabbi evolved from one in which the rabbi supported himself with some unrelated craft or occupation and served the community as rabbi on the side, into a full-time, all-consuming career, the attitude toward rabbinic "monopolies" changed. By the 17th century, it was argued that one rabbi did not have the right to encroach upon the livelihood of another rabbi, based on "tradition". By the 19th century, this "tradition" was made into law, which regarded rabbis as craftsmen, dependent on their community for their livelihood, and so barring any others from encroaching upon his business territory.[11]

Hasagat gevul, which in its literal sense seems aimed to protect agrarian societies from corruption and land robbery, is thus applied to new forms of business and even to new developments within old occupations, such as the rabbinate. It is invoked as the root of the ethical injunction against violating another person's rights to earn a living, and thus ends up protecting all Jews—from the independent handmill operator to the owner of a monopoly to the tax-collector to the rabbi—from competition which might threaten the welfare of each individual and their families.

Intellectual Property and Copyrights

Ownership of incorporeal property was recognized in Judaism as early as the Mishnaic period. It was not until the 16th century, however, with the invention of the printing press, that copyright became a legal right—and even then it was based on *hasagat gevul*. In the middle of the 15th century, a man by the name of Meir Katzenellenbogen printed Maimonides' seminal work, *Mishneh Torah*. Much to his chagrin, someone else printed a rival edition shortly after his own came on the market. Katzenellenbogen complained to the great Rabbi Moses Isserles, who imposed a ban on anyone buying the rival edition. With this as a precedent, *Sefer HaBahir* by Elijah Levita was printed in 1518 with a warning: anyone reprinting the book within 10 years would be banished from the community. Thereafter, warnings printed at the beginning of books proscribing reprinting for a specified period of time became common, and the threat contained in them was usually of banishment. The nature of the ban was hotly debated: should it be imposed on the printer of the rival edition, or on the purchasers of such a book? Moreover, could a rival edition be printed before the specified period was completed, if the original publisher had already recovered his costs and turned a profit? What if all of the original copies were already sold?

Copyright laws grew out of a double concern: concern for the printer's livelihood on the one hand, and for the affordability of books on the other. A printer would typically lay out large sums of money in order to print a book, and the rabbis were concerned that he (or she) be able to recover the funds spent. If competition were permitted, and several editions of the same book printed at once, then printers would be forced to raise their prices in order to cover their costs. This, they feared, would lead to prohibitively high book prices. Expensive books were — and continue to be! — a hardship and obstacle to rabbis, as not only they, but their students and potential students, are forced to be frugal with their learning. Thus in a sense, their concern for book prices was not solely based on their good-will toward printers, but also grew from their own self-interest and love of learning.

The related issue of intellectual property rights came to be governed by the same set of laws pertaining to copyrights. Thus the author's rights were in time protected as well as those of the publishers. "Wrong attributions of rabbinic dicta"[12] (as Rabbi Tigay put it) came to be as surely prohibited as any other false encroachment of another person's property, based on the concept of *hasagat gevul*.

Notes

1 Plaut, *The Torah* 1472.
2 Hertz 830.
3 Cohen 1088.
4 Tigay 183.
5 Schreiber 1037.
6 Menahem Elon, "Hassagot Gevul" in *Encyclopaedia Judaica* XI, 1459-66.
7 Ibid. 1462.
8 Ibid.
9 Ibid.
10 Ibid. 1462-3
11 Ibid. 1463-4.
12 Tigay 183.

42

Deuteronomy 20:19

דברים כ,יט:

כִּי תָצוּר אֶל עִיר יָמִים רַבִּים לְהִלָּחֵם עָלֶיהָ לְתָפְשָׂהּ
לֹא תַשְׁחִית אֶת עֵצָהּ לִנְדֹּחַ עָלָיו גַּרְזֶן כִּי מִמֶּנּוּ תֹאכֵל
וְאֹתוֹ לֹא תִכְרֹת כִּי הָאָדָם עֵץ הַשָּׂדֶה לָבֹא מִפָּנֶיךָ בַּמָּצוֹר.

JPS (1916) — "When thou shalt besiege a city a long time,
in making war against it to take it, thou shalt not destroy
the trees thereof by wielding an axe against them; for thou
mayest eat of them, but thou shalt not cut them down; for is
the tree of the field man, that it should be besieged of thee?"

NJV (1961) — "When in your war against a city you have
to besiege it a long time in order to capture it, you must not
destroy its trees, wielding the ax against them. You may eat
of them, but you must not cut them down. Are trees of the
field human, to withdraw before you into the besieged city?"

This law is given as part of the rules pertaining to warfare
and the conquest of the Promised Land. At its most basic level, it
introduces into Judaism a respect for nature and an ecological
sensibility. However, the rabbis expanded this law to create an
even larger Jewish principle, the principle against wasting anything useful or beneficial. This law is known as *bal tashhit*, from
the Hebrew in this verse, "you must not destroy" (*lo tashhit*).

What is the Principle of *Bal Tashhit*, "You Must Not Destroy"?

Literally, the commandment given in Deuteronomy 20:19 prohibits the destruction of fruit-bearing trees during the siege of a

city. More specifically, it bans the destruction of fruit-bearing trees during the siege of a city by cutting them down with an ax. As such, it seems to be a very specific commandment with little relevance beyond war-time sieges. However, the rabbis sensed in it a larger moral principle, the principle against wastefulness.

That principle was first discerned in the juxtaposition of Deuteronomy 20:19 and 20:20. While Deuteronomy 20:19 proscribes destroying trees, the very next verse permits it, with a slight change of focus: "Only trees that you know do not yield food may be destroyed; you may cut them down for constructing siege works against the city that is waging war on you, until it has been reduced." The distinction is clear: the wanton destruction of fruit-bearing trees is not allowed, whereas the purposeful and necessary destruction of trees that do not bear fruit is permitted. In other words, the only destruction allowed is the destruction of trees that are "useless" and, furthermore, whose destruction would be militarily beneficial.

Once the verse was understood in this general sense as prohibiting the destruction of otherwise useful trees, its greater principle was uncovered. The first step toward expanding its reach was to enlarge the list of prohibited means of destruction. Thus, the rabbis decided, not only is chopping down a tree with an ax prohibited, but so is killing a tree through purposeful dehydration or by drawing off too much sap. In this manner, the rabbis removed the focus from the verse's literal meaning toward a more general understanding of its larger point.

Beyond its application to trees, however, the rabbis discerned in this verse a greater ethical principle. Ibn Ezra and others reasoned that if one must not destroy trees because they are useful to humans, so too one must not destroy anything useful to humans. This is the essence of the law known as *bal tashhit*, "do not destroy." The rabbis considered Deuteronomy 20:19 as a statement against destruction for destruction's sake. As Rabbi Samson Raphael Hirsch put it, "You may not destroy trees just to cut them down . . . so that your whole purpose is destruction."[1] Based on this reasoning, they developed the law of *bal tash-hit* into a general principle, forbidding wastefulness.

In the Talmud, this principle seems already established as applying to more than just trees. "Rabbi Eliezer said, 'I heard that a person who rends his garments for the dead more than is necessary transgresses the commandment against destructiveness'" (*Bava Kama* 91b). Thus it is extended to clothing, and its unnecessary ruin. Elsewhere, the Talmud takes an even more radical view of the law: "A person who could get along on corn but insists on eating wheat (a rarer commodity), or a person who could drink mead but drinks wine instead infringes on the ordinance of *bal tash'hit*" (*Shabbat* 140b). While this seems contrary to the general non-ascetic attitude of mainstream Judaism, it demonstrates how far the rabbis (some rabbis, at any rate) were willing to extend the law of *bal tash'hit*. It also shows a sensitivity to the distinction between necessity and luxury, on which in a certain sense the understanding of utility and wastefulness is based.

In his *Mishneh Torah* (*Hilhot Melakhim* 6:10), Maimonides expanded on Rabbi Eliezer's idea, stating that the law of *bal tash'hit* applies in every case, not merely in times of war, and extends the principle of *bal tash-hit* to utensils, clothing, buildings, wells, and food — and by implication all others useful items. Whereas in the Torah's formulation, the only benefit of a tree was its fruit on the one hand or its wood (to be used for military purposes) on the other, Maimonides exhibits a more sophisticated economic understanding, one which includes the sale of trees and the possibility that a tree might itself be destructive as it causes damage to other trees or fields.

Nehama Leibowitz has a very beautiful rendering of the *bal tash'hit* principle. She understands the commandment as a reminder that God is the ultimate owner of all things, and therefore it is not up to humans to destroy anything. "Everything is granted to us in trust," she writes, and so we must use what is granted to us wisely and keep it in good condition for its true Owner and Creator. She also senses in the law an important personal lesson. She quotes the *Sefer HaHinukh* as teaching that

> this precept is designed to inculcate love of the good and beneficial. This will lead to the avoidance of destructiveness and the promotion of our well-being. This is the way of the pious and the worthy who love peace and rejoice in the well-being of all people, bringing them near to the Torah. They do not suffer the loss of even a grain of mustard, being distressed at the sight of any loss or destruction. If they can help, they prevent any destruction with all the means at their disposal. But it is otherwise with the wicked, the embodiments of destructive spirits who revel in the corruption of the world, corrupting themselves. One is measured by one's own yardstick. In other words, one is always affected by one's own attitude, and one who desires good and rejoices in it, will always be granted to enjoy it.[2]

Thus, the principle of *bal tash'hit* is not only a war-time ecological commandment, but also a timeless personal lesson and ethical teaching.

What are the Ecological Implications of this Verse?

The Torah does not have a concept of "ecology" the way we do today. It does, however, understand the ways in which nature and humanity are dependent upon one another as well as on God. Deuteronomy 20:19 is one of many laws demanding respect for the earth. For example, during the Sabbatical Year (falling every seven years), farmers must let their fields lie fallow in order to allow the soil to recuperate and replenish itself. The holidays of Shavuot (The Festival of Weeks) and Sukkot (The Festival of Booths) celebrate the first-fruits and harvest, respectively. *Tu BeShvat*, the New Year for Trees, while not of Biblical origin, celebrates trees and their fruits. Judaism, a religion whose central myth,[3] or defining narrative, is the story of a people's journey to a Promised Land, has always been centered on the earth and people's relationship to it.

The Torah's laws commanding respect for the earth stand in contrast to the prevailing practice of the ancient near east. Most ancient religions worshipped the earth itself, and believed in an array of gods who oversaw its different geological features. The Torah's theology is radically different. It insists that the earth is created by the One True God. Therefore, God is to be worshipped and the earth is to be cared for. The fundamental theology of Jewish ecology is given in Psalms 24:1: "The earth is the Lord's and all that is in it." This tempers God's instructions to Adam and Eve in Genesis 1:28: "Be fertile and increase, fill the earth and master it…." On the one hand, we are at the top of the food and brain chain; on the other hand, we are merely part of God's Creation. Thus the Torah teaches: while we have been created such that we master the earth, we must remember that God is the earth's only True Master, and we must act within God's laws. Deuteronomy 20:19 reminds us that while we are capable of mastering the earth and taking down its trees for the sake of our wars and other whims, we must not.

What Does the Verse Teach us about War?

Deuteronomy 20:19 is part of a larger section of laws pertaining to warfare. From the general section on warfare (Deuteronomy 20:1-20) one sees that Israel is required to display human kindness even in wartime: the betrothed is exempt from military service; offers of peace must be made to a city before it is attacked; and fruit-trees cannot be destroyed during a siege. The rules of war are to be infused with reason and mercy. The Torah's laws are designed not to encourage war, but to temper it and make it as humane as possible.

In ancient — and not so ancient — warfare, it was common to destroy the enemy's fruit trees and fields. Deforestation was also a common technique of war, similar to today's practice of defoliation. These practices aimed to weaken the enemy's economy and hamper its ability to fight in the near future. It was also intended as pressure on cities to surrender. This occurred as recently as the Civil War in the United States, when the people of Savannah, Georgia, surrendered to General Sherman during his "March to the Sea" — west to east — through the Confederacy in 1864-1865, burning everything in sight — fields, houses, cities. The point was to demoralize the South by destroying its way of life and thus to prompt an earlier surrender. The citizens of Savannah surrendered from a distance, rather than give him the opportunity to burn down their beloved city.

Rabbi Hertz sees the verse as a sort of warning: the Israelites should not be so reckless as to devastate the very land they were trying to conquer.[4] Sforno points out that while armies unsure of their victory might cut down fruit-trees to harm the enemy, Israel was assured by God of victory. Thus destroying the trees would hurt only themselves. As Midrash *Sifrei Devarim* put it, "When in your war against a city you have to besiege it a long time in order to capture it — 'to capture it, and not to destroy it.'" W. Gunther Plaut writes, "Creating was seen as an ongoing process, and humans at all times were God's co-partners in safeguarding its potential. The Torah uses the example of behavior during warfare to demonstrate the importance of this principle."[5]

"Are Trees of the Field Human, to Withdraw Before you into the Besieged City?"

The Hebrew of the last phrase of Deuteronomy 20:19 is difficult to understand. Its strange syntax renders its meaning and translation uncertain. Over the ages, rabbis have come to use this uncertainty to derive different lessons from the verse.

One school understands this phrase as teaching about humanity, rather than utility. If the first part of the verse focused on the benefits and usefulness of fruit-bearing trees, and was designed to teach about wastefulness, this phrase aims to teach about benevolence. Sforno writes:

> Is then the tree of the field a human, who is capable of submitting to you, that the city be besieged on its account, and be

forced to surrender because of the siege? This is obviously not so, and although it is acceptable to inflict damage upon the inhabitants of a city with implements of war and other kinds of tactics so as to besiege the city, since you will not attain this goal by destroying the trees, it is improper to destroy them.

Thus we are to act with kindness toward the land and its trees even as we wage war on its inhabitants. While focusing on humanity, this reading is in a sense not so far from the discussion of utility. Destroying trees is futile in terms of winning the battle, the argument goes, and so therefore there is no reason to commit such an act. We are to have compassion with the trees and treat them with kindness and mercy.

Another school sees this phrase not as a question, but as a statement. Because there is no punctuation in the original Torah text, both readings are valid. The Midrash *Sifrei Devarim*, for example, translates the phrase "A human is [like] a tree...". This reading stresses human dependence on vegetation. It reminds us that we must co-exist peacefully with the earth, even when we wage war with its inhabitants. Rabbi Samson Raphael Hirsch similarly teaches, "The tree of the field is the human being, the products of the soil are the condition for human existence."[6]

Notes

[1] Hirsch V, 394.

[2] Leibowitz, *Devarim* 197.

[3] For a discussion on the definition and function of myth, see Neil Gillman, *Sacred Fragments: Recovering Theology for the Modern Jew* (Philadelphia: Jewish Publication Society, 1990) 26-32, 84-8.

[4] Hertz 833.

[5] Plaut, *The Torah* 1479.

[6] As quoted by Fields III, 144.

43

Deuteronomy 21:1-9

כִּי־יִמָּצֵא חָלָל בָּאֲדָמָה אֲשֶׁר ה' אֱלֹהֶיךָ נֹתֵן לְךָ לְרִשְׁתָּהּ
נֹפֵל בַּשָּׂדֶה לֹא נוֹדַע מִי הִכָּהוּ: וְיָצְאוּ זְקֵנֶיךָ וְשֹׁפְטֶיךָ
וּמָדְדוּ אֶל־הֶעָרִים אֲשֶׁר סְבִיבֹת הֶחָלָל: וְהָיָה הָעִיר הַקְּרֹבָה
אֶל־הֶחָלָל וְלָקְחוּ זִקְנֵי הָעִיר הַהִוא עֶגְלַת בָּקָר אֲשֶׁר לֹא־
עֻבַּד בָּהּ אֲשֶׁר לֹא־מָשְׁכָה בְּעֹל: וְהוֹרִדוּ זִקְנֵי הָעִיר הַהִוא
אֶת־הָעֶגְלָה אֶל־נַחַל אֵיתָן אֲשֶׁר לֹא־יֵעָבֵד בּוֹ וְלֹא יִזָּרֵעַ
וְעָרְפוּ־שָׁם אֶת־הָעֶגְלָה בַּנָּחַל: וְנִגְּשׁוּ הַכֹּהֲנִים בְּנֵי לֵוִי כִּי
בָם בָּחַר ה' אֱלֹהֶיךָ לְשָׁרְתוֹ וּלְבָרֵךְ בְּשֵׁם ה' וְעַל־פִּיהֶם
יִהְיֶה כָּל־רִיב וְכָל־נָגַע: וְכֹל זִקְנֵי הָעִיר הַהִוא הַקְּרֹבִים אֶל־
הֶחָלָל יִרְחֲצוּ אֶת־יְדֵיהֶם עַל־הָעֶגְלָה הָעֲרוּפָה בַנָּחַל: וְעָנוּ
וְאָמְרוּ יָדֵינוּ לֹא שָׁפְכוּ אֶת־הַדָּם הַזֶּה וְעֵינֵינוּ לֹא רָאוּ:
כַּפֵּר לְעַמְּךָ יִשְׂרָאֵל אֲשֶׁר פָּדִיתָ ה' וְאַל־תִּתֵּן דָּם נָקִי בְּקֶרֶב
עַמְּךָ יִשְׂרָאֵל וְנִכַּפֵּר לָהֶם הַדָּם: וְאַתָּה תְּבַעֵר הַדָּם
הַנָּקִי מִקִּרְבֶּךָ כִּי־תַעֲשֶׂה הַיָּשָׁר בְּעֵינֵי ה'.

*JPS (1916) — "If one be found slain in the land that the
LORD thy God giveth thee to possess it, lying in the field,
and it be not known who hath smitten him, then thy elders
and thy judges shall come forth, and they shall measure
unto the cities that are round about him that is slain. And it
shall be, that the city which is nearest unto the slain man,
even its elders of that city shall take a heifer of the herd,
which hath not been wrought with, and which hath not
drawn in the yoke. And the elders of that city shall bring
down the heifer until a rough valley, which may be neither
plowed nor sown, and shall break the heifer's neck there in
the valley. And the priests the sons of Levi shall come
near — for them the LORD thy God hath chosen to minister
unto Him, and to bless in the name of the LORD; and according to their word shall every controversy and every
stroke be. And all the elders of that city, who are nearest*

unto the slain man, shall wash their hands over the heifer, whose neck was broken in the valley. And they shall speak and say: 'Our hands have not shed this blood, neither have our eyes seen it. Forgive, O LORD, thy people Israel, who Thou hast redeemed, and suffer not innocent blood to remain in the midst of Thy people Israel.' And the blood shall be forgiven them. So shalt thou put away the innocent blood from the midst of thee, when thou shalt do that which is right in the eyes of the LORD."

NJV (1961) — "If, in the land that the LORD your God is assigning you to possess, someone slain is found lying in the open, the identity of the slayer not being known, your elders and magistrates shall go out and measure the distances from the corpse to the nearby towns. The elders of the town nearest to the corpse shall then take a heifer which has never been worked, which has never pulled in a yoke; and the elders of that town shall bring the heifer down to an overflowing wadi, which is not tilled or sown. There, in the wadi, they shall break the heifer's neck. The priests, sons of Levi, shall come forward; for the LORD your God has chosen them to minister to Him and to pronounce blessing in the name of the LORD, and every lawsuit and case of assault is subject to their ruling. Then all the elders of the town nearest to the corpse shall wash their hands over the heifer whose neck was broken in the wadi. And they shall make this declaration: 'Our hands did not shed this blood, nor did our eyes see it done. Absolve, O LORD, Your people Israel whom You redeemed, and do not let guilt for the blood of the innocent remain among your people Israel.' And they will be absolved of bloodguilt. Thus you will remove from your midst guilt for the blood of the innocent, for you will be doing what is right in the sight of the LORD."

With the prescribing of this strange ritual, *Parshat Shoftim* comes to a close. The Torah portion of *Shoftim*, or "judges," delineates the rules and regulations pertaining to the judges and officials of Israel. It is therefore significant, as Rabbi Hirsch notes, that the *Sidrah* ends with a case in which these very officials must publicly clear themselves from suspicion for having breached one of the Torah's most basic laws, "You shall not murder" (Exodus 20:13). This ritual is known as the *eglah arufah*, the "broken-necked heifer."

The text does not explicitly state why a heifer, and no other animal, must be used. The ceremony recalls the ritual of the *parah adumah* (the red heifer) of Numbers 19, where a red heifer (as with the *eglah arufah*) that had never been trained to work a yoke, was slaughtered outside the camp. It was then burned to ashes, which were sprinkled on anyone who had become ritually defiled through contact with a dead body. In both cases, the heifer is used ritually to purify. Still, in neither case does the text explain why a heifer is specified as the required animal.

A heifer is a cow that has not produced a calf. Rashi explains that it must be only one or two years old. The Rabbis taught, "Let the heifer which has never produced fruit (i.e., which has never born offspring nor been set to do any work) be killed in a spot which has never produced fruit (i.e., a wadi, a rough, uncultivated ground), to atone for the death of a man who was debarred through his premature death from producing fruit." Others thought that the heifer symbolized the murderer, and what would be done to him if found. The Talmud (*Sanhedrin* 52b) states: "All shedders of blood are compared to the *eglah arufah*. Just as it is killed by the sword and at the neck, so are they to be killed by the sword and at the neck."

Why Does the Torah Establish the *Eglah Arufah* Ritual?

Murder is taken very seriously in the Torah, which teaches that life, and human life in particular, is sacred. It is no surprise, therefore, that premeditated murder is considered the worst crime a person can commit. Premeditated murder (as opposed to killing in self-defense) is punished with the death penalty.

Just as human life is sacred, so too is the Land of Israel. Murder, the shedding of innocent blood, defiles the land just as it defiles the person who commits such an act. This principle is set forth in Numbers 35:33: "You shall not pollute the land in which you live; for blood pollutes the land, and the land can have no expiation for blood that is shed on it, except by the blood of him who shed it." This principle is portrayed vividly in Genesis, when, after Cain kills his brother Abel, God says to Cain, "What have you done? Hark, your brother's blood cries out to Me from the ground!" (Genesis 4:10). Similarly, Job cries out, "Earth, do not cover my blood; let there be no resting place for my outcry!" (Job 16:18).

Of course a problem arises when the murderer is not known or caught. How, in that case, can expiation be made to purify the land? What can be done to end the outcry of innocent blood when the murderer cannot be tried and executed? As Malbim points out, because we cannot kill the murderer, we must substitute something else: the heifer. Thus, the *eglah arufah* ritual seeks to atone for a murder that has not been brought to justice.

What Were the Conditions Under Which the *Eglah Arufah* Ritual Would Take Place?

The ritual of the *eglah arufah* took place only under very specific conditions. First, the discovered corpse must have been obviously murdered. There had to be marks of human violence on the body, barring the possibility that the person died of natural causes while traveling. Second, the person must be dead, and not dying, when found. He or she must be lying openly in the field, and not floating in a river or buried or hidden. While these rules seem somewhat arbitrary and picayune, Rabbi Hirsch interprets them as pointing to a case where the murderer openly flaunted the law. Hiding or trying to get rid of the body, or not finishing off the job, betrays some fear of the authorities and the law. This case shows the perpetrators to be acting with no regard to humanity, society, law or the authorities, he explains. Therefore, some ritual involving those very authorities and law-makers is necessary near the scene of the crime.[1]

Moreover, the ritual of the *eglah arufah* was only performed in places where Jewish courts ruled. First, a body found near a non-Jewish city was presumed to have been killed by non-Jews, in which case the Jewish community did not need to seek atonement. Second, it was assumed that in non-Jewish cities, murderers and bandits might feasibly reside undisturbed, as other law codes of the ancient world were less stringent about murder than the Torah. Therefore if a dead body were found near the border of a non-Jewish city (or a city where non-Jewish courts ruled), the *eglah arufah* ritual was not performed. Once murder became commonplace even in Jewish cities, however, the rabbis abolished the ritual altogether, as no longer serving a purpose in educating the people or in expiating the land from its sins. The ritual was never performed in Jerusalem, which was considered to belong to all of the tribes of Israel and therefore did not qualify as a "land that God is assigning you to possess."

The *eglah arufah* ritual was to take place in a wadi, a rough valley that had never been cultivated. There also needed to be a body of running water, as prescribed in verse 5 (where the elders wash their hands over the heifer). As Rabbi Hertz wrote, the running water carrying away the heifer's blood would "symbolize the removal of defilement from the land."[2] The corpse was to be buried where it was found, and the land where it was found was never to be farmed. Maimonides understood this as added impetus for the discovery of the murderer: the owner of the land would surely do everything he could to find the murderer, so that the body could be buried elsewhere and his land used for agriculture.[3]

The *eglah arufah* ceremony was to be performed by kohanim (priests) and the elders of the nearest town, even if there existed no evidence that the murderer came from there. The Rabbis interpreted this to be a token of the responsibility borne by leaders of a community. The Talmud (*Makkot* 11a) suggests that truly righteous people prevent calamities in the surrounding area. If the elders were truly righteous, no evil would have occurred, even in the fields surrounding their city.

While we do not know if the ritual of the *eglah arufah* was ever regularly practiced, we do know how and when it came to be abolished. The Talmud (*Sotah* 47a) explains that the practice was eliminated in the first century C.E., because murder, even in the Jewish community, had become so widespread then that it was no longer feasible that no one in the city knew anything of the crime. As the Midrash *Sifrei* put it, "*If there be found* [a dead body], but not *at a time when it is generally found* — whence it was derived: when murderers proliferated, the breaking of the heifer's neck was abolished."[4]

What is the Deeper Significance and Meaning of the *Eglah Arufah* Ritual?

The reason for the *eglah arufah* is not given in the text. As the *Interpreter's Bible* points out, "The reasoning behind these carefully specified actions is not openly expressed. Clearly, from a practical viewpoint, it was an acknowledgment that the crime was taken seriously, but that nothing further could be done to identify the circumstances of the death or to apprehend the person, or persons, responsible for it."[5] The Rabbis listed the mitzvah of the *eglah arufah* in the category of *hukkim*, commandments for which there is no apparent reason.

However, several commentators do see the *eglah arufah* ceremony as embodying a larger ethical principle. It underscores the sanctity of human life and the seriousness with which mocking that sanctity through murder is taken. One of the highest goals of the whole of God's plans for the people of Israel is that the life of every human is sacred and should be treated as such, and a murdered body found on the soil of God's land is the greatest mocking rebelliousness of that Torah. Nehama Leibowitz sees the *eglah arufah* as a call to each of us to take responsibility for those in our community:

> The public as a whole and the city nearest to the slain and its elders are all responsible for the terrible deed committed in the field. Their whole way of life, their social order, economic, educational, and security institutions are answerable for the murder...Thus responsibility for wrong-doing does not only lie with the perpetrator himself and even with the accessory. Lack of proper care and attention is also criminal. Whoever keeps to his own quiet corner and refuses to have anything to do with the "evil world," who observes oppression and violence but does not stir a finger in protest, cannot proclaim with a clear conscience that "our hands have not shed this blood."[6]

Similarly, the commentary known as *Me'am Lo'ez* finds meaning in the fact that this case, of a murder taking place in an open field, is listed in the Torah immediately after a section dealing with warfare:

> This juxtaposition is intended to emphasize that we are never to become unconcerned or apathetic about death, despite the unfortunate need to participate in military campaigns. Each death is to disturb and affect us profoundly, bringing in its wake a ritual that involves the participation of the nation's leaders to try to discover what moral breakdown occurred in the nation as a whole to permit murder to take place.[7]

What Were the Social Implications of this Ritual?

In today's overpopulated and sprawling society, we are used to not knowing our neighbors and townspeople. In the ancient world, however, cities were smaller and life was more communal than it is today; everyone could be easily accounted for until the murderer was found. It was therefore rare to have an unsolved murder.

The *eglah arufah* ceremony was required for murder cases committed in open fields, far from a city, with no witnesses. It was unlikely that the murderer could be found in such a case.

Unlike most murder cases, in which two witnesses are required, the testimony of even one witness was sufficient to prevent the *eglah arufah* ritual from taking place. Still, with surprisingly modern sensitivity to the phenomenon of publicity, many commentators see the *eglah arufah* as designed to draw attention to a case that might otherwise fall by the wayside. As Nehama Leibowitz put it, "We know too well the indifference that prevails among people regarding the miseries of others. Anyone hearing of a murder, either then or now, would shake his head, go his own way, and the world would continue as before."[8]

Abravanel and others felt that the sensational nature of the *eglah arufah* would capture the public's interest such that the search for the murderer would be kept alive. The strange ritual, involving all of the area's elders and judges, would shock the residents of the neighboring cities with the news that someone had been murdered in their area. In fact, the publicity around such a strange ceremony would equal that of the execution of the murderer, thereby raising communal awareness of responsibility and the moral code. Moreover, it would ensure that all of the neighboring cities would be forced to take some responsibility for the murder—otherwise, a murder in an open field lying between urban districts might go uninvestigated as no city would be willing to take responsibility for it.

There might also be a lesson taught in the ritual itself. For the elders who must take part in the ceremony, witnessing the killing of the heifer might serve to forcefully remind them what would happen to them should their confession of innocence prove to be untrue and of how important their moral leadership of the community is. A breach of their own word or conduct would result in bloodshed similar to that taking place before them with the killing of the heifer.

"Our Hands Did Not Shed This Blood, Nor Did Our Eyes See it Done"

The final step of the *eglah arufah* ritual is the prayer for expiation. Deuteronomy typically emphasizes prayer as the means for forgiveness and communication with God (as opposed to ritual acts), and so it is not surprising here that the strange ceremony culminates in a communal prayer for God's forgiveness. Still, the language of the elders' oath is odd: "Our hands did not shed this blood, nor did our eyes see it done." After all, no one is accusing the highly respected elders of having committed the murder. Why should they be required to declare their own innocence?

The oath of the elders teaches the importance of communal responsibility. While no one is accusing the elders of having actually committed murder, their prayer shows them taking responsibility for the fact that a murder took place in their neighborhood—on their watch, as it were. The Talmud understands the oath as a vow that the elders did not permit lawlessness and violence to hold sway in their community (*Sotah* 45b). They were vowing to God that they had acted rightfully to ensure an ethical society, such that there was no "blood on their hands," even in any indirect way.

The Midrash *Sifrei Devarim* explains: "Could it possibly occur to anyone to suspect the elders of murder? No! By this avowal the elders of the town declare, He did not come to us hungry, and we failed to feed him; he did not come to us friendless, and we failed to befriend him."[9] The Talmud (*Sotah* 45b) considers that the possible failure to feed him refers to not giving him food for his journey, such that he would be forced to resort to highway robbery and risk being killed in the process of trying to steal food for his survival. In a more general sense, this would mean that the elders were vowing that no poor person in their community went so "unaided as to be driven to a life of crime"[10]. Ibn Ezra understands the oath of the elders to concern the safety of the highways. He sees the elders as vowing that they ensured the guarding of the highways to prevent violence on their stretch of the road.

The Palestinian Talmud (circa 400 C.E) has a slightly different understanding of the elders' oath. There, the oath is considered to be about the murderer, not the murdered. Thus, the phrase "our hands have not shed this blood, neither have our eyes seen it" is a declaration that the elders had never met the murderer, had never imprisoned him and then let him go free. As Rabbi Hirsch paraphrased, "the murderer did not come into our hands and we allowed him to go free, we did not see him and close our eyes to his guilt."[11]

What is the Role of the Priests in this Ritual?

While the text takes pains to ensure that the Levite priests will take part in the *eglah arufah* ritual, their exact role is in the ceremony is unclear. Many commentators understand the verses to mean that the priests are the ones who utter the oath and atonement prayer. According to this view, the Sanhedrin (the rabbis of the Great Assembly who served as judges) were responsible for measuring the distances to the nearby cities, the elders washed their hands over the *eglah arufah,* and the priests spoke the oath. However, the text does not make explicit the role of the Levites, and so their exact function in the ceremony is uncertain.

What is certain is that the *eglah arufah* ceremony is not a ritual sacrifice. In a ritual sacrifice, the Levites perform the slaughtering of the animal. Here, the Levites become involved in the ceremony only after the heifer's neck is broken, barring the possibility that this was some kind of sacrificial offering to God. At the bare minimum, it seems that the priests were present as religious representatives at the ceremony.

Modern scholars see the verses about the Levites as a later addition to the text. Most likely, an older tradition about the *eglah arufah* existed, which the Deuteronomist (the source of the Book of Deuteronomy) included in his text, adding on to it an element of prayer. The Priestly author, whose main interest was the Priests and their ritual duties, probably inserted the Levites into the ceremony at a later date.

Notes

[1] Hirsch V, 396-7.
[2] Hertz 834.
[3] Ibid.
[4] as quoted in Epstein V,197.
[5] Keck II, 445.
[6] Leibowitz, *Devarim* 207.
[7] Jacob Culi, *The Torah Anthology: Me'Am Lo'ez* (New York, Maznaim Publishing Corp., 1977) V/3, 279.
[8] Leibowitz, *Devarim*. 204.
[9] as quoted in Hertz 835.
[10] Leiber 1105.
[11] Hirsch V, 403.

44

Deuteronomy 22:1-3

דברים כב,א-ג:

לֹא תִרְאֶה אֶת שׁוֹר אָחִיךָ אוֹ אֶת שֵׂיוֹ נִדָּחִים וְהִתְעַלַּמְתָּ
מֵהֶם הָשֵׁב תְּשִׁיבֵם לְאָחִיךָ: וְאִם לֹא קָרוֹב אָחִיךָ אֵלֶיךָ וְלֹא
יְדַעְתּוֹ וַאֲסַפְתּוֹ אֶל תּוֹךְ בֵּיתֶךָ וְהָיָה עִמְּךָ עַד דְּרֹשׁ אָחִיךָ
אֹתוֹ וַהֲשֵׁבֹתוֹ לוֹ: וְכֵן תַּעֲשֶׂה לַחֲמֹרוֹ וְכֵן תַּעֲשֶׂה לְשִׂמְלָתוֹ
וְכֵן תַּעֲשֶׂה לְכָל אֲבֵדַת אָחִיךָ אֲשֶׁר תֹּאבַד מִמֶּנּוּ וּמְצָאתָהּ,
לֹא תוּכַל לְהִתְעַלֵּם.

JPS (1916) — "Thou shalt not see thy brother's ox or his sheep driven away, and hide thyself from them; thou shalt surely bring them back unto thy brother. And if thy brother be not nigh unto thee, and thou know him not, then thou shalt bring it home to thy house, and it shall be with thee until thy brother require it, and thou shalt restore it to him. And so shalt thou do with his ass; and so shalt thou do with his garment; and so shalt thou do with every lost thing of thy brother's, which he hath lost, and thou hast found; thou mayest not hide thyself."

NJV (1961) — "If you see your fellow's ox or sheep gone astray, do not ignore it; you must take it back to your fellow. If your fellow does not live near you or you do not know who he is, you shall bring it home and it shall remain with you until your fellow claims it; then you shall give it back to him. You shall do the same with his ass; you shall do the same with his garment; and so too shall you do with anything that your fellow loses and you find: you must not remain indifferent."

These verses are part of the sidrah (Torah portion) known as *Ki Tetze*, which contains the highest number of *mitzvot* (commandments) of any portion in the entire Torah (according to

Maimonides, there are 72 separate *mitzvot* commanded here). Deuteronomy 22:1-3 is included in a section that discusses burying the hanged corpse of a criminal on the same day as the hanging; restoring lost property to its owner; and helping fallen animals right themselves. These verses, commanding the return of lost property, are a good example of the way the Rabbis of the Talmud (living circa 100 C.E.-600 C.E.) developed a practical code of *halakhah*, or Jewish law, from the commandments given in the Tanakh.

As the two JPS translations offered above suggest, the Hebrew verb *"hitalamta"* has a wide variety of meanings. In the well-respected *Alcalay Hebrew-English Dictionary*, its translation is given as "to overlook, ignore, disregard, neglect, close an eye to, deny; to disappear, hide oneself, be concealed." The earlier JPS translation preferred to translate the Hebrew as "thou mayest not hide thyself"; the later translation (NJV) preferred the less formal "you must not remain indifferent."

No matter how this verb is translated, however, its meaning is insightfully placed here, at the end of a law commanding the return and interim safekeeping of all lost objects and animals. As the JPS *Torah Commentary* notes, it is an "interesting anticipation of one's psychological reaction"[1] to the law. It is an admission that the natural human response is to "hide oneself," to pretend that one did not notice the stray animal or lost object. The natural reaction is to shirk the responsibility the law requires of us, and to do so through pretending not to notice a given situation or, worse, feigning indifference to our ethical obligations. The Torah warns against such behavior in several places. For example, Deuteronomy 15:9, regarding the sabbatical year in which all debts are canceled: "Beware lest you harbor the base thought, 'The seventh year, the year of remission, is approaching,' so that you are mean to your needy kinsman and give him nothing..." Or Deuteronomy 15:18, regarding a slave's right to leave his master after seven years service: "When you do set him free, do not feel aggrieved; for in the six years he has given you double the service of a hired man..."

Why is the Law of Returning Lost Property Repeated Several Times in the Torah?

In addition to Deuteronomy 22:1-3, God commands the return of lost property at two other points in the Torah. The first is Exodus 23:4: "When you encounter your enemy's ox or ass wandering, you must take it back to him." The second is Leviticus 5:20-25:

The Lord spoke to Moses, saying: When a person sins and commits a trespass against the LORD by dealing deceitfully with his fellow in the matter of a deposit or a pledge, or through robbery, or by defrauding his fellow, or by finding something lost and lying about it; if he swears falsely regarding any one of the various things that one may do and sin thereby — when one has thus sinned and, realizing his guilt would restore that which he got through robbery or fraud, or the deposit that was entrusted to him, or the lost thing that he found, or anything else about which he swore falsely, he shall repay the principal amount and add a fifth part to it. He shall pay it to its owner when he realizes his guilt. Then he shall bring to the priest, as his penalty to the LORD, a...guilt offering.

One reason for the repetition is the different thrust each version gives the law. The first version, in Exodus, is the most basic. It requires the return of wandering animals, a common occurrence in biblical times. Leviticus' main concern is the expiation ritual involved with transgression of the law; this is typical of the Book's preoccupation with the Temple and Priestly cult. Deuteronomy is the most expansive of the three, extending the law given in Exodus beyond its narrow application to animals and requiring the return of all lost property.

In fact, there is a good lesson embedded in the different phrasing of the law as it is given in Exodus and in Deuteronomy. Exodus requires the return of wandering animals to one's "enemy." Deuteronomy's language specifies that one must return lost property to one's "fellow." In this way, all bases are covered: whether friend or foe, the lost property must be returned to its rightful owner. In fact, Deuteronomy is perhaps the most practical of the three versions, legislating what to do in case the finder does not know who the owner is. Certainly this is the most likely lost-and-found scenario, at least in modern times when travel is common and we do not always know our neighbors or those passing through our towns.

Traditionally, when a law is given more than once in the Torah, the rabbis understood the repetition to be purposeful and full of halakhic significance. Thus, they derive from each version of the law different teachings. On the other end of the spectrum, a more literary-critical approach would understand the repetition to be the result of careless editing or as evidence of multiple authors who were unaware of each other's work.

What *Halakhot* (Jewish laws) are Derived from These Verses?

The Jewish code of law touches on every aspect of life, and it is no surprise that the area of lost property is thoroughly covered. The Torah, in all three versions of its law regarding the return of lost property, takes into consideration and legislates a variety of situations. What if the owner of the lost property is a friend, and what if he or she is an enemy? What if the finder does not know the owner? What if the lost property is an animal, and what if it is something else, like clothing? What if the animal just seems to be wandering off, but is not definitely lost? Still, the Bible leaves many questions open. For instance, we are told that the finder must keep the object until the owner comes to claim it. How long must the finder keep the property? What if it costs money to keep the property — an animal, after all, must be housed and fed? Does the owner of the property have any responsibilities in searching for the lost property, or does it all fall on the shoulders of the finder to contact the owner? These questions are thoroughly debated by the rabbis of the Talmud, and those debates have in turn been debated by generations of rabbis and scholars through the present day. In order to give a feel for Talmudic legal discussion, a few of those issues will be explored here.

The second chapter of the Talmudic tractate *Bava Metzia* (21a) begins: "Which objects may a person keep, and which is he obligated to try and return?" The question betrays a certain discomfort with the law as set forth in the Torah. After all, is a person really obligated to return all lost objects? A wallet, or a cat with a collar, fine; but what about loose change scattered on the ground of a public park? What about that single glove left on a seat of a public bus? Does a person's obligation to return lost objects really extend that far?

The rabbis mitigate the Torah's injunction to return all lost objects by introducing a concept known as *ye'ush* (pronounced *yay*-oosh). *Ye'ush* is the owner's giving up hope of ever recovering the lost object. For example, I find a child's marble lying underneath a park bench. I can safely assume that the child, and his or her parents, gave up hope of recovering that marble when they left the park. So too with the coins scattered on the ground. These are objects of relatively little value which under most circumstances would not be seriously mourned. It is said of these objects that the owner has "gone through *ye'ush*" [literally, "despair"] for them. The finder of such an object is, according to the law, not required to return it to its rightful owner. Such objects are considered ownerless, and take on an "up for grabs" status.

A wallet or a pet, however, are property which an owner would reasonably miss and not give up hope of recovering, at least not for a while after the loss—and so loss of those objects is not considered *ye'ush* and they must be returned.

However, not all objects fall neatly into the category of *ye'ush* or not-*ye'ush*. The glove on the bus, for example. It may be that that glove belonged to someone well-off, accustomed to losing an occasional glove during the winter, and who ran off to buy another one as soon as the first one was missing. The owner gave up caring about the glove as soon as it was discovered as missing—that is, he or she went through *ye'ush* over it. In that case, the finder of the glove would not be obligated to try and return it. But, what if the glove belonged to someone who could not afford a new pair of gloves, or who had strong sentimental attachment to it, and truly missed that lost glove? It cannot be said that that person went through *ye'ush* for the glove, or that that person gave up caring about the glove when it was discovered to be lost. In which case, the finder would be obligated to return it. The point is that while *ye'ush* helps the rabbis mitigate the burden of the law, it does not entirely remove its reach or clear up every possible case.

Assume a person finds an object that does not fall under the category of *ye'ush*. What then? We do not live in a society where we would know or even have any means of finding the rightful owner. If my child comes home from camp with a bunk-mate's bathing suit, I know how to return that bathing suit to its owner. But if I find a gold earring on the sidewalk, how do I even go about returning it? Because it is something valuable, I must assume that the owner has not gone through *ye'ush*, and so I am obligated to return it—but the Torah has not told me what I am to do, beyond "taking it back to your fellow" (Deuteronomy 22:1) or bringing it home and keeping it until the owner claims it (22:2). The rabbis of the Talmud legislated that the finder of a lost object (which is not *ye'ush*) must publicize the find. Thus, in the case of the earring on the sidewalk, I might post a sign in the windows of the nearest stores advertising the found earring, or I might run an ad in the local paper. The Talmud describes an elaborate "lost and found" system that, according to the rabbis describing it, took place on the pilgrimage festivals at the Temple. A certain rock was designated the "lost and found" center, and everyone who had lost or found an object since the previous pilgrimage festival would announce the loss or find. In this way, the lost and found objects were publicized and all those claiming or returning objects knew where to go to recover them.

Thus far the rabbis of the Talmud have answered what kinds of objects must really be returned, and, moreover, how to facilitate that return when the finder does not know who the owner is (namely, by publicizing the find). But the story continues; for after all, the finder is obligated to keep the object until the owner claims it. This gives rise to several good questions. Is the finder allowed to use the object while it is in his or her safekeeping? The rabbis' answer reveals much about their worldview and what they valued as important:

> If a person finds books, he must read from them every thirty days. If he does not know how to read, he must unroll them. But he may not read them for the first time…If a person finds clothing, he must shake the dust from it every thirty days, but he may not wear it for his splendor [i.e., he may not wear the clothing just because he thinks it is flattering to him or stylish]. If he finds items of silver or copper, he may use them as necessary, but he may not wear them out. Items of gold or of glass, he may not even touch until Elijah the Prophet comes to herald the coming of the Messiah. (Talmud, *Bava Mezia* 29b)

The hierarchy is amazing—after gold or glass objects, which one must safeguard but not even touch, the next most precious item on the list is books! Books must be read from, or at least unrolled, only once a month (books were obviously in the form of scrolls at the time). But a person cannot even use them to learn something new from them—lest one's excitement over the book cause it to tear. In general terms, then, the law is that the finder must safeguard the found object, but must be careful not to damage it. If using the object might damage it, then it should not be used.

What about animals? The Biblical verses are primarily concerned with the return of wandering animals. In today's world, aside from agricultural areas, most wandering animals are strays or lost pets, and with community-run animal shelters there is less question what to do with them. In Talmudic times, however, the question of what to do with a stray animal carried serious financial import. Animals were valuable, and sure to be sorely missed by their owners. On the flip side, they are expensive to maintain. The Torah states that a person is required to keep the animal until its owner claims it, but is he or she really expected to feed it, milk it, do whatever is necessary to keep it alive and well until the owner tracks it down? Rashi clarifies the rabbis' answer: if the animal eats and works, then let it eat and work. If it eats but does not work, then the finder may sell it and save the money, which is given to the owner in place of the animal when the owner comes to claim it. This way, the finder does not lose money in doing his or her duty of returning lost animals.

An example of this is related in the Talmud, in *Ta'anit* 25a:

> A man passed by the door of Rabbi Hanina ben Dosa's house and left there (by mistake) some hens, which were found by Rabbi Hanina's wife. The former said to her, "Eat not of their eggs." The eggs and hens accumulated, causing them inconvenience. Whereupon he sold them and bought with the proceeds some goats. Once that same man who had mislaid his hens passed by and said to his fellow: Here I left my hens. Rabbi Hanina overheard and said to him: Have you a mark of identification (that the hens are yours)? He said yes. He gave him the mark of identification, and took the goats.

This story introduces another aspect of the lost-and-found process regulated by the rabbis: the mark of identification. After all, if I post a sign in a local store announcing that I've found a valuable gold earring, anyone might come to claim it as theirs. Thus a system of identifying marks was established, to weed out any deceitful claimants. Someone coming to claim a found object as their own must be able to describe it accurately and in detail; otherwise the finder is not obligated, in fact is not permitted, to return it to that person.

In this manner, the rabbis created a complete code of law dealing with the return of lost objects from the basic Biblical injunction. From the Biblical law, we know only the principle, that lost objects must be returned; but from the rabbinic law, we know the details of how to put that principle into practice.

Note

1 Tigay 199.

45

Deuteronomy 22:6-7

דברים כב,ו-ז:

בִּי יִקָּרֵא קַן צִפּוֹר לְפָנֶיךָ בַּדֶּרֶךְ בְּכָל עֵץ אוֹ עַל הָאָרֶץ
אֶפְרֹחִים אוֹ בֵיצִים וְהָאֵם רֹבֶצֶת עַל הָאֶפְרֹחִים אוֹ עַל
הַבֵּיצִים לֹא תִקַּח הָאֵם עַל הַבָּנִים: שַׁלֵּחַ תְּשַׁלַּח אֶת הָאֵם
וְאֶת הַבָּנִים תִּקַּח לָךְ לְמַעַן יִיטַב לָךְ וְהַאֲרַכְתָּ יָמִים.

*JPS (1916) — "If a bird's nest chance to be before thee in the
way, in any tree or on the ground, with young ones or eggs,
and the dam sitting upon the young, or upon the eggs, thou
shalt not take the dam with the young; thou shalt in any
wise let the dam go, but the young thou mayest take unto
thyself; that it may go well with thee, and that thou mayest
prolong thy days."*

*NJV (1961) — "If, along the road, you chance upon a bird's
nest, in any tree or on the ground, with fledglings or eggs
and the mother sitting over the fledglings or on the eggs, do
not take the mother together with her young. Let the mother
go, and take only the young, in order that you may fare well
and have a long life."*

There is in Judaism a high respect for all living things —
plant, animal, and human. While human life is held as the most
precious of the three, animals and plant life are also to be treated
with kindness and respect. Respect for God's Creation is, in Judaism, one way to show respect for God.[1] The Hebrew term for
the value of kindness to animals is *tza'ar ba'alei hayim,* or "pain to
living creatures." Obviously, the value is to avoid causing pain
to living things. This means avoiding not only physical pain to
animals, but emotional pain as well.

When God created Eve and Adam, God gave them mastery over all the earth. In fact, the first commandment given in the Torah (Genesis 1:28) is God's instructions to the first human beings: "God blessed them and God said to them, 'Be fertile and increase, fill the earth and master it; and rule the fish of the sea, the birds of the sky, and all the living things that creep on earth.'" Ruling the animal world, however, does not mean acting cruelly.

In several other places in the Torah, Jews are commanded to treat animals with kindness, even as we use them for work and food. For example: "When you see the ass of your enemy lying under its burden and would refrain from raising it, you must nevertheless raise it with him" (Exodus 23:5) or "You shall not muzzle an ox while it is threshing" (Deuteronomy 25:4). These injunctions, designed to protect both the physical and emotional well being of animals, are an important balance to humanity's right to rule over the animal world given in Genesis.

There are also three laws that involve not only kindness to animals, but also respect for the parent-child relationship common to humans and animals. These include

Exodus 23:19, "You shall not boil a kid in its mother's milk" and Leviticus 22:28, "No animal from the herd or from the flock shall be slaughtered on the same day with its young" as well as our verses at hand (Deuteronomy 22:6-7). That the parent-child relationship is held sacred even in regard to animals is an important aspect of Jewish ethics, as will be seen below, regarding the reward of a long, good life promised for honoring parents.

If Kindness to Animals is so Important, Why Aren't All Jews Vegetarians?

If animals are to be treated with respect, then why are people allowed to rule over them in the first place? This question rings especially true in regard to food. Why are we permitted to eat animal flesh at all?

In the Creation story of Genesis 1, humans were in fact supposed to be vegetarian. Immediately after God's blessing and command to rule over animal life, God said to the newly created humans:

> See, I give you every seed-bearing plant that is upon all the earth, and every tree that has seed-bearing fruit; they shall be yours for food. And to all the animals on land, to all the birds of the sky, and to everything that creeps on earth, in which there is the breath of life, [I give] all the green plants for food. (Genesis 1:29-30)

God gave plant life to sustain humans and animals; animals, however, are not given as food for humans. However, soon after Adam and Eve were created, humanity took a moral turn for the worse. Cain kills his brother Abel, Cain's descendant Lamekh commits murder, and 10 generations later, "the Lord saw how great was human wickedness on earth, and how every plan devised by the human mind was nothing but evil all the time." (Genesis 6:5). This is the generation of Noah.

God, angry and disappointed over morally corrupt humanity, destroys all life on the planet, except for one fertile couple of every animal species and Noah's children, who were allowed to join their parents on the ark. After the flood, God repented of the destruction God had caused, and vowed never to repeat such an act. By this point, God has also learned a bit about humanity. God realizes that humans are drawn to killing and blood, and so decides to give them animals to eat, so they will refrain from killing one another. In a passage reminiscent of God's first blessing and commandment to the first humans in chapter 1, God says to Noah and his sons,

> Be fertile and increase, and fill the earth. The fear and the dread of you shall be upon all the beasts of the earth and upon all the birds of the sky—everything with which the earth is astir—and upon all the fish of the sea; they are given into your hand. Every creature that lives shall be yours to eat; as with the green grasses, I give you all these…But for your own life-blood I will require a reckoning…Whoever sheds the blood of a human, by humans shall this blood be shed; for in God's image did God make humans. (Genesis 9:1-3, 5-6)

Jews, and all humanity, are therefore permitted to eat meat and fish as well as plants. It is true that according to the Torah eating meat is a concession for our moral weakness; but the story tells us that such a weakness is permitted, as long as we satisfy it by being carnivores and not murderers.

Notwithstanding God's permission to eat meat, Jews are troubled by the potential cruelty and disrespect for life inherent in a carnivorous lifestyle. The system of *kashrut* (the Jewish dietary laws), whose goal is to elevate the basic and necessary action of eating into an act of holiness and respect for life and the Source of All Life, mitigates this threat. Many of the laws of *kashrut* are devoted to treating the animal with respect and mercy. For example, animals must be slaughtered with a very sharp knife across the throat, in a single, lightening-quick motion. This is considered to be the fastest and least painful method for killing the animal. Hunted animals are not permitted; as a result, historically one found relatively few Jews who hunted for sport. The consumption of an animal's blood is not permitted (in fact, this is a law which the rabbis consider is incumbent upon all people, not just Jews). The blood is drained from the slaughtered animal and covered with earth, a gesture of respect for lost life. The meat must also be salted until all traces of blood are removed before cooking.

The treatment of the animal during its life is also an important consideration. For example, there is currently a debate among rabbis as to whether veal is kosher. Some rabbis argue that the conditions in which veal is bred and raised in this country are inhumane, and conclude that veal (American veal, at any rate) is not kosher. Others disagree. Still, the basic principle of *tza'ar ba'alei hayim*, causing pain to animals, is an important factor in Jewish ethics and eating.

Despite the measures the system of *kashrut* takes to guard against callousness, many Jews feel that vegetarianism is ethically preferable to eating meat. This is a valid Jewish attitude, one which has become increasingly popular in recent years, undoubtedly aided by medical research advocating a diet low in red meat.[2]

What Other Ethical Lessons Do These Verses Teach?

One view, described in the JPS *Torah Commentary*, argues that there is no ethical teaching to be found in the law of sending away the mother bird. The mother bird will be caused the pain of separation from her children (whether eggs or chicks); therefore, proponents of this view argue, this law cannot be about kindness to animals at all. According to this view, the Torah finds the act of taking the eggs or chicks from their nest in the presence of their mother in and of itself callous. There is no ethical lesson in this law, beyond the narrow teaching that the act of taking eggs or chicks in the presence of the mother is "callous".[3] While this is one valid interpretation of the text, others interpret the verse more broadly and derive from it different ethical teachings, above and beyond the value of kindness to animals (*tza'ar ba'alei hayim*) discussed above.

Sefer HaHinnukh holds that the mitzvah (commandment) of sending away the mother bird teaches that it is forbidden to cause any animal to become extinct. If we insist on taking the eggs or young birds, we must leave the parents, so that another generation will come into being despite our greed. That is why we are told to shoo away the mother, rather than take her and leave the chicks. The chicks, which still need their mother to survive, might die on their own, and another generation would not necessarily be born to replace them.

Nahmanides sees these verses as aiming to arouse mercy in human beings. He disagrees with most scholars, who see the verses as an injunction toward kindness to animals. If the Torah wanted us to refrain from killing or eating animals, Nahmanides argues, it would have stated so explicitly. Rather, these verses teach compassion. We are to avoid cruelty precisely in those situations where we have the capacity to be cruel. We can and do kill animals; however, Nahmanides felt, we need laws such as this one to remind us to be compassionate in doing so. Similarly, Maimonides writes:

> Since therefore the desire of procuring good food necessitates the killing of animals, the Torah enjoins that this should be done as painlessly as possible. It is not allowed to torment the animals by slitting the throat in a clumsy manner, by pole-axing, or by cutting off a limb whilst the animal is still alive. It is also prohibited to kill an animal with its young on the same day, to prevent people from killing the two together in such a manner that the young is slain in the sight of the mother; for the suffering of animals under such circumstances is very great.... The same reason applies to the sending away of the dam. . . . If the Law provides that such grief should not be caused to cattle and birds, how much more careful must we be that we should not cause grief to our fellowmen![4]

Maimonides thus discerns two lessons in this law. First, he feels that the law is designed to discourage people from taking birds and their eggs/chicks. The mother is forbidden, and then the eggs or chicks, Maimonides argues, are generally not so appealing by themselves. People therefore will not bother taking them, and the family of birds will find themselves generally unharmed. Second, he sees in this law a lesson for all human interaction. We should treat each other with at least as much care and compassion as we treat a mother bird, remaining always mindful of the pain and grief we are capable of causing and doing our utmost to avoid hurting our friends and neighbors.

Why is a Long, Happy Life Promised in Return for Sending Away the Mother Bird?

The latter half of the verses at hand reads: "Let the mother go, and take only the young, in order that you may fare well and have a long life." If the mitzvah of sending away the mother bird is in and of itself remarkable, then it is all the more noteworthy for the great reward promised in return for its fulfillment. Such a reward is offered in only two other place in the Torah: the Ten Commandments and in Deuteronomy 25:15 as a reward for having just weights. Exodus 20:12 and Deuteronomy 5:16 states: "Honor your father and your mother, as the LORD your God has commanded you, that you may long endure, and that you may fare well, in the land that the LORD your God is assigning to you." The Torah is making an important argument, that honoring parents — whether your own or even those of an animal or bird — is crucial to one's own life. The quality, and perhaps even the length, of one's life, depends on respecting the parent-child relationship, not only in one's own life but also among all humanity and even beyond that, among all species. Ibn Ezra understands the promise of a long life to be a just reward for the respect for life demonstrated in shooing away the mother bird and honoring one's parents. He understands the mother bird to be "the essence of the nest," such that letting her live is tantamount to fundamentally respecting life.

Maimonides, Rashbam and others see an intrinsic connection between the sending away of the mother bird and the other verses relating to animal parents, Exodus 23:19 ("do not boil a kid in its mothers milk") and Leviticus 22:28 (against slaughtering offspring and their parents on the same day). All three cases involve the parent-child relationship, and the potential anguish caused to the parent animal. The relationship between parent and child is sacred. That sanctity is guarded by a set of laws regulating human action, especially in dealing with animals where people might forget such things in their relishing of human dominance over the animal kingdom.

Of course, it is dangerous to make promises, especially where theology is concerned. In a story told in the Talmud (*Hullin* 142a) and made famous by Milton Steinberg's novel *As a Driven Leaf*, the breaking of the promise of length of days causes one young rabbi, Elisha ben Abuya, to question, and ultimately abandon, his faith in God. The story recounts how a father sent his son to fetch eggs from a nest high up in a tree. The father, a devout Jew, instructed his son to send away the mother bird before collecting the eggs. As a group of rabbis passed (among them Elisha ben Abuya), the young boy dutifully carried out his father's instructions. But then, on his way back down the tree trunk, he fell, and died. Horror-struck, the rabbis begin a theological debate over what had happened. How could the boy have died, when he should have been granted long life in return for fulfilling the mitzvah of sending away the mother bird (and that of honoring his own father by carrying out his instructions)? For Elisha ben Abuya, the incident served to sever his faith in Torah and its theology. Others, such as Rabbi Yaakov, argued that the reward of "length of days" refers to the World to Come, not this world. Still others find in this story fuel for the theory that rewards and punishments are not linked to performance of specific *mitzvot*.

Rashi quotes one particular Sage of the Talmudic debate in his comment to this verse (Deuteronomy 22:7). "If the Torah says, 'that it may go well for you and you may prolong you days' for an easy mitzvah which does not involve any monetary hardship for you, how much greater the reward for a difficult mitzvah!" This is perhaps the most helpful approach to the promise of a long and good life. We are to understand it as emphasizing the importance of the mitzvah of sending away the mother bird, of honoring one's own parents and the parent-child relationship in general, and use it as a guide with which to approach the performance of all of God's commandments and ethical injunctions.

Notes

[1] For more on the Jewish attitude toward plants and ecology, see Verse #23, Leviticus 25:10, regarding the Sabbatical and Jubilee Years, and Verse #42, Deuteronomy 20:19, regarding the mitzvah of *bal tashhit*, "do not destroy."

[2] For more information on Judaism and vegetarianism, see Louis A. Berman, *Vegetarianism and the Jewish Tradition* (New York: KTAV Publishing House, Inc., 1982) and Richard H. Schwartz, *Judaism and Vegetarianism* (New York: Lantern Books, 2001).

[3] Tigay 201.

[4] Maimonides, *Guide* III:48.

46

Deuteronomy 24:14-15

דברים כד,יד-טו:

לֹא תַעֲשֹׁק שָׂכִיר עָנִי וְאֶבְיוֹן מֵאַחֶיךָ אוֹ מִגֵּרְךָ אֲשֶׁר
בְּאַרְצְךָ בִּשְׁעָרֶיךָ: בְּיוֹמוֹ תִתֵּן שְׂכָרוֹ וְלֹא תָבוֹא עָלָיו הַשֶּׁמֶשׁ
כִּי עָנִי הוּא וְאֵלָיו הוּא נֹשֵׂא אֶת נַפְשׁוֹ וְלֹא יִקְרָא עָלֶיךָ
אֶל ה' וְהָיָה בְךָ חֵטְא.

*JPS (1916) – "Thou shalt not oppress a hired servant that is
poor and needy, whether he be of thy brethren or of thy
strangers that are in thy land within thy gates. On the same
day thou shalt give him his hire, neither shall the sun go down
upon it, for he is poor, and setteth his heart upon it; lest he
cry against thee unto the LORD, and it be sin in thee."*

*NJV (1961) – "You shall not abuse a needy and destitute
laborer, whether a fellow countryman or a stranger in one of
the communities of your land. You must pay him his wages
on the same day, before the sun sets, for he is needy and ur-
gently depends on it; else he will cry to the LORD against
you and you will incur guilt."*

What is Judaism's Attitude toward Work and Workers?

The *mitzvah* regarding treatment of employees is included in a
section of Deuteronomy dealing generally with what Rabbi Joseph H. Hertz termed "laws of equity and humanity."[1] These
mitzvot include the exemption of men from military service during their first year of marriage, laws against kidnapping, and injunctions against committing injustice to the stranger, orphan,
and widow. Prompt payment of a poor laborer is one aspect of a
larger system of ethical conduct the Torah sets forth.

It is wrong, the *mitzvah* states, to keep workers waiting beyond the customary time frame for their wages. The law applies

to both Israelite and non-Israelite workers, and specifically to poor laborers. Judaism recognizes the potential for an employer to exploit his or her workers, especially those who are poor or of a different culture (and therefore especially vulnerable to such situations), and seeks to protect them. The Hebrew verb translated by *JPS* as "oppress" or "abuse" means literally to take advantage of, exploit, or withhold something due somebody. The *mitzvah* that employers must pay their workers promptly lies at the heart of Judaism's democracy and sense of justice, demanding that all people — Israelite or non-Israelite, rich or poor — be treated fairly by those who have the power to exploit or take advantage of them.

While such a democratic demand for justice in the workplace may not seem so revolutionary today, Rabbi Hertz points out that in the ancient world, in Greece and Rome especially, such a law did not exist. In fact, quite the contrary. Ancient Greek and Roman society did not assign any dignity to the act of working, nor to those who worked to earn their living. Slaves, Rabbi Hertz writes, were seen as "'animated tools' without any human rights or claims."[2] Work was dishonorable, done by the lowest members of society, who were barely considered human. Judaism, on the other hand, had from its very roots laws to protect the worker and imbue working people with dignity and respect. Work dignifies and consecrates according to the Jewish attitude, and so too the worker is dignified and consecrated.[3]

Even the great rabbis of the Talmud worked to earn their living as laborers — they were tailors, carpenters, masons, etc. Hillel the Elder, one of the most renowned rabbis in the history of Judaism, earned his living as a woodcutter, which did not take away from his dignity. People remained the masters of labor; and labor did not mean enslavement. It was only in such a culture that Shabbat, a weekly day of rest, could come into existence. It was Judaism's way of crowning working people with supreme human dignity.

What are the Moral Obligations of an Employer in Judaism?

Because Jewish law is designed to honor and protect working people, employers are bound by certain moral obligations. An employer may not oppress his or her employees, especially in the area of their salaries. The Talmud extends the Torah's injunction regarding prompt payment to cover the disbursement of rental fees due for animals and machinery (*Bava Metzia* 111a), and also forbids keeping a person in suspense regarding his or her wages (*Bava Metzia* 3a). Maimonides, writing in the dark Middle Ages, went even further: "Obligatory kindness to one's workman goes so far that neither he nor his animal is to be prevented from eating of the food in the preparation of which they have been engaged."[4]

Another verse in the Torah, Leviticus 19:13, commands a similar law regarding prompt payment of employees. Leviticus 19:13 states: "You shall not defraud your fellow. You shall not commit robbery. The wages of a laborer shall not remain with you until morning." The *mitzvah* of prompt payment is linked there to robbery and fraud, imbuing the topic with an extra layer of moral severity. Taking the two verses together makes an employer who does not promptly pay his or her employees culpable of a serious breach of Jewish ethics. In fact, the Talmud considers such a person to have transgressed a total of six *mitzvot*: do not withhold from your fellow; do not rob; do not withhold the wages of a poor person; do not keep wages overnight; the sun shall not set upon him [the unpaid laborer]; and you must give his wages on that day (*Bava Metzia* 111a). The ethical obligations of an employer are not taken lightly, and the tradition does its utmost to ensure that employees are paid on time for their labor.

The *halakhic* (legal) requirements regarding the payment of wages were developed by the rabbis in their consideration of these verses, in conjunction with Leviticus 19:13. Despite the similarity of the Leviticus and Deuteronomy laws, there is a key difference between the two: the time frame for payment is different. Deuteronomy states that workers must be paid before the sun sets; Leviticus states that they must be paid before morning (i.e., before dawn). It is obvious from either verse that prompt payment is what is meant, and many take the *mitzvah* to be payment as soon as possible after the work day is over.

Still, the rabbis felt there needed to be some deadline imposed on the employer, who might be inclined to cite one or the other verse in his or her defense, arguing that he or she really had until the next morning or evening to pay. Therefore, the rabbis established a 12-hour pay period, beginning upon completion of the day's work, in which an employee must be paid. Someone who works during the day must be paid before dawn of the following day (Rashi on Leviticus 19:13), and someone who works at night must be paid before sunset (Nahmanides on Deuteronomy 24:14-15). Though this *halakhic* extension of time in which wages must be paid seems somewhat contrary to the Torah's intention, the idea of prompt payment is maintained. In fact, it is perhaps a more balanced system than the one laid forth in the

Torah; the rabbinic interpretation gives employers a bit of breathing-room in which to run to the bank or do whatever else is necessary to procure funds in order to pay his or her workers without transgressing this very important and ethics-laden *mitzvah*.

It is also important to note that the Torah seems to presuppose that workers are paid on a daily basis. The rabbis thus saw fit to exclude from this law cases where it was pre-arranged for a worker to be paid later. In contemporary society, where workers are generally paid by "check in the mail" after the completion of a project or on a weekly or bi-monthly basis, this understanding is especially important. The value of prompt payment still applies, and one must be careful to uphold this moral injunction. However, in a world that does not generally operate on a daily payment schedule, one should feel comfortable making arrangements with one's employees to be paid on a regular basis. As long as one pays promptly according to the pre-arranged schedule, one is fulfilling the *mitzvah* set forth in Deuteronomy 24 of just employment practices. Of course, an employer must also always be sensitive to the financial needs of his or her employees; if it comes to an employer's attention that an employee is in fact on the brink of poverty it is the employer's duty to do the utmost to help that person — including establishing a more generous payment practice.

Why Specify "Needy and Destitute" Laborers as Deserving of Payment?

While "fair treatment must be meted out to every hireling, rich or poor",[5] Deuteronomy 24:14-15 specifies that destitute workers especially must be paid on the day of their work. The rabbis tend to understand this as suggesting that employers must be sensitive to the needs of their employees, especially poor ones who may in fact be living from one day to the next. As the *Stone Chumash* put it, poor people are defenseless and more vulnerable to exploitation; they cannot risk losing their job by speaking up or arguing over their payment schedule, and yet need their daily wages more than anybody else.[6]

This is the sense of the Hebrew expression "he sets his heart upon it" (verse 15). Literally, the Hebrew is "raising his soul (or life) towards it." Rhetorically, it is an expression meaning "longing intensely for something," as it has come to be used in English as well. However, commentators feel that in the usage in this verse the expression implies something even more serious than longing. Ibn Ezra writes that it means "he relies on his daily earnings for sustenance," that is, he needs to be paid at the end of the day in order to buy food for the night or next day. Rashi understood the phrase to mean that a poor person accepts even dangerous work, thereby risking his or her very life, in order to have enough money to live.

The bottom line of the *mitzvah* is that: "Employers should be sensitive to the fact that poor laborers need their pay immediately; they do not have the wherewithal that an employer does that would enable them to wait for their pay."[7] Or, as the Talmud states (*Bava Metzia* 112a): "One who withholds the wages of a worker is taking his life from him."

Why Would God React Only if the Wronged Worker Cried Out in Prayer?

It seems somewhat odd that Deuteronomy 24:15 threatens God's wrath against employers about whom God has heard complaints. After all, should God really wait for someone to cry out in prayer before rendering justice?

The rabbis were wary of what such a verse might suggest, that God might not see or act upon injustice unless it is reported. Their answer is that God would act to render justice whether called upon by the exploited workers or not; but that God will act more quickly upon hearing the pleas of those being taking advantage of. Rashi writes, "Even if [the worker] does not cry to God [the employer will be punished], but if he does call out, God will hasten more quickly to punish [the employer]." Rashi's comment is based on the Midrash *Sifrei Devarim* 279, which states, "My punishment will come more quickly if you have caused one to cry up to Me."

Indeed, the Torah gives a similar warning of God's wrath upon hearing the cries of the mistreated in several other instances. Exodus 22:21-23 and Deuteronomy 15:9, for example, warn against the exploitation of orphans and widows, and the refusal of loans to the poor: "You shall not ill-treat any widow or orphan. If you do mistreat them, I will heed their outcry as soon as they cry out to Me, and My anger will blaze forth, and I will put you to the sword, and your own wives shall become widows and your children orphans" (Exodus 22:21-23). "Beware lest you harbor the base thought, 'The seventh year, the year of remission, is approaching,' so that you are mean to your needy kinsman and give him nothing. He will cry out to the LORD against you, and you will incur guilt" (Deuteronomy 15:9). Malachi 3:5 also refers to such a phenomenon.

Judaism cherishes a long-standing tradition of crying out to God for help, from the cries of the Israelite slaves in Egypt to these verses and beyond. There is in fact a midrash on this verse, related in Munk's *The Call of the Torah*:

> To the end of his life, Moses prayed to enter the Holy Land. The Midrash recounts that on his last day, he gathered all of his arguments and declared, "O HaShem, if I do not enter [the Holy Land], you will cause the Torah to give a false teaching, for You stated, 'On that day shall you pay hire; the sun shall not set upon him." Is this the payment of my wages? And yet I made this people into a holy nation, faithful to HaShem. And how much trouble it took to do so!' HaShem answered him, "Enough! You will have all the payment for your labors in the World to Come" (*Devarim Rabbah* ch. 11).[8]

Indeed, while the idea of a God who acts only when called upon may be anathema to many of us, the teaching probably is not so far off from our own practice. After all, it is precisely in time of crisis and need that we find ourselves praying, calling out to God for help. The lesson of these verses is that God protects those who are suffering, and renders justice—even, as the midrash suggests, if that justice is not seen or felt until the World to Come.

Notes

[1] Hertz 851.
[2] Hertz 929.
[3] Ibid.
[4] Maimonides, *Guide* III:42
[5] Cohen 1110.
[6] Schreiber 1061.
[7] Tigay 226.
[8] Munk V, 256-7.

47

Deuteronomy 25:17-19

דברים כה,יז-יט:

זָכוֹר אֵת אֲשֶׁר עָשָׂה לְךָ עֲמָלֵק בַּדֶּרֶךְ בְּצֵאתְכֶם מִמִּצְרָיִם.
אֲשֶׁר קָרְךָ בַּדֶּרֶךְ וַיְזַנֵּב בְּךָ כָּל הַנֶּחֱשָׁלִים אַחֲרֶיךָ וְאַתָּה
עָיֵף וְיָגֵעַ וְלֹא יָרֵא אֱלֹהִים. וְהָיָה בְּהָנִיחַ ה' אֱלֹהֶיךָ לְךָ
מִכָּל אֹיְבֶיךָ מִסָּבִיב בָּאָרֶץ אֲשֶׁר ה' אֱלֹהֶיךָ נֹתֵן לְךָ נַחֲלָה
לְרִשְׁתָּהּ תִּמְחֶה אֶת זֵכֶר עֲמָלֵק מִתַּחַת הַשָּׁמָיִם, לֹא תִּשְׁכָּח.

JPS (1916) — *"Remember what Amalek did unto thee as ye came forth out of Egypt; how he met thee by the way, and smote the hindmost of thee, all that were enfeebled in thy rear, when thou wast faint and weary; and he feared not God. Therefore, it shall be, when the LORD thy God hath given thee rest from all thine enemies round about, in the land which the LORD thy God giveth thee for an inheritance to possess it, that thou shalt blot out the remembrance of Amalek from under heaven; thou shalt not forget."*

NJV (1961) — *"Remember what Amalek did to you on your journey, after you left Egypt — how, undeterred by fear of God, he surprised you on the march, when you were famished and weary, and cut down all the stragglers in your rear. Therefore, when the LORD your God grants you safety from all your enemies around you, in the land that the LORD your God is giving you as a hereditary portion, you shall blot out the memory of Amalek from under heaven. Do not forget!"*

T he *mitzvah* of "remembering Amalek" is strange, troubling, and unfortunately, sadly relevant. The *mitzvah* is strange, because it is unclear what exactly the Amalekites did to warrant such annihilation. It is troubling, because God's instruction to

destroy an entire people runs counter to the notion of a compassionate and loving God. And it has proven sadly relevant throughout Jewish history, as the Jewish people are met generation after
generation with anti-Semitic attacks reminiscent of Amalek's
Biblical one. To Jews living after the Holocaust, the cry "do not
forget!" feels oddly contemporary. Indeed, in every generation
there has been an Amalek seeking to destroy the Jewish people.

Who was Amalek?

The Amalekites were a nomadic tribe who lived in the Negev
and Sinai deserts. Although nothing is known of them aside
from the Biblical account, it is known that there were nomadic
tribes dwelling in Southern Israel at that time, who often attacked travelers.

Within the Biblical account, careful attention is paid to Amalek's genealogy. The Torah takes pains to mention that Amalek is
an enemy of Israel by his very birth and blood: Amalek is a
grandson of Esau, Jacob's brother and arch enemy (Genesis
36:12). The rivalry and aggressive fighting between Jacob and
Esau, this genealogy suggests, will be continued by their descendants, the children of Israel and the Amalekites. The text also refers to Amalek's mother, Timna, who was a concubine of Esau's
son Eliphaz (Genesis 36:12). According to some Bible scholars,
the Bible often uses matrilineal concubinage to denote nomadic
status of the son. Ishmael, for instance, was a nomad born to
Abraham's concubine Hagar; so too with the sons of Nahor
(Abraham's brother and Rebekah's grandfather) and the sons of
Keturah (Abraham's second wife, whom he married after the
death of Sarah). In this way, the Biblical account of Amalek's
geneology and parentage signals to the reader certain key factors
about Amalek's personality: that he and his descendants will be
a nomadic people and will be aggressive enemies of Israel.

These hints regarding Amalek's personality hold true not
only for the battle of Exodus and the command given in Deuteronomy, but for the rest of biblical history and indeed all of Jewish
history. Thus, in I Samuel, King Saul sets out to defeat the enemy
Amalekites, led by King Agag (I Samuel 14:48, 15). Throughout
the reigns of Saul and David, the Bible recounts that the Amalekites raided Israel; David eventually conquers them in I Samuel
27:8 and they are not mentioned much thereafter. In the story of
Purim recounted in the Book of Esther, Haman is a descendant of
the Amalekite King Agag; and so too throughout history enemies of the Jewish people have been called "Amalekites."

Why did Amalek Attack the Israelites?

Why did Amalek attack the Israelites? And what did the Israelites do to inspire such an attack? While the Bible offers no clear answer to this question, the rabbis had several ideas. One answer, offered in the midrashic collection *Peskihta de Rav Kahana*, is found by looking at what directly preceded the Amalekites' brutal attack. The first verses of Exodus 7 recount the episode of Moses' drawing water from the rock, in response to the people's complaints of thirst. At the end of this episode, Amalek attacks Israel. The Midrash explains that God allowed the Amalekites to attack precisely because the Israelites doubted and struggled against God in their complaints. As Hertz notes, "It is the invariable lesson of Jewish history that whenever Israel begins to doubt God and itself, asking 'Is the Lord among us or not?' an Amalek unexpectedly assails it."[1]

Others explained that God permitted Amalek to attack because of moral (not specifically theological or religious) flaws in Israel. Rashi, for instance, writes that the Amalekites attacked because the Israelites used false weights and measures. Others argue that Amalek may have attacked for purely practical reasons, seeing the Israelites as a threat to their control of the pasturelands of the area, or as easy targets for plunder as they passed through the land. One Midrash explains that Amalek did not want to fight Israel alone, and actually approached the other nations, suggesting that they join in the attack. At first the other nations resisted out of fear, but Amalek persuaded them: "Come," he said, "and I will tell you what to do. If they defeat me, you'll flee, and if not, come and help me defeat them" (*Mekhilta Beshalah*).[2] Thus, explains the Midrash, Amalek was the first in a long line of nations who attacked Israel, and was the original instigator of anti-Israelite and anti-Semitic actions.

If the Midrash insists on Amalek's basic evilness, it also insists on the goodness and mercy of the Israelites. In another story from the *Mekhilta Beshalah*, Moses appointed Joshua to lead the battle against Amalek in order to train him in warfare. Joshua immediately proved his moral worthiness to lead the children of Israel into the Promised Land by renouncing the common practice of abusing the slain enemies. Rather, says the Midrash, Joshua treated even his slain enemies with mercy.[3] This story highlights the moral difference between the Amalekites and the Israelites: the Amalekites were so merciless and ruthless as to attack, unprompted, the weak and weary travelers. By contrast, the Israelites, led by Joshua, would not even abuse the enemies they wounded or killed in this war of self-defense. Their commitment to leading morally upright lives, marked by the qualities of mercy and compassion, stands as an important lesson to warring nations in every generation and in marked opposition to the aggressive and ruthless behavior of the Amalekites.

What Did Amalek Do that was so Terrible as to Merit Such Harsh Judgment?

It is difficult for modern minds to accept a commandment to "blot out" another nation. Modern, post-Holocaust sensibilities shudder at the thought of genocide, and are offended if not horrified at a verse in the Torah that seems to suggest such action be taken by Israelites against another nation. Martin Buber, the 20th century philosopher, understood and shared this sensitivity. He wrote that this horror stems as much from the difficulty many people have today with the idea of Divine will as from their heightened sensitivity to genocide. If we are uncomfortable with the idea of Divine will, then the notion of Divine war, which undoubtedly underlies the Torah's injunction to destroy Amalek, is even more foreign and troubling.[4]

Why does the Torah, which is so filled with humane and ethical injunctions and teachings, and seems to have as one of its goals the establishment of a just society, include the mitzvah of destroying Amalek? No other enemy of Israel is punished in such strong terms. Even the Egyptians, who enslaved the Israelites and were the nation's first oppressor, did not receive such harsh judgment from God. In fact, God commands "You shall not abhor an Egyptian, for you were a stranger in his land" (Deuteronomy 23:8). Amalek's crime against Israel must have been even more serious than that of the Egyptians or any other Biblical enemy of Israel to merit such a sentence.

Curiously, the nature of the Amalekites' crime is not fully described in the Torah. The verses at hand, Deuteronomy 25:17-19 mention an incident: "he [Amalek] surprised you on the march, when you were famished and weary, and cut down all the stragglers in your rear." This must be a reference to the battle with the Amalekites in Exodus, although there is no mention of an underhanded attack on the "weak and weary" there. This battle, the first to be mentioned in the Torah, is recounted as follows:

> Amalek came and fought with Israel at Rephidim. Moses said to Joshua, "Pick some men for us, and go out and do battle with Amalek. Tomorrow I will station myself on the top of the hill, with the rod of God in my hand." Joshua did as Moses told him and fought with Amalek, while Moses, Aaron,

and Hur went up to the top of the hill. Then, whenever Moses held up his hand, Israel prevailed; but whenever he let down his hand, Amalek prevailed. But Moses' hands grew heavy; so they took a stone and put it under him and he sat on it, while Aaron and Hur, one on each side, supported his hands; thus his hands remained steady until the sun set. And Joshua overwhelmed the people of Amalek with the sword. Then the LORD said to Moses, "Inscribe this in a document at as a reminder, and read it aloud to Joshua: I will utterly blot out the memory of Amalek from under heaven!" And Moses built an altar and named it Adonai-nissi [the LORD is my banner]. He said, "It means, Hand upon the throne of the LORD!" The LORD will be at war with Amalek throughout the ages. (Exodus 17:8-16)

Another battle occurs in Numbers, following the incident of the spies (the very incident that ultimately kept the generation of the Exodus from Egypt from reaching the Promised Land). Moses, as per God's instruction, sent spies to scout out the Promised Land and give a report as to the kind of land it was and what kind of people dwelt there. When the spies returned, they gave a favorable report about the land itself, but were afraid of the "giants" who inhabited it and advised not attacking them. Upon hearing that they were faced with such a strong enemy, the children of Israel became afraid; they spent the night crying and wishing they were back in Egypt. God became so angry at their ingratitude and lack of trust and faith that God declared none of them (with the exception of Caleb and Joshua bin Nun, who had given good reports) would enter the Promised Land.

The Israelites, upon hearing such a harsh sentence, changed their minds and told Moses they would enter the Promised Land and fight its giant inhabitants. But it was too late; Moses warned that God was not with them and if they chose to fight it would be on their own, with no Divine help: "Do not go up, lest you be routed by your enemies, for the LORD is not in your midst. For the Amalekites and the Canaanites will be there to face you, and you will fall by the sword...." The Israelites nonetheless decided to fight: "Defiantly they marched toward the crest of the hill country, though neither the LORD'S Ark of the Covenant nor Moses stirred from the camp. And the Amalekites and Canaanites who dwelt in that hill country came down and dealt them a shattering blow at Hormah" (Numbers 14:42-44; the story of the spies begins in Numbers 13:1).

While in both of these instances—in Exodus and Numbers—the Amalekites are the enemy of Israel, engaging in harsh battle with them, in neither case is an attack on the "weak and weary" mentioned. Nonetheless, tradition holds that the attack on the weak and weary took place in the Exodus account; that what instigated the battle fought by Joshua was the Amalekites' attack on the rear of the caravan. As Rabbi Hertz notes, an attack on non-combatants, the sick and weak, the very young and the very old, is considered to be devoid of humanity and mercy.

In fact, Deuteronomy 25:18 states that Amalek was "undeterred by fear of God." This expression suggests that Amalek lacked the basic principles of humanity and compassion by which all other peoples and religions live. In Rabbi Hirsch's estimation, Amalek attacked either out of "pure joy of massacre,"[5] so threatened were they by the ethical teachings of the Israelites that they chose to ruthlessly attack the Israelites rather than risk living in a world where morality ruled over the sword.[6] Another interpretation of the phrase "undeterred by the fear of God" has to do with Amalek's ruining the Israelite's reputation as God's protected people. Attacking the Israelites and damaging Israel's reputation as "untouchable" also meant diminishing people's fear of God.

One final idea must be explored. "Blotting out the memory" of an entire nation is an action that can never be condoned. However, it might be sanctioned if it were done in self-defense. Along that line of reasoning, tradition assumes that the Amalekites intended to commit genocide against the Israelites (Psalm 83:4-9). As the JPS *Torah Commentary* suggests, if the Amalekites intended to commit genocide and "blot out" the Israelites, then perhaps God's injunction to "blot out the memory" of the Amalekites is the only just punishment for them.[7]

How does the Jewish Tradition Connect Anti-Semitism to the Amalekites?

The sad truth of Jewish history is that anti-Semitism and anti-Semites have existed in almost every generation. Jewish tradition has dubbed these anti-Semites "Amalek." Just as the Jewish people are the descendants of the children of Israel whose story is recounted in the Torah, so too the Jews' enemies are seen as the descendents of that first biblical adversary, Amalek.

Thus, in the Book of Esther, Haman, the bitter enemy of the Jews in the Purim story, is a descendant of Amalek (via King Agag, Saul's enemy in I Samuel 15). Later, in the 1st century C.E., early rabbinic literature uses the term "Amalek" to refer to the Romans. This practice continued in every generation since including modern day enemies such as the Nazis, who were often referred to in Jewish literature as Amalek as well.

If Amalek is the original anti-Semitic enemy of the Jews, however, Judaism is careful not to glean a message of warlike aggression from the Torah's injunction to "blot out" their memory. First of all, Israel's experience with the Amalekites had shown them to be unreliable people with whom to have any transactions at all, and a nation with whom it was not possible to make bona fide peace, in spite of their attempts to do so. Peace is always the first choice and only when no peace can be found can belligerent action be used or justified. Moreover, according to Maimonides' code of law, the *Mishneh Torah* (*Hilkhot Melakhim* 6:1,4), the Amalekites were to be offered the option of surrender and were to be spared if they accepted.

Unfortunately, the fact of Jewish history from the times of the Torah until today is that the struggle against anti-Semitism rarely ends peacefully. Rabbi Hirsch wrote that the struggle against anti-Semitism requires constant attention and work; therefore God did not just blot out Amalek in one stroke as God did with the Egyptians.[8] The survival of Amalek in the Torah is meant to teach us how to handle anti-Semitism in the future: strive for peace, resort to war when necessary for national self-defense, and never forget to be on guard against unwarranted attack.

The Midrash took a somewhat more optimistic view of Amalek's place in Jewish history. According to the *Mekhilta* (*Beshalah*), God instructed Moses to write God's judgment of Amalek in the Torah in order to let the world know that all who harm Israel will come to a bitter end. As much as Amalek's presence in every generation is an undeniable truth of history, so too is the secret of Israel's survival against such a persistent enemy and the reality of God's protection and Israel's ultimate victory.

What are the Mitzvot of "Remembering Amalek" and "Do Not Forget"?

The mitzvah of remembering Amalek is one of the 613 *mitzvot* required of all Jews. In fact, the language of Deuteronomy 25:17-19 suggests that there are two *mitzvot* involved: one is to "remember what Amalek did to you" (verse 17) and the other is "do not forget" (verse 19). What exactly does this mitzvah entail? What must one do to fulfill the *mitzvah* of "remembering," and how might this be different from "do not forget"?

The text itself makes it clear: the Israelites are to remember to take revenge on the Amalekites once they are settled in the

Promised Land. The phrase "blot out their memory" means "wipe them out." At first glance, this seems to require actual genocide. Rashi comments that the commandment includes women, children, and even animals, lest the existence of something belonging to an Amalekite cause one to accidentally say Amalek's name (i.e. "Whose animal is that? — It belonged to Amalek"), which would be a transgression of the *mitzvah*. King Saul waged a successful battle against the Amalekites, but did not fully carry out the proscription. He allowed King Agag to live, and took the best of the Amalekites' livestock. For this, God removes Saul from power (I Samuel 15:11).

Rabbinic Judaism managed to mitigate somewhat the performance of the *mitzvah* of remembering Amalek. Using the ambiguous phrase "blot out the memory," they focus less on actual murder and more on wiping out all recollection and of the Amalekites. Given that today there is no clear historical trace of the Amalekite people, it seems that the Israelites managed to fulfill this commandment. Nahmanides, quoting the *Sifra*, claims that the mitzvah of "remember Amalek" means "remember to speak about Amalek, about the terrible things he did to the Israelites." He writes: "I might think that it means [remember Amalek] 'in your heart.' But when Scripture states 'do not forget,' forgetfulness of heart is already stated. How then can I fulfill the injunction 'remember'? It must mean 'by verbal utterance.'" Talking about Amalek and teaching each generation about Amalek's unjust attack is therefore the way to fulfill the command "remember."

Other rabbis read the commandment as an ethical lesson. Samson Raphael Hirsch, for example, comments that "remember Amalek" is a commandment to keep away from evil, a warning not to forget and become like Amalek, through not fearing God and taking advantage of your position of superiority to the detriment of others weaker than you.[9] Rabbi Elie Munk quotes the *Shelah* (Rabbi Isaiah ben Avraham ha-Levi Horowitz, d. 1630, Land of Israel) as saying: "If Israel is in a position of dominance with the freedom to act, then it must remember and wage war against Amalek; however, if Israel is subjugated, then at least it must not forget."[10] The *Zohar*, based on Midrash, understands the war against Amalek as an internal struggle. The battle against Amalek, and the command to always remember it, is symbolic of the war against our inner, spiritual and ethical weakness, which often come under attack.

Another Midrash interprets the mitzvah to mean that is it forbidden to show mercy foolishly on irreconcilable enemies of Israel, on people wholly committed to Israel's destruction.[11]

While we are to always strive for peace, the mitzvah is to remember that peace is impossible with those who insist on Israel's destruction.

In order to fulfill the mitzvah of remembering and not forgetting, the story of Amalek's attack is read every year on the Shabbat before Purim, called *Shabbat Zakhor*, "Sabbath of Remembrance." While the Shabbat before Purim was chosen because Haman was a descendant of Agag, king of the Amalekites, the reading was instituted in order that the memory of what Amalek did to the Israelites not be forgotten. As Nahmanides wrote, the story of the Amalekites' attack must be related to each generation in order that we as a people do not forget the tragedy that happened to us. In this way, the mitzvah of "remembering Amalek" became a separate obligation, a public, fixed event. Some *siddurim* (prayerbooks) even include Deuteronomy 25:17-19 at the end of the morning prayer service, suggesting that people fulfill the mitzvah of "remembering Amalek" on a daily basis through re-reading the Torah's story.

No matter how we understand this mitzvah, one overarching lesson emerges: at all stages of Jewish life, Jews must remember their history and transmit it to the next generation. Remembering Amalek is as much about collective memory (remembering) as it is about war and destruction (Amalek). As such, it belongs to a larger category of *mitzvot* designed to preserve the Jewish heritage, by "teaching your children" — a value so central to Judaism that it is repeated in the *Shema* prayer twice every day and celebrated yearly at the intergenerational Passover seder table.

Notes

[1] Hertz 280.
[2] Elimelech Epstein Halevy, "Amalekites" in *Encyclopedia Judaica* I, 791.
[3] Ibid.
[4] Martin Buber, "Samuel and Agag," in *Commentary* January 1962: 63-4.
[5] Hirsch V, 524.
[6] Ibid.
[7] Tigay 236.
[8] in Munk V, 268.
[9] Hirsch V, 523-6.
[10] Munk V, 268.
[11] see Epstein Halevy I, 787-91.

48

Deuteronomy 29:13-14

דברים כט,יג-יד:

וְלֹא אִתְּכֶם לְבַדְּכֶם אָנֹכִי כֹּרֵת אֶת הַבְּרִית הַזֹּאת וְאֶת
הָאָלָה הַזֹּאת: כִּי אֶת אֲשֶׁר יֶשְׁנוֹ פֹּה עִמָּנוּ עֹמֵד הַיּוֹם
לִפְנֵי ה' אֱלֹהֵינוּ וְאֵת אֲשֶׁר אֵינֶנּוּ פֹּה עִמָּנוּ הַיּוֹם.

*JPS (1916) – "Neither with you only do I make this cove-
nant and this oath; but with him that standeth here with us
this day before the LORD our God, and also with him that
is not here with us this day."*

*NJV (1961) – "I make this covenant, with its sanctions, not
with you alone, but both with those who are standing here
with us this day before the LORD our God and with those
who are not with us here this day."*

Moses is nearing the end of his final speech to the children
of Israel. His final act as leader of the Jewish people is to bring the
Israelites into a covenant with God, one that will last not just for
the generation who was brought out of Egypt but also for Jews of
all time. The covenant ceremony taking place at this point in the
Torah is marked by this statement of intent.

Who Are "Those Who are Not with Us Here This Day"?

The text is striking in its mystery: God is entering into a covenant
with the Israelites taken out of Egypt, and with "those who are
not with us here this day." What does that mean? Who might
those people be?

The real problem lies in the fact that just a few verses earlier (29:9-10), the Torah explains that the entire people was present for Moses' speech and his reiterating the covenant with God: "You stand this day, all of you, before the LORD your God—your tribal heads, your elders and your officials, all the men of Israel, your children, your wives, even the stranger within your camp, from woodchopper to water drawer—to enter into the covenant of the Lord your God...." If the whole people were present, then who are "those not present"?

The most prevalent understanding of this phrase is that it refers to the descendants of the Israelites taken out of Egypt—namely, the Jews, including our own generation and those yet to come. The Talmud (*Shevu'ot* 39a) says, " 'Those who are standing here'—this tells me only of those standing at Mount Sinai. From where is it derived that the generations to come are included in the covenant and the oath? From 'and also with him that is not here with us this day.'" Rashi and Nahmanides, the medieval commentators, also understand this verse as referring to future generations of Jews, making it a crucial proof-text for the basic claim of the Jewish tradition that Jews have a special covenant with God from generation to generation for all time.

While obviously future generations of Jews were not physically present at Sinai and for Moses' final speech, the Midrash tells us that, spiritually speaking, all Jews were there. " 'Those not here with us' refers to those "spiritually present: the souls of all future generations of Jews (and, adds Bekhor Shor, of proselytes) were present and bound themselves to God by this covenant."[1] The notion that converts were also present is important, as it confirms their place in the Jewish community—they too were spiritually present and so take part in the covenant with God.

Why Are Future Generations of Jews Bound to This Ancient Covenant?

While the notion of the Jewish people sharing a covenant with God for all time is beautiful and inspiring on the one hand, for many people it poses a serious religious problem. After all, why should one generation be compelled to follow the traditions of those who came before it? As the *Etz Hayim* commentary notes, "those who are not here with us this day" even includes those Jews who reject Judaism.[2] And so the question is: What right did our ancestors have to obligate us?

Of course, religion is not the only aspect of our lives determined by our parents and direct ancestors. Our parents determine for us when we are born, where we grow up, what type of education we receive, etc. As Rabbi Plaut notes, the past influences the present; we are committed in the present and in the future because of what has occurred in the past.[3] The *Etz Hayim* writes that "maturity consists in accepting those conditions as facts of our lives, rather than fantasizing about how our lives would have been easier had we been born otherwise."[4]

Still, Rabbi Plaut asks, "May a child not reject its inheritance? May a future Israel not choose to abandon God and Torah?"[5] This is the question many Jews ask, resenting being obligated to live Jewish lives simply because they were counted among those "not present" in Deuteronomy 29:14. To a certain extent, the split of American Judaism into denominations (Reform, Reconstructionist, Conservative, Orthodox) reflects different attitudes toward inherited religion: those who are totally comfortable with the notion of obligation passed on from generation to generation, and those who reject that idea. In between — and covering most of the Jewish population — lie Jews who struggle with what it means to be obligated, to have inherited this Jewish tradition and this covenant with God.

Struggling with and questioning the Jewish tradition and one's relationship and obligation to it is an important part of deepening one's religious identity and conviction. If the verse teaches us that all Jews were spiritually present when our ancestors entered into the covenant with God, then we can understand that to mean that each Jew's spirit must struggle with the meaning of that same covenant. On Passover, we learn that each person must consider him or herself to have personally left Egypt (Exodus 13:8), that is, we must each come to our own understanding of what Exodus means for us personally. Abravanel noted that Israel is like a debtor: the original man who took the loan might have died long ago, but the estate is still responsible for the unpaid loan. So too, it is the responsibility of every generation of Jews, and every individual Jew, to figure out how their relation to the "unpaid loan" of the Jewish tradition which they have inherited.

Why Is the Covenant Ceremony Itself Not Described in the Torah?

The verse clearly states that a covenant is being created between God and the People of Israel; but oddly enough, the ceremony of which it seems to be a part is not described anywhere in the text. Given how thoroughly the text describes other ceremonies — of making sacrifices to God, for example, or the receiving of the law at Mount Sinai — the absence here is striking.

However, scholars tend to see the absence of any description of the ceremony as typical of ancient Near Eastern treaties. According to the JPS *Torah Commentary*, ancient Near Eastern treaties followed a standard format: first a proclamation, then the writing out of the terms of the covenant or treaty, followed by a list blessings and curses associated with the fulfilling or breaking of the treaty, and finally the erecting of a stele or the sacrifice of an animal in conclusion.[6] This is in fact the exact format followed here: Moses gives a lengthy introduction, the terms of the covenant with God are written out, blessings and curses are listed. The fact that the ceremony in which the Israelites came to be bound by this covenant is not described is normal given this format.

In fact, while there is no animal sacrificed at the end of this covenant agreement, the language of this verse makes a reference to the practice. The verb translated as "make" (as in, "I make this covenant with you today") is from the Hebrew root k'r't, which literally means to cut. Many scholars see this as a linguistic remnant of the ritual act of slaughtering animals at covenant ceremonies (see for example: Genesis 15:9-18, where Abraham slaughters birds to God as part of their covenant; and Jeremiah 34:18-20). The expression to "cut" a covenant came to mean "to enter into a covenant," regardless of the means used or the absence of an actual sacrifice involving cutting.

What Sort of "Oath" or "Sanctions" Were Involved in This Covenant?

The verse states that the covenant between God and the People of Israel was made "with its sanctions," or in the earlier translation as an "oath." Nahmanides noted that God placed the Israelites under oath lest they turn away from God as they did with the golden calf. He bases this idea on the fact that there is no oath mentioned or given in Exodus prior to the incident of the golden calf, and so feels that God has "learned a lesson" and decides to add an oath the next time a covenant is made with the Israelites.

The Talmud distinguishes between the type of oath made here and a vow, which requires some qualifying condition. With an oath, as the one in this verse, there are no terms of agreement that might change and alter that pact. Therefore, one is forever bound by an oath — just as the Jews are forever bound by the covenant made in the Torah. "Just as there is no condition in the hearts of the generation destined to come after you, so with you, there is no condition in your hearts."[7]

Traditionally, this verse is seen as the basis on which Jews are bound by Torah laws. The Israelites' acceptance of the covenant here is understood by the rabbis as an acceptance of Torah Law generally. It is only much later in the Tanakh, in the Book of Esther, that the Jews accept upon themselves Rabbinic Law as well. There, the Jews "undertook and irrevocably obligated themselves and their descendants, and all who might join them...." (Esther 9:27). While in context that verse is referring to the observance of the holiday of Purim, in rabbinic literature that verse becomes the Scriptural basis for the authority of Rabbinic Law.

Notes

[1] Tigay 278.
[2] David Lieber et al., eds., *Etz Hayim: Torah and Commentary* (Philadelphia: Jewish Publication Society, 2001) 1166.
[3] Plaut, *The Torah* 1542.
[4] Libier 1166.
[5] Plaut, *The Torah* 1542.
[6] Tigay 277.
[7] Talmud Yerushalmi, *Nedarim* 3b, as quoted in *Torah Temimah*.

49

Deuteronomy 30:11-14

דברים ל,יא-יד:

כִּי הַמִּצְוָה הַזֹּאת אֲשֶׁר אָנֹכִי מְצַוְּךָ הַיּוֹם לֹא נִפְלֵאת הִוא
מִמְּךָ וְלֹא רְחֹקָה הִוא: לֹא בַשָּׁמַיִם הִוא לֵאמֹר מִי יַעֲלֶה לָּנוּ
הַשָּׁמַיְמָה וְיִקָּחֶהָ לָּנוּ וְיַשְׁמִעֵנוּ אֹתָהּ וְנַעֲשֶׂנָּה: וְלֹא מֵעֵבֶר
לַיָּם הִוא לֵאמֹר מִי יַעֲבָר לָנוּ אֶל עֵבֶר הַיָּם וְיִקָּחֶהָ לָּנוּ
וְיַשְׁמִעֵנוּ אֹתָהּ וְנַעֲשֶׂנָּה: כִּי קָרוֹב אֵלֶיךָ הַדָּבָר מְאֹד
בְּפִיךָ וּבִלְבָבְךָ לַעֲשֹׂתוֹ.

JPS (1916) — "For this commandment which I command thee this day, it is not too hard for thee, neither is it far off. It is not in heaven, that thou shouldest say: 'Who shall go up for us to heaven, and bring it unto us, and make us to hear it, that we may do it?' Neither is it beyond the sea, that thou shouldest say: 'Who shall go over the sea for us, and bring it unto us, and make us to hear it, that we may do it?' But the word is very nigh unto thee, in thy mouth, and in thy heart, that thou mayest do it."

NJV (1961) — "Surely, this Instruction which I enjoin upon you this day is not too baffling for you, nor is it beyond reach. It is not in the heavens, that you should say, 'Who among us can go up to the heavens and get it for us and impart it to us, that we may observe it?' Neither is it beyond the sea, that you should say, 'Who among us can cross to the other side of the sea and get it for us and impart it to us, that we may observe it?' No, the thing is very close to you, in your mouth and in your heart, to observe it."

The words *"Lo bashamayim hi,"* "It is not in heaven," have become a cornerstone of Judaism. From them we discern the attitude, prevalent in every generation, that each Jew is responsible for living a Jewish life.

Rabbis from Talmudic times to our own day have interpreted these verses, and this expression specifically, as the Torah's way of reminding every Jew that living Jewishly is within their grasp. To those who desire to deepen their Jewish living, these verses provide comfort. Rabbi Samson Raphael Hirsch wrote in his commentary that "it is not in heaven" means that "it [Judaism] is not inaccessible or supernatural, making it necessary for a man to scale the heights of heaven to find it, and bring it down to earth!" and that "it contains no secret metaphysical references to anything beyond the grasp of the ordinary human mind."[1] The medieval commentator Sforno noted that the phrase in Verse 14, "it is very close to you," teaches that we do not need prophets or great wisdom to understand Torah or Jewish tradition. "It is not in heaven" reminds us that in our times of searching for meaning in Judaism, meaning is close at hand and available to all, regardless of religious upbringing or educational background.

To those who seek a justification for abandoning Judaism, however, these verses are full of admonition. Judaism, they tell us, is not "too baffling," nor is it too distant, to be lived in every generation and in every country. No Jew can resort to the inaccessibility of the teachings of Torah; rather, the Torah is here with us for our own teaching and doing. The commentaries that focus on this interpretation of the verse give a powerful response to those who claim that certain Jewish laws were important only in the shtetls [towns and villages] of Europe, or applicable only in ancient times. While Jewish law must certainly be made relevant and imbued with new meaning in every generation and in every new place where Jews reside, no one can claim that Judaism is outdated or completely foreign. Indeed, it is incumbent upon each generation of Jews to imbue Judaism with meaning and make it worthy of living in the present. "It is not in heaven" means that the Torah is here with us on earth, and must be integrated into our lives as it sheds new meaning on our own existence, and we shed new meaning on it and the traditions it engenders.

What do These Verses Teach us about Judaism's Attitude Toward Learning?

The Talmud (*Temurah* 16a) recounts the following story: Rabbi Judah said in the name of Samuel that 3,000 *halakhot* (Jewish laws) were forgotten in the days of mourning following the death of Moses. After the period of *shivah* (seven days of mourning), the Jews turned to Joshua, placed in charge by Moses, and demanded of him that he "inquire of the Lord" as Moses would do. Joshua answered them: "*lo bashamayim hi* — it is not in heaven." In other words, now that the Jews had been given the Torah, they were to look for answers there, and not rely on prophets to speak directly to God on their behalf.

While prophecy was maintained among Jews throughout the biblical period, once the Tanakh was complete prophetic activity ceased. Since that time, it has been up to Jews to study and learn the Torah and the Bible, the record of prophecy in which all of the answers are said to be contained. The Oral Torah, or Talmud, is also considered part of this sacred revelation. According to tradition, the Talmud was given by God to Moses along with the Torah, only it was given as an oral tradition, not a written one. The term "Torah" is often used to denote all of classical Jewish literature, including the Five Books of Moses, the Bible, and the Talmud, all of which are considered to be God's Teaching. In fact, Rashi, in his comment on these verses, writes that the phrase "it is near to you" indicates that the Torah was given to the Jews both in written and in oral forms. The fact that we have them here on earth means "it is not in heaven" — it is here with us, to be studied and learned.

Because Judaism places such emphasis on learning and specifically on Torah learning, education and scholarship have always held a coveted place in the Jewish community. As long as 2,000 years ago, Jewish Law ruled that parents are forbidden to live in a city without proper schools. Moreover, a teacher/student ratio of more than one teacher for every twenty-five students is considered too high, and thus forbidden by the Talmud. Further, the poor must be educated free of charge. During the Middle Ages, when the rest of Europe was almost entirely illiterate, nearly all Jewish men and women could read and write, with some achieving much higher levels of knowledge. A twelfth-century monk wrote that "a Jew, however poor, even if he has ten sons, would put them all to letters, not for gain, as the Christians do, but for the understanding of God's Law, and not only his sons but his daughters."[2]

Of course, the education of Jewish daughters was more often than not neglected. While testimonies such as the monk's do exist, the norm was generally to educate sons at a higher level than daughters. While Jewish girls were taught to read and write in most communities, they were often not taught Talmud, which was reserved for the boys, and their education often terminated at an earlier age. However, in recent times the education of girls has taken a central place in most denominations of Judaism, with Jewish women becoming Torah and Bible scholars, earning their doctorates in Talmud, and becoming rabbis.

If "it is not in heaven" is the basis for Judaism's *attachment* to learning, it is also the basis for Judaism's *approach* to learning as well. While in many religions, Scripture is taken as something to be memorized but never challenged, in Judaism the tradition of *interpreting* Torah is as strong as the tradition of *learning* it. "It is not in heaven" means that the Torah is no longer in God's hands alone. It is also in our hands. And once in our hands, it is ours to interpret, to wrestle with, to challenge. It is, as the JPS *Torah Commentary* notes, the "halakhic counterpart of the idea that the intent of the original framers of the Constitution is not determinative for its interpretation."[3]

This idea is taught in one of the Talmud's most famous passages (*Bava Metzia* 59b), in which Rabbi Eliezer is debating some matter of Jewish law with the Sages. In his frustration to prove he is correct, he declares: "If the law is as I say it is, may this carob tree prove it!" At which the carob tree uprooted itself and jumped forward 100 cubits. Still, the Sages did not concede: "You don't bring proof from a carob tree!" they argued. Rabbi Eliezer then declared, "If the law is as I say it is, may this stream prove it!" At which the water of the stream reversed course. Still the Sages did not concede, again arguing that no proof could be had by a river changing course. Rabbi Eliezer, exasperated, declared a third challenge: "If the law is as I say it is, may the walls of this House of Study prove it!" At which the walls of the house began to collapse inward on the Sages. One of them, Rabbi Yehoshua, shouted out to the walls: What do you stand to gain from the Rabbis winning arguments of halakhah like this?" At which the walls stopped collapsing inward, and stayed where they were, leaning in over the heads of the Rabbis inside. Rabbi Eliezer, still not content, declared again: "If the law is as I say it is, may proof be brought from heaven!" At which point a Heavenly Voice rang forth: "Why are you giving Rabbi Eliezer such a hard time? The law is as he says it is!" Upon hearing this, Rabbi Yehoshua jumped to his feet and shouted the phrase from our verse, "It is not in heaven!" The Talmud goes on to explain that because the Torah was given in full at Mt. Sinai, Heavenly Voices no longer decide Jewish debates. It is rather up to "*rabim*" — a word that can be translated as either "rabbis" or as "the masses." The story ends with God smiling down on the Sages, delighted with their intellectual vigor, saying "My children have defeated me! My children have defeated me!"

"It is not in heaven" thus teaches us that it is up to us to engage in learning Torah, for God has given the Torah for exactly that purpose, and delights in watching us discuss and debate its lessons. In fact, the idea of not wanting to learn Torah was so foreign to the Sages of the Talmud that one of them taught, " 'It is not in heaven' — but even if it were, it would still be your duty to go up after it and learn it!" (Talmud *Eruvin* 55a).

What does this Verse Teach Us about Judaism's Attitude Towards Christianity and Islam?

The above story teaches that learning trumps claims of prophecy. Because the Torah was given at Sinai, no further revelations are needed--that is the meaning of the phrase "it is not in heaven." Rabbi Hirsch quotes the Midrash (*Devarim Rabbah*), which tells us: you are never to claim that another Moses has arisen to bring us a new Torah from heaven — for nothing of the Torah was left in heaven![4]

This means that Judaism rejects the claims of post-biblical prophets. While the founders of other religions, such as Jesus or Mohammad, may have had important and valuable lessons to teach about humanity and the sanctity of life, they have no place in official Judaism law or theology. Christianity and Islam are religions built "on top" of Judaism — they borrowed from Judaism and claimed to have supplanted it with a new message from God. Judaism, however, rejects the premise that any new message was given. Indeed, the lessons of these "new prophets," if true, would already be contained in the Torah itself. Thus Judaism rejects the assertions of any people who claim to be prophets, bringing a "new message" from God. God has already given the entire message in the Torah.

Similarly, the elevation of a religious leader to the status of "prophet" is also contrary to Judaism. Individuals of great learning or compassion are respected in Judaism precisely because they are normal human beings, even when they exhibit exceptional qualities. No one person is considered to have a "direct line" to God that is inaccessible to anyone else; in Judaism, everyone has direct access to God via prayer, study, good deeds and meditation.

Of course, the fact that Judaism rejects the claims of "new prophets" does not mean that Jews in any way must reject the people who follow such religions. Peace and respect for one's neighbors are two of Judaism's most important principles. Peaceful co-existence with one's non-Jewish neighbors, based on mutual respect and recognition that all humanity is created in God's image, has always been and remains at the core of Jewish values.

What Specific "Commandment" or "Instruction" are these Verses About?

Commentators on the Torah have long struggled with what commandment Verse 11 is specifically referencing. The verse begins: "For this commandment which I command you this day," and so we must ask "Which commandment?"

There have emerged two main answers to this question. The first takes the reference to "this commandment" in its most general sense, understanding it to mean all of God's commandments generally. This interpretation underlies the NJV translation of the verse, which renders it in English: "Surely, this Instruction which I enjoin upon you this day." Translating "*mitzvah*" as "Instruction," with a capital I, makes it refer to the Torah in general. According to this understanding, the Torah as a whole is not too difficult or "far away" to be learned or lived. "It is not in heaven" means that Judaism as a whole is accessible to all.

The explanation, championed by Nahmanides, holds that "this commandment" is a reference to the commandment of repentance (*teshuvah*, meaning return). This understanding is based on the fact that the initial verses of Chapter 30 are in fact dealing with repentance: "When all these things befall you––the blessing and the curse that I have set before you––and you take them to heart amidst the various nations to which the LORD your God has banished you, and you return to the LORD your God, and you and your children heed His command with all your heart and soul, just as I enjoin upon you this day..." (30:1-2). Nahmanides notes that the reference to repentance here is in the future tense, suggesting that the destiny of Israel and all Jews is to find their way back to God. The "commandment" of Verse 11 is thus none other than the command to return.

"'If your outcasts are in the uttermost parts of heaven' (30:4) and you are under the power of the nations, you can yet return to God and do 'according to what I enjoin upon you this day' (30:2), for the thing is not hard, nor is it too far off from you," he writes. Moreover, Nahmanides sees the phrase "in your mouth and in your heart" as indicating confession and return. "It is not in heaven," accordingly, means that no one should despair of repenting, of turning a new leaf and returning to God and the Jewish values from which they have strayed. Return is neither too difficult nor too far to be achieved by any Jew.

This is the point of Rabbi Hirsch's inspiring words: "The Torah…is about you yourself, and its contents concern your own life here on earth. To understand them you have only to delve into your innermost self, and to look at your material human conditions with open eyes."[5] Return to God and a Jewish way of life requires nothing more or less than realizing that the answers are "not in heaven," but rather have been given to us to discover during our time here on earth.

Notes

[1] Hirsch V, 602.
[2] Telushkin, *Literacy* 556.
[3] Tigay 286.
[4] Hirsch V, 603.
[5] Ibid. 602.

50

Deuteronomy 31:19

דברים לא,יט:

וְעַתָּה כִּתְבוּ לָכֶם אֶת הַשִּׁירָה הַזֹּאת וְלַמְּדָהּ אֶת
בְּנֵי יִשְׂרָאֵל שִׂימָהּ בְּפִיהֶם לְמַעַן תִּהְיֶה לִי הַשִּׁירָה הַזֹּאת
לְעֵד בִּבְנֵי יִשְׂרָאֵל.

*JPS (1916) — "Now therefore write ye this song for you, to
teach thou it the children of Israel; put it in their mouths,
that this song may be a witness for me against the children
of Israel."*

*NJV (1961) — "Therefore, write down this poem and teach it
to the people of Israel; put it in their mouths, in order that
this poem may be My witness against the people of Israel."*

Moses' life is drawing to a close, and he spends his final
days preparing the Israelites for the next stage of their journey
without him. He appoints Joshua as his successor, and writes a
"Farewell Song" recounting Israel's history and God's greatness.
Finally, just before his death at the close of the Book of Deuteronomy, Moses climbs Mt. Nebo, where he sees from afar the Promised Land he will never enter.

Deuteronomy 31:19 is God's injunction to Moses to write the
"Farewell Song" for the Israelites. From a broader perspective, it
is God's ultimate lesson for the Israelites and their descendants:
the Torah, this "song," is the legacy of the Jews for all time.

What Specific Commandment did the Rabbis Deduce from this Verse?

There is something curious about the grammar of this verse. The
first verb, "write," is in the plural, suggesting that God is ad-

dressing both Moses and Joshua. However, the rest of the verbs in the verse are singular. This implies that God is addressing only one of them, or perhaps (as the medieval commentator Ibn Ezra suggests) God is addressing each individual Israelite.

The Rabbis of the Talmud felt, as did Ibn Ezra, that the singular verbs indicate that God was in fact commanding every Israelite individually. This understanding led them to deduce that while the writing of the first *Sefer Torah* (book of Torah, or Torah scroll) was done by Moses with Joshua's assistance, God's intention and command was actually for every Jew to write his or her own *Sefer Torah*.

Of course, not every Jew is a *sofer* (scribe), someone who is trained to write holy manuscripts such as the Torah scroll, or the parchments that are placed inside the *mezuzah* or in the *tefillin*. The rabbis therefore decided that one who commissions a Torah scroll to be written, or who contributes to such a commission by donating the amount to pay the *sofer* for writing even one letter, has fulfilled this mitzvah (*Menahot* 30a). In recent times, there is a custom for the *sofer* to leave the final letters of a Torah scroll traced in outline only, and then at a festive celebration upon the completion of the writing of the new scroll, different members of the community have a turn to fill in the final letters, thereby fulfilling the mitzvah of writing their own *Sefer Torah*.

To What "Song" is this Verse Referring?

Another ambiguity of the text is the reference to "this song" or "this poem" (*hashirah hazot*). In its most general sense, the verse seems to be an injunction regarding the entirety of Jewish tradition, that it should be taught to the Israelites, or "placed in their mouths," as a reminder of God's special care for them.

However, there is in fact a song Moses writes in the very next chapter, chapter 32 of Deuteronomy, known as *Ha'azinu* (from the first word of the song). Rashi and many other commentators feel that the phrase refers to "this song" (*Ha'azinu*). Nahmanides points out that the *Ha'azinu* song is written in the special manner reserved for chanted poetry, with special spacing for each line (similar to the way English poems or song lyrics are written in a manner different from ordinary prose). *Ha'azinu* has come to be referred to in English as Moses' "Farewell Song." According to this reading, then, God is instructing Moses and Joshua in Deuteronomy 31:19 to write down the *Ha'azinu* song, and to teach it to the Israelites so that it will serve as a "witness" of God's covenant with them.

There are, however, other opinions as to what "this song" refers. These are generally based on the recognition that the verse as a whole seems to be pointing to something much larger than the narrow *Ha'azinu* song. After all, why should one part of the Torah, namely *Ha'azinu*, be so much more important than any other part, that it alone serves as God's witness and should be "put in the mouths" of the Israelites?

Rashi's grandson, Rabbi Shmuel ben Meir, disagreed somewhat with his grandfather. Rashbam tended to look carefully at the grammar and precise wording of the Biblical text, which often led him to very different conclusions than other, less literal-minded commentators. Rashbam picked up on the fact that two words are used to refer to the "song": *hashirah hazot*, "this song." Working from the rabbinic assumption that no word of Torah is superfluous, he deduced that the words "this" (*hazot*) and "song" (*hashirah*) must indicate two separate works. "Song," he decided, must be a more general term, while "this" must indicate something much more specific. His conclusion: "this" refers to *Ha'azinu*, while "song" refers to the entire book of Deuteronomy. To Rashbam, the book of Deuteronomy is of a different quality than the rest of the Torah; it is read as a song. Modern scholars agree with Rashbam that Deuteronomy is markedly different than the other four books but offer a different explanation: it is from a completely different source than the rest.[1]

Few people agreed with Rashbam on this verse. In fact, the rabbis of the Talmud (who lived nearly a millennium before him) took a much more general, inclusive approach to interpreting it. Looking ahead a bit in the text, they saw that in 31:26, the whole Torah is said to serve as God's witness before the Israelites: "Take this book of Teaching and place it beside the Ark of the Covenant of the LORD your God, and let it remain there as a witness against you." They deduced from this that the "song" referenced in 31:19 must therefore be this same witness, namely, the entire Torah. After all, *Ha'azinu* would hardly be adequate for telling the children of Israel all of God's will and commandments! (Talmud *Nedarim* 38a).

How Does the Song Serve as a "Witness" for God?

Written prophecy serves a two-fold purpose. At the time of the prophecy, it serves as a warning or prediction of things to come. Later, after those prophesied events have come to pass, it serves as a kind of proof of the veracity and power of the prophet and God. In that sense, all written prophecy serves as a witness.

The idea that written records of prophecy can serve as testimony on God's behalf is reflected in several places in the Bible. For example, from the book of Isaiah:

Long ago, I foretold things that happened,
From My mouth they issued, and I announced them;
Suddenly I acted, and they came to pass.
Because I know how stubborn you are
(Your neck is like an iron sinew
And your forehead bronze),
Therefore I told you long beforehand,
Announced things to you ere they happened —
That you might not say, "My idol caused them,
My carved and molten images ordained them"

(Isaiah 48:3-5).

Both here and in Deuteronomy 31:19, the parts of the Torah and Bible which foretell future events are seen not only as miraculous prophecies, but more importantly as proof that God is ultimately in charge of Israel's destiny. God alone can foretell what will happen, and how things will turn out. A witness testifying that events were foreseen prevents misinterpretation of the events. Lest anyone suspect that some foreign gods caused some disaster or miracle, or that it was a matter of chance and coincidence, the prophecy can be held up as a "witness" that God is the all-powerful Knower of Israel's future.

And how does this theory play out with regard to the *Ha'azinu* song (assuming that we take Rashi's interpretation, that "this song" indicates the *Ha'azinu* song of Chapter 32)? *Ha'azinu's* main theme is that God treats and has treated Israel with kindness and justice, but that Israel has repaid God with betrayal and disobedience. The song therefore serves as an answer to the Israelites when they complain to God during times of distress. Specifically, it speaks to the Israelites who witnessed the destruction of the Temple and the exile of the Jews from their land. Contemporary prophets such as Second Isaiah made it clear that these events were the direct result of Israel's idolatry, corruption, and immorality. Lest they find in their situation some proof that their idols and false gods had some real control over their lives, the legacy of *Ha'azinu* stood as witness for the God of Abraham, Isaac, and Jacob — that God alone knew in advance what was to be Israel's future, from its sinfulness to God's punishment to God's ultimate mercy and redemption. As Sforno suggested, such a "witness" might cause people to repent when disaster comes, because they will see that their fate was foretold and they will realize what they must do to avert the harsh decree.

What Does this Verse Mean for Us?

"And you who cling to the LORD your God, you are all alive to-day." That verse, recited in synagogue every time the Torah is read, rings true of the Jewish heritage passed on for 3,000 years. For those who have chosen to uphold the tradition of Torah and to pass it on to their children and their children's children, the Torah is their legacy. This is the ultimate lesson of Deuteronomy 31:19. Rabbi Akiva once asked: "From where is it derived that one must repeat a lesson to his disciple until he learns it? From the verse, 'and teach it to the children of Israel.'" (Talmud *Eruvin* 54b) The idea that we must teach the tradition we have inherited, and teach it well, lies at the foundation of Judaism. It is the secret to Judaism's survival through exile, Diaspora, and persecution for 3,000 years.

The verses preceding Deuteronomy 31:19 instruct the Israel-ites to read the Torah every seven years, so that "the people—men, women, children, and the strangers in your communities—may hear and so learn to revere the LORD your God and to ob-serve faithfully every word of this Teaching. Their children, too, who have not had the experience, shall hear and learn to revere the LORD your God" (Deuteronomy 31:12-13). Over time, the custom of reading Torah was reduced to an annual cycle, so that today the Torah is read in its entirety every year (some commu-nities read it on a triennial cycle, taking three years to read it in its entirety). The reading of the Torah has become the centerpiece of the weekly Shabbat morning service, and is also read in syna-gogue on Monday and Thursday mornings and Shabbat after-noons, as well as on holidays and *Rosh Hodesh*, the first day of the new Hebrew month.

Beyond its public readings, however, Torah study has formed the backbone of Jewish culture since the religion's earliest days. There is a well-known passage in the Talmud, which lists the acts that earn a person a place in the World to Come. The list in-cludes honoring one's parents, performing acts of kindness, pro-viding hospitality to guests, visiting the sick, and making peace between one's friends. The passage ends with the signature cli-max: "And the study of Torah is equal to them all." Studying To-rah is the most important mitzvah of all, because it leads to all of the other mitzvot. Learning is what enables Jews to deepen their spiritual lives and make their religion and culture worthy of their time, energy, and souls.

Indeed, this is perhaps the symbolic meaning of the Rabbis' injunction, based on Deuteronomy 31:19, that each person is commanded to write their own *Sefer Torah* (Torah scroll). Rabbah, a great rabbi of the Talmud, once said: "Though one's parents may have left one a Torah scroll, it is a mitzvah for a person to write one for oneself, as it is written, 'And now, write for yourselves this song.'" (Talmud *Sanhedrin* 21b). Whatever we inherit from our parents is only the beginning; it is up to us to write our own copy of the tradition, in our own handwriting and with our own mistakes and flourishes. We must begin with Torah study, from which all Jewish life stems. From there, we must take it upon ourselves to write our own tradition, to take ownership of that which has been passed on to us and make it our own. We must add our own voices to it, and then pass on this old-new tradition to our children, that Torah may be the Jews' legacy for all time.

Note

[1] See Verse 1 for a fuller explanation of the different sources of the Bible.

References

Traditional Commentaries

Rabbi Don Isaac Abravanel, b. Lisbon 1437, d. Venice 1508

Rabbi Moshe ben Hayim Alshekh, Safed, 1508-1593

Rabbi Yehudah Leib Alter, Poland, 2nd Gerer Rebbe, also known as the *S'fat Emet*, 1847-1905

Rabbi Yitzhak ben Moshe Arama, Spain, 1420-1494

Rabbi Haim ben Moshe Attar, author of commentary on the Torah, *Or Ha-Haim*, b. Morocco 1696, d. Jerusalem, 1743

Rabbenu Bahya ben Asher ben Halava, Saragossa, Spain, 1263-1340

Bahya ben Yosef ibn Pakuda, author of *Hovot HaLevavot* (*Duties of the Heart*), Spain, 1050-1120

Gaon of Vilna, Eliyahu ben Shlomo Zalman, Lithuania, 1720-1797

Rabbi Samson Raphael Hirsch, Frankfurt, Germany, founder of neo-Orthodoxy, 1808-1888

Rabbi Abraham ibn Ezra, b. Toledo, Spain, 1092-1167

Rabbi David Kimhe, or "Radak;" Narbonne, France, 1160-1235

Rabbi Shmuel David Luzzatto (common acronym is ShaDaL) Padua, Italy, 1800-1865

Maimonides, Rabbi Moshe ben Maimon, or Rambam — Spain & Egypt, 1135-1204

Rabbi Moshe ben Nahman, Nahmanides, or Ramban; Gerona, Spain, 1194-1270

Natziv, acronym for Rabbi Naphtali Zevi Yehuda Berlin, head of the yeshivah at Volozhin, Lithuania; 1817-1893

Ralbag, Rabbi Levi Ben Gershon, Provence, France, 1288-1344

Rashbam, Rabbi Shmuel ben Meir, Rashi's grandson; School of "Tosafot," 1085-1174

Rashi, Troyes, France, 1135-1204

Rabbi Menahem ben Binyamin Recanati, Kabbalist, Italy, 1217-1305

Saadya ben Yosef, b. Egypt , Gaon (head of academy) of Pumbedita, Babylonia, 882-942 C.E.

Rabbi Moses Schreiber, known as the "Hatam Sofer, the Hebrew title of his book "Seal of the Scribe", Pressburg, Slovakia — 1762-1839

Rabbi Ovadiah Sforno , Bologna, Italy, 1475-1550

Bibliography

Adler, Morris. *The Voice Still Speaks*. New York: Bloch Publishers, 1996.

Alcalay, Reuben. *The Complete Hebrew-English Dictionary*. Brooklyn: Hamed Books NewYork Branch, 2000.

"Chosen People" by Henri Atlan, in *Contemporary Jewish Religious Thought*, ed. Arthur A. Cohen & Paul Mendes-Flohr (New York: Scribner's Sons, 1987)

Alter, Robert. *The Art of Biblical Poetry*. New York: Basic Books, 1985.

Eleazar ben Judah of Worms, *Sefer HaRoke'ah*. Lemberg: Shalom Tsverling, 1910.

ben Maimon, Moses. *Mishneh Torah: Hilkhot Shabbat, Hilkhot Tzedakah, Hilkhot Rotzei'ah Ushmirat HaNefesh, Hilkhot De'ot, Hilchot Mada, Hilkhot Yesoday Torah, Hilkhot Teshuvah*.

— —. *Shemonah Perakim: Hakdamah le'Avot*.

— —. *Guide of the Perplexed* Vol. III.

Berkowitz, William. "Jacques Lipchitz: An Interview" in *Reconstructionist*, February 1974.

Berman, Louis A. *Vegetarianism and the Jewish Tradition*. New York: KTAV Publishing House, Inc., 1982.

Blumenthal, David. *God at the Center: Meditations on Jewish Spirituality*. San Francisco: Harper & Row, 1988.

Bleich, J. David. *Contemporary Halakhic Problems*. Vol. II. New York: Ktav, 1983.

Buber, Martin. *Moses: The Revelation and the Covenant*. New York: Harper & Row, 1958.

— —. *Israel and the World: Essays in a Time of Crisis*. New York: Schocken, 1948.

— —. *Tales of the Hasidim* (New York: Schocken Books, 1948)

Martin Buber, "Samuel and Agag," in *Commentary* January 1962

Buttrick, George Arthur et al., eds. *The Interpreter's Bible: The Holy Scripture in the King James and Revised Standard Articles and Introduction, Exegesis, Exposition for Each Book of the Bible* Vols. I-IV. (New York, Nashville: Abington Press, 1952)

— —. *The Interpreter's Dictionary of the Bibl e: An Illustrated Encyclopedia*. Vol. III. New York: Abingdon Press, 1962.

Campbell, Joseph. *The Hero With A Thousand Faces*. Princeton: Princeton University Press, 1972.

Cassuto, Umberto. *The Commentary on the Book of Exodus*. Jerusalem: Magnes Press, 1967.

Chill, Abraham. *The Mitzvot: The Commandments and Their Rationale*. Jerusalem: Keter Books, 1974.

Cohen, A., ed. *Soncino Books of the Bible*. Vol I. London, New York: Soncino Press, 1947.

Cohen, Jeffrey M. *Blessed Are You: A Comprehensive Guide To Jewish Prayer*. Northvale: Jason Aronson, 1993.

Culi, Jacob. *The Torah Anthology: Me'Am Lo'ez*. Vol. V/3. New York, Maznaim Publishing Corp., 1977.

Driver, S. R., ed. *The Cambridge Bible: The Book of Exodus in the Revised Version*. Cambridge: The University Press, 1911.

Elkins, Dov Peretz. *So Young To Be A Rabbi*. New York: Thomas Yoseloff, 1969.

— —. *Moments of Transcendence: Inspirational Readings for Yom Kippur*. Northvale: Jason Aronson, 1992.

— —. *Glad To Be Me: Building Self-Esteem in Yourself and Others*. Princeton: Growth Associates, 1989.

— —. *Humanizing Jewish Life*. South Brunswick: A.S. Barnes, 1976.

— —. "The Influence of Hebrew on the English Language," unpublished paper.

Elon, Menahem. "Hassagot Gevul." *Encyclopaedia Judaica*. 1972.

Epstein, Boruch Halevi. *The Essential Torah Temimah*. New York and Jerusalem: Feldheim Publishers, 1989.

Epstein Halevy, Elimelech. "Amalekites." *Encyclopaedia Judaica*. 1972.

Fields, Harvey J., *A Torah Commentary for Our Time*. Vols. I-III. New York: UAHC Press, 1990.

Finkelstein, Louis. "Judaism As a System of Symbols." *Mordecai M. Kaplan Jubilee Volume*. Ed. by Moshe Davis. New York: Jewish Theological Seminary of America, 1953.

Frankel, Ellen. *The Classic Tales – 4000 Years of Jewish Lore*. Northvale: Jason Aronson, 1989.

Frick, Frank S. *A Journey Through the Hebrew Scriptures*. Harcourt Brace College Publishers, 1995.

Gillman, Neil. *Sacred Fragments: Recovering Theology for the Modern Jew*. Philadelphia: Jewish Publication Society, 1990.

Ginzberg, Louis. *Legends of the Bible*. Philadelphia: Jewish Publication Society of America, 1956.

— —. *Legends of the Jews*. Vol. II. Philadelphia: Jewish Publication Society of America, 1909-1938.

Goldman, Solomon. *In the Beginning*. Philadelphia: Jewish Publication Society of America, 1949.

Greenberg, Aharon Yaakov. *Torah Gems*. Tel Aviv: Yavneh Publishing House, 1992.

Greenstone, Julius H. *Numbers with Commentary*. Philadelpiah: Jewish Publication Society of America, 1939.

Haran, Menahem. *Olam HaTanakh*. Vol III. Tel Aviv: Davidzon-Iti, 1993.

Hertz, Joseph H. *Pentateuch and Haftorahs: Hebrew Text, English Translation and Commentary*. London: Soncino Press, 1960.

— —. *The Authorized Daily Prayer Book* (New York: Bloch Publishing Co., 1975)

Heschel, Abraham Joshua *God in Search of Man: A Philosophy of Judaism*. New York: Farrar, Straus and Cudahy, 1955.

— —. *The Prophets*. Philadelphia: Jewish Publication Society, 1962.

— —. *The Sabbath: Its Meaning for Modern Man*. New York: Farrar, Straus, & Giroux, 1951.

Hirsch, Samson Raphael *The Pentateuch*. Vols. I-V. London: Isaac Levy, 1959.

Hoffman, Edward. *The Heavenly Ladder: A Jewish Guide to Inner Growth*. San Francisco: Harper, 1985.

The Holy Bible: New Revised Standard Version. New York: National Council of the Churches of Christ, 1989.

Humash Torah Shleimah. Jerusalem: Beit Torah Sheleimah, 1992.

ibn Pakudah, Bahyah. *Duties of the Heart*. NewYork: Feldheim, 1978.

Jacobs, Louis. *A Jewish Theology*. New York: Behrman House, Inc., 1973.

— —. *Jewish Values*. Hartford: Hartmore House, 1969.

James, William. *The Varieties of Religious Experience*. New York: Random House, 1929.

Kadushin, Max. *Worship And Ethics*. Chicago: Northwestern University Press, 1964.

Kaplan, Aryeh. *The Living Torah: The Five Books of Moses*. New York: Maznaim, 1981.

— —. *Jewish Meditation: A Practical Guide*. New York: Schocken Books, 1985.

Kaplan, Mordecai M. *The Future of the American Jew*. New York: Macmillan Co., 1948.

Kaplan, Tuvia. *Fathers and Sons: The Chassidic Masters on Pirkei Avos*. Southfield: Targum Press, 1992.

Karo, Joseph Shulkhan Arukh: Orat Haim, Yoreh Deah.

Kasher, Menachem M. *Encyclopedia of Biblical Interpretation*. Vol. VII. New York: American Biblical Encyclopedia Society, 1967.

Kaufmann, Yehezkel, *The Religion of Israel*. Chicago: University of Chicago Press, 1960.

Keck, Leander E. et al., eds. *The New Interpreter's Bible: General Articles & Introduction, Commentary, & Reflections for Each Book of the Bible*. Vols. I-II. Nashville, Abingtion Press, 1998.

Kierkegaard, Soren. *Fear and Trembling*. New York: Penguin Books, 1985.

Kook, Abraham Isaac. *Abraham Isaac Kook: The Lights of Penitence, The Moral Principles, Lights Of Holiness, Essays, Letters, And Poems*. New York: Paulist Press, 1978.

Kushner, Lawrence S. *God Was in This Place and I, i Did Not Know*. Woodstock, Vermont: Jewish Lights Publishing, 1991.

Lamm, Norman. *The Shema: Spirituality and Law in Judaism*. Philadelphia: Jewish Publication Society, 1998.

Lieber, David, et al., eds. *Etz Hayim: Torah and Commentary*. Philadelphia: Jewish Publication Society, 2001.

Lieberman, David. *The Eternal Torah: A New Commentary Utilizing Ancient and Modern Sources in a Grammatical, Historical, and Traditional Explanation of the Text.* Vol. I. River Vale: Twin Pines Press, 1979.

Leibowitz, Nehama *Studies in Bamidbar (Numbers): In the Context of Ancient and Modern Jewish Bible Commentary.* Jerusalem: World Zionist Organization, Department for Torah Education and Culture, 1974.

— —. *Studies in Bereshit (Genesis): In the Context of Ancient and Modern Jewish Bible Commentary.* Jerusalem: World Zionist Organization, Department for Torah Education and Culture, 1980.

— —. *Studies in Devarim (Deuteronomy): In the Context of Ancient and Modern Jewish Bible Commentary.* Jerusalem: World Zionist Organization, Department for Torah Education and Culture, 1980.

— —. *Studies in Shemot (Exodus): In the Context of Ancient and Modern Jewish Bible Commentary.* Jerusalem: World Zionist Organization, Department for Torah Education and Culture, 1976.

— —. *Studies in Vayikra (Leviticus): In the Context of Ancient and Modern Jewish Bible Commentary.* Jerusalem: World Zionist Organization, Department for Torah Education and Culture, 1974.

Leibowitz, Yeshayahu. *The Jerusalem Report.* 2 June 1994: 56.

Levine, Baruch. *Leviticus: The Traditional Hebrew Text with New JPS Translation, The JPS Torah Commentary.* Philadelphia: Jewish Publication Society, 1989.

Lunshtam, Shemuel E. "Yovel" in *Entziklopediah Mikra'it.* Ed. Shemu'el Ahitov. Jerusalem: Mosad Bialik, 1958.

Hyam Maccoby, "Sanctification of the Name," in *Contemporary Jewish Religious Thought.* Ed. Arthur A. Cohen and Paul Mendes-Flohr. New York: Charles Scribner's Sons, 1987.

Meeks, Wayne and Jouette Bassler, eds. *The HarperCollins Study Bible: New Revised Standard Version, with the Apocraphal/Deuterocanonical Books.* New York: HarperCollins Publishers, 1993.

Meier, Richard. "Synagogue: Contemporary Period." *Encyclopaedia Judaica.* 1972.

Metzger, Bruce M. and Roland E. Murphy, eds. *The New Oxford Annotated Bible with the Apocryphal/Deuterocanonical Books.* Oxford, New York: Oxford University Press, 1991.

Millgram, Abraham. *Jewish Worship.* Jewish Publication Society, Philadelphia, 1971.

Milgrom, Jacob. *Numbers: The Traditional Hebrew Text with New JPS Translation, The JPS Torah Commentary.* Philadelphia: Jewish Publication Society 1990.

The Mishnah: A New Translation with a Commentary by Rabbi Pinhas Kehati. Jerusalem: Eliner Library, Dept. for Torah Education and Culture in the Diaspora, 1987.

Munk, Elie. *The Call of the Torah: An Anthology of Interpretation and Commentary on the Five Books of Moses*. Vol. V. Brooklyn: Mesorah Publications, Ltd., 1995.

Newman, Louis I. *The Hasidic Anthology: Tales and Teachings of the Hasidim*. New York: Bloch, 1934.

Nulman, Mary. *The Encyclopedia of Jewish Prayer: Ashkenazic and Sephardic Rites*. Northvale: Jason Aronson, 1993.

Orlinsky, Harry M. *Notes on the New Translation of The Torah*. Philadelphia: Jewish Publication Society of America, 1969.

Pasachoff, Naomi. *Great Jewish Thinkers: Their Lives and Work*. West Orange: Behrman House, 1992.

"*Parashat Vayishlach*." *Reflections*. 2 November 1991: 3.

Peli, Pinchas. *Torah Today: A Renewed Encounters With Scriptures*. Washington, DC: B'nai B'rith Books, 1987.

Pinchas Peli, "Blessing—The Gateway to Prayer," *Tradition* Fall, 1973
— —. *Jerusalem Post*, 17 August 1985.

Plaut, W. Gunther. *The Torah: A Modern Commentary*. New York: Union of American Hebrew Congregations, 1981.

— —. *The Case for the Chosen People*. Garden City: Doubleday, 1965.

Rabinowitz, Louis Isaac. "Mezuzah." *Encyclopaedia Judaica*. 1972.

Rackman, Emanuel. *American Examiner-Jewish Week* 10 February 1972: 11.

Riskin, Shlomo. *Jerusalem Post* 10 August 1990.

Roth, Sol. "Towards A Definition of Humility." *Tradition* Spring-Summer 1973: 5-21.

Sanford, John A. *Dreams: God's Forgotten Language*. Philadelphia and New York: J.B. Lippincott Co., 1968.

— —. *The Man Who Wrestled With God: Light from the Old Testament on the Psychology of Individuation*. New York: The Paulist Press, 1981.

Speiser, E. A. *The Anchor Bible: Genesis*. Garden City: Doubleday, 1995.

Spiro, Ken. *World Perfect: The Jewish Impact on Civilization*. Deerfield Beach: Simcha Press, 2002.

Sarna, Nahum. Exodus: *The Traditional Hebrew Text with New JPS Translation, The JPS Torah Commentary*. Philadelphia: Jewish Publication Society 1991.

— —. *Genesis: The Traditional Hebrew Text with New JPS Translation, The JPS Torah Commentary*. Philadelphia: Jewish Publication Society 1989.

— —. *Understanding Genesis*. New York: Schocken Books, 1966.

Scherman, Nosson, et al., eds. *The Chumash: The Torah, Haftaros and Five Megillos with a Commentary Anthologized from the Rabbinic Writings*. Brooklyn: Mesorah Publications, Ltd., 1994.

Schwartz, Richard H. *Judaism and Vegetarianism*. New York: Lantern Books, 2001.

Steinsaltz, Adin. *Biblical Images: Men and Women of the Book*. New York: Basic Books, 1984.

Torah, Nevi'im, Ketuvim 'im perush Rashi ve'Da'at Mikra.' Vols. II, IV. Jerusalem: Mosad haRav Kook, 1969.

"Torah Thoughts" on Kee Tavo. *B'nai B'rith Messenger*. 19 September 1986.

Torat Elohim: Hamisha Humshe Torah im Perush Ha-Amek Davar. Vol. II. Jerusalem: Yeshivat Valozin, 1998.

Telushkin, Joseph. *Jewish Wisdom: Ethical, Spiritual, and Historical Lessons from the Great Works and Thinkers*. New York: William Morrow & Co, 1994.

— —. *Jewish Literacy: The Most Important Things to Know About the Jewish Religion, its People, and its History*. New York: William Morrow & Co., 1991.

Tigay, Jeffery H. *Deuteronomy: The Traditional Hebrew Text with New JPS Translation, The JPS Torah Commentary*. Philadelphia: Jewish Publication Society, 1996.

Tishby, Isaiah and Fischel Lachower. *The Wisdom of the Zohar: An Anthology of Texts*. Oxford, New York: Oxford University Press, 1989.

Unterman, Alan. *Dictionary of Jewish Lore and Legend*. New York: Thames & Hudson, 1991.

Weinfeld, Moshe. *The Anchor Bible: Deuteronomy 1-11*. New York: Doubleday, 1991.

— —. "Pentateuch." *Encyclopaedia Judaica*. 1972.

Wiesel, Elie. *Messengers of God*. New York: Random House, 1976.

Wigoder, Jeffery et al., eds. *Illustrated Dictionary and Concordance of the Bible*. New York: Macmillan, 1986.

Wright, Christopher J. H. "Sabbatical Year." *The Anchor Bible Dictionary*. Ed. David Noel Freedman. New York: Doubleday, 1992.

Yehuda, Zvi. *Cleveland Jewish News.*12 June 1987: 42.

About the Author

DOV PERETZ ELKINS

Dov Peretz Elkins was born in Philadelphia. He is a graduate of Gratz College for Hebrew Teachers, received his BA in literature from Temple University, and his M.H.L. and rabbinic ordination from the Jewish Theological Seminary. He received his doctorate in counseling and humanistic education in 1976 at Colgate Rochester Divinity School. In 1989 he was given an honorary Doctor of Divinity degree for distinguished rabbinic service by his alma mater, the Jewish Theological Seminary.

After 2 years as military chaplain at Fort Gordon, Georgia, Rabbi Elkins became Associate Rabbi of Har Zion Temple of Philadelphia. From 1970 to 1972, he served as spiritual leader of the Jacksonville Jewish Center in Florida. From 1972 to 1976, he occupied the pulpit of Temple Beth El, Rochester, New York, one of America's largest and most prestigious congregations. From 1976 to 1984, he maintained a private practice in Pastoral Counseling, and was consultant to synagogues and many national Jewish and non-Jewish organizations, as well as in the corporate world, such as Xerox, Kodak, IBM, etc.

During the 1984-85 year Rabbi Elkins was interim rabbi at Har Zion Temple, Penn Valley, PA, and from 1985 to 1987, he was spiritual leader at Beth El Temple, Norfolk, Virginia. From 1987-1992, he was Senior Rabbi at The Park Synagogue, Cleveland, Ohio, and since 1992 has been Senior Rabbi at The Jewish Center, Princeton, NJ. He will complete 13 years of service in Princeton at his retirement in the summer of 2005.

A nationally known lecturer, educator, workshop leader, human relations trainer, organizational consultant, author, and book critic, he has written widely for the Jewish and general press, including such journals as *Reader's Digest, New Woman, The Christian Century, Judaism, Hadassah Magazine, Religious Educa-*

tion, Conservative Judaism, The Reconstructionist, and many others. He is a regular book reviewer for several Anglo-Jewish weeklies throughout the country.

Dr. Elkins is the author of over thirty books. His *Chicken Soup For The Jewish Soul®,* co-edited with Jack Canfield and Mark Victor Hansen was on the NY Times best-seller list two weeks after publication, and has already been acclaimed as one of the best in the 70-volume Chicken Soup series. It is one of the best selling books in the Jewish world in this decade.

Dr. Elkins has been trained in group dynamics, human development, and humanistic education at leading growth centers throughout North America, including Esalen Institute, at Big Sur, California, NTL (National Training Labs) at Bethel, Maine, and the Gestalt Institute of Cleveland. He is a certified instructor of Parent Effectiveness Training (P.E.T.) and Teacher Effectiveness Training (T.E.T.).

Dov Peretz Elkins is a member of the Rabbinical Assembly, the Council for Jewish Education, the Jewish Educators Assembly, the Coalition for the Advancement of Jewish Education (CAJE), the Conference of Jewish Communal Service, and the Association for Humanistic Psychology. He was honored by Gratz College in 1996 with the "Distinguished Alumnus Award."

Rabbi Elkins and his wife, Maxine reside in Princeton, NJ. Their children and grandchildren live in Los Angeles, Tel Aviv, Cleveland, and Philadelphia.

Rabbi Elkins can be reached at DPE@JewishGrowth.org. His web site is www.JewishGrowth.org.

S.P.I. Books—NEW / RECENT RELEASES:	Ret. Price

New Release!

AL-QAEDA'S ARMIES: *Middle East Affiliate Groups &*
The Next Generation Of Terror
by Jonathan Schanzer, Foreword by Ambassador Dennis Ross

$17.95

Jonathan Schanzer dissects Al-Qaeda and offers surprising recommendations for how to counter their threat. Mr. Schanzer is a senior fellow at The Washington Institute, specializing in radical Islamic movements. Ambassador Dennis Ross played a leading role for 12 years in two Presidential administrations in shaping U.S. involvement in the Mideast peace process.

Trade Paper • 6" x 9" • 224 pgs • ISBN: 1-56171-884-X

New Release!

BIBLE DREAMS: *The Spiritual Quest—How the Dreams in the Bible*
Speak to Us Today **by Rabbi Seymor Rossel**

$23.95

This intriguing work explores the meaning of the dreams and visions found throughout the Bible. Rabbi Rossel examines the prophetic spirit in dreaming that has transformed human beings through the ages. It has been said, G-d reaches out to us through dreams bringing us guidance, sustaining and nourishing our spirits, healing and refreshing us. This book demonstrates how!

Hard • 6" x 9" • 380 pgs • ISBN: 1-56171-939-0

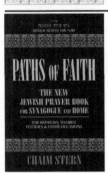

Recent Release!

PATHS OF FAITH: *The New Jewish Prayer Book* **by Rabbi Chaim Stern**

$24.95

Here is the long-awaited new prayer book for Jewish Sabbath and religious weekday services, which was recently completed by Rabbi Chaim Stern, noted author of *Gates of Prayer* and *Gates of Repentence*. (These books have been used for the past 30 years in most of the 800+ Reform and Liberal Conservative Congregations). In the words of the author: "I consider *Paths of Faith* my masterwork, the prayer book I always wanted to create. It is the summation of a lifetime devoted to creating liturgy".

Hard • 6"x 9" • 448 pgs • ISBN: 1-56171-933-1

Recent Release!

CLASSIC JEWISH TALES
by David Sokoloff

$8.95

Perfect for the coming Holidays, this is a delightful introduction to the remarkable range of stories which have enriched Jewish life throughout the generations. Adapted from Jewish Folklore, the Talmud and Hasidic tradition and illustrated with dozens of charming drawings, CLASSIC JEWISH TALES welcomes kids to the world of Jewish literature.

Trade paper • 8.5"x 11" • 96 pgs • B&W Illustr. • ISBN: 1-56171-948-X

S.P.I.Books • 99 Spring Street, 3rd FL • New York, NY 10012
Tel: (212) 431-5011 • Fax: (212) 431-8646 • E-mail: publicity@spibooks.com

S.P.I. Books—HUMOR / RELATIONSHIP:	Ret. Price
IT HAPPENED IN CHELM: A Story of The Legendary Town Of Fools **by Florance Freedman** (Winner of a National Jewish Book Award) An engaging tale about the mythical town in Poland, whose inhabitants are renowned for being simpletons. The classic Jewish story is retold here accompanied by beautiful illustrations on every page. Ages 6 through adult. For Ages 5 to 8. Hard • 7"x 10" • 96 pgs, Illust. throughout • ISBN: 0-944007-00-7	$9.95
THE JEWISH RIDDLE COLLECTION: A Yiddle's Riddle **by Rabbi Reeve Robert Brenner** In this delightful collection of Jewish riddles Reb Reeven provides answers to questions you've always been too afraid to ask: On what planet in our solar system did the people of Israel first appear? What is the correct Jewish greeting to the Pope on Christmas? (How about stating: **Good Yuntiff Pontiff!**) There are 1,000's of additional brain teasing riddles packed into this humorous and entertaining book! Trade Paper • 9"x 6" • 136 pgs • ISBN: 0-933503-38-5	$7.95
1. THE FUNNIEST MAN IN THE WORLD: **2. MORE OF THE FUNNIEST MAN IN THE WORLD** The Wild and Crazy Humor of Ephraim Kishon **by Ephraim Kishon** These two separate books contain hilarious stories full of life's everyday Characters by Israel's most famous humorist–who also happens to be the World's bestselling humor writer with 64 million books sold in 50 languages! These are the best and funniest stories culled from the author's past 25 books. For Ages 10 to Adult. 1.Cloth • 6"x 9" • 224 pgs • ISBN: 0-944007-47-3 2. Cloth • 6"x 9" • 200 pgs • ISBN: 0-944007-48-1	1. $12.95 2. $12.95

Call S.P.I Books : 212-431-5011 for details.

S.P.I.Books • 99 Spring Street, 3rd FL • New York, NY 10012
Tel: (212) 431-5011 • Fax: (212) 431-8646 • E-mail: publicity@spibooks.com

S.P.I. Books—CHILDREN'S TITLES:		Ret. Price
	**THE NEW JEWISH HOLIDAY ACTIVITY BOOK:** **by David Sokoloff** This book is designed to stimulate children's interest and appreciation of jewish holidays and traditions in a way that is both fun and educatonal. Features: **Jewish word puzzles • mazes • match games • holiday quizzes • find-the-mistake • coloring pages • connect-the -dots, and much more.** For Ages 4 to 8. Soft • 8.5"x 11" • 96 pgs, B&W Illust. throughout • ISBN: 1-56171-949-8	$6.95
	***CREATION:*** *The Book / Game With Questions & Answers About the Bible* **by F. Oelbaum** This unique book features 3,600 brain-teasing questions & answers on the Bible. In addition, it can also be played as a game which folds out from the book's flaps. Questions for ages 6-Adult. An ideal learning and quiz book. For Ages 6 to Adult. Trade paper • 9"x 12" • 380 pgs • ISBN: 0-944007-15-5	$10.95
	**THE BIBLE STORY ACTIVITY BOOK** **by J. Pliskin** A hands-on educational book that brings the ancient stories of the Bible to life for children. Includes the actual Bible stories, plus word searches based on each story, coloring fun, brain teasers, fill-in-the-blanks, and more. For Ages 5 to 8. Trade paper • 8.5"x 11" • 96 pgs • Illust. throughout • ISBN: 0-944007-67-8	$5.95
S.P.I. Books HUMOR / RELATIONSHIP:		Ret. Price
MENSCH OR SHLEMIEL???	***MENSCH OR SHLEMIEL? IS HE FOR REAL?:*** *Knowing Sooner What A Man Will Be Like Later* Millions of Jewish women incorrectly believe they have limited choices in love. They think finding the perfect guy is just destiny or luck. Well perhaps it was, until now. Because finally, with the help of this serious relationship book, you can take the uncertainty out of dating–and learn how to tell if he's a Mensch or a Shlemiel! Now you can learn to understand his secret signals of romance. For Ages 16 to Adult to Grandparents (if they are single)! Hard • 7"x 7" • 160 pgs • B&W Illustrations • ISBN: 1-56171-986-2	

S.P.I.Books • 99 Spring Street, 3rd FL • New York, NY 10012
Tel: (212) 431-5011 • Fax: (212) 431-8646 • E-mail: publicity@spibooks.com

S.P.I. Books COOKING:	Ret. Price

I MUST HAVE THAT RECIPE: *A Unique Collection Of Treasured Recipes* **by Hirschhorn & Katz** — $22.95

This book was created with the assistance of the Albert Einstein College of Medicine of Yeshiva University. The result of years of compiling, these proven Jewish recipes are truly the "best of the best". Features over 400 recipes that will delight your family and guests. Also features a unique section of recipes from the best restaurants in North America.

Hard • 10" x 10" • 466 pgs • ISBN: 1-56171-166-7

ENTERTAINING ON THE JEWISH HOLIDAYS **by Israela Banin** — $24.95

The only book that helps you plan your Jewish Holiday tables & meals in high style and with minimal efforts. You'll learn how to create an effective and original motif for each holiday–using items that are readily available and inexpensive. Includes: explanations on **backgrounds and significance of each Jewish Holiday** • **checklists of traditional ceremonial objects & foods** • **recipes** • **color photos showing proper implementation** and **a selection of appropriate holiday songs**. This author is the Jewish Martha Stewart!

Hard • 9"x 12" • 224 pgs • color photos throughout • ISBN: 1-56171-018-0

TZEDAKAH: *Can Jewish Philanthropy Buy Jewish Survival?* **by Jacob Neusner**   (A Rossel Publishers book) — $9.95

This book is about "tzedakah", the righteousness that is charity. Dr. Jacob Neusner presents the Jewish sources from Talmud to Maimonides, and raises issues important to all segments of American Jewry. Can Jewish philanthropy mold a future made up not only of "good" works, but of holy works? Or has the emphasis on giving and on "checkbook Judaism", split the community into religious and secular camps?

For Ages 8 to Adult.

Trade paper • 6"x 9" • 150 pgs • ISBN: 0-940646-07-2

EASY AND ELEGANT: *300 International Jewish Recipes* **by Mindy Ginsberg** — $24.95

An extraordinary collection of today's most popular gourmet dishes including 300 rare and delicious recipes that are all winners. From Greek Moussaka to Italian Eggplant Parmeasan to Moroccan Apricot Chicken to Israeli Salads. Includes a special section on the "Greatest Desserts on Earth" that could be a book in itself! And this tome is packed with large full color photos of all the major dishes.

Hard • 9"x 12" • 224 pgs • Color photos throughout • ISBN: 1-56171-024-5

S.P.I.Books • 99 Spring Street, 3rd FL • New York, NY 10012
Tel: (212) 431-5011 • Fax: (212) 431-8646 • E-mail: publicity@spibooks.com

S.P.I. Books—JUDAICA–SPORTS / GIFT BOOKS:	Ret. Price

Recent Release!
THE BIG BOOK OF JEWISH BASEBALL: *An Anecdotal Encyclopedia*
by Peter Horvitz & Joachim Horvitz

The Baseball Bible Is Here! A lively and complete reference of the topic with a comprehensive list of literally every Jewish athlete who has played in the Major Leagues–from Hall of Famers Sandy Koufax and Hank Greenberg to players who spent a short time in the big leagues... It's generously illustrated with baseball memorabilia & cards and many previously unpublished photos.

For Ages 8 to Adult.
Trade Paper • 8.5"x 11" • 200 B&W photos • 308 pgs • ISBN: 1-56171-973-0

$19.95

New!
THE JEWISH BASEBALL CARD SET: *8 Full Color Jewish Baseball Cards*
by Joachim Horvitz

The first collection of Jewish Baseball Cards ever created! These collector's items feature the 8 top players, including: **Hank Greenberg, Moe Berg, Lipman Pike, Jesse Levis, Harry Shuman, Harry Danning, Cy Malis and Hy Cohen.**

This is from a limited edition of 500 sheets that are not cut out.
For Ages 5 to Adult.
Coated Card Stock (printed on both sides)
8.5"x 11" • 8 Color cards/per sheet • ISBN: 1-56171-905-6

$ 4.00

($3.95 per sheet of 8 color cards Min. order is 5 sheets, retail Value: is $15.80

Note:
1 set = 4 sheets containing 8 cards each

THE JEWISH BOXER'S HALL OF FAME
by Ken Blady

This one-of-a-kind Jewish sports book includes rare interviews, anecdotes, photos and records of past and current Jewish boxers. From the 1800's to the present, the greatest are all featured here along with unique memorabilia.

For Ages 8 to Adult.

Hard • 6"x 9" • Rare photos throughout • 336 pgs • ISBN: 0-93503-87-3

$14.95

The Big Book Of Jewish Sports Heroes: *Biographies, Anecdotes & Rankings Of The 150 Greatest Jews In Sports* **by Peter Horvitz**

Meet the most accomplished and interesting Jewish athletes in the history of sports in this entertaining new title by the author of *The Big Book Of Jewish Baseball.*

They are all featured: yesterday's legends and today's rising stars, including the **150 Greatest Jewish Athletes** of all time rated according to their achievements. For Ages 8 to Adult.

Trade paper • 6"x 9" • 150 pgs • ISBN: 0-940646-07-2

$19.95

S.P.I.Books • 99 Spring Street, 3rd FL • New York, NY 10012
Tel: (212) 431-5011 • Fax: (212) 431-8646 • E-mail: publicity@spibooks.com